Communicating Meaning

The Evolution and Development of Language

Communicating Meaning

The Evolution and Development of Language

Edited by

Boris M. Velichkovsky
Duane M. Rumbaugh

LONDON AND NEW YORK

First published 1996 by Lawrence Erlbaum Associates, Inc.

Published 2019 by Routledge
2 Park Square, Milton Park, Abingdon, Oxon OX14 4RN
52 Vanderbilt Avenue, New York, NY 10017

First issued in paperback 2019

Routledge is an imprint of the Taylor & Francis Group, an informa business

Copyright © 1996 Taylor & Francis.

All rights reserved. No part of this book may be reprinted or reproduced or utilised in any form or by any electronic, mechanical, or other means, now known or hereafter invented, including photocopying and recording, or in any information storage or retrieval system, without permission in writing from the publishers.

Notice:
Product or corporate names may be trademarks or registered trademarks, and are used only for identification and explanation without intent to infringe.

Cover design by Gail Silverman

Library of Congress Cataloging-in-Publication Data

Communicating meaning: the evolution and development of language / edited by Boris M. Velichkovsky, Duane M. Rumbaugh.
    p. cm.
   With few exceptions, this work documents a conference at the Center for Interdisciplinary Research (ZiF), Bielefeld, held in Jan. 1992.
   Includes bibliographical references and indexes.
   ISBN 0-8058-2118-X
   1. Language and languages—Origin—Congresses. 2. Biolinguistics—Congresses. 3. Language acquisition—Congresses. 4. Human evolution—Congresses. I. Velichkovsky, B. M. (Boris Mitrofanovich) II. Rumbaugh, Duane M., 1929—
    P116.C66 1996
    400—dc20
                                             96-2147
                                                   CIP

ISBN 13: 978-1-138-97117-2 (pbk)
ISBN 13: 978-0-8058-2118-5 (hbk)

CONTENTS

PREFACE vii

1 Language Development at the Crossroad
of Biological and Cultural Interactions 1
Boris M. Velichkovsky

PART I TOWARD A NEW THEORETICAL FOUNDATION

2 The Origins of Words: A Psychophysical Hypothesis 27
Stevan Harnad

3 What Knowledge Must Be in the Head
in Order to Acquire Language? 45
William Bechtel

PART II PHYLOGENETIC PREREQUISITES

4 Was Speech an Evolutionary Afterthought? 79
Alexandra Maryanski

5 Prefrontal Cortex and Symbol Learning: 103
Why a Brain Capable of Language Evolved Only Once
Terrence W. Deacon

PART III ONTOGENESIS OF LANGUAGE

6 Origins of Communication in Infancy 139
Marc H. Bornstein

7 The Temporal Organization of Language: 173
Developmental and Neuropsychological Aspects
Angela D. Friederici

Part IV Environment and Culture as Shaping Forces

8   Genetic Histories and Patterns of Linguistic Change   187
    Alberto Piazza

9   Orality, Literacy, and Cognitive Modeling   211
    Eckart Scheerer

In Place of a Conclusion

10 Biobehavioral Roots of Language: 257
    Words, Apes, and a Child
    Duane M. Rumbaugh and E. Sue Savage-Rumbaugh

11 The Cultural Roots of Language   275
    Michael Tomasello

List of Authors   309

Author Index   311

Subject Index   323

PREFACE

The search for the biological foundations of human culture inevitably leads to language. Superficial intuition suggests that language is a *sine qua non* for the evolution of sociality. Without it, the diversity and sophistication of today's social systems would be unthinkable. However, there is the opposite hypothesis that the evolution of human language may in part be the result of our being thoroughly social entities: our sociality itself may have amplified the evolution of a capacity we share with other primates but developed to a degree unequaled as yet by any other species.

To date, the issues involved have been the subject of intriguing discussions within linguistics, paleoanthropology, and so forth. Most of these discussions have been restricted to the narrow confines of a single discipline and its methodological arsenal. Yet, the presumed interdependence of the evolution of language as a biological capacity and its growing significance for human culture calls for an interdisciplinary effort to explore the processes involved both on a phylogenetic and ontogenetic scale.

This is the aim of the following volume. With few exceptions, it documents a Conference at the Center for Interdisciplinary Research (ZiF), Bielefeld, which took place in January 1992. This conference was organized within the framework of a research group working on the overarching theme of "Biological Foundations of Human Culture." Throughout the academic year 1991–1992, scholars from areas as different and far apart as biology, psychology, sociology, anthropology, economics, primatology, history, and philosophy of science presented and discussed recent approaches toward a biologically and sociologically founded understanding of human culture. In outlining plausible pluralistic accounts of phenomena such as the evolution of social intelligence, psychological dispositions such as trust, and the detection of cheating, or of basic social institutions such as the family, the group explicitly avoided biological as well as sociological reductionisms. This pluralistic perspective was considered a prerequisite of the project by all participants and made it possible to bring the diverse intradisciplinary approaches into fruitful interdisciplinary dialogue. The results of the project are published in three books, of which this is one.

Advances in the study of the evolution of language as presented in this volume will certainly contribute to further insights into the intricacies of the biological and the social realms. Inevitably, new problems and questions will also arise. Interdisciplinarity, for that matter, is not a new answer to old questions. Rather, it is a new framework, considered to provide a more plausible "language" in which to pose questions and evaluate the answers.

In my dual role as convener of the research group and executive director of the ZiF, I want to thank Duane Rumbaugh and Boris Velichkovsky for taking on the task of editing this volume, and Sabine Maasen for assuming a major share of the burden of planning and organizing the conference as well as this book. Thanks also go to William Durham for co-organizing the conference, and finally to the staff of the ZiF, notably Lilo Jegerlehner, for her indispensable technical assistance.

—Peter Weingart

CHAPTER

1

LANGUAGE DEVELOPMENT AT THE CROSSROAD OF BIOLOGICAL AND CULTURAL INTERACTIONS

Boris M. Velichkovsky
Dresden University of Technology

Once banned by the *Société Linguistique de Paris* and the *Philological Society of London* as notoriously unscientific, the problem of the origin of language today seems to have become one of the most intensely discussed topics at the intersection of several highly respected scientific disciplines. With the emergence of language as a part of anthropogenesis as well as of individual development, new, specifically human forms of communication, learning, and problem solving have become possible, which are transforming the relatively slow pace of the biological evolution of behavior and its control mechanisms into a rather static background of cumulative cultural changes. Indeed, language has always been regarded as the most distinctive attribute of our species. Its analysis, therefore, is indispensable for any serious study of the biological foundations of human culture.

This was the topic of an International Conference on Biological and Cultural Aspects of Language Development organized at the Center for Interdisciplinary Research of the University of Bielefeld in 1992 and generously supported by the Volkswagen-Stiftung (Hannover). The core of the present volume consists of the updated papers presented at this Conference. This volume, however, does not detail the proceedings of the Bielefeld Conference. Whereas the chapters included preserve similarity to the delivered talks, some of the Conference papers are not considered. Furthermore, a number of new contributions have been added to make the interdisciplinary discussion of the evolution and development of language more relevant and coherent. As a product of the project on Biological Foundations of Human Culture, the volume appears now in the series with the same title.

TOWARD A NEW THEORETICAL FOUNDATION

The chapters of this volume deal, first of all, with the consequences of the Chomskyan Revolution of the early 1960s (Chomsky, 1972; Fodor, 1983; Pinker, 1994). In struggling with early behaviorist attempts to explain internal psychological processes by contingencies of external events and reactions of organisms, this new approach postulated abstract symbolic representations and logical operations on them in virtually every domain of cognition and communication. In the field of language studies the information processing paradigm for symbols, in particular, has brought about several claims that have immediate relevance to the present discussion. The most important claims are thorough nativism, the priority of grammar over all other aspects of language, and the assumption that there is computational and often also neurophysiological modularity of underlying processes, (for an analysis of the neuropsychological validity of these views, see Farah, 1994).

A revolution at one point in history, however, may become an outdated orthodoxy at the next. Fascination with the computer metaphor turns out to be a constraint on the discussion of intricated biological and cultural issues in the interdisciplinary field of language studies. The fact that the same program can run on somewhat differently designed versions of von Neumann machines (see Fodor & Pylyshyn, 1988) seems to be an insufficient reason for abandoning evolutionary and social approaches to human language. Because they are committed to this self-sufficient formal conception, leading proponents of the theory often simply ascribe corresponding computational resources to a hypothetical linguistic module of the brain. As William Bechtel (chap. 3, this volume) stresses, however, the problem has just been postponed and arises again when we try to explain how such a computational module could have evolved. He adds that formal symbol manipulation is profoundly different from the kinds of processes we observe elsewhere in the biological domain. That is the reason why its emergence in humans appears mysterious: Arguments for the biology of language rest on biologically implausible claims (E. A. Bates, Thal, & Marchman, 1991). Indeed, although demonstrating perfectly well how logical-sentential formulas could be computed, symbol information approach leaves little, if any, space to explain the development. In a rather direct way this has been spelled out by Chomsky (1967), who admitted that he presented "an instantaneous model of language acquisition" (p. 441). Years later, Fodor (1985) made a similar confession: "Deep down, I am inclined to doubt that there is such a thing as cognitive development in the sense that developmental cognitive psychologists have in mind" (p. 35).

The view of language as an informationally encapsulated, syntactic module of the brain is relativized already by perceptual categorization studies. Rosch (1973), in dealing with ethnographic material, and Bornstein (1979), in investigating early ontogenesis, discovered that it is perceptual processing that determines the type of lexical distinctions, not vice versa. This conclusion disproves, at least in the field of color terms, the age-old linguistic relativity hypotheses (see also Berlin & Kay, 1969). The visual information processing account for semantics of color terms can be valid also for that part of the lexicon that is responsible for the description of location as well as the identities of objects (Jackendoff & Landau, 1991). Taking the perspective of simulation of the early stage of language development, Harnad (1990; chap. 2, this volume) described this field of study as an investigation of the "symbol grounding problem." Beyond this psychophysical perspective, cognitive linguistics has in the last decade postulated massive visual and spatial involvement in semantic processing: More concrete visual meanings may have been extended by analogical processes to deal with abstract objects and relations, including pragmatic aspects of discourse (Fauconnier, 1985; Lakoff, 1987; Langnacker, 1987). Obviously, this is a correction of the modularity view, because it shows a profound coordination of processing in presumably separate domains of language and visual cognition.

The new connectionist paradigm seems to be better suited to capture precisely this heterogeneous and context-dependent character of meaningful linguistic processing (Hinton & Shallice, 1991; Ramsey, Stich, & Garon, 1991). Again, this new approach seems to be more appropriate for the simulation of pattern recognition, the ability that connects us with our mammalian ancestors, thus warranting continuity in evolution and leading to human forms of communication and cognition (Harnad, Hanson, & Lubin, 1995). An even stronger aspect of connectionism is its role in learning and change. This explains why neural networks are increasingly used to model different aspects of language performance development, including syntactic effects (for an overview see Bechtel, chap. 3, this volume). One of the theoretical perspectives discussed in several contributions (Bechtel, chapt. 3, Scheerer, chap. 9, and Tomasello, chap. 11, this volume) links the connectionist argumentation with the ecological approach and with Vygotskian cultural-historical psychology. In both cases, the emphasis is not so much on "What is inside of your head?" but on "What is your head inside of?" The main difference is that, whereas ecological psychology deals with physical aspects of the environment (for biological positions of "ecological physics" see Kugler, Shaw, Vincente, & Kinsella-Shaw, 1990), the Vygotskian approach presupposes that cultural products of activity influence our behavior, brain, and mind (Vygotsky, 1985).

In this search for a new theoretical foundation, nobody denies that mature linguistic processing has a *prima facie* symbolic character. The question is whether this should be explained by properties of an inborn "language of the thought" with its "universal grammar" or whether it is a result of an extended evolution that ultimately interacted with human culture. Although individual preferences in reacting to this theoretical dilemma may still differ, development and adaptive plasticity of language are moving into the foreground of discussion.

Within and Beyond the Transition Field

The previously discussed indication of a paradigmatic change is caused, not only by the new horizons of philosophical, logical, and linguistic analysis, but also by recent empirical discoveries. What seemed to be a result of a sudden change can now be traced in more detail and be seen as evolving over time. Interdisciplinary research conducted during the recent decades has produced significant, often spectacular insights into the nature of the early stages of language development, whether it is the reconstruction of the vocal facilities of early *hominids*, the experimental demonstration of the perceptual categorization in human infants, the investigation of behavior and learning in modern higher primates, or the discoveries of linguistic and genetic research showing that the roots of the big families of modern languages can be traced back to the Paleolithic period.

Thus, the data show that nearly all human vocalizations, especially in the production of consonant sounds (Duchin, 1990), might have been available much earlier than is postulated in the conventional analysis done by Lieberman (1984, 1991), who argued that Neanderthals did not have the faculty of speech because of their vocal tract anatomy. Some authors such as Conroy (1990) see evidence for speech prerequisites already in *Homo erectus* (nearly 1.5 million years ago), well before Neanderthals appeared about 100,000 years ago. This is, of course, quite a substantial gap, especially if we take into account that the archaeological data on which Lieberman based his theory are even "younger," going back some 50,000 years. The recent finding of a complete Neanderthal hyoid bone, which is apparently very similar to that of modern humans, only adds fuel to the fire, suggesting that at least Middle Paleolithic populations were anatomically fully capable of modern speech (Arensburg, Schepartz, Tillier, Vandermeersch, & Rak, 1990).

However, the evolution of speech—glossogenesis—seems to be neither the whole nor even the main story. Contemporary neuropsychology provides an appropriate analogy suggesting that relative phonetic and grammatical fluency can be accompanied by severe language disturbances, such as those in Wernicke's type of aphasia (Luria, 1976, 1980), and Williams' syndrome (Bellugi, Bihrle, Jerigan, Trauner, & Doherty, 1990). For the evolutionary analysis it is important to note that, despite all the controversy over endocast finds, there appears to be a major agreement on the basic steps leading from Miocene apes to modern humans. In all recent sources, these breakpoints are shown to coincide with transition periods leading to the specification of *Homo erectus* and archaic *Homo sapiens* (Bickerton, 1990; Corballis, 1991; Donald, 1991; Lieberman, 1991). Within this broad framework of evolutionary investigations one also can easily recognize two tendencies: Late-language models start to prevail over early-language models, and lexically driven models of language evolution overcome more traditional linguistic emphasis on phonology and on grammar (see Deacon, chap. 5, and Tomasello, chap. 11, both in this volume).

The discussion of the origin of language has been greatly diversified in recent years by considering some of its additional framing conditions. For many authors linguistic abilities depend on previous motor control refinement, a point of view reminiscent of Piaget's (e.g., 1983) theory of the child's intellectual development in which sensorimotor coordinations are shown to form a basis for later, symbolic stages of intelligence. The proposals include wholistic "mimetic" (Donald, 1991), hierarchically organized manual (Greenfield, 1991), and gestural-expressive (Corballis, 1991; Kendon, 1991) movements. Some evidence testifies, however, that there is probably no continuous line from sensorimotor activity, specifically gesture, to language either in phylogenesis (Burling 1993) or ontogenesis (Karmiloff-Smith, 1992). Another process under consideration is episodic recollection (Bridgeman, 1992; Donald, 1991), although Tulving (1983), who introduced the notion of episodic memory, preferred to consider episodic recollection as a late and not as an intermediary stage of cognitive development. Other authors have invoked even more complicated determinants, such as generativity (Corballis, 1991), lexical creativity and a readiness to negate associative experience (Deacon, chap. 5, this volume) as well as "second-order" or "reflective" intentionality (Noble & I. Davidson, 1991). Propositional speech, therefore, may depend in its development on pragmatics in the broad sense of the word. Even literacy is now intensively discussed as a factor in shaping not only semantics but also the phonology and syntax of language (Donald, 1991; Scheerer, chap. 9, this volume). Of course, literacy is a purely cultural, continuing stage in the historical memory of humankind.

In a seemingly different endeavor, historical and comparative linguistics provide new arguments, as formulated by the theory of language monogenesis. In elaborating the pioneering arguments of William Jones formulated as early as in 1786 (for more details, see Durham, 1992), the descent relationships of languages were used to infer the historical pattern of sound shifts, and thereby to reconstruct words and expressions of the protolanguages. This procedure was widely applied, generating word lists and associated cultural inferences for many ancestral languages, including Proto-Athapaskan, Proto-Indo-European, Nostratic, Austronesian and Proto-Polynesian, to name a few (Dolgopolsky, 1992; Renfrew, 1988; Ruhlen, 1994). The tentative conclusion is that the human languages form "what is very likely a single language family" (Greenberg, 1987, p. 337) that might converge to a single source somewhere between 30,000 and 100,000 years ago. This approach has reached its ultimate expression for both historical linguistics and biological anthropology in a recent comparison of the global phylogenies of gene pools and languages. Using linguistic evidence on the one hand and populational genetic data on the other, Cavalli-Sforza and his colleagues found that the genetic family tree correlates "surprisingly well" with its still somewhat incomplete linguistic counterpart (see Cavalli-Sforza, Menozzi, & Piazza, 1994; Durham, 1992; Piazza, chap. 8, this volume).

In another recent venture, the very understanding of language as the *differentia specifica* of our species has been questioned. The main insight enabling investigations into primate language consists of diverting attempts in the study of primarily vocal speech to the investigation of comprehension and communication with the help of manual signs (R. A. Gardner & B. T. Gardner, 1969), plastic tokens (Premack, 1986), or computer-recorded lexigrams (Savage-Rumbaugh et al., 1993). These studies prove that higher primates are able to use referential semantics. Recent results of primate language studies go even further, including the narrow definition of language as a combinatorial grammar system introduced by Chomskyan linguistics and propagated in a symbol information processing approach. Experiments with the bonobo chimpanzee *(Pan paniscus)* Kanzi, in particular, demonstrated that his learning abilities amount to understanding phrases despite their grammatical transformations (Greenfield & Savage-Rumbaugh, 1990; Rumbaugh & Savage-Rumbaugh, chap. 10, this volume). Even Terrace (1985), whose efforts led to the ape-language controversy, contended that "there is little question that apes overlap with human beings with respect to their ability to learn arbitrary rules regarding the use of symbols. Both species learn to make requests by using arbitrary symbols, and both species are able to use symbols to communicate intentionally" (p. 1021). These results, often ignored by the symbol information processing camp, suggest that in one way or another the concept of an inborn linguistic processing module of the human brain is in need of revision.

SOME UNRESOLVED PARADOXES

Despite all of this progress, the problem of relationships between biological and cultural factors of language development remains controversial and, in a sense, more paradoxical than ever. An emerging understanding is that neither nativist nor empiricist accounts seem to tell the complete story of the origins and early development of language. Perhaps the main paradox is that such little change in genetic endowment could produce the tremendous differences in behavior, communication, and cognition that have led to our technologies and culture.

How Much Genetic Change Makes the Difference?

It seems to be only a minor variation that separates humans from the two closest evolutionary outgroups: chimpanzees and gorillas (Lewin, 1989; R. D. Martin, 1990). Only slightly more than 1% of the genome is found to be different in a comparison between *Homo* and *Pan*. This 1% is scattered throughout the genome so that there simply are no human versus chimpanzee genes. This is demonstrated in a study by Lisitsyn and his coworkers (Lisitsyn et al., 1990). After breaking up chimpanzee DNA by heating and melting it into single strands, human DNA from brain tissue was allowed to reallele. It was expected that about 99% would reallele well because the match did not need to be perfect. The other 1% would then be the unique human genetic material. Instead, it was found that no material remained except highly redundant DNA that, in addition, was widely distributed across the genome (see also Ueda, Washio, & Kurosaki, 1990). Prehumans were nearly there. Furthermore, they had the genetic variation to produce the "tweaks" that pushed them over the edge.

The studies showing an affinity of linguistic and genetic changes (Cavalli-Sforza, Menozzi, & Piazza, 1994; Piazza, chap. 8, this volume) simultaneously led to the conclusion that there is a lack of direct effect of genes on language. Of course, some aspects of linguistic functioning can be interpreted as if they resulted from the action of specific genetic mechanisms that evolved via the conventional neo-Darwinian process (Pinker & P. Bloom, 1990). Besides classical data on the existence of the critical, or at least the sensitive period for the acquisition of language (e.g., Hurford, 1991), one recent example is the case of specific disturbances of phonology and morphology that has been traced by Gopnik (1990) in three generations of a large family. On the other hand, experiments with *Pan paniscus* Kanzi seem to suggest that an appropriate social support, together with instrumental means (e.g., keyboards with lexigrams; see Rumbaugh, Savage-Rumbaugh, chap. 10, this volume), may help to overcome differences in genetic material. This conclusion comes close to the actual results of a centuries-old investigation in other fields of behavioral genetics (Horgan, 1993).

The correlation of linguistic and genetic changes hardly goes beyond some parallel changes of two comparably complex systems. Being itself a very interesting marker of evidence concerning the paths and pace of development, this correlation has no causal significance, as in the case of the correlation of data on the populational frequency of blood Rh factor and similarities of European languages discussed by Piazza (chap. 10, this volume). A common argument today is that language massively uses already existing structures of the brain that had initially evolved for purposes other than oral communication (Bridgeman, 1992; Donald, 1991; Greenfield, 1991). These genetically determined structures had other cognitive and sensorimotor functions before they became "residues" of the linguistic mechanisms.

Does Our Brain Really Matter?

If the genetic changes in the evolution of humans are so small, how were these minor changes connected with the growth of specific neurophysiological tissue? Although textbooks on neuropsychology connect language ability with a specific core region, including the famous Broca and Wernicke areas around *planum temporale* of the left cortical hemisphere, the data on this seemingly obvious topic remain controversial. Putting aside rather anecdotal evidence of preserved linguistic and cognitive abilities in persons with severely reduced overall brain geometry (see Lenneberg, 1967; Lewin, 1980), one easily finds firm neuropsychological results testifying that lesions in the core region of language, first of all, do not preclude all vocalizations (Jackson, 1874; Van Lancker, 1987), and, second, usually do not completely disturb an understanding of the communicative situation and its adequate evaluation (Huber, Poeck, & Weniger, 1989; Luria, 1980).

Some low-level as well as higher-level linguistic phenomena thus seem to survive the destruction of the language zones. This fact, together with the data on developmental changes of the functional brain localization of linguistic processes (within the left hemisphere as well as between hemispheres; Goldberg & Costa, 1981), suggests that the localization of language is a very plastic matter evolved in the course of time. The initial plasticity of neural networks, which have so far been left unstructured by learning, can explain the existence of the sensitive period in the development of language (Marchman, 1993). With respect to the possible brain localization of grammar, this developmental dynamic is especially clearly demonstrated by Friederici (chap. 7, this volume). According to this, Broca's area takes over relatively automatized syntactic operations, a process that is relatively slow (because it can last for the first 10 years of life).

Another problem is that there are, in fact, no serious differences in the structural organization of human and nonhuman primate brains (Bridgeman, 1992; Soreno, 1991). Provided that language is a relatively recent capacity, one can hardly imagine any big evolutionary changes, so our attention has to be directed even to a relatively minor neurophysiological development. Paradoxically, this development does not take place directly within the language core area, but at least one step higher on the evolutionary scale in the prefrontal lobes of the neocortex.

It has long been known that "the entire period of human evolutionary existence could be considered as the 'age of the frontal lobe'" (Tilney, 1928, p. 13). The problem of the development of prefrontal regions and the interpretation of their unusual functions is the subject of heated debates (Deacon, chap. 5, this volume; Stuss & Benson, 1990). In evaluating prefrontal functions, it is necessary to see both the difference and similarity between humans and nonhuman species. What Deacon calls the "family resemblance in prefrontal functions" consists in executive control of behavior with an implicit negative attitude toward actual perception or earlier memory associations. This attitude is, of course, the minimal requirement for an intellectually inquiring organism, not just a knowing one. One can speculate that this type of control, such as the rule "Do not look for it there where you have found it previously!" could have supported the lives of early hominids in the savanna: In view of sparsely distributed food, a typical "savanna task" presupposes some form of negation of previous perceptual experience (see Jacobsen, 1936). Acquisition of such heuristics would simultaneously be a step to rule-governed behavior.

Of course, there are profound dissimilarities of prefrontal functions between humans and nonhuman primates. In humans the prefrontal brain is involved in personal and reflective control; changes of mental attitudes; and thoroughly social and cultural, higher order pragmatics: irony, sarcasm, metaphorical speech, and poetic language. This form of executive control is based on the use of conceptual (i.e., primarily verbal) means. Human prefrontal functions are interwoven with language —if not in their actual execution, then at some earlier, formative phases of individual development (Bridgeman, 1992; Luria, 1976). Recent evidence that neocortex size in primates is correlated with group size (Dunbar, 1993) seems to suggest the same social driving forces. Turbulences and mild, though permanent, challenges to life in a large group can be an especially powerful catalyst for the development of "Machiavellian" intelligence (Whiten & Byrne, 1988) requiring a flexible evaluation of the situation from different perspectives. Eventually, this situation contributes to the emergence of an internal "theory of mind" (Perner, 1991) in other group members, which, in turn, could generate a selective pressure for the evolution of the prefrontal neocortex in anthropogenesis.

Where Are Symbols "Grounded"?

Although the orthodox version of the symbol information approach praised "methodological solipsism" (Fodor, 1979) as the favorite research strategy, all reformed trends acknowledge that the internal symbol system underlying human language needs some form of grounding in the real world or, at least, in the perception of the latter (Harnad, chap. 2, this volume). Does the grounding presuppose perceptual categorization or still something else such as reference to culture? This volume contributes to the discussion of the issue. Three complementary approaches are represented. According to the first, semantics and syntax grow up "from below" relatively continuously from visual and intermodal perceptual experience (see Harnad, chap. 2, Bechtel, chap. 3, and Maryanski, chap. 4, this volume).

The second approach, in line with the earlier philosophical analysis of Wittgenstein and Quine, argues against a continuous transformation of perceptual categorization into linguistic categories. From this point of view, semantics is growing out of thinking (i.e., in a sense "from above"; Deacon, chap. 5, this volume). Perceptual categorization is undoubtedly one of the major steps on the way to advanced forms of cognition and communication. However, even though categorical perception can be one prerequisite for the development of symbolic representations and language, it is undoubtedly a rather primitive prerequisite, because it apparently is shared by nonprimate apes and even such mammals as chinchillas (for an overview of comparative studies on categorical perception, see Massaro, 1987). If referential and lexical semantics could grow from low-level perceptual and mnemonic functions, then language should occur in many species, not only, as it is, in humans (Deacon, chap. 5, this volume). This means that perceptual categorization does probably not directly underlie the development of semantic categories of language.

The third approach relativizes the dichotomy of continuous versus discontinuous models of language evolution and consists of a sociocultural analysis of the problem (Tomasello, chap. 11, this volume). Semantic reference and syntax are considered here as developing within the field of social interaction. "Joint attention" (Bruner, 1978; Vygotsky, 1934, 1962) is the most important phenomenon of such interaction, creating the earliest "zone of proximal development" for cognitive, behavioral, and specifically linguistic development. Thus, communicative interaction between mother and child presupposes a sophisticated control of mutual eye movements. Indeed, there are specific prefrontal mechanisms in pointing and in coordinated eye movements that in humans seem to be instrumental in serving communication and cooperative activity. The question as to whether such a symbolic gaze use (e.g., pointing to an object for others) can be observed in primates is a subject of current discussions (see Tomasello, Krueger, & H. H. Ratner, 1993).

Some rather radical suggestions about the role of cultural factors in language development are beginning to appear in the literature. Bechtel (chap. 3, this volume) argues that the complexity of formal operations of early linguistic processing has been exaggerated because it had been supposed that all these operations were happening in the child's head. Language is an objective, external symbol system that exists within culture, supporting any individual use of it. Visual languages with their enduring properties can be of special importance to such an external support (Donald, 1991; Scheerer, chap. 9, this volume). Literacy, furthermore, presupposes evolving new "functional systems" in the brain (Luria, 1976), such as subserving reading or counting skills. A more controversial thesis is that a phonological (not just phonetic) type of perception can be found only in literate persons (Scheerer, chap. 9, this volume). This suggestion may be too revolutionary, however, as it presupposes that categorical perception of phonemes is possible before the development of oral speech. Evidence of differences in neuropsychological mechanisms of language in literate and illiterate persons is more promising, but such evidence is still fragmentary (Hu, Qiou, & Zhong, 1990; Lecours, Mehler, Parente, & Beltrami, 1988).

There is another possibility of bridging biological and cultural phases of development (Biben, Symmes, & Bernhards, 1989; Papoušek & Papoušek, 1991). This possibility can be found in early mother-child communication. Its most salient aspect is "motherese": the slow, stylized way most people adopt when talking to babies (Bornstein, chap. 9, this volume; Grieser & Kuhl, 1988). Along with emerging mutual activities of mother and child (Bruner, 1978), motherese may well be the main vehicle for early linguistic development. This is evidenced by its properties: typical prosodic melodies, accentuation of phonemic features, simplified semantics, distinctiveness of syntactic boundaries, and, in particular, control of the child's attentional reactions. Indeed, there are data showing that motherese affects the infant's gaze movements much more than does usual conversational speech (Bornstein, chap. 9, this volume). Socialization of attentional control, therefore, seems to be one of the major preconditions of language acquisition.

EVOLUTIONARY PERSPECTIVE CULTURALLY AMPLIFIED

What kind of unifying framework would then explain the appearance of language? Biobehavioral roots of communication and cognition are different. So are their initial brain mechanisms: limbic and subcortical regions control non-propositional vocalizations, while neocortical mechanisms are responsible for perception and problem solving. A convergence of both lines creates a basis for the emergence of language and symbolic thought, provided that newly evolved prefrontal structures can mediate social control necessary for the acquisition of language and its cultural transmission.

Stages in Language Evolution and Development

The multiplicity in which the language emerged would make its explanation a hopeless venture if we were restricted by the theoretical framework of language as a closed formal system. Fortunately, in view of the aforementioned advances we are not forced to keep the model. The existence of early nonpropositional forms of language (that we call

P-languages to differentiate them from the notion of *protolanguage* used in paleolinguistics) is supported by phenomena such as speech automatisms, emotional vocalizations, or synpractical reference. In general, one can say that P-language has no syntax, but knows a form of primitive semantics. This semantics is determined mainly by emotional context, associative experience and, of course, by the processes of visuospatial recognition and categorization which humans share with other primates (Maryanski, this volume; Soreno, 1991; Velichkovsky, 1982).

Even the normal language of a child may be an example in this respect because it has no clear-cut-division of semantics and syntax. Tomasello (1992, chap. 11, this volume) argues that children's early grammatical competence can be explained by deep semantics of verbs, without resorting to adultlike linguistic rules. Friederici (1983) as well as other authors (e.g., Akhutina, Velichkovsky, & Kempe, 1989) demonstrated that during development a marked interaction can be observed between syntactic and semantic variables up to the ages of 10 to 12. This interaction of syntax and semantics is valid for adults, too: Even proponents of the modularity view would spend some more dozens milliseconds to processing the sentence "The boy bites the dog" instead of the reversed version. This means that, at least in the beginning, syntactic rules are bound by their meaningful context of application.

In addition to P-language and language, there may well be later, or higher—in evolutionary and logical terms—forms of *M-language* (a name we use to avoid the term *metalanguage,* which has a different connotation within linguistics). Ample evidence comes from research on situational pragmatics (Herrmann, 1983), semantics of "mental spaces" (Fauconnier, 1985), and poetic theory (Shcheglov & Zholtkovsky, 1987). In ontogenesis, M-language has to be based on the "theory of mind" stage of cognitive development (Karmiloff-Smith, 1992; Perner, 1991), when at about age 4, cognitive and also linguistic (mainly in the form of propositional attitudes) manifestations of understanding other people's beliefs, desires, deceptions, and intentions become common. At the same age, one observes in different languages of the world nonmonotonic changes in the linguistic development caused by metalinguistic discoveries of the type, "the first noun is the agent" (see Akhutina, Velichkovsky & Kempe, 1989).

This is also the age when major changes in myelinization of prefrontal regions of the brain occur (Luria, 1980; see also Stuss, 1992).

Data such as these argue in favor of a hierarchical model of the functional organization of the brain, in which different cognitive processes and forms of language are described as distributed over three different levels (Velichkovsky, 1990). Accordingly, at Level 1 (P-Language) we note only prerequisites of propositional language that are split between two separate lines of evolution: emotional communication and elementary problem solving. At Level 2 (Language), these lines are united (i.e., manifested by communication and understanding of propositional contents). Level 3 (M-language) fulfills the metainstrumental function: generation, monitoring, adaptation, and repair of processing at the lower levels. All three levels can simultaneously undertake the task-dependent distribution of roles for leadership and background coordination (see Bernstein, 1947; Werner, 1948). This is only an abstract static picture, however, in need of further elaboration.

The Multiple-Level Evolutionary Model

The neuropsychological data allow us to localize protolinguistic processes outside the classical anterior part of the language core area (Broca) in the subcortical and paleocortical brain as well as in the posterior neocortex. This is the reason why even in severe cases of Broca and global aphasia, which are characterized among other things by agrammatism, different manifestations of nonpropositional P-language are still possible (Van Lancker, 1987). MacLean (1988), in particular, argued for phylogenetic roots of the early emotional vocalization within the limbic paleocortex, as coming only with the transition from reptiles to early mammals, with still a long way to a convergence with cortical mechanisms of perceptual and intellectual processing (Maryanski, chap. 4, this volume).

From this multilevel perspective, it is possible also to look anew at some well-known, but nevertheless paradoxical changes in the brain that occur in anthropogenesis. The development and functioning of language are usually examined in connection with the enlarged perisylvan region of the left hemisphere (Geschwind & Galaburda, 1987), but this type of asymmetry is very old. It was evidently found in our fossil ancestor, *Homo erectus*, and, ontogenetically, can be documented already in the fetus. Nonhuman primates also seem to have some analogue to the region.

Other changes, however, are unique in human evolution. They consist of prefrontal growth, but above all in an enlargement of the right frontal and left posterior regions of the neocortex (Bradshaw, 1989; Holloway & De la Coste-Larymondie, 1982). Although they are always considered "silent" with respect to speech, both of these regions seem to be important for metalinguistic and meta-cognitive operations, namely, for changing the truthvalues of the verbal and visuospatial representations of knowledge (for an overview, see Velichkovsky, 1994). Indeed, prefrontal regions outside Broca's area, and especially within the right hemisphere, provide firm neuropsychological evidence of the existence of M-language. Recent findings show that injuries of these regions in the right hemisphere produce characteristic disorders in metalinguistic and metacognitive coordination. For example, a patient with such an injury may no longer be able to detect the irony or understand the metaphorical meaning of a phrase (H. Gardner, Brownell, Wapner, & Michelow, 1983). Similar problems arise in connection with the processing of the macrosemantics of a text, such as distinguishing between the description of fictitious and real episodes (Chernigovskaya, 1990).

The existing experimental data testify that Level 3 functioning is unavailable for monkeys (Cheney & Seyfart, 1991) and even for the brightest of primates (Premack, 1988; Tomasello, Kruger, & H. H. Ratner, 1993). The same, of course, can be said about the normal human child 2.5 years of age, who served as control in language understanding tests in experiments with Kanzi, as reported by Rumbaugh and Savage-Rumbaugh (chap. 10, this volume). Although processes leading to the "theory of mind" stage can well be documented in a preverbal child, there is no evidence that either the developed "theory of mind" or the reflective "second-order" intentionality could be available before language comes to the scene (Karmiloff-Smith, 1992; see also Rosenthal, 1986, for compelling logical arguments). Both "theory of mind" phenomena and manifestations of M-language demonstrate very similar intersubjective semantics (Velichkovsky, 1990). This also can be seen in the fact that the siblings' group size is a valid predictor of the time when the "theory of mind" appears in a child's development (Jo Perner, personal communication, 1994).

Although higher primates seem to possess the major structures that could support Level 2 linguistic functioning (i.e., language per se), they do not regularly reach that level of performance. The reason for that is, of course, the big question dominating the investigation of language evolution. It is probable that the emergence of language is possible only through a loop "from above", via the internal meta-cognitive control executed by the prefrontal brain, or—still an exceptional situation—by an external, social substitute for the prefrontal control.

Loops of Evolution and Cultural Amplification

The segment of human evolution leading to full-blown language was not a monotonous unidirectional progression. It testifies to numerous reiterations, amplifications, and coevolution of its heterogeneous components (Bridgeman, 1992; Deacon, 1991). Every progressive change leads, not only to an anatomical expansion of new areas, but also to the "downstream" waves along the whole vertical dimension of the brain. This secondary reorganization mainly induces functional alterations, whereby the functions can be modernized or completely changed. For instance, the "reptilian" part of our brain (basal ganglia and midbrain; MacLean, 1985) is massively involved in bipedal locomotion and executes some background coordinations of expedient piano playing (Bernstein, 1947). Similarly, structures that evolved for the recognition of perceptual categories and for the control of fine motor coordination become sites of our direct linguistic capacities (Greenfield, 1991; Soreno, 1991) where the Level 2 processes reside. As in the example of the "reptilian brain" playing piano, this happens only in the second run which, in the case of language, is primarily caused by the prefrontal expansion and its sociobehavioral correlates (i.e., after structures of Level 3 were, in the first run, delineated).

This nonmonotony can be helpful in explaining paradoxes in this field of study. To find the origins of language one tends to look for preconditions, whereas one actually needs to look for consequences of language evolution, including changes in social interactions and material culture. The last requirement seems to have become accepted by all recent multilevel evolutionary theories (Donald, 1991; Plotkin, 1988; Tomasello, Krueger, & H. H. Ratner, 1993). These "extracerebral components" greatly diversify the possibility of supporting linguistic performance via external loops, which, in terms of individual development, means that the child grows up into a world of mature culture and its symbolic forms, so different and so much easier in comparison with the mystery of the initial evolution of language.

An additional complexity is that the prefrontal brain, too, could not remain the same after the second-run change of lowerlevel mechanisms. The careful reconstruction given by Deacon (chap. 5, this volume) shows how difficult it is to define the basic preverbal functions of this brain region. The task is not made easier in the case of the early functioning of the verbal (second-run) prefrontal brain. Whether it immediately became an organ of higher order thought, M-language, and reflective consciousness is in serious doubt (see Rosenthal, 1986). The long history still lying ahead brought further qualitative changes (e.g., the distinction between everyday and scientific concepts that is crucial for an analysis of consciousness and different forms of metacognition; however, owing to Scribner & M. Cole, 1981; Vygotsky, 1934, 1962. In any case, its own "second-run," the prefrontal brain supported by language becomes a true organ of culture and verbally mediated symbolic thinking. This emerging cognitive power (not just the freeing of the hand for manufacturing and art after the manual gesture was replaced by oral speech, as suggested recently by Corballis, 1992) was at the heart of the technological "creative explosion" of the Upper Paleolithic period (Marshack, 1989).

If the present analysis is correct, we can expect that vocal propositional language has evolved on the eve of these major cultural changes in the evolution of humankind, perhaps in the Lower-Middle Paleolithic period, together with the appearance of the archaic *Homo sapiens*. This is a temporal zone in which the reconstruction lines of the "Eve tongue" seem to converge. The previous, great historical phase, that of *Homo erectus,* was mostly a preparatory period of coevolution of prefrontal functions and social organization. These processes created forms of attentional control necessary for the emergence of symbolic language as well as prerequisites for its social transmission and external, cultural storage. From this point of view, it would be wrong to localize language only within biology and not within culture. The only justification for that would be an artificial narrowing of the scope of language functions to a meaningless vocalization or grammar (see Pinker, 1994). Emerging language was nonseparate from emerging culture, although direct neuroanatomical prerequisites for language had evolved at least an epoch earlier.

CONCLUSION

In the cryptic story of the origins of language, the crucial impetus may come from above, from the sphere of interindividual metacognitive coordination, which is neuroanatomically connected, not with the language core area around the *planum temporale* of the left hemisphere, but with the prefrontal brain. In other words, we should seriously consider the possibility that early the evolution and ontogenesis of language do not proceed only in the "upstream," but also, to a critical degree, in the "downstream" fashion. It can therefore be assumed that language as a formal system is generated primarily through the functioning of the metacognitive coordination level.

Different lines of research presented in this volume approach this conceptual problem by means of new empirical data and fresh theoretical hypotheses. These concepts are often rather speculative from the mainstream cognitive community point of view, but will undoubtedly contribute to the interdisciplinary dialogue between the different approaches to the problem of the biological foundations of human culture. As a manifestation of the flexibility and adaptive power of human nature, language transcends any one-sided attempt at its explanation. If this were to be formulated as a new paradigm, or as the currently emerging *Zeitgeist*, it would involve a change of the perspective: At the very center of the investigations are precisely those interactions of biological and cultural factors that make the development of formal properties of language possible.

ACKNOWLEDGMENT

Thanks are due to all coworkers at the Center for Interdisciplinary Research, University of Bielefeld. The contribution of Peter Weingart, who initiated the project, Biological Foundations of Human Culture, was especially significant. A valuable collaboration on the part of Duane Rumbaugh, along with the authors of this volume and many other colleagues in Atlanta, Bielefeld and Toronto is also greatly appreciated. The preparation of this chapter was supported by the Natural Sciences and Engineering Research Council of Canada and by the Deutsche Forschungsgemeinschaft (DFG SFB 360/B4).

REFERENCES

Akhutina, T. V., Velichkovsky, B. M., & Kempe, V. (1989). Semantic syntax and orientation on the word order in ontogenesis. In M. Shakhnorovich (Ed.), *Semantics in speech activity* (in Russian) (pp. 5–23). Moscow: Nauka.

Arensburg, B., Schepartz, L. A., Tiller, A. M., Vandermeersch, B., & Rak, Y. (1990). A reappraisal of the anatomical basis for speech in Middle Paleolithic hominids. *Journal of American Physical Anthropology, 89,* 137–146.

Bates, E. A., Thal, D., & Marchman, V. A. (1991). Symbol and syntax: A Darwinian approach to language development. In N. A. Krasnegor, D. M. Rumbaugh, R. L. Schiefelbusch, & M. Studdert-Kennedy (Eds.), *Biological and behavioral determinants of language development* (pp. 29–65). Hillsdale, NJ: Lawrence Erlbaum Associates.

Bellugi, U., Bihrle, A., Jernigan, T., Trauner, D., & Doherty, S. (1990). Neuropsychological, neurological, and neuroanatomical profile of Williams' syndrome. *American Journal of Medical Genetics Supplement, 6,* 115–125.

Berlin, B., & Kay, P. (1969). *Basic color terms: Their universality and evolution.* Berkeley: University of California Press.

Bernstein, N. A. (1947). *On the construction of movements.* Moscow: Medgiz.

Biben, M., Symmes, D., & Bernhards, D. (1989). Contour variables in vocal communication between squirrel monkey mother and infants. *Developmental Psychobiology, 22*(6), 617–631.

Bickerton, D. (1990). *Language and species.* Chicago: University of Chicago Press.

Bornstein, M. H. (1979). Perceptual development: Stability and change in feature perception. In M. H. Bornstein & W. Kessen (Eds.), *Psychological development in infancy: From image to intention* (pp. 37–82). Hillsdale, NJ: Lawrence Erlbaum Associates.

Bradshaw, J. L. (1989). *Hemispheric specialization and psychological functions.* New York: Wiley.

Bridgeman, B. (1992). On the origin of consciousness and language. *Psycoloquy (refereed electronic journal), 92.315.consciousness.1.bridgeman.*

Bruner, J. (1978). On prelinguistic prerequisites of speech. In R. N. Campbell & P. T. Smith (Eds.), *Recent advances in the psychology of language: Language development and mother-child interaction* (pp. 17–35). New York: Plenum.

Burling, R. (1993). Primate calls, human language, and nonverbal communication. *Current Anthropology, 34*(1), 25–53.

Cavalli-Sforza, L. L., Menozzi, P., & Piazza, A. (1994). *History and geography of human genes*. Princeton, NJ: Princeton University Press.
Cheney, D. L., & Seyfarth, R. M. (1991). Truth and deception in animal communication. In C. A. Ristau (Ed.), *Cognitive ethology: The minds of other animals* (pp. 127–151). Hillsdale, NJ: Lawrence Erlbaum Associates.
Chernigovskaya, T. N. (1990, April 19–22). *Modes of consciousness: Cultural, functional, and neuropsychological dimensions.* Paper presented to the Conference on Interdisciplinary Investigation of Consciousness, Center for Interdisciplinary Research, University of Bielefeld, Bielefeld, Germany.
Chomsky, N. (1967). The formal nature of language. In E. H. Lenneberg (Ed.), *Biological foundations of language* (pp. 397–442). New York: Wiley.
Chomsky, N. (1972). *Language and mind.* New York: Harcourt, Brace and World.
Conroy, G. (1990). *Primate evolution.* New York: Norton.
Corballis, M. (1991). *The lopsided ape: Evolution of the generative mind.* New York: Oxford University Press.
Corballis, M. (1992). On the evolution of language and generativity. *Cognition, 44,* 197–226.
Deacon, T. W. (1992). Brain-language co-evolution. In J. A. Hawkins (Ed.), *The evolution of human languages* (pp. 76–91). Redwood City, CA: Addison-Wesley.
Dolgopolsky, A. (1992, January). *Language relationship and the history of mankind.* Paper presented at the Conference on Biological and Cultural Aspects of Language Development, Center for Interdisciplinary Research, University of Bielefeld, Germany, January 20–23, 1992.
Donald, M. (1991). *Origins of the modern mind: Three stages in the evolution of culture and cognition.* Cambridge, MA: Harvard University Press.
Duchin, L. E. (1990). The evolution of articulate speech: Comparative anatomy of the oral cavity in *Pan* and *Homo*. *Journal of Human Evolution, 19,* 687–697.
Dunbar, R. I. M. (1993). Co-evolution of neocortex size, group size and language in humans. *Behavioral and Brain Sciences, 16,* 751–792.
Durham, W. H. (1992). *Applications of evolutionary cultural theory.* Report Nr.12/92 Center for Interdisciplinary Research, University of Bielefeld, Germany
Farah, M. J. (1994), Neuropsychological inference with an interactive brain: A critique of the "locality assumption". *Behavioral and Brain Sciences, 17*(1), 43–60.
Fauconnier, G. (1985). *Mental spaces.* Cambridge, MA: MIT Press.

Fodor, J. A. (1979). Methodological solipsism considered as a research strategy in cognitive psychology. *Behavioral and Brain Sciences, 3,* 63–110.
Fodor, J. A. (1983). *The modularity of mind.* Cambridge, MA: MIT Press.
Fodor, J. A. (1985). Fodor's guide to mental representation: The intelligent auntie's vademecum. *Mind, 94,* 76–100
Fodor, J. A., & Pylyshyn, Z. (1988). Connectionism and cognitive architecture: A critical analysis. *Cognition, 28,* 3–71.
Friederici, A. D. (1983). Children's sensitivity to function words during sentence comprehension. *Linguistics, 21,* 717–739.
Gardner, H., Brownell, H., Wapner, W., & Michelow, D. (1983). Missing the point: The role of the right hemisphere in the processing of complex linguistic materials. In E. Perecman (Ed.), *Cognitive processing in the right hemisphere* (pp. 169–191). New York: Academic Press.
Gardner, R. A., & Gardner, B. T. (1969). Teaching sign language to chimpanzees. *Science, 165,* 664–672.
Geschwind, N., & Galaburda, A. M. (1987). *Cerebral lateralization: Biological mechanisms, associations, and pathology.* Cambridge, MA: MIT Press.
Goldberg, E., & Costa, L. D. (1981). Hemispheric differences in the acquisition and use of descriptive systems. *Brain and Language, 14,* 144–173.
Gopnik, M. (1990). Feature-blind grammar and dysphasia. *Nature, 314,* 715.
Greenberg, J. H. (1987). *The languages of America.* Stanford, CA: Stanford University Press.
Greenfield, P. M. (1991). Language, tools, and the brain: The ontogeny and phylogeny of hierarchically organized sequential behavior. *Behavioral and Brain Sciences, 14,* 531–595.
Grieser, D. L., & Kuhl, P. K. (1988). Maternal speech to infants in a tonal language: Support for universal prosodic features in motherese. *Developmental Psychology, 24*(1), 14–20.
Harnad, S. (1990). The symbol grounding problem. *Physica, 42,* 335–346.
Harnad, S., Hanson, S. J., & Lubin, J. (1995). Learned categorical perception in neural nets: Implications for symbolic grounding. In V. Honovar & L. Uhr (Eds.), *Symbol processing and connectionist network models in artificial intelligence and cognitive modelling: Steps toward principled integration* (pp.191–206). New York: Academic Press.
Herrmann, T. (1983). *Speech and situation: A psychological analysis of situated speaking.* Berlin: Springer.
Hinton, G. E., & Shallice, T. (1991). Lesioning an attractor network: Investigations of acquired dyslexia. *Psychological Review, 98,* 74–95.
Holloway, R. L., & De la Coste-Larymondie, M. (1982). Brain endocast asymmetry in pongids and hominids. *American Journal of Physical Anthropology, 58,* 108–110.

Horgan, J. (1993). Eugenics revisited. *Scientific American, 268,* 92–100.
Hu, Y.-H., Qiou, Y.-G., & Zhong, G.-Q. (1990). Crossed aphasia in Chinese: A survey. *Brain and Language, 39,* 347–356.
Huber, W., Poeck, K., & Weniger, D. (1989). Aphasie. In K. Poeck (Ed.), *Clinical neuropsychology,* 2nd ed. (pp. 89–136). Stuttgart, Germany: Thieme.
Hurford, J. R. (1991). The evolution of the critical period for language acquisition. *Cognition, 40*(3), 159–201.
Jackendoff, R., & Landau, B. (1991). Spatial language and spatial cognition. In D. J. Napoli & J. A. Kegl (Eds.), *Bridges between psychology and linguistics: A Swarthmore Festschrift for Lila Gleitman* (pp. 145–169). Hillsdale, NJ: Lawrence Erlbaum Associates.
Jackson, H. J. (1874). On affections of speech from disease of brain. *Brain, 1,* 304–330.
Jacobsen, C. (1936). Studies of cerebral function in primates. *Comparative Psychology Monographs, 13,* 1–68.
Karmiloff-Smith. A. (1992). *Beyond modularity: A developmental perspective on cognitive science.* Cambridge, MA: MIT Press.
Kendon, A. (1991). Some considerations for a theory of language origins. *Man (N.S.), 26*(2), 199–222.
Kugler, P. N., Shaw, R. E., Vincente, K. J., & Kinsella-Shaw, J. (1990). Inquiry into intentional systems, I: Issues in ecological physics. *Psychological Research, 52*(2/3), 98–121.
Lakoff, G. (1987). *Women, fire, and dangerous things.* Chicago: University of Chicago Press.
Langacker, R. (1987). *Foundations of cognitive grammar.* Stanford, CA: Stanford University Press.
Lecours, A. R., Mehler, J., Parente, M. A., & Beltrami, M. A. (1988). Illiteracy and brain damage: III. A contribution to the study of speech and language disorders in illiterates with unilateral brain damage (initial testing). *Neuropsychologia, 26*(4), 575–589.
Lenneberg, E. H. (1967). *Biological foundations of language.* New York: Wiley.
Lewin, R. (1980). Is your brain really necessary? *Science, 210,* 1232–1234.
Lewin, R. (1989). *Human evolution.* 2nd ed. Oxford, England: Blackwell.
Lieberman, P. (1984). *The biology and evolution of language.* Cambridge, MA: Cambridge University Press.
Lieberman, P. (1991). *Uniquely human: The evolution of speech, thought, and selfless behavior.* Cambridge, MA: Harvard University Press.

Lisitsyn, N. A., Launer, G. A., Wagner, L. L., Akopyanz, N. S., Martynov, V. I., Lelikova, G. P., Limborska, S. A., Polukarova, L. G., & Sverdlov, E. D. (1990). Isolation of rapidly evolving genomic sequences: Construction of a differential library and identification of a human DNA fragment that does not hybridize to chimpanzee DNA. *Biomedical Science, 1*, 513–516.

Luria, A. R. (1976). *Basic problems of neurolinguistics.* The Hague: Mouton.

Luria, A. R. (1980). *Higher cortical functions in man.* 2nd ed. New York: Basic Books.

MacLean, P. D. (1985). Evolutionary psychiatry and the triune brain. *Psychological Medicine, 15*, 219–221.

MacLean, P. D. (1988). The midline frontolimbic cortex and evolution of crying and laughter. In E. Perecman (Ed.), *The frontal lobes revisited* (pp. 121–140). Hillsdale, NJ: Lawrence Erlbaum Associates.

Marchman, V. A. (1993). Constraints on plasticity in a connectionist model of the English past tense. *Journal of Cognitive Neuroscience, 5*(2), 215–234.

Marshack, A. (1989). Evolution of the human capacity: The symbolic evidence. *Yearbook of Physical Anthropology, 32*, 1–34.

Martin, R. D. (1990). *Primate origins and evolution: A phylogenetic reconstruction.* London: Chapman and Hall.

Massaro, D. W. (1987). Psychophysics versus specialized processes in speech perception: An alternative perspective. In M. E. N. Schouten (Ed.), *The psychophysics of speech perception* (pp. 46–65). Dordrecht, Netherlands: Martinus Nijhoff.

Noble, W., & Davidson, I. (1991). The evolutionary emergence of modern human behavior: Language and its archeology. *Man (N.S.), 26*, 223–253.

Papoušek, H., & Papoušek, M. (1991). Innate and cultural guidance of infants' integrative competencies: China, the United States, and Germany. In M. H. Bornstein (Ed.), *Cultural approaches to parenting* (pp. 23–44). Hillsdale, NJ: Lawrence Erlbaum Associates.

Perner, J. (1991). *Understanding the representational mind.* Cambridge, MA: MIT Press.

Piaget, J. (1983). Piaget's theory. In P. H. Muessen (Ed.), *Handbook of child psychology* (Vol.1, pp. 103–128). New York: Wiley.

Pinker, S. (1994). *The language instinct: How the mind creates language.* New York: William Morrow.

Pinker, S., & Bloom, P. (1990). Natural language and natural selection. *Behavioral and Brain Sciences, 13*, 707–784.

Plotkin, H. (1988). An evolutionary epistemological approach to the evolution of intelligence. In H. J. Jerison & I. Jerison (Eds.), *Intelligence and evolutionary biology* (pp. 73–92). New York: Springer.

Premack, D. (1986). *"Gavagai!" or the future history of the animal language controversy.* Cambridge, MA: MIT Press.
Premack, D. (1988). "Does the chimpanzee have a theory of mind?" revisited. In R. W. Byrne & A. Whiten (Eds.), *Machiavellian intelligence* (pp. 160–179). Oxford, England: Clarendon Press.
Ramsey, W., Stich, S. P., & Garon, J. (1991). Connectionism, eliminativism, and the future of folk psychology. In W. Ramsey, S. P. Stich, & D. E. Rumelhart (Eds.), *Philosophy and connectionist theory* (pp. 315–339). Hillsdale, NJ: Lawrence Erlbaum Associates.
Renfrew, C. (1988). Archeology and language: The puzzle of Indo-European origins. *Current Anthropology, 29*(3), 437–468.
Rosch, E. (1973). Natural categories. *Cognitive Psychology, 4*(3), 328–350.
Rosenthal, D. (1986). Two concepts of consciousness. *Philosophical Studies, 49*(3), 329–359.
Ruhlen, M. (1994). *On the origin of languages: Studies in linguistic taxonomy.* Stanford, CA: Stanford University Press.
Savage-Rumbaugh, E. S., Murphy, J., Sevcik, R. A., Brakke, K. E., Williams, S. L., & Rumbaugh, D. M. (1993). Language comprehension in ape and child. *Monographs of the Society for Research in Child Development, 58*(3–4), 1–256.
Scribner, S., & Cole, M. (1981). *The psychology of literacy.* Cambridge, MA: Harvard University Press.
Shcheglov, Y., & Zholtkovsky, A. (1987). *Poetics of expressiveness: A theory and applications.* Amsterdam: Benjamins.
Soreno, M. I. (1991). Language and the primate brain. In *Program of the 13th Annual Conference of the Cognitive Science Society* (pp. 39–45). Hillsdale, NJ: Lawrence Erlbaum Associates.
Stuss, D. T. (1992). Biological and psychological development of exucutive function. *Brain and Cognition, 20,* 8–23.
Stuss, D. T., & Benson, D. F. (1990). The frontal lobes and language. In E. Goldberg (Ed.), *Contemporary neuropsychology and legacy of Luria* (pp. 29–49). Hillsdale, NJ: Lawrence Erlbaum Associates.
Terrace, H. S. (1985). In the beginning was the name. *American Psychologists, 40,* 1011–1028.
Tilney, F. (1928). *The brain, from ape to man.* New York: Harper.
Tomasello, M. (1992). *First verbs: A case study of early grammatical development.* Cambridge, MA: Cambridge University Press.
Tomasello, M., Kruger, A. C., & Ratner, H. H. (1993). Cultural learning. *Behavioral and Brain Sciences, 16,* 495–552.
Tulving, E. (1983). *Elements of episodic memory.* Oxford, England: Clarendon Press.

Ueda, S., Washio, K., & Kurosaki, K. (1990). Human-specific sequences: Isolation of species-specific DNA regions by genome substraction. *Genomics, 8,* 7–12.
Van Lancker, D. (1987). Non-propositional speech: Neurolinguistic studies. In A. W. Ellis (Ed.), *Progress in the psychology of language* (Vol. 3, pp 49–118). Hillsdale, NJ: Lawrence Erlbaum Associates.
Velichkovsky, B. M. (1982). Visual cognition and its spatial-temporal context. In F. Klix, J. Hoffmann, & E. van der Meer (Eds.), *Cognitive research in psychology* (pp. 55–64). New York: North-Holland.
Velichkovsky, B. M. (1990). The vertical dimension of mental functioning. *Psychological Research, 52*(2/3), 282–297.
Velichkovsky, B. M. (1994). The levels endeavour in psychology and cognitive science. In P. Bertelson, P. Eelen, & G. d'Ydewalle (Eds.), *International perspectives on psychological science: Leading themes.* Hove, UK: Lawrence Erlbaum Associates.
Vygotsky, L. S. (1962). *Thought and language.* Cambridge, MA: MIT Press (original work published 1934).
Vygotsky, L. S. (1985). *Mind in society: The development of higher psychological processes.* Cambridge, MA: Harvard University Press.
Werner, H. (1948). *Comparative psychology of mental development.* New York: International University Press.
Whiten, A., & Byrne, R. W. (1988). Machiavellian intelligence hypotheses. In R. W. Byrne & A. Whiten (Eds.), *Machiavellian intelligence* (pp. 1–9). Oxford, England: Clarendon Press

PART

I

TOWARD A NEW THEORETICAL FOUNDATION

CHAPTER

2

THE ORIGINS OF WORDS:
A PSYCHOPHYSICAL HYPOTHESIS

Stevan Harnad
University of Southampton

When speculating about the origins of language we do well to remind ourselves just what we are pondering the origins of: For some, a language is something so general that just about every form of human activity qualifies: music, dance, even emotional expression (Agawu, 1991; Goodman, 1968; Pribram, 1971). For others, it is a very specific and complex mental organ that allows us to produce and recognize grammatically correct sentences (Chomsky, 1980). I would like to take a third road and consider language to be only that form of human activity that is intertranslatable with English (or any other language) plus whatever mental capacity one must have in order to produce and understand it. The intertranslatability criterion, however, although rather powerful, is still too vague and general. So let me add that one of the principal features of language is that it allows us to categorize the world and its parts in what appears to be an infinity of different ways, among them, possibly, a way that comes close to the way the world really is.

It is hypothesized that words originated as the names of perceptual categories, and that two forms of representation underlying perceptual categorization—iconic and categorical representations—served to *ground* a third, symbolic form of representation. The third form of representation made it possible to name and describe our environment, chiefly in terms of categories, their memberships, and their invariant features. Symbolic representations can be shared because they are intertranslatable. Both categorization and translation are approximate rather than exact, but the approximation can be made as close as we wish. This is the central property of that universal mechanism for sharing descriptions that we call natural language.

TRANSLATION AND CATEGORIZATION

In pondering the origins of language, then, we are pondering the origins of an intertranslatable form of classifying ability. It is an ability that allows us to say: That is an apple; an apple is a round, red fruit, etc. Now this view of language is dangerously reminiscent of positions that are reputed to have been discredited by philosophers—by Wittgenstein (1953) and Quine (1960), for example. Wittgenstein was at pains to show us that the Look, this is an X and that is a Y model of language is wrong, or woefully simplistic: What matters is not what words stand for, but how they are used by a speech community. Quine even held that the X in Look, that is a rabbit (uttered while pointing to a rabbit) is so hopelessly ambiguous that it could mean just about anything to anybody: rabbit parts, rabbit stages, unique instants, or what have you. There is simply no way of arriving at the fact of the matter—or perhaps no fact of the matter to arrive at.

How then is one to defend the glossable-classificatory view of language being proposed here in the face of such prominent criticism? Fortunately, there is always a point of retreat to which one can safely repair as long as one is willing to abandon realism about word meaning: There may be no way of settling on the fact about what people mean when they say Look, that is an X, but we can certainly describe the regularities in the external conditions under which they tend to do so, along with the requisite internal conditions that would make it possible for them to do so under those external conditions. This position is not behaviorism, for it is very much concerned with what is going on inside the head. A behaviorist can never explain how an organism manages to classify its inputs as it does; he must take that success for granted. All he can tell you is what kind of a history of rewards and punishments

2. THE ORIGINS OF WORDS

shaped the organism to do so, given that it can and does do so (Catania & Harnad, 1988).

Obviously it is a form of cognitivism that is being proposed here (Harnad, 1982): People use language to classify the world in a shared and modifiable way. The internal structures that allow them to do so are the physical substrate of language, and hypotheses about the origins of language are hypotheses about the origins of those structures, so used. There is room for functionalism here, too (Fodor, 1975; Pylyshyn 1984): The most important property may not be the specific physical realization of the structure underlying language, but its functional principles, which may be physically realizable in many different ways. The question, "What is language?" becomes the question, "What functional substrate can generate the expressive power of language?" This in turn becomes (according to what we have just agreed), "What functional substrate can generate our glossable classifying ability?"

Let us return to Quine's underdetermined rabbit, which he chose to call, in an undetermined language, *Gavagai*. Gavagai is meant to stand holophrastically for our expression, "Look, that's a rabbit." According to the glossability criterion, the two phrases must be intertranslatable. Now let me inject an important qualifying note right away: Intertranslatability is never exact; it is only approximate. However, the approximation can be made as close as one desires—not necessarily holophrastically—perhaps using a profligate quantity of words, but with the resultant meaning coming as close as need be, reducing uncertainty to whatever level satisfies the demands of the shared external communicative context for the time being (Steklis & Harnad, 1976). (People presumably communicate in order to *inform* one another, and to inform is to reduce uncertainty about competing possibilities among which a choice must be made.) It is an interesting and suggestive parallel fact that categorization, like translation, is provisional and approximate rather than exact (Harnad, 1987b).

Consider the first of Quine's variant readings, "undetached rabbit parts." On this reading, Gavagai could mean, "Look, that's undetached rabbit parts." Of course, all that is needed to disambiguate the two is a larger sample of classification problems because a language with an expressive power that allows full intertranslatability with English must be able to capture the difference between the external circumstances in which we are speaking of rabbits and those in which we are speaking of undetached rabbit parts. "Rabbit," for example, is no good for distinguishing detached from undetached rabbits: They are both rabbits, as far as that goes. "Detached rabbit," on the other hand, is a closer approximation, but now we are unpacking the holophrastic side of English. "Rabbit" is indifferent to the distinction between intact and disassembled rabbit conditions. In English, we need two words to mark that difference; but if in Gavagese the holophrastic "Gavagai" really means, "Look, that's undetached rabbit parts," then (to meet our stern criterion of intertranslatability) there will have to be another lexical item in Gavagese for "Look, that's detached rabbit parts," "Look, that's rabbit parts," "Look, that's a part," and "Look that's a rabbit." One can certainly continue to play this game holophrastically (*Bavagai, Travagai,* etc.), and the more synthetic languages such as German and Innuit (Pullum, 1989) certainly go further in this direction than, say, English or Chinese do. But there are limits to what it is practical to do in this holistic way, and most languages seem to have elected instead to go analytic, coining small, detached, portable words to mark important classes, and making combinations of them in the form of phrases and propositions to mark complex or composite conditions.

The point does not depend on practicality, however, for whether it does so analytically, synthetically, or even entirely holophrastically, a language must provide the resources for marking distinctly all the categories we distinguish (in English, say). Now Quine could argue that, even with all distinctions marked, there can always be higher order ambiguities that we have not yet thought of. But then at that point one must revert to the approximationism mentioned earlier: All that is needed is that language have the resources to mark all potential distinctions as they arise; preemptive ambiguities with respect to inchoate future distinctions (such as Goodman's [1954] green vs. "grue") do not count as underdetermination for they are differences that do not yet make a difference.[1] It is also a rather vague conjecture that a language as a whole is open to multiple interpretations, say, English as it is, ver-

---

[1]Behaviorism is right in at least one respect. Our experience does shape us to mark the differences that make a difference for us (Harnad, 1987b). This, I take it, is the core of truth in Skinner's notion of "selection by consequences" (Catania & Harnad, 1988). To put it information-theoretically, linguistic communication can only resolve the actual uncertainties one has encountered so far, not all potential uncertainties yet to be encountered. For one thing, language and cognition can themselves always generate new uncertainties by formulating questions and distinctions that no one has encountered or thought of (hence been "uncertain" about) before.

2. THE ORIGINS OF WORDS

sus Fenglish, in which the meanings of "true" and "false" are swapped, and all other meanings are suitably adjusted so that everything remains coherent: If one said "'That is a rabbit' is true" in Fenglish, "true" would mean what "false" means in English, but only because in Fenglish "is" means what in English "isn't" means, "rabbit means" nonrabbit, and so on. Yet in order to have English and Fenglish speakers continue to discourse with one another coherently in the same world of objects and events without ever suspecting that their words do not mean the same thing, so many adjustments seem to be needed that to conjecture that the deception is even possible may be equivalent to assuming that formal "duals" of meaning exist (analogous to the duals of logic and mathematics, where it can be proved that certain formal operations can be systematically swapped under a transformation in such a way as to yield coherent dual interpretations).[2] Such a strong conjecture calls for a proof, and as far as I know, no one has offered a proof of the existence of semantic duals in language.

Apart from the absence of a formal proof, another reason for suspecting that coherent dual interpretations of languages may not be possible is that the systematic adjustments would have to go beyond linguistic meaning. They would have to encompass perception too, and would thereby inherit the problems of the "inverted spectrum" conjectures (e.g., D. Cole, 1990): Could you and I be walking around the same world speaking and behaving identically, even though I see the sky as blue and the earth as green, whereas you see the sky as green and the earth as blue? Again, if our classifications are always approximate, it may be a long time before we discover the difference.[3] If there is ever a difference, however, it will disambiguate us forever. Until then, there is no difference between identity and approximate identity, or at least no difference that makes a difference, no uncertainty on which any actual outcome depends.

---

[2] For example, in propositional calculus, and/not and or/not are duals, and in group theory we have the duals +/0 and x/1. In both cases the interpretations of all the formulas can be systematically swapped in a way that preserves truth values.

[3] Saul Kripke (personal communication) has pointed out that the similarity structure of the two-dimensional color wheel would have to be gerrymandered quite radically in order to make all of our perceptual similarity judgments come out identically; hence there may be an unproved psychophysical dual conjecture (blue-green vs. green-blue) implicit here too.

THE GROUNDING OF WORD MEANINGS
IN PERCEPTUAL CATEGORIES

The problem of the underdetermination of meaning has taken us rather far afield from our original intention merely to say informally what it is that a language-origin theory is a theory of the origin of. However, the fact that conjectures about semantic duals turn out to be related to conjectures about perceptual duals is not, I think, coincidental, and it also happens to be closely related to the hypothesis to be put forward in this chapter. To contemplate swapping the meaning of words is also to contemplate swapping experiences. True–false is a rather abstract distinction, but blue–green is just about as concrete as a distinction can get. Is there a way to ground the former in the latter: to ground abstract semantic categories in concrete perceptual categories, and thereby to ground the meanings of the names of abstract categories (the words denoting them) in the meanings of the names of concrete categories? This is the kind of theory of the origin of words and word meanings that is put forward here. Furthermore, although the theory is primarily a bottom-up psychophysical model for the representation of word meaning, it has some rather straightforward implications for the origin and nature of language.

Psychophysics is the branch of psychology concerned with our perceptual capacity: (a) What stimuli can we detect? (b) What stimuli can we tell apart (discriminate)? (c) What stimuli can we identify (categorize)? The first two questions pertain primarily to the sensitivity of our sense receptors, although limits on our ability to make sensory discriminations (and to extend them with instruments) will also influence our ability to make conceptual and semantic distinctions. The third question, about identification or categorization, however, coincides squarely with a large segment of our linguistic capacity: the naming of sensory categories.

The connection between language and perception is at the heart of the *Whorf hypothesis* in linguistics and anthropology, a conjecture that has had a checkered history. The hypothesis suggests that language influences (or perhaps even determines) our view of reality. To state it less vaguely: The way things look to us (and what things we believe really exist) depends on how we name and describe them in our language. Whorf's (1956) original example concerned the Hopi language, which apparently lacks a future tense. He accordingly inferred that the

Hopi lacked a concept of the future. It turns out that Whorf was wrong in that case, partly because of his imperfect understanding of the Hopi language, and partly because the absence of a concept of the future seems to be too radical a deficit to attribute to a human culture living in an Einsteinian universe, given all the ways that the temporal dimension impinges ineluctably on human life.

Having adopted the intertranslatability constraint, we might already have suspected that something was amiss in Whorf's inferences, because English ought to be fully intertranslatable with Hopi. Hence, whatever concepts an Englishman might have, a Hopi should likewise be eligible to have. The Hopi language might lack, for example, the vocabulary for discussing quantum mechanics or general relativity, but this lexical deficit is trivial, and should be remediable by providing the requisite information and instruction *in* Hopi (albeit perhaps with the help of a few coinages or semantic extensions for the sake of convenience and economy). The same should hold true for the concept of the future (Steklis & Harnad, 1976).

Whorf might have replied that he was not suggesting that the Hopi could not acquire a concept of the future (perhaps even in Hopi), but simply that they did not have one at the time. Unfortunately, it is likely (on account of the universal temporal contingencies mentioned earlier) that they did. Let us suppose, however, that they might not have had one—although only in the sense that they (and most people without an advanced education) likewise do not have the concepts of quantum mechanics or general relativity. In that form, the Whorf hypothesis would really only be a rather obvious statement about the relation between one's lexicon and one's conceptual repertoire. We tend to have names for the kinds of things that we think there are and that we tend to talk about; if the existence of new things is pointed out, we can always baptize them with a new name, not thereby changing our language, but only extending its lexicon. Hence, on the face of it, the real causal story seems to be the reverse of the Whorf hypothesis: Reality influences language, which was presumably the commonsense view in the first place. I think there may be more to the Whorf hypothesis than this, however, so let us pursue it a bit further.

The second specific case in which the hypothesis has been investigated is that of color terms (Berlin & Kay, 1969).[4] The prediction was that the visible spectrum was subdivisible in many different ways, and that the qualities of the colors and the differences among them should be influenced by the way we partition the spectrum into the named color categories of the language we speak. Berlin and Kay studied color terms in different cultures. They found that whereas languages did differ in how and where they subdivided the spectrum (although the differences were not quite as radical as one might have hoped), the effects on color perception seemed to be minimal, if indeed there were any effects at all. Our color perception, and hence the quality of the colors we can identify and discriminate, is determined largely by the physiology of our color receptors, which is, for all practical purposes, identical across cultures and languages (Boynton, 1979).

CATEGORICAL PERCEPTION

The universality of color perception would appear to represent another defeat for the Whorf hypothesis, with reality (this time internal rather than external reality) again influencing language, rather than the reverse. However, a closer look at the actual processes and mechanisms involved suggests that there may also be some Whorfian effects in the predicted direction (language on perception, rather than perception on language) in color perception after all. The area of research in which these subtler effects have been investigated is a specialized subfield of psychophysics called *categorical perception* (Harnad, 1987a). It has been found that although the boundaries of color categories are governed primarily by the physiology of the color receptor system, their exact location can be modulated by experience with seeing and naming colors. Boundaries can be moved somewhat; they display some plasticity, and secondary boundaries can perhaps be created on the basis of subcategorization and naming alone (Bornstein, 1987). How qualitative these effects are is open to different interpretations, but they are certainly *quantitative*, in the sense that equal-sized physical differences are more easily discriminated across named category boundaries than

---

[4]A related case that is often mentioned, although not the data on which it is based, is Eskimo snow terms, but unfortunately that seems to have turned out to be a Whorfian canard too (Pullum, 1991).

within them. This is really a Whorfian manifestation of perceptual learning theory's old interest in the "acquired distinctiveness" and "acquired similarity" of cues: The idea was that two stimuli would look more alike if they had the same name, and more different if they had different names (E. J. Gibson, 1969; Lawrence 1950).

It is the subject of another book (Harnad, 1987a) how categorical perception works in detail. An even more closely investigated case of categorical perception than that of color categories is the perception of speech sounds. Another theory related to the Whorf hypothesis—the "emic–etic" distinction in phonology and anthropology—turns out to be closely related to the work on the categorical perception of phonemes. The emic–etic distinction is a somewhat metaphorical extension of the phonemic–phonetic distinction in phonology (Pike, 1982). The speech sounds of a given language vary in many ways. Only some of these differences signal a difference in meaning in the language. These are called "phonemic" differences. The rest of the differences are "phonetic" differences—nonsignaling differences that are less salient, less readily perceived, and less easily produced than the phonemic differences.

In categorical perception terms, phonemic differences are differences across a phoneme category boundary, and phonetic differences are differences within a phoneme category. By analogy with color terms, the difference between blue and green is an emic difference, whereas differences among various (unnamed) shades of green are etic. The metaphoric extension underlying emic–etic theory is that the emic distinctions are the salient ones in a culture, the ones that have been underwritten by language, whereas the etic distinctions have not (or have not yet) become bounded, named categories.

So one way to reconstruct the Whorf hypothesis is to state it thus: Naming a category generates an emic (i.e., qualitative) distinction along an etic continuum of (quantitative) differences. Language does not create the etic differences. These are furnished by our sensory apparatus; however, it does create the emic distinctions, and these become the salient ones, the ones that govern our (provisional) view of reality. Let us recall, at this midpoint of our discussion, the informal criteria we adopted for language at the outset: A language is an approximately intertranslatable system for approximately categorizing the world. We have spoken a little about categorization and approximation. What about intertranslatability?

Names of perceptual categories are trivially intertranslatable. All one need do is coin a gloss: "rabbit" = "gavagai." However, naming categories is not all that language involves. Even if the principle function of language is conceded to be classificational, not all classification takes the form, "This is an X," or "X = Y." Language can also describe properties, chief among them being category membership itself.[5]

NAMING AND DESCRIBING

If I say, "Rabbits are white," I am actually making a statement about category membership: The members of the category "rabbits" are members of the category "white." I want to conjecture here that any assertion in any language can be reformulated as a statement about category membership. (For example, the preceding sentence would assert that members of the category, "assertion in any language," are members of the category, "statement about category membership.") Other speech acts are simply assertions with special markers, such as interrogative or imperative. If this conjecture is correct, then it follows that, after *naming*, the second critical linguistic function is *describing*; a description always takes the form of a statement about category membership. Note that even an ostensive (pointing) statement such as the holophrastic *Gavagai* is actually a description—"This is a rabbit,"—in which the deictic "this" refers to the member of a singular category, namely, "the thing I am pointing to right now." The assertion is that "that thing" is a member of the category "rabbit." Hence ostensive statements are simply special cases of descriptions in which the item for which the deictic term (this, that) stands is present and available to the senses. So although it is true that names must precede descriptions in the sense that they provide the atomic terms of a description, it is also true that some (possibly holophrastic) ostensive assertions must be primitive in all category naming. No chicken–egg worries need arise here. If all assertions are statements about category membership, and the assertion is the minimal linguistic utterance, then all one need note is that there are two

---

[5]Whether all are members or just some is simply another higher order category-membership matter, this time having to do with the membership of the categories "some," and "all." It may be that one or the other of these, like negation and two-valued logic, has to be an innately given primitive in any categorization system, but these are formal details on which I am not expert and fortunately need not commit myself for present purposes.

2. THE ORIGINS OF WORDS 37

kinds of assertions: ostensive and descriptive (or "de re" and "de dicto," respectively). Both say something of the form, "The members of X are members of Y," but in the ostensive case, X is a sensory event that is available and can be pointed to (or, for the realist, an object that is present and can be pointed at by means of the sensory event) and Y is simply "things that are called Y," whereas in the descriptive case, X is "things that are called X," and Y is "things that are called Y."

At this point my psychophysical hypothesis about the origin of words can be presented explicitly: Words originate by ostensive experience with concrete sensory categories. This "grounds" them psychophysically. They can then enter into descriptions of higher categories, including abstract ones. Here is a simple example that I have used before (Harnad 1990): .

1. That is a "horse" (naming by ostension).
2. That is "stripes" (naming by ostension).
3. A "zebra" is a "horse" with "stripes" (description).

All the important features of the remarkable expressive power of language and its grounding in prior sensory experience are captured by this exceedingly simple example. "Horse" is named on the basis of direct sensory acquaintance. "Stripes" likewise. Then these grounded terms can be used to ground a new term, "zebra," by description alone, and so on.[6]

Is this just an empiricist (sense–datum) theory of meaning, and hence vulnerable to the many existing objections to such theories?[7] To avoid those objections, my hypothesis has actually been put forward in the form of a black-box theory of object sorting and word use rather than a theory of perception and meaning. Without getting involved in side issues, this means that this kind of theory can only hope to explain word-use behavior that is Turing-indistinguishable from the use of meaningful language. There is always the possibility that the theory only describes the inner workings of a mindless, meaningless robot that

---

[6] I am not claiming that "horse," "stripes," and "zebra" are actually learned in this way, only that knowledge by description must be grounded in some primitive concrete categories named on the basis of direct acquaintance in this way.

[7] Chief among these is the "vanishing intersections" objection that most categories have no common sensory properties (and perhaps no common properties at all). I will return to this in my discussion of sampled variation later (see footnote 10).

simply acts exactly as if it were speaking meaningfully. This is a limitation that I am happy to accept (Harnad, 1991).

I have not yet said much of inner workings, however, and "ostension" is not a very satisfactory account of the way of concrete categories are learned from sensory experience. What must be noted in order to see that ostension is a far from trivial candidate for the grounding of words is that the problem of *category acquisition* is itself far from trivial. It is at least as general as the problem of induction and pattern recognition. What a category-learning device must be able to do is to sample a finite number of sensory instances of Xs and thereafter name Xs correctly—for all the Xs that human beings can name. This is something that no man-made pattern-learning device can even come close to doing at the present time. Nor do I claim to have solved the categorization problem. I have merely proposed a representational model that has some features that I think the ultimately successful model will need to have, too. These features are described more fully elsewhere (Harnad, 1987b, 1991; Harnad, Hanson, & Lubin, 1991, 1996). For present purposes, the brief description that follows should be sufficient.

SYMBOLIC REPRESENTATIONS

Learning to categorize all Xs will require three kinds of internal representation. The first, *iconic representations,* are analogs of the physical patterns that concrete objects project onto the surfaces of our sensory receptors. These representations are used primarily to discriminate among stimuli that occur simultaneously or in rapid succession. They allow judgments to be made about whether two sensory projections or traces are the same or different, and if different, about the degree of difference between them. The second kind of representation, *categorical representations,* do not preserve the analog shape of the sensory projections; they preserve and encode only the invariant sensory properties shared by all the members of a concrete perceptual category. These invariant properties are learned by sampling positive and negative instances of the category in question (i.e., members of the category and its complement: the set of alternatives with which the members could be confused[8]) and finding the features that will correctly sort that par-

---

[8]Intertranslatability is what makes category learning difficult. If category invariance were not underdetermined—if categories wore all their invariant

2. THE ORIGINS OF WORDS

ticular sample as well as future samples. Such features are converged on by a learning algorithm[9] that generates successful categorization. The invariant features are always provisional, however, and the categorization always approximate, because the context of confusable alternatives could always be widened.[10]

The names for the categories that have iconic and categorical representations then go on to furnish the primitives for the third kind of representation, *symbolic representations*. These include the primitive category names (including names of invariant features) and combinations of names in the form of propositions about category membership. Most of the names correspond to the lexicon of a natural language; their combinations take the form of sentences (descriptions).

This three-level representational system is grounded bottom-up in psychophysical categories. Top-down influences occur through categorical perception. Similarity judgments are not mediated purely by iconic representations (or perhaps iconic representations are not pure). Belonging to the same category (i.e., having the same name) makes things look more similar, and belonging to a different category (i.e.,

---

features "on their sleeves," so to speak—then category learning would be trivial, and so would all linguistic communication, because there would be no appreciable uncertainty to reduce. To "inform" someone would simply be to point to something he already knew, and to give it an arbitrary label for future common reference. In reality, however, categories are underdetermined (nontrivially interconfusable); hence both ostension and description are informative because they induce us to resolve the confusion (provisionally) by revising our representations.

[9] A possible candidate for this learning algorithm may emerge from contemporary connectionistic research (Hanson & Burr, 1990; Harnad, 1991, 1993a, 1995; Harnad, Hanson, & Lubin, 1991, 1994) or from related work on statistics and general induction.

[10] According to the "vanishing intersection" critique, there exist no shared features for most of our categories. But then how do we nonetheless succeed in sorting their members? It is assumed in this chapter that where there is successful categorization performance, there must be invariant features. The grounding process, however, being recursive and potentially highly embedded, can quickly reach levels of abstraction quite remote from their sensory invariants, which may not even be consciously accessible. Moreover, most invariants are also provisional, the categories they pick out being based on a finite sample of interconfusable members and nonmembers. With a widening of the sample, however, it is not that the invariants vanish, but rather that the approximation becomes tighter, sometimes by replacing or revising some or all of the prior invariants, but always by subsuming them as a special case - if, that is, successful categorization performance continues to be possible. Otherwise, it is the category rather than the invariance that has vanished.

having a different name) makes them look more distinct. Most of the symbolic component consists of internal translation (e.g., "An X is a Y," A Y is a Z," etc.). It is the primitive symbols, which are grounded in nonsymbolic representations—iconic and categorical ones—that prevent this symbolic circle from being vicious.[11] Two different systems of grounded symbolic representation are, in principle, intertranslatable, and their respective groundings can be tested against ostensive experience in the real world.

THE ORIGIN OF WORDS

As the foregoing discussion shows, my hypothesis about the origin of words is really a hypothesis about the origin of symbolic categories: They originate in sensory categories and are grounded in the iconic and categorical representations that make it possible for you to pick out those sensory categories. Abstraction occurs first with the extraction of invariant sensory features that takes place in concrete perceptual category learning, and then proceeds to abstract higher order categories by symbolic description. The grounding hypothesis, in turn, has some implications for the way language may have begun. It suggests that language evolved along lines similar to the way it is learned: Concrete categories were assigned names because of a collective utility that shared names had for the community as a whole.

Many categories come to mind that it would have been useful to name and describe: kinfolk, tribesmen, enemies, foods, predators, weather conditions, tools, places, discomforts, dangers. Simply naming these categories, then sharing and using the names would seem to have been its own obvious reward under easily imaginable primitive conditions in which people would benefit from the sharing of information (reducing uncertainty) about future contingencies. Names could at first have been shared "iconic" responses (both verbal and gestural, as sug-

---

[11] As an example of a symbolic circle that is vicious, consider the hopeless task of a nonspeaker of Chinese trying to learn the meaning of Chinese from nothing but a Chinese-Chinese dictionary (Harnad, 1990). The fact that cryptographers (e.g., those who deciphered cuneiform writing or the Enigma code) seem to be able to break out of such a circle owes itself, if one thinks about it, to the fact that they already speak at least one grounded language that is intertranslatable with the target language. The rest is just the exploitation of shared statistical regularities.

2. THE ORIGINS OF WORDS

gested by the "bow-wow" [imitation] and "yo-he-ho" [motor-correlate] theories of language origin (cf. Harnad, Steklis, & Lancaster, 1976). These iconic names could then have taken the usual path to arbitrariness as their linguistic function, because of its powerful consequences, took precedence over their original imitative, instrumental, and expressive origins. Name concatenation would have been a natural development (as would the converse process of dismantling holophrastic expressions), particularly with the object–name serving as the first model in ostension. "That 'cat'" and "that 'dog'" lead quite naturally to the superordinate category statement: "'Cat', 'dog': 'animal.'"[12]

Intertranslatability did not, I suggest, require a separate development, because translation is a lexical-lexical matter for the most part, and that is what the internal translation performed by the symbolic representations really is. Once there is a representational system that allows things to be reliably sorted into named categories, with their names going on to figure in (symbolic) descriptions of still more categories, their membership and their invariant features, then intertranslatability is trivial: It depends only on a shared grounding, which can always be checked and adjusted to as close an approximation as necessary for successful coherent interaction and joint operations on objects (e.g., sorting them into categories). Given a "common ground" of primitive categories and the capacity to name and describe them, all the rest can be settled verbally (as in Kenneth Pike's "magic show," in which, on stage, before an audience, he learns to converse in a language he has never before encountered, by interacting with a native speaker who speaks only that language).

Could two symbolic representational systems fail to be intertranslatable? If two organisms were capable of human-scale categorization, naming, and describing performance, could a Quinean indeterminacy nevertheless leave them lost in Babel-like confusion and uncertainty about whether they were really understanding one another or just talking at cross purposes?[13] I think not. The approximateness of categoriz-

---

[12]Note that much of this seems explicable as operant shaping by consequences—categorization and naming being, after all, operant responses—except that the critical component, the underlying representational system that makes it all possible, is anything but behavioristic. Nevertheless, shaping by consequences no doubt played a role in the origin of language, just as it does in its development (Catania & Harnad, 1988).

[13]Or worse, could a radical Kuhnian gap of incommensurability (Kuhn, 1970) separate some symbolic systems from others?

ing and describing may be a liability, but the capacity to revise and tighten the approximation as closely as necessary (as dictated by "consequences") through further ostension and discourse seems a much more powerful countervailing asset, and a universal one.

What a theory of language origin cannot resolve, of course, is the mind–body problem. One source of indeterminacy accordingly remains (Harnad, 1993b, 1996): There is no way to know (because of the inverted-spectrum conjecture, for example) that the qualitative sensory experience in which our words are grounded is a shared experience—or even that anyone other than oneself has any qualitative experience at all, rather than merely going mindlessly through the behavioral motions. That, however, is a distinction on which this hypothesis must remain approximate, at least until it can be shown to have differential consequences for the way we sort, name, and describe things and then go on to share our names and descriptions with one another through that universally glossable classificatory system we call language.

REFERENCES

Agawu, V. K. (1991) *Playing with signs: A semiotic interpretation of classic music.* Princeton, NJ: Princeton University Press.

Berlin, B., & Kay, P. (1969). *Basic color terms: Their universality and evolution.* Berkeley: University of California Press.

Bornstein, M. H. (1987). Perceptual categories in vision and audition. In S. Harnad (Ed.), *Categorical perception: The ground work of cognition* (pp. 287–300). New York: Cambridge University Press.

Boynton, R. M. (1979). *Human color vision.* New York: Holt, Rinehart, Winston.

Catania, A. C., & Harnad, S. (Eds.). (1988). *The selection of behavior. The operant behaviorism of B.F. Skinner: Comments and consequences.* Cambridge, MA: Cambridge University Press.

Chomsky, N. (1980). Rules and representations. *Behavioral and Brain Sciences, 3,* 1-61.

Cole, D. (1990). Functionalism and inverted spectra. *Synthese, 82,* 207–222.

Fodor, J. A. (1975). *The language of thought.* New York: Crowell.

Gibson, E. J. (1969). *Principles of perceptual learning and development.* Englewood Cliffs, NJ: Prentice-Hall.

Goodman, N. (1954). *Fact, fiction and forecast.* London: Athlone Press.

Goodman, N. (1968). *Languages of art: An approach to a theory of symbols.* Indianapolis, IN: Bobbs-Merrill.

Hanson, S. J., & Burr, D. J. (1990). What connectionist models learn: Learning and representation in connectionist networks. *Behavioral and Brain Sciences, 13,* 471-518.

Harnad, S. (1982). Neoconstructivism: A unifying theme for the cognitive sciences. In T. Simon, R. Scholes (Eds.), *Language, mind and brain* (pp. 1–11). Hillsdale, NJ: Lawrence Erlbaum Associates.

Harnad, S. (Ed.). (1987a). *Categorical perception: The groundwork of cognition.* New York: Cambridge University Press.

Harnad, S. (1987b). The induction and representation of categories. In S. Harnad (Ed.), *Categorical perception: The groundwork of cognition* (pp. 535–565). New York: Cambridge University Press.

Harnad, S. (1990). The symbol grounding problem. *Physica D, 42,* 335–346.

Harnad, S. (1991). Other bodies, other minds: A machine incarnation of an old philosophical problem. *Minds and Machines, 1,* 43–54.

Harnad, S. (1992). Connecting object to symbol in modeling cognition. In A. Clarke & R. Lutz (Eds.), *Connectionism in context* (pp. 75–90). New York: Springer-Verlag.

Harnad, S. (1993a). Grounding symbols in the analog world with neural nets. *Think* (Special issue on machine learning), *2(1),* 12-78)

Harnad, S. (1993b, June). *Turing indistinguishability and the blind watchmaker.* Presented at the Conference on Evolution and the Human Sciences, London School of Economics, Centre for the Philosophy of the Natural and Social Sciences.

Harnad, S. (1995a). Grounding symbolic capacity in robotic capacity. In L. Steels & R. Brooks (Eds.), *The artificial life route to artificial intelligence. Building embodied situated agents* (pp. 277-286). Hillsdale, NJ:Lawrence Erlbaum Associates.

Harnad, S, (199b). Does the mind piggy-back on robotic and symbolic capacity? In H. Morowitz (Ed.), *The mind, the brain, and complex adaptive systems* (pp. 204–220). Cambridge, MA: MIT Press.

Harnad, S., Hanson, S. J., & Lubin, J. (1991, March). Categorical perception and the evolution of supervised learning in neural nets. In D.W. Powers & L. Reeker (Eds.), *Working papers of the AAAI Spring Symposium on Machine Learning of Natural Language and Ontology* (pp. 65-74). Presented at Symposium on Symbol Grounding: Problems and Practice, Stanford University. March 1991; also reprinted as Document D91-09, Deutsches Forschungszentrum für Künstliche Intelligenz, Kaiserslautern. Stanford, CA.

Harnad, S. Hanson, S. J., & Lubin, J. (1995). Learned categorical perception in neural nets: Implications for symbol grounding. In V. Honavar & L. Uhr (Eds.), *Symbol processing and connectionist network models in artificial intelligence and cognitive modelling: Steps toward principled integration* (pp. 191-206). Academic Press.

Harnad, S., Steklis, H. D., & Lancaster, J. B. (Eds.). (1976). Origins and evolution of language and speech. *Annals of the New York Academy of Sciences, 280,* 445-455.

Kuhn, T. (1970). *The structure of scientific revolutions.* Chicago: University of Chicago Press.

Lawrence, D. H. (1950). Acquired distinctiveness of cues: II. Selective association in a constant stimulus situation. *Journal of Experimental Psychology, 40,* 175–188.

Pike, K. L. (1982). *Linguistic concepts: An introduction to tagmemics.* Lincoln: University of Nebraska Press.

Pribram, K. H. (1971). *Languages of the brain.* Englewood Cliffs, NJ: Prentice-Hall.

Pullum, G. K. (1989). The great Eskimo vocabulary hoax. *Natural Language and Linguistic Theory, 7,* 275–281.

Pullum, G. K. (1991). *The great Eskimo vocabulary hoax, and other irreverent essays on the study of language.* Chicago: University of Chicago Press.

Pylyshyn, Z. W. (1984). *Computation and cognition.* Cambridge, MA: MIT/Bradford.

Quine, W. V. O. (1960). *Word and object.* Cambridge, MA: MIT Press.

Steklis, H. D., & Harnad, S. (1976). From hand to mouth: Some critical stages in the evolution of language. *Annals of the New York Academy of Sciences, 280,* 445–455.

Whorf, B. L. (1956). *Language, thought and reality.* Cambridge, MA: MIT Press.

Wittgenstein, L. (1953). *Philosophical investigations.* New York: Macmillan.

CHAPTER

3

WHAT KNOWLEDGE MUST BE IN THE HEAD IN ORDER TO ACQUIRE LANGUAGE?

William Bechtel
Washington University, St. Louis

LOCALIZATIONIST DANGERS IN THE STUDY OF LANGUAGE

Many studies of language, whether in philosophy, linguistics, or psychology, have focused on highly developed human languages. In their highly developed forms, such as those employed in scientific discourse, languages have a unique set of properties that have been the focus of much attention. For example, descriptive sentences in a language have the property of being "true" or "false," and words of a language have senses and referents. Sentences in a language are structured according to complex syntactic rules. Theorists focusing on language are naturally led to ask questions such as what constitutes the meanings of words and sentences and how the principles of syntax are encoded in the heads of language users. Although there is an important function for inquiries into the highly developed forms of these cultural products

(Abrahamsen, 1987), such a focus can be quite misleading when we want to explain how these products have arisen or account for the human capacity to use language. The problem is that focusing on the most developed forms makes linguistic ability seem to be a *sui generis* phenomenon not related to, and hence not explicable in terms of, other cognitive capacities. Chomsky's (1980) postulation of a specific language module equipped with specialized resources needed to process language and possessed only by humans is not a surprising result.

The strategy of identifying a specific component within a system and assigning responsibility for one aspect of the system's behavior to that component is a common one in science. Richardson and I (Bechtel & Richardson, 1993) referred to this as *direct localization*. To see that direct localization is not a strategy unique to language studies or to explaining cognitive functions, we need only to consider the earliest attempts to explain fermentation. In the wake of Pasteur, many researchers doubted whether any chemical explanation of fermentation was possible. They thought that it was a unique capacity of yeast cells. However, in 1897 Buchner demonstrated that fermentation continued in extracts after the cell membrane had been destroyed. He then posited that there was a single enzyme, zymase, that was responsible for the chemical process. Buchner's explanation soon proved to be inadequate as chemists recognized that fermentation was a many-step process.

Because I am emphasizing the limitations of direct localization, I should also stress that it is often a fruitful first step in developing a more adequate understanding of how a complex system operates. Moreover, sometimes the concept of direct localizations is correct: There is a component in the system that performs the task assigned to it. The point to recognize then is that one still has not explained the system's activity until a decomposition is effected, because, until then, we do not understand how something is able to perform that activity. If the identified direct localization is correct, at least in a first approximation, then research typically proceeds at a lower level in which researchers try to take that component apart.

As research on fermentation continued, researchers developed a *complex localization* in which many different enzymes as well as coenzymes were identified as responsible for different components of the overall chemical transformation. The result, by the 1930s, was a complex model of interacting components that achieved the overall reaction of fermentation. Richardson and I have identified two heuristics that

3. KNOWLEDGE NECESSARY TO ACQUIRE LANGUAGE

figured in this and other cases of developing complex localizations: the *decomposition* of a complex activity into simpler activities and the *localization* of responsibility for these activities in different components. It would seem that the goals in the effect to explain human linguistic abilities are similar: We want to know the various sorts of processes involved in language processing (task decomposition) and to identify the cognitive-neural components responsible for each (function localization).

In fact, such a program is in place in the study of language. A person's understanding of language is frequently decomposed into different kinds of knowledge: knowledge of syntax, semantics, pragmatics, and so on. Psycholinguists attempt to identify component processes in human comprehension and production of language. A similar enterprise is pursued in artificial intelligence, with researchers trying to develop parsers that can enable programs to extract useful representations of information from natural language inputs. Much of this work is very sophisticated and very impressive. In this chapter, however, I want to raise a worry about the conceptualization of these projects and advance a different perspective from which to think about human linguistic ability. The worry can be focused by noticing that there is a step to be performed even before one attempts a direct or complex localization: One must identify a system that is responsible for the phenomenon. Richardson and I refer to this as identifying the *locus of control* for the phenomenon. In the case of language, it seems to many that this system is the mind–brain. The case for this seems to be overwhelming: Humans comprehend and produce language, and the activities involved in doing this surely must be occurring inside their heads. To recognize that this could be controversial, though, we only have to consider the approach against which Chomsky (1959) was reacting: Skinner's (1957) proposal to explain language by using the tools of operant conditioning. Skinner's program was to minimize the contribution of the mind and to explain linguistic behavior in terms of environmental processes conditioning particular forms of behavior. The alternative to Chomsky that I urge, however, is not Skinner's. My goal is not to discount the mind as playing a significant role in explaining linguistic capacities, but to suggest that linguistic ability be understood in terms of interactions between the mind and features of the environment.

Before beginning to develop my alternative proposal, let me note one consequence of localizing linguistic capacity in the mind. The mind itself is construed as working on linguistic principles. Chomsky's transformational grammar employed procedures for manipulating strings of symbols composed in particular ways. (Often a tree structure is used to provide a more perspicuous representation.) Psychologists such as George Miller were attracted to the idea that the mind might process language by performing such transformations, and more generally by the idea that the mind might operate by performing formal operations on strings of symbols. The availability of the computer, a device that can be interpreted as operating by performing formal operations on symbol strings, combined with Chomskyan linguistics to inspire the development of the information processing tradition in psychology. The key to the information processing tradition is that the mind–brain is a representational device, and that it operates by performing operations on the symbols serving as its representations. These symbolic representations reflect the character of linguistic representations, and Fodor (1975), in fact, referred to the internal representational system of the mind as a *language of thought*.

For Fodor, the language of thought hypothesis is important, not just because the mind uses representations, but because these representations are structured in much the way that natural language representations are structured by principles of grammar. In fact, for him this is part of what marks the difference between modern cognitivist theories and associationism. He contends that the mind must employ a compositional syntax and semantics (i.e., there must be syntactic principles for composing mental representations such that the semantic interpretation of a composed string is governed by the syntactic rules by which it is composed); otherwise crucial features of cognition such as productivity and systematicity could not be explained (Fodor, 1987; Fodor & Pylyshyn, 1988). It should be noted that Fodor characterized productivity and systematicity first as features of natural languages, and then applied them to the mind. *Productivity* refers to the fact that it is always possible to create new sentences in a language. Fodor argued that it is similarly always possible for a mind to think a new thought. *Systematicity* refers to the fact that for any expression that is part of a language, there are others related to it in systematic ways that are necessarily also part of the language. Thus, if "the florist loved Mary" is a sentence of English, so also of necessity is "Mary loved the florist." Fodor contended that the same principle applies to thought: Any mind

3. KNOWLEDGE NECESSARY TO ACQUIRE LANGUAGE

that could think "the florist loved Mary" could also think "Mary loved the florist."

What is noteworthy is that rather than using principles of the mind to explain human capacity in language, Fodor's approach used language to explain thought. Unfortunately, this has the effect of making language even more mysterious for we cannot hope to explain it by decomposing it in terms of other simpler mental capacities. Since for Fodor this language like representational system underlies language learning, linguistic capacity cannot be explained by learning; rather, it must be part of the person's native cognitive endowment. In itself this is not an insuperable problem. It might, for example, be possible to give an evolutionary explanation of how the language module came to be. Unfortunately, Fodor blocked this move as well by arguing that animals that demonstrate cognitive capacities must already have a language of thought. Moreover, Fodor did not offer a proposal to explain how a process of variation and selective retention would have generated an internal language of thought. Finally, such a proposal seems seriously at odds with current theories of how the brains of other animals operate. Formal symbol manipulation is profoundly unlike the kinds of processes we observe elsewhere in the biological domain, and its emergence in humans appears mysterious (Churchland, 1986).

Given the problematic aspects of this approach, it is worth at least considering some alternatives. One way to open up alternatives is to consider again the path that led to this approach. I have stressed two elements: First, one starts with the most complicated form of language use and makes that the basis for study; second, one localizes the capacity to use language in a particular system or subsystem. By focusing on the most highly developed form of language, we are led to the properties of languages that seem hardest to explain in terms of anything simpler. By attributing language use to a particular system (the mind) or subsystem (the language module), we are led to attribute to that system the very characteristics that distinguish the phenomenon itself. This makes the mind or the language module incredibly powerful and renders its operation mysterious. The suggested alternative, then, is to focus on simpler forms of language use and to consider how the control of language use might be distributed, not localized. I have discussed the first strategy elsewhere (Bechtel, 1993a, 1993b) and approaches to studying how less complex forms of language can be acquired by other species are explored by Rumbaugh and Savage-Rumbaugh (chap. 9, this volume). In this chapter, I explore the second strategy by investigating whether it is possible to distribute the control of language in such a manner that one can more readily explain its development. I then show that this can have the beneficial effect of reducing the resources we must attribute to the cognitive system in order to process language.

DISTRIBUTING CONTROL OF LANGUAGE

The motivation for localizing the control of language use in the mind or brain is because it is human cognizers who comprehend and produce linguistic structures. How could they accomplish this if the control of language use were not internal to them? The alternative is to construe linguistic ability as an emergent product of the mind or brain and a certain kind of environment. Complex products often emerge from the interaction of two or more entities, none of which itself exhibits the requisite complexity to account fully for the phenomenon. A clear example of how interaction can produce an emergent product out of simpler components is found in the work of Herbert Simon. Simon (1980) invited us to consider the path of an ant as it traverses an uneven terrain on its way to its goal. The path might appear to be very complex, but the ant does not have to represent this complexity. The ant must just use relatively simple procedures for detecting and following the flattest course that is roughly in the direction of its goal. The complex trajectory is the product of the ant's relatively simple procedure for deciding on a course of motion and a structured environment.

In the case of language, there are two pertinent environments external to the cognitive system. One is provided by the physical symbols (sound patterns, manual signs, written characters) used in language. These physical symbols afford certain sorts of use (e.g., referring to objects) and composition (e.g., linear concatenation either in time or space) and thereby make composed structures available to language users. The second is provided by other users of the language. The communal use of language serves to maintain a system of using particular symbols to refer to specific objects and of employing particular ways of putting linguistic symbols together to achieve certain ends.

I do not here develop a comprehensive account of the way that both the physical symbols and the social context of the cognitive system in-

3. KNOWLEDGE NECESSARY TO ACQUIRE LANGUAGE

teract in the development of language, because I want rather to explore the implications of this perspective for assumptions about what must go on in the head of the language user. As preparation for my primary endeavor, however, I will offer a speculative sketch of how external symbols and social contexts interact with the cognitive system. To see the importance of external symbols, consider first some rather high-level cognitive skills and how the use of written symbols supports those activities. Rumelhart, Smolensky, McClelland, and Hinton (1986) provided an example from arithmetic. For most people, multiplying two three-digit numbers is too complex a task to carry out in one's head. To simplify the task, we make use of conventions such as the following for writing numbers on a page:

$$343$$
$$\underline{822}$$

This technique permits us to decompose the multiplication task into component tasks, each of which we are able to perform simply by knowing the multiplication tables. The procedure we were taught in school enables us to proceed in a stepwise manner. We begin with the problem 2×3, whose answer we have already memorized. As a result we write 6 directly beneath these two numbers:

$$343$$
$$\underline{822}$$
$$6$$

The external representation of the problem then points us to the next step of multiplying 2×4. What we have learned is a routine for dealing with the problem in a step-by-step manner in which each step requires limited cognitive effort (remembering an already learned result). A problem that would be quite difficult if external symbols were not available is rendered much simpler with external symbols.

The main challenge in mastering such a task is learning to write the symbols in the canonical format and to proceed in the designated step-by-step manner. There are, of course, other ways in which the problem could be represented, and other procedures through which it could be solved. For example, we could encode the problem and the steps for solving it in the following manner:

$$343 \times 822$$
$$686 + 6{,}860 + 274{,}400$$
$$281{,}946$$

This representation, however, requires the use of appropriate procedures, and this involves some relearning of basic skills.

I have described the performance of each step as the remembering of an already learned result; it could just as well be described as a process of pattern recognition and completion. This characterization seems highly suited for other cognitive tasks such as evaluating formal arguments and developing proofs in formal logic. In *Connectionism and the Mind*, Abrahamsen and I discussed the problems of teaching students to use the argument forms of formal logic (e.g., modus ponens), and we argued that what students must learn is to recognize patterns in external symbols. Here the patterns are a bit more difficult because they have slots for variables, and what is required to instantiate the pattern is for the symbols filling the slots to stand in the right relation to each other. Students who have difficulty distinguishing valid from invalid forms often have not determined what property a pattern must have to be an instance of a pattern type. For example, they fail to appreciate that the same filler must fill both the slots for A in the following argument in order to constitute an instance of modus ponens:

$$\text{If } A, \text{ then } B$$
$$\underline{A}$$
$$\therefore B$$

Once students recognize this and thus have mastered the patterns of various valid and invalid arguments, they are able both to evaluate arguments and to construct arguments of their own. Constructing proofs, we contend, is an extension of this ability. Now, in addition to recognizing and completing valid argument forms, students must learn the patterns that specify when steps of particular kinds are fruitful in order to derive the desired conclusion.

I want to emphasize the crucial role that external symbols seem to play in both arithmetic and logic. As we are learning skills, such as those of logic, it seems necessary to have the symbolic structures externally represented. Students often require much practice in learning to distinguish basic valid and invalid logical forms. In teaching these, I have relied on computer-aided instruction in which students confront

3. KNOWLEDGE NECESSARY TO ACQUIRE LANGUAGE 53

large numbers of simple arguments in English prose and must determine their form and validity. Students performing exercises on the computer find it helpful to write out templates of each argument form and compare explicitly the prose argument to each of their templates. The cognitive demands of comparing two external symbolic structures seem to be much less than internally representing the symbols and performing the comparison. Even advanced symbol users often rely on external representations when the forms get complex. For example, it is much easier to apply the de Morgan laws to determine that the statement, "It is not the case that both the legislation will pass and the courts will not block it" is equivalent to the statement, "The legislation will not pass or the courts will block it" when the sentences are written on paper than when we have merely heard them and must perform the operation internally. When the comparison is yet more complex, we often find it useful to write the intermediate forms on paper. Pattern recognition, completion, and comparison seem to place relatively low demands on our cognitive system in comparison with high-level computations.

The challenge is to see whether, in fact, by use of external symbols we can perform the high-level computations of logic and arithmetic using only pattern recognition, completion, and comparison abilities. In Bechtel and Abrahamsen (1991), I reported on the ability of a connectionist network to recognize and complete simple argument forms of sentential logic. Recently I demonstrated the ability of a connectionist network to construct simple derivations in sentential logic by successively writing new steps onto units of the input layer (Bechtel, 1994). In the following sections I describe connectionist simulations by others suggesting that a similar approach might work in the case of language. First, though, I need to sketch more theoretically how the framework advanced here might apply in the case of language.

As mature language users, we often think to ourselves linguistically. This reinforces the idea that our mental representations are languagelike and that the rules for using language are natively encoded in our cognitive system. How could it be that we rely on external symbols in the case of language? One clue is found in the comparison of spoken and written language. Not only does our spoken language often deviate from syntactical norms, but generally we fail to notice these deviations when we listen to speech. However, when the same speech is transcribed, the deviations stand out clearly. Thus, precise conformity to principles of grammar seems to be much easier when we use external written symbols.

Written words are, however, only one form of external symbol. Spoken words also constitute external symbols, albeit more transient ones, that persist momentarily as sounds. With the aid of echoic memory, humans are able to maintain a trace of those spoken symbols over a period that lasts a bit longer than the sounds themselves. These external symbols are available to us not only when we listen to others, but as we speak. As mature language users we may not rely greatly on feedback from the sounds we have uttered, but this feedback may be far more important to language learners.

The child learning a first language must learn not only to utter the sounds of a language, but also to order the sounds to fit the established patterns used in that language. At first the child's insertion into the ongoing use of language may be a single sound or what to us is a single word. Even without the child having a specific intention in mind, the community may interpret this utterance, and thus it may have consequences (Lock, 1980). Having learned that individual sounds can be used in communication, the child gradually masters the conventions or patterns for putting them together. What the child is learning is to generate and respond to patterns in external symbols.

Having suggested that linguistic symbols may be construed as symbols external to language users, I want to stress two things. First, language use is first embodied in a social context. Eventually humans learn to use language privately as a tool for thought, but this is derivative from the public use of language. Much of the process of learning to use a language depends on interacting in this social context that exhibits the particular principles of language use of the community. Moreover, there is incentive for the language learner to master the patterns of a particular language, because only then can the individual learn from the sentences uttered by others and use language to gain personal objectives. Second, the external symbols of language (sounds, manual signs, lexigrams, written words) themselves permit a certain kind of composition. Sounds, for example, can be strung together sequentially and uttered with different intonations and modulations. Grammatical principles of word order and case endings are natural devices that can be applied to these kinds of entities. Manual signs provide additional dimensions for variation (e.g., place where the sign is made), and these dimensions are employed for grammatical purposes in

3. KNOWLEDGE NECESSARY TO ACQUIRE LANGUAGE

various sign languages. The grammatical devices "chosen" by the linguistic community are exemplified in the linguistic strings employed in that community. What the language learner must do is learn to conform to these structures: to extract the meaning encoded in these structures and to produce linguistic strings of his or her own.

What are the implications of such an approach for the psychological explanation of language processing? I would argue that with a distributed conception of language, we do not need to posit nearly so rich a structure of internal representations as has often been thought. In particular, we might not need to posit a syntactically structured representation of language in the head and then view language processing as the performance of computations on this structure. Part of the strategy for reducing what needs to be posited within the language user is to envision the linguistic community, and not the cognitive system, as being the primary enforcer of principles of compositionality in the language and the external medium in which language is encoded (sound patterns, hand movements, ink blots on a page) as being the locus in which composition is achieved. The cognitive system exists in a linguistically structured environment, and must therefore conform to the demands of that environment. At least at the outset, the symbols used are the symbols of natural language, typically physical sounds. What the cognitive system must learn to do is to use these symbols and put them together in appropriate ways. This requires recognizing and using patterns. The task that remains for the cognitive system is certainly not trivial, but it is a task different from that projected when the cognitive system is construed as have a native, languagelike representation system on which formal operations are performed.

LOWERING THE REQUIREMENTS ON A MIND THAT CAN PROCESS LANGUAGE

Fodor and Pylyshyn's (1988) arguments for a syntactically structured internal representational system are directed against recent connectionist models of cognition. Connectionist networks consist of units or nodes that have activation values and are connected to each other by weighted connections. They operate by having units excite or inhibit each other as they pass their activations along the connections, thereby causing changes in the activations of other units (see Fig. 3.1). (For an introduction to connectionism, see Bechtel & Abrahamsen, 1991.) Fodor and Pylyshyn's chief complaint against connectionism is that it represents a return to associationism, and they contend that associationism has already been demonstrated as inadequate to model cognition.

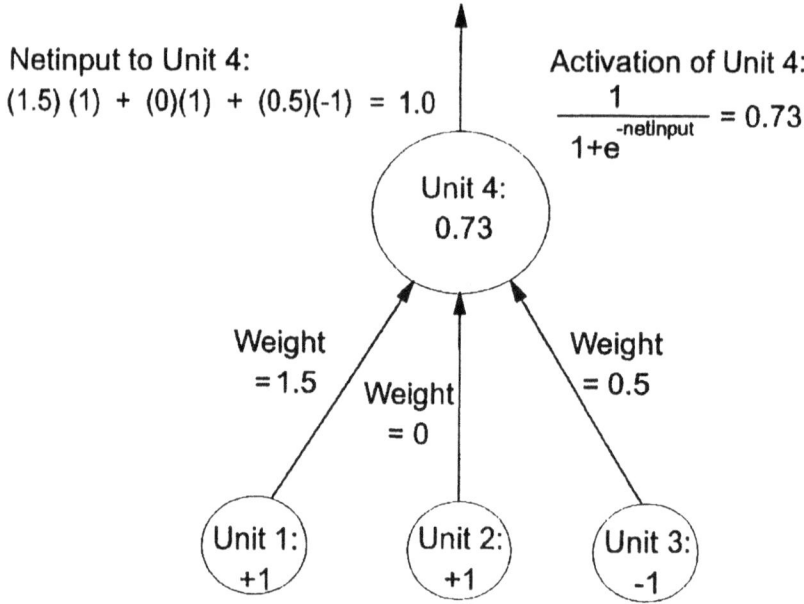

Fig. 3.1. An illustration of processing in a connectionist network. The activation levels of the four units are shown beneath their labels. The weights on the three connections leading to Unit 4 are also shown. The Netinput to Unit 4 is determined by multiplying the activation of each feeding unit by the weight on the connection and summing across the three feeding units. The activation of Unit 4 is then determined according to the logistic activation function shown in the upper right.

The reason for seeing connectionism as associationist is that the connections between units in networks constitute associative links between what is represented by these units. The central arguments against associationism stem from Chomsky (1965), who evaluated the potential of various automata to instantiate grammars and argued that automata operating on merely associationist principles lacked the computational power required for the grammars of natural languages. My reference to grammatical principles as patterns and to pattern recognition as the basic skill required to learn a language may seem like an attempt to reduce grammars to associative principles and thus to run afoul of Chomsky's arguments. However, connectionism and the program for

3. KNOWLEDGE NECESSARY TO ACQUIRE LANGUAGE 57

accounting for language that I am proposing here are not so easily undermined.

First, I have been emphasizing external symbols and suggesting that the cognitive system must learn to use these external symbols. The external symbols give the cognitive system increased computational power. Using the model of a Turing machine, we might see the cognitive system as comparable to the read head of the turning machine. The read head is a finite state device, but obtains its much greater power by reading and writing symbols on a tape. For the cognitive system, the role of the tape is performed by the medium in the external world from which it can read symbols and to which it can write them. Thus, supplemented by a medium for external symbols, a connectionist system has capacities equivalent to a Turing machine.

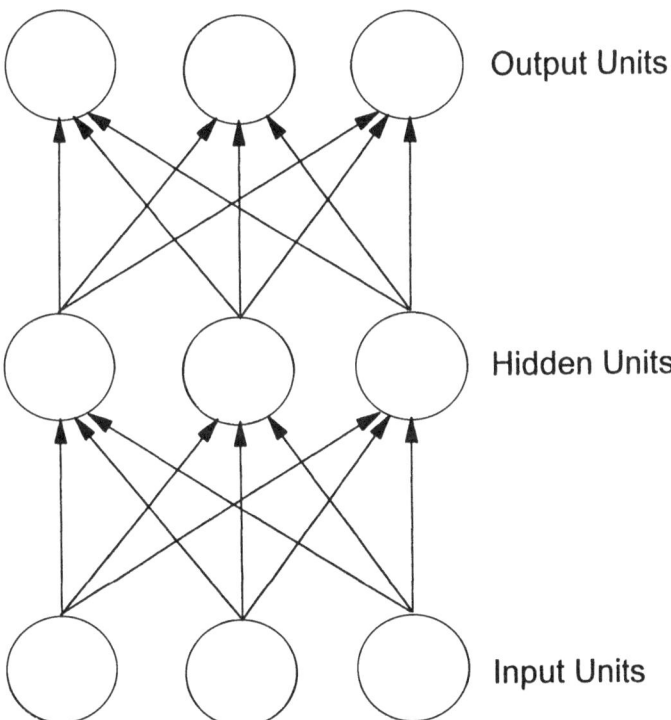

Fig. 3.2. A simple three-layer feedforward network. Each unit in the input layer is connected to every unit in the hidden layer, and each unit in the hidden layer is connected to every unit in the output layer. The hidden units serve to transform the input pattern into a new pattern from which the output pattern can be constructed.

Second, a connectionist system with hidden units (see Fig. 3.2) is more than a simple association device. Hidden units are typically used to transform the input pattern into a different pattern from which the target output pattern can be generated. With sufficient hidden units, a multilayer network can be trained to generate any designated output for any given input pattern, and is thus a powerful computational device.

However, although a network is of the same computational power as a Turing machine, connectionist models do not operate in the same way as Turing machines or symbolic computers. The differences between connectionist systems and computers running traditional programs have attracted many researchers to connectionism. For example, connectionist systems exhibit content-addressable memory and graceful degradation, and lead themselves to tasks requiring satisfaction of multiple soft constraints. Moreover, insofar as connectionist networks are neural-like in structure, they constitute an architecture that can more reasonably be thought of as having evolved. My interest in using connectionism in this project, however, is not to defend connectionism per se. Rather, I invoke connectionist systems as exemplars of a class of dynamical systems in which we might model cognition. What is important for my purposes is that these systems differ from those that have classically been used to model cognitive performance in that they do not employ languagelike internal representations and formal operations on these representations. If such systems could, nonetheless, learn to use external linguistic symbols, they can help us lower the requirements on a mind that can process language.

Although they do not use internal languagelike representations, connectionist systems do employ representations. The patterns on input and output units are construed as representing information. Moreover, the patterns on hidden units serve representational roles (Hinton, 1986). Critics of connectionism, such as Fodor and Pylyshyn, have focused on these representations, and have argued that connectionism must fail because these representations are inadequate. Because they are not built up according to compositional rules, the representations are not syntactically structured in a manner that permits structure-sensitive processing rules to be applied to them. This is the case because activation patterns in networks can only represent the presence or absence of features of objects or events, not relations between those features. Multiple units having positive activation values, for example, can indicate that multiple features are present, but cannot show whether the features are in-

3. KNOWLEDGE NECESSARY TO ACQUIRE LANGUAGE

stantiated in one object, or in many. For example, units representing *red*, *blue*, *circle* and *square* are active in Fig. 3.3, but from this one cannot tell whether the circle is being represented as red or blue; neither can the color for the square be determined. The consequence, according to Fodor and Pylyshyn, is that connectionist models will fail to exhibit productivity and systematicity, the two features that they had claimed all cognitive systems exhibit. By way of contrast, linguistic representations are structured. In particular, they employ compositional syntactic rules for composing strings of symbols, and the semantic interpretation of a string adheres to these principles.

red blue green brown square triangle circle

Fig. 3.3.   An illustration of a problem facing connectionist representations. The units for *red*, *blue*, *square*, and *circle* are all active, but there is no way to indicate whether it is the circle or square that is red.

Many connectionists have struggled with the question of how they should answer Fodor and Pylyshyn. In what follows I examine two strategies that connectionists are exploring. The first accepts the demand that mental representations employ a system of compositional structure, albeit not a system such as classical syntax, whereas the second departs more radically from that framework. In reviewing these programs, I aim to explore the potential for developing connectionist networks that, although not employing linguistically structured internal representations, nonetheless are able to learn (via application of rules for changing weights between units) to extract information from and encode information in external linguistic symbols.

NETWORKS THAT EMPLOY FUNCTIONAL REPRESENTATIONS OF SYNTACTICAL STRUCTURE

What distinguishes a classical linguistic representational system is that each of the components is explicitly designated by words in a sentence, and the relationship between the different entities mentioned is specified by the grammatical principles on which the sentence is structured. Connectionists have pursued an alternate strategy of building connectionist systems in which compositional structure is preserved functionally, but not structurally (van Gelder, 1990). As with syntactic structures, the goal is to build up complex structures, but not ones in which representations of the components' entities can be identified in the compound representation. The goal is to recover the components and their relations from the compound pattern that is created. This will make it possible to keep clear, for example, whether it is the circle that is blue, or the square, and to perform computational operations on these representations roughly comparable to those that can be performed on syntactically structured sentences.

One exemplar of this approach is Pollack's (1990) recursive autoassociative memory (RAAM). (Another exemplar employs the tensor product operation to build compound representations. These bind components of a representation into a compound from which they can later be extracted. See Dolan, 1989; Smolensky, 1990.) In addition to developing connectionist representations that would respect the order found in a symbolic representation, Pollack sought to develop representations of complex structure that could be of fixed length. This is important because the input layer of any given network is of fixed size, unlike a sentential representation which can grow in size as additional clauses are embedded or as propositions are linked by logical operators.

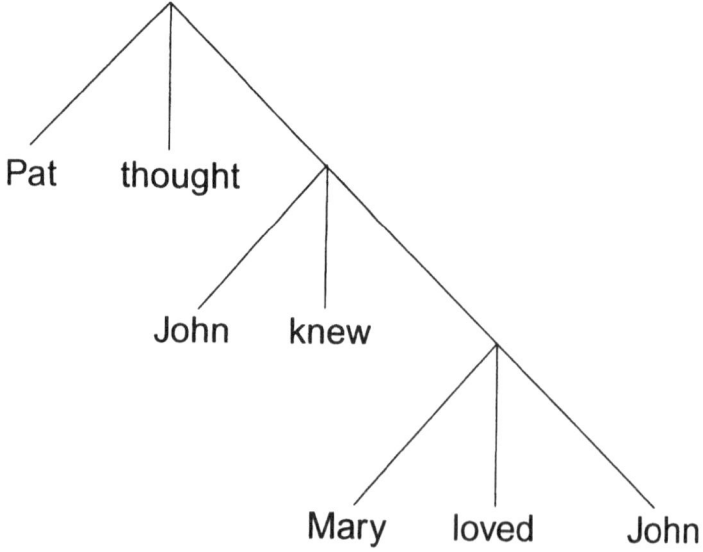

Fig. 3.4. A tree representation of the sentence, "Pat thought John knew Mary loved John."

3. KNOWLEDGE NECESSARY TO ACQUIRE LANGUAGE 61

A standard way to depict structured symbolic representations such as sentences, for which Pollack wants to construct compressed representations, is to show it as a tree structure (see Fig. 3.4). For each word in a string or tree, Pollack assigned a 16-bit activation pattern. The task for the RAAM is to develop a 16-bit activation pattern that represents the whole tree.

To accomplish this, Pollack used the encoder network shown on the left in Fig. 3.5. It has 48 units (3 sets of 16) on the input layer, and 16 units on the output layer. The bit patterns for the words on the terminal nodes on the lowest branches of the tree (*Mary*, *loved*, and *John*) are supplied to the three sets of input units, and the pattern created on the output units constitutes the compressed representation of that branch.

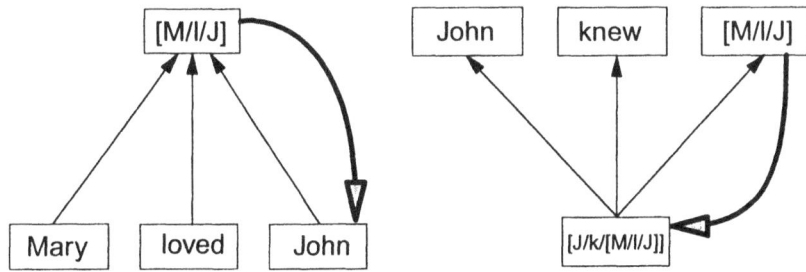

Fig. 3.5. Encoder and decoder networks. The network on the left is an encoder network; a representation of three components is supplied on the input units, and a compressed representation is generated on the output units. If the compressed component is only part of a larger structure, the compressed representation can be used as an input to the network on a subsequent cycle. The decoder network is on the right. A compressed representation is supplied as input to this network and a decompressed representation is produced on the output units. If the output representation is still a compressed representation, it can again be used as an input.

The process is repeated at the next higher branch. (The tree used in this discussion branches only to the right. However, if the tree also branched to the left or from the center, then the compressed representations for all the nodes with branches extending from them at a given level would first be formed; then these, plus any terminal nodes at the level, would be supplied to form the compressed representation at the next higher level.) In this case, the patterns for *John knew* and the compressed representation for *Mary loved John* are supplied to the input nodes for the second cycle. This is a recursive procedure, so it can be applied for as many branches as are found in a particular tree. The decoder network on the right in Fig. 3.5 is then used to uncompress the representation. This involves supplying the compressed representation for the whole sentence to the input units; the uncompressed representation are then constructed on the output units. If the representation on the output units is not itself a terminal representation, it is again supplied to the input units, and another uncompressed representation is constructed on the output units.

To obtain from the decoder network what was supplied to the encoder network, appropriate weights must be found for all of the connections. To train these weights, the two networks shown in Fig. 3.5 are joined as in Fig. 3.6, creating an autoassociative network. An autoassociative network is one that is trained to construct on its output units the very same pattern as was presented on its input units. As long as

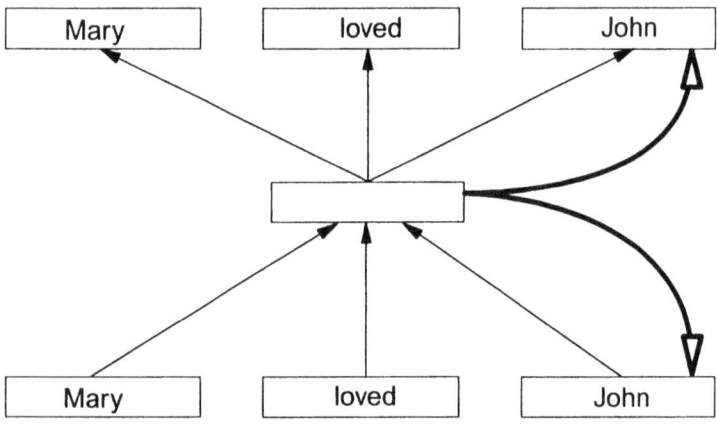

Fig. 3.6. Pollack's (1990) full RAAM network, that combines the two networks shown in Fig. 3.5. In this case the network is trained to reproduce on its output units the same pattern presented on the input units. The pattern on the hidden units is the compressed representation. If the pattern being compressed is itself part of a larger pattern, the compressed representation can then be used as part of the input and output pattern for the larger pattern.

the hidden layer has fewer units than the input and output layers, but still enough to recreate the patterns employed on those layers, an autoassociative network can be used to create compressed representations from which the whole can be recreated. The procedure for training the network is parallel to the one described earlier. One starts with the terminal nodes on the lowest branch, and supplies each of them to the input units. The network generates a pattern of activation on the output units. This is compared to the target output values (which are the same as the input values), and the difference (known as the *error*) is used to change weights through the network according to a procedure known as backpropagation (Rumelhart, Hinton, & R. J. Williams,

3. KNOWLEDGE NECESSARY TO ACQUIRE LANGUAGE 63

1986). This procedure uses a derivative of the error with respect to the activation values of the output units, thus changing weights in such a way that the network is more likely to produce the target output when given the same input in the future. After applying this procedure at the lowest branches, one proceeds to the higher branches, using the compressed representation generated on the hidden units as the input for the appropriate node at the higher level. This actually is a rather complex procedure, because when the same tree is processed again in the future, the weights will have been changed, and the pattern created on the hidden units for the terminal nodes will be different. Hence, at the higher nodes a different pattern will be used as input and target output. Thus, during training the network is chasing a moving target. However, through repeated applications of this procedure, the network is able to acquire weights that permit nearly perfect autoassociation. The two parts of the network can then be detached and used in the manner indicated in the previous paragraph.

Pollack trained his RAAM on 14 sentences similar to the one shown in the tree in Fig. 3.4. After training, the encoder network was able to develop compressed representations from which the decoder network could reconstruct all 14 sentences. The network's abilities were not limited to the sentences in its training set. Pollack tested the ability of the network to encode and decode variations of sentences in the training set correctly. For example, in the training set, four of the sentences of the form "X loved Y" were employed. Because four names were available in the lexicon that the network used, 16 such sentences were possible. When the network was tested on these, it was able to develop compressed representations from which it could regenerate the original sentence for all of them. Thus, the network's ability is not punctate, but seems to exhibit systematicity. On somewhat more complex sentences, the network made some errors. For example, when given the new input sentence "John thought Pat knew Mary loved John," the network returned "Pat thought John knew Mary loved John," which had been one of the sentences in the training set. One might argue, however, that this kind of error is precisely the sort we expect from humans as well (e.g., you might have needed to go back to reread the sentence to notice the difference).

The first significant feature of the compressed representations formed by the RAAM is that they do not employ explicit compositional syntax and semantics. There is no obvious representation of "Mary" in the compressed presentation of "Mary loved John." Yet, the network's capacity seems to be systematic to a significant degree. However, there is a second aspect to these compressed representations. It turns out that they can be used for other computational processes. Chalmers (1990), for example, used a similar RAAM to encode active and passive sentences, and then trained an additional transformation network to construct the compressed representation of the active sentence from a compressed representation of the passive sentence. Even when the transformation network was trained on only a subset of the sentences on which the RAAM had been trained, it was able to generalize perfectly and create a compressed encoding of the passive sentence from which the RAAM decoder network could create the correct uncompressed representation. (The performance was less impressive, achieving only 60% correct on those sentences on which neither the RAAM nor the transformation network had been trained.)

Blank, Meeden, and Marshall (1992) performed a variety of additional tests to exhibit the usefulness of compressed representations developed by RAAM networks. They employed a variation on the strategy used by Pollack and Chalmers. Their RAAM formed a compressed representation from two input patterns at a time, and they encoded sentences by proceeding through them word by word. When the first word of the sentence was encoded, it was supplied to the left-hand set of input units, and the right-hand units were left blank. Subsequently, the compressed pattern created on the hidden units was supplied to the right-hand input units, and the next word to the left-hand input units. In one simulation the researchers trained the network to encode 20 sentences each of the form "X chase Y" and "Y flee X" as well as 110 miscellaneous sentences. Then they trained a feedforward network to generate the compressed form of "Y flee X" from the compressed form of "X chase Y" using 16 of the compressed patterns. The network generalized perfectly to the four remaining cases, and correctly handled three out of four additional sentences of the form "X chase Y" that were not in the training set of the RAAM. (The one error consisted of the substitution of one word for another.) Blank and his colleagues also demonstrated other operations that could be performed on compressed representations. For example, they used the compressed representations as inputs to networks that were trained to determine whether a particular feature was present in the encoded sentence (a noun of the "noun-aggressive" category or a combination of a noun of the "noun-

3. KNOWLEDGE NECESSARY TO ACQUIRE LANGUAGE 65

aggressive" category and a noun of the human category). The network was 88% correct in detecting nouns of the "noun-aggressive" category on sentences on which the RAAM (but not the detector network) had been trained, and 85% correct on sentences on which neither network had been trained. The scores were nearly identical in the combination feature test.

These demonstrations are limited and the degree of generalization is modest, but they do suggest that one might be able to use functional representations of the grammatical structure of the sentence to perform operations that otherwise would seemingly require an explicit representation of the grammar. Although Fodor and Pylyshyn contended that an explicit compositional syntax and semantics were required to model cognition, RAAM networks indicate that connectionists can develop and employ representations in which the compositional structure is only functionally present. The RAAM architecture offers a potentially important advance beyond classical modes of representation because the connectionist functional representations may have very useful properties. For example, the RAAM network may develop similar compressed representations of similar sentences. This is important because connectionist systems generally handle new cases by treating them in the same manner as similarly represented cases. This explains their ability to generalize. One result is that networks do not crash on new cases. A second result is that when networks make errors, the errors generally are intelligible. For example, when Chalmer's network was tested on sentences on which neither the RAAM nor the transformation network had been trained, all but one of the resulting errors involved substitution of one word for another in the same grammatical category.

In a sense, however, research with RAAM networks is still in the spirit of classical cognitive modeling that employs languagelike representations. The RAAM builds up a complete representation of the linguistic input on which operations can then be performed. Although the representations do not exhibit explicit compositional structure and the operations performed on them are performed by connectionist networks, the representations nonetheless appear to play the same role as linguistically structured internal representations, and the operations performed on them are comparable to those performed by applying formal rules in classical systems. In the following section I discuss a far more radical approach, one that does not involve an attempt to build up a complete representation of the syntactic structure of a sentence.

DOING AWAY WITH INTERNAL REPRESENTATIONS OF SYNTACTICAL STRUCTURE

The perspective I suggested earlier was that the cognitive system might be viewed as extracting information from externally encoded sentences and encoding information in them, but without developing an internal representation of the sentence. One way to pursue this is by training a network to perform a task that is not one of encoding the structure of the sentence, but of using the information presented in the sentence to perform another task. Both of the simulations I discuss here employ what are known as *recurrent networks* (Elman, 1990), which are designed to take advantage of the fact that linguistic input, either from

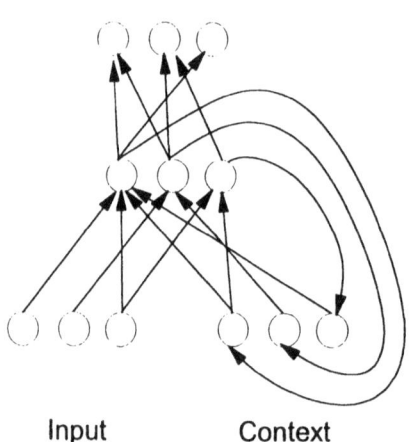

Fig. 3.7. Elman's (1990) recurrent network. Patterns generated on hidden units during one cycle of processing are copied onto the context units, and thus provide part of the input on the next cycle.

speech or writing, is usually sequential in nature. Yet, there are dependencies between different elements in the sequential input, with both the meanings and grammatical function of given words being affected by preceding and succeeding words. Standard feedforward networks are not able to accommodate this because, after the network processes a given input, it starts fresh with the next input. Thus, the whole linguistic structure must be presented at once if the network is to utilize the dependencies between items. This has the disadvantage of letting the number of input units determine a maximum length of an input sentence. The solution employed in a recurrent network is to copy the activations on the hidden unit on a given cycle of processing back onto a special set of input units, designated as *context units* (Fig. 3.7). The

3. KNOWLEDGE NECESSARY TO ACQUIRE LANGUAGE

activations on the context units thus provide a trace of processing on the previous cycle. Because the activation of hidden units on the previous cycle was itself partly determined by the context units whose activation values were copies of hidden unit activations on yet a previous cycle, the recurrent network can provide a trace of processing several cycles back.

The potential of recurrent networks to process sequential inputs such as those that occur in language is illustrated in a simulation by Elman in which a recurrent network was trained to predict as output the next item in a sequence. In one simulation the input was a corpus of 10,000 two- and three-word sentences employing a vocabulary of 29 words. The sentences were constructed to fit 15 different sentence templates, of which the following are two examples: NOUN-HUMAN VERB-INTRANSITIVE (e.g., Woman thinks) and (NOUN-HUMAN VERB-EAT NOUN FOOD (e.g., Girl eats bread). The 15 sentences were concatenated, with no indication of the beginning or end of individual sentences, to form a corpus of 27,524 words, which were then presented to the network one at a time. The network was trained to produce on its output units the next word in the sequence, and after only six passes through the training sequence, its outputs closely approximated the actual probabilities of the next words in the training corpus. Note that in the actual corpus used in training a given word could be followed by several different words, so its predictions should reflect the frequency of successive words. This is what was found. Moreover, it is not enough for the network to attend simply to the current word. What follows a given word may depend on what proceeds it. For example, *woman eats* will be followed by *sandwich, cookie*, or *bread*, whereas *dragon eats* can be followed by *man, woman, cat, mouse, dog, monster, lion, dragon*, as well as by *sandwich, cookie*, or *bread*.

How did the network obtain this level of performance? The recurrent connections provided the hidden units with relevant information about what had preceded the current input. The statistical technique of cluster analysis provides a useful way of analyzing the information contained on the hidden units. This technique recursively groups together those inputs which produce the most similar activation patterns on the hidden units; a hierarchical tree structure is then constructed to exhibit the clusterings of inputs. Thus, nouns employed patterns on the hidden units that were more similar to other nouns than to verbs.

Among nouns, those referring to animate objects formed one subclass; those referring to inanimate objects made up another. Among animates, nonhuman animals were distinct from humans, and aggressive animals were distinguished from nonaggressive ones. Verbs were also categorized into groups, with intransitive verbs distinguished from transitive verbs for which a direct object is optional and from those in which it is mandatory. It is interesting to note that the network learned to distinguish these categories while performing a quite different task: predicting the next word in a sequence. Identifying grammatical categories was not a task explicitly taught to the network. Knowing how the sentences in the corpus were constructed, of course, we can see why these are useful distinctions for the network to make. It is also interesting to note that there is was sufficient regularity in word sequences that a simple network could pick up on it. This network had no access to any of the word's meanings. Elman cited McClelland's characterization of this task as comparable to trying to learn a language by listening to a radio. Chomsky appealed to the poverty of the stimulus in linguistic input to argue that language learning was possible only with a native understanding of grammar, but the network has induced grammatical distinctions from a limited input (albeit one generated from a quite simple grammar).

Elman's goal was simply to show that a recurrent network could become sensitive to temporal dependencies, and he used linguistic input to illustrate this. He was not trying to model a realistic language-processing task. In a more realistic language task, the network should be trying to extract appropriate information from a structured sequence. The challenge is to see whether a network that does not develop an explicit representation of the sequence can accomplish this.

A simulation by St. John and McClelland (1990) shows how this goal might be pursued. One way to interpret the processing of sentences is to construe it as a task of developing a conceptual representation of an event. From such a conceptual representation one can determine what thematic role the entities mentioned in the sentence are playing. Thematic roles are different from grammatical roles. The grammatical subject of a sentence might be the agent (e.g., the cat chased the mouse), the patient (e.g., the mouse was chased by the cat), or the instrument (e.g., the rock broke the window) of an activity. In their simulation, the available case roles are these: agent, action, patient, instrument, coagent, copatient, location, adverb, and recipient. Sentences are

3. KNOWLEDGE NECESSARY TO ACQUIRE LANGUAGE

presented to the network one word at a time, and the network answers questions about what entity or activity filled a particular thematic role or about what thematic role an entity or activity filled. Thus, the input to the network might be the sentence "The schoolgirl spread something with a knife." In response to queries, the network should output *schoolgirl* when queried as to the agent, and *knife* when queried as to the instrument. If queried with *spread* it should respond with *action*. In addition to specifying the actual filler, the network was also trained to respond with several features of the filler, such as *person*, *adult*, *child*, *male,* or *female* for agents. Thus, when queried as to the agent in the previous sentence, the network should not only indicate *schoolgirl*, but also *person*, *child*, and *female*.

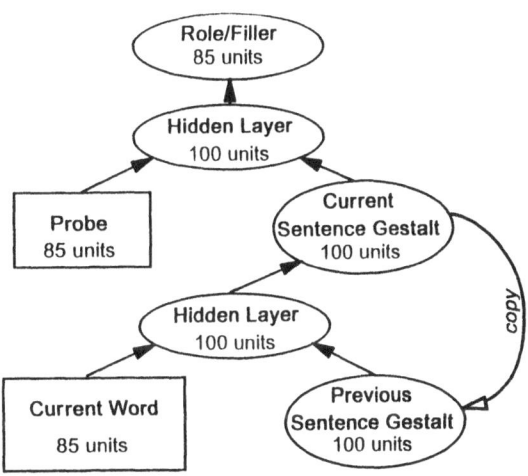

Fig. 3.8. St. John and McClelland's (1990) network for determining thematic roles and fillers from sentences. The two square boxes indicate input units. The input on the probe units specifies either the thematic role or the filler to be generated. The final output units must then designate the combination of thematic role or filler. The sentence is copied one word at a time on the current word input units. This pattern is processed through a set of hidden units to create a *current sentence gestalt*. When a subsequent word is presented, the current sentence gestalt is copied onto the previous sentence gestalt and provides part of the input. This recurrent connection serves to provide the network with a representation of the sentence part that has already been copied.

In their simulation, St. John and McClelland employed a rather complex network (see Fig. 3.8), that can be analyzed into two parts. The top part responds to the queries put to it on the probe units, which specify either a given thematic role or a given filler. This probe and the units designated as the *sentence gestalt* feed into a layer of hidden units, which in turn generate a pattern on the output units that should specify both the thematic role and its filler. The key to the operation of the network is clearly the construction of the sentence gestalt by the lower part of the network. The inputs to this part of the network are the current word of the sentence and the previous sentence gestalt, which represents a copy of the pattern constructed on the sentence gestalt units when the previous word was copied. These are fed through a layer of hidden units to create a new sentence gestalt.

The whole network is trained by backpropagation so that the correct answer is generated to the probes. The training procedure requires the network to generate responses to all of the case role and filler probes for the whole sentence after each word is copied. Thus, from the very first word of the sentence, the network is required to guess all of the role–filler combinations for the whole sentence. The psychological interpretation St. John and McClelland offer for this procedure is that the network is to be thought of as experiencing real world scenes that the sentences describe; its task is to interpret the sentences in accord with the scenes. The functional significance of the training procedure, though, is to force the network to attend to the dependencies between words in its corpus so that it can predict what is likely to follow given words of a sentence. It is this training procedure that accounts for a significant part of the network's ability to develop semantic sensitivity.

St. John and McClelland trained the network on a corpus of over 22,000 sentences describing 120 different events. Multiple sentences could be constructed for each event because different words that could be used for the same entity or action (e.g., *someone*, *adult*, and *bus driver* could all be used to designate the bus driver), and not all components of the event had to be mentioned in each sentence (e.g., if the bus driver is eating, the instrument may be included or omitted). The events were constructed from frames associated with the 14 verbs in the vocabulary (four of which could also be used in the passive). The procedures used to construct the events made some events far more likely than others, exposing the network to a number of rather sexist stereotypes. For example, the bus driver (always a male) was described as eating steak more frequently than soup, and was generally portrayed as eating with gusto, whereas the teacher (always a female) more commonly ate soup and did so daintily. During its training, 330,000 random sentence trials were presented to the network. The network learned to make correct thematic role–filler assignments to the active sentences more quickly, but at this point it also began to make assignments for the passive sentences.

The network was able to process a wide variety of sentences. In some cases, such as "The schoolgirl stirred the kool-aid with a spoon,"

3. KNOWLEDGE NECESSARY TO ACQUIRE LANGUAGE   71

the semantics was sufficient to determine the thematic role–filler assignments, but in passive sentences such as "The bus driver was given the rose by the teacher," the syntax is crucial. (To ensure that the network was relying on syntactic information, it was trained with equal numbers of instances of the bus driver giving a rose to the teacher, and the teacher giving a rose to the bus driver.) The network also made correct thematic role–filler assignments in ambiguous sentences such as "The pitcher hit the bat with the bat," in sentences with concepts that were not explicitly instantiated such as "The schoolgirl spread something with a knife," and in sentences with role fillers that were not explicitly mentioned such as "The teacher ate the soup" (instrument not specified). One of the most interesting abilities of the network was its ability to revise earlier assignments when later information in the sentence required it. In the sentence, "The adult ate the steak with daintiness," the network had to supply the individual for the general category *adult*. When only "The adult ate" was presented, the network assigned equal response values to *bus driver* and *teacher* as agents and to *steak* and *soup* as patients. But after the word *steak* was presented, the network judged *bus driver* and *steak* to be the two most likely fillers, because the *bus driver* was described far more often as *eating steak*. The network at this point also supplied the filler *gusto* for the adverb role. Supplying *daintiness* as input, however, brought a reversal. Now, not only did *daintiness* surpass *gusto* in activation strength, but *teacher* received more activation than *bus driver*. Although *steak* received more activation than *soup*, *steak* declined in activation and *soup* increased. The network was thus able to update its interpretation of previous information as new information became available to it.

Limitations in the manner of encoding output to queries made it impossible to test this network's abilities to process complex grammatical constructions such as embedded clauses. However, in a further simulation St. John and McClelland demonstrated the ability of such networks to handle complex syntactical structures. In this case the network was trained on 56 different sentences using forms of the word *give*. The following show some examples:

> The bus driver gave the rose to the teacher.
> The bus driver gave the teacher the rose.
> The teacher was given the rose by the bus driver.
> The rose was given to the teacher by the bus driver.
> The rose was given by the bus driver to the teacher.

The network was able to extract proper thematic roles and fillers from this corpus. Thus, the model seems to be well on the way to extracting information from the syntactical structure of English sentences.

St. John and McClelland's network must extract a representation of an event from sentences whose words are presented sequentially. The classical way of approaching this task is to build a structured representation of the input, then perform computations on it to answer the queries. This is not, however, what this network does. It does construct an internal representation (the current sentence gestalt) in the course of processing the sentence, and it uses this representation to construct its output. However, this representation is not a classical representation with combinatorial syntax and semantics. Moreover, it is not even a representation designed to be functionally equivalent to the whole. It is a representation that captures only information in the input that is relevant to the task on which it was trained.

This simulation demonstrates that, at least in limited cases, a network can extract information from syntactically structured representations without employing internal syntactically structured representations. This raises the prospect that humans, too, can comprehend sentences without representing the sentences in a syntactically structured internal code and performing formal operations on it. Of course, this prospect may turn out to be illusory. St. John and McClelland's network can only process a small fragment of English, and it remains a question whether networks of this kind could eventually handle the full range of complexity found in human natural languages. The answer to the question will only come from further empirical investigation. In conducting such investigations, however, we should be careful not to exaggerate human ability. In written prose we can retrace our steps as necessary when dealing with extremely complex sentences. In oral communication, however, we often make mistakes in comprehending complex sentences. Reviewing the pattern of external symbols is not something that a network of this design could perform, and we should not expect the network to do better than people can with oral input.

Another limitation of this network is that it is only potentially capable of comprehending sentences. Can such a design work for production as well as for comprehension? I can only speculate as to how linguistic production might be modeled by a network that does not employ an internal representation of the syntactic structure of the sentences it is producing. In a simulation one could develop a network that uses for its input a sentence gestalt of the form used in St. John and McClelland's simulation, then train it to produce proper sentential outputs. The speech output network again might be a recurrent network with activations on a layer between the input and output units being recycled as input. However, the sentence gestalt, or some other semantic representation, might remain as a constant input during all the cycles of processing until a sentence is complete. On the output units the network would be trained to issue the words of a sentence in sequential order. In such a simulation, the connection weights would need to acquire the knowledge of how to produce grammatically correct speech, but there would be no internal grammatically structured representation. (Note added in proof: Since this paper was written, a report of a network which works in much this way has been published by Miikkulainen, 1993.)

It is not clear how good a performance a connectionist network could achieve on such a task. However, we must again bear in mind what standards we should use in judging such a network. We should not expect it to produce the full range of sentences that linguists judge to be correct sentences of a language. Rather, we should only expect it to obtain levels found in actual human speech. Even this is a quite unrealistic expectation for a relatively simple, totally interconnected network. It is already apparent that more highly structured networks (in which, for example, modules perform different parts of an overall task) achieve better performances than vanilla feedforward networks (R. A. Jacobs, Jordan, Nowlan, & Hinton, 1991). Realistic performance on such language tasks will likely await new developments in network design, but the goal is clear: to teach a network to produce proper linguistically structured sentences without employing an internal representation of the linguistic product that is itself syntactically structured.

FINAL REFLECTIONS ON MODELING THE INTERNAL COMPETENCIES NEEDED FOR LANGUAGE

In my discussion I contend that the requirements on the cognitive system responsible for language might be significantly fewer than they have often been portrayed to be. Human languages do have complex structures such as those that linguists have identified in the course of developing grammars for natural languages. Nevertheless, responsibility for comprehending and producing grammatical speech may not lie exclusively with the internal cognitive system. Rather, it can utilize the resources of external symbols and can be constrained by social processes supporting and governing language use. As a result, the fluent use of a language may not require internal representations of the grammatical structures upon which formal operations can be performed, but only the ability to extract and encode meanings in such structures. This does not mean that the internal processes used by the cognitive system might not be quite complex. Yet they need not be of the same sort that linguists have developed for describing language. The cognitive system may only be part of the system responsible for language, and its internal organization may be quite different from that of the emergent product.

Abrahamsen (1987) argued that the tasks of linguistics and psycholinguistics are quite different. Linguists are analyzing language as a cultural product. Grammars such as Chomsky's provide representations of that product, but these grammars need not characterize the processing that occurs when people comprehend or produce sentences of a language. Abrahamsen argued that psycholinguists should expect that they will need to reformat the grammars developed by linguists when they try to account for the psychological processes involved in language use. I propose that psycholinguists may need to go a step further. The systems involved in processing languages may be dynamic systems that do not employ grammatically structured representations internally, but that do generate and comprehend external symbols. It is these external symbols that afford syntactic structuring, and it is the communities of language users who must develop and regulate the use of these structures. Cognitive systems can interact with syntactically structured symbols by producing and comprehending them, but language is an emergent product of cognitive systems, external symbols, and communities of language users.

The simulations I have described here are meant only to demonstrate how abilities to utilize grammatically structured linguistic items might be accounted for without internal syntactic representations. These simulations are not meant to be serious models of language processing ready to be evaluated by human data. I am not even convinced that they represent the most fruitful way of exploring linguistic ability within a connectionist or nonsymbolic framework. They approach the task of language processing in isolation from other cognitive activities and the needs of the organism to control its body in its environment.

3. KNOWLEDGE NECESSARY TO ACQUIRE LANGUAGE 75

Thus, there is no real semantics for such models. A far more realistic approach might begin with a model of a system functioning in an environment, that is, a system with sensory capacities to absorb information from its environment and motor capacities to change its environment. Given such a system, the challenge would be to extend these capacities by making it possible for the system to extract information from linguistic symbols present in the environment or to produce linguistic symbols as a means of manipulating its environment. Such a system would presumably develop the capacity to use symbols semantically before it began to focus on the syntax of linguistic structures. Once the system had developed the processing ability to recognize the semantic import of linguistic structures, though, it might notice that the grammatical structure provided additional information, and it might learn to respect the grammatical structure as it sought to extract information.

I close with two qualifying comments. First, by arguing for the reduction of demands on the internal processing system responsible for language, I may seem also to be endorsing an empiricist view of language according to which linguistic ability is simply acquired by the use of more generally applicable cognitive abilities. My position, however, is also compatible with a form of nativism (E. A. Bates & Elman, 1992; Bechtel & Abrahamsen, 1991). Although I have argued for an approach that does not posit internal syntactically structured representations, I have not denied that the cognitive system that learns to comprehend and produce language may be highly structured and have processing capacities quite different from those involved in other cognitive abilities. Presumably the neural hardware underlying language processing had to evolve first in a context in which it was not used for language, and has only in recent evolution become specifically used for language processing (see Deacon, chap. 5, this volume). Nonetheless, the system might well have been preadapted to the demands of language processing to such a degree that language learning seems almost inevitable among humans. We know that even children who lack linguistic models begin to develop language systems so long as they have an appropriate medium for symbol development (Golden-Meadow & Feldman, 1977). This argues for a system predisposed to develop language, but not for a specific analysis of the internal nature of this system.

Second, I have emphasized the external symbols such as sounds and inscriptions that figure in language use. We have, however, learned to use language internally. It is salient for my purposes, though, that the use of external symbols comes first in children's linguistic development, and that using language privately in our thinking is a later development (Vygotsky, 1934, 1962). I expect that private linguistic thought will utilize many of the same computational resources as overt speech in much the same way that visual imaging utilizes the same neural substrates as visual perception (Farah, 1988). Having learned to produce speech, we may have learned to go through all but the steps of overtly pronouncing words, and to have used this aborted production in much the same way as we have learned to use external symbols. We might, for example, use this production capacity to create echoic memories of symbols. If this speculation is correct, then even in private thinking we are using symbols as if they were external, and are manipulating them in the same manner as we might manipulate truly external symbols such as inscriptions on a page. That is, we might try to produce a symbol string, and then determine appropriate modifications of it. The symbols remain external to the cognitive system that is producing and recognizing them, and that production and comprehension system might not need a syntactical representation of the syntactically structured output it produces and comprehends.

REFERENCES

Abrahamsen, A. A. (1987). Bridging boundaries versus breaking boundaries: Psycholinguistics in perspective. *Synthese, 72*, 355–388.

Bates, E. A., & Elman, J. L. (1992). *Connectionism and the study of change.* CRL Technical Report No. 9202. San Diego: Center for Research in Language, University of California.

Bechtel, W. (1993a). Decomposing intentionality: Perspectives on intentionality drawn from language research with two species of chimpanzees. *Biology and Philosophy, 8*, 1–32.

Bechtel, W. (1993b). Knowing how to use language: Developing a rapprochement between two theoretical traditions. In H. Roitblat, L. Herman, & P. Nachtigall (Eds.), *Language and Communication: Comparative perspectives* (pp. 65–83). Hillsdale, NJ: Lawrence Erlbaum Associates.

Bechtel, W. (1994). Natural deduction in connectionist systems. *Synthese, 101*, 433–463.

Bechtel, W., & Abrahamsen, A. A. (1991). *Connectionism and the mind: An introduction to parallel processing in networks.* Oxford, England: Basil Blackwell.

Bechtel, W., & Richardson, R. C. (1993). *Discovering complexity: Decomposition and localization as strategies in scientific research.* Princeton, NJ: Princeton University Press.

Blank, D. S., Meeden, L., & Marshall, J. B. (1992). Exploring the symbolic/subsymbolic continuum: A case study of RAAM. In J. Dinsmore (Ed.), *Closing the gap: Symbolism vs. connectionism* (pp. 113-148). Hillsdale, NJ: Lawrence Erlbaum Associates.

Chalmers, D. J. (1990). Mapping part–whole hierarchies into connectionist networks. *Artificial Intelligence, 46,* 47–75.

Chomsky, N. (1959). Review of Verbal Behavior. *Language, 35,* 26–58.

Chomsky, N. (1965). *Aspects of a theory of syntax.* Cambridge, MA: MIT Press.

Chomsky, N. (1980). *Rules and representations.* New York: Columbia University Press.

Churchland, P. S. (1986). *Neurophilosophy: Toward a unified science of the mind-brain.* Cambridge, MA: MIT Press.

Dolan, C. P. (1989). Tensor manipulation networks: Connectionist and symbolic approaches to comprehension, learning, and planning. *AI Lab Report.* Los Angeles: University of California.

Elman, J. L. (1990). Finding structure in time. *Cognitive Science, 14,* 179–212.

Farah, M. J. (1988). Is visual perception really visual? Overlooked evidence from neuropsychology. *Psychological Review, 95,* 307–17.

Fodor, J. A. (1975). *The language of thought.* New York: Crowell.

Fodor, J. A. (1987). *Psychosemantics: The problem of meaning in the philosophy of mind.* Cambridge, MA: MIT Press.

Fodor, J. A., & Pylyshyn, Z. W. (1988). Connectionism and cognitive architecture: A critical analysis. *Cognition, 28,* 3–71.

Hinton, G. E. (1986). Learning distributed representations of concepts. *Proceedings of the Eighth Annual Conference of the Cognitive Science Society* (pp. 1–12). Hillsdale, NJ: Lawrence Erlbaum Associates.

Golden-Meadow, S., & Feldman, S. (1977). The development of language like communication system without a language model. *Science, 197,* 401–3.

Jacobs, R. A., Jordan, M. I., Nowlan, S. J., & Hinton, G. E. (1991). Adaptive mixtures of local experts. *Neural Computation, 3,* 79–87.

Lock, A. (1980). *The guided reinvention of language.* London: Academic.

Miikkulainen, R. (1993). *Subsymbolic natural language processing.* Cambridge, MA: MIT Press.

Pollack, J. (1990). Recursive distributed representations. *Artificial Intelligence, 46,* 77–105.

Rumelhart, D. E., Hinton, G. E., & Williams, R. J. (1986). Learning internal representations by error propagation. In D. E. Rumelhart, J. L. McClelland & the PDP Research Group (Eds.), *Parallel distributed processing: Explorations in the microstructure of cognition. Vol. 1: Foundations* (pp. 318–362). Cambridge, MA: MIT Press.

Rumelhart, D. E., Smolensky, P., McClelland, J. L., & Hinton, G. E. (1986). Schemas and sequential thought processes in PDP models. In J. L. McClelland, D. E. Rumelhart, & the PDP Research Group (Eds.), *Parallel distributed processing: Explorations in the microstructure of cognition. Vol. 2: Psychological and biological models* (pp. 5–57). Cambridge, MA: MIT Press.

Simon, H. A. (1980). *The sciences of the artificial*. Cambridge, MA: MIT Press.

Skinner, B. F. (1957). *Verbal behavior*. Englewood Cliffs, NJ: Prentice-Hall.

Smolensky, P. (1990). Tensor product variable binding and the representation of symbolic structures in connectionist systems. *Artificial Intelligence, 46*, 159–216.

St. John, M. F., & McClelland, J. L. (1990). Learning and applying contextual constraints in sentence comprehension. *Artificial Intelligence, 46*, 217–257.

van Gelder, T. (1990). Compositionality: A connectionist variation on a classical theme. *Cognitive Science, 14*, 355–384.

Vygotsky, L. S. (1962). *Thought and language* Cambridge, MA: MIT Press. Original work published in 1934.

PART

II

PHYLOGENETIC PREREQUISITES

CHAPTER

4

WAS SPEECH AN EVOLUTIONARY AFTERTHOUGHT?

Alexandra Maryanski
University of California at Riverside

It is a very convenient habit of kittens that whatever you say to them, they always purr. If they would only purr for "yes" and mew for "no," or any rules of that sort, so that one could keep up a conversation! But how can you talk with a person if they always say the same thing?

—Lewis Carroll

Beginning in the late 19th century, teaching apes an oral language became an intellectual challenge. Virtually every means was tried but an ape capable of speech was never forthcoming, with the result that this line of inquiry was abandoned (C. Hayes, 1952; W. N. Kellogg & L. A. Kellogg, 1933). Nonetheless, when acquisition and production were channeled through other sensory modalities, chimpanzees and gorillas were able to associate symbols with objects and to perform some syntactical "linguistic operations" using both natural language sign (Ameslan) and artificial (e.g., computer-assisted) languages. Although the linguistic production of apes is modest compared to that of adult humans, it is clear that both *(Pan)* chimpanzees and (Gorilla) gorillas can acquire large vocabularies of arbitrary symbols and use them referentially for constructing new words and for denoting objects that are not present. Recently, bonobo chimpanzees *(Pan paniscus)* set a new course by revealing a capacity for English speech comprehension at the level of a normal 2½- to 3-year-old human child. Seemingly, when young bonobos are nurtured in a verbally rich environment, their auditory systems respond by selecting and organizing significant sounds into phonemes, then combining these elements for the perception of words and meaningful sentences (see Rumbaugh & Savage-Rumbaugh, chap. 9, this volume; Savage-Rumbaugh et al., 1993).

The latent capacity of apes to use language has revived interest in the genesis of language, that is, in how and why language evolved in humans. Yet, paradoxically, many scholars disregard ape research, despite the fact that apes are doing *something* linguistic. Just what that something is, however, invites controversy, even acrimony among scholars. Part of this controversy results from a lack of an agreed upon definition of what constitutes language, another part from a reluctance by language researchers to consider anything less than a full-blown production system with formal syntax as "real" language, and still another because of a bias toward oral languages. Yet, Darwinian theory would indicate that, like other features of organisms, language (or its components) evolved over time and perhaps, in a stair-step evolutionary process. The linguist, Edward Sapir (1933), certainly pressed this point some time ago when he proposed that language was the "slowly evolved product of a particular technique or tendency," which he called the "symbolic one," and while speech was a "distinctly human achievement ... its roots probably lie in the power of the higher apes to solve specific problems by abstracting general forms or schemata from the details of a given situation" (p. 13).

This chapter is devoted to a consideration of Sapir's proposal that clues to the genesis of language may lie in examining the phyletic components of language, especially in determining why hominoids (i.e., apes and humans) acquired the necessary neurological equipment to engage in linguistic activity. The story of how hominoids and hominid ancestors (i.e., near to or on the line to humans) acquired the capacity for language forces us to examine the sense modalities of primates (i.e., auditory, visual, generalized somatic [here: haptic], and olfactory) and the ways that these are structured and integrated in the brain. The story begins with the adaptation of primates in the arboreal niche and then turns to the selection pressures on the African savanna that reintegrated the sensory organs in ways that provided the neurological foundation for propositional speech. These capacities, it is argued, evolved originally for reasons having little to do with social communication, per se, but rather with object recognition and learning in the diversified niches inhabited by primates for 60 million years. When selection favoring language, whether visual or verbal, eventually occurred, the neurological wiring was already in place.

ON THE NEUROBIOLOGY OF PRIMATE SENSE MODALITIES

The Nature of Perception in Mammals

Until 65 million years ago, most organisms had relatively sparse sensory equipment, but that changed with placental mammals when a six-layered cerebral cortex or *neocortex*, evolved over older *limbic cortex*. The limbic system (a nomenclature introduced to designate specialized, inner-core structures and related brain stem connections) is phylogenetically ancient cortex that envelopes the gustatory and olfactory modalities and other structures involved with such visceral functions as feeding and sexual behaviors, aggression, motivational functions and expressions of emotion (Isaacson, 1982; Lovilot, Tagifzouti, Simon, & Le Moal, 1989; MacLean, 1990). As the cerebral cortex became elaborated, specialized regions developed: the motor area in the frontal lobe (for specific, goal-directed voluntary movement), the somatosensory system in the parietal lobe (notably haptic or tactile discrimination), the auditory system in the temporal (for hearing), and the visual system in the occipital (and partly in temporal cortex). In simple mammals the cerebral cortex is composed mostly of motor and sensory zones, whereas in advanced mammals, the bulk of the neocortex is composed of specialized regions, often referred to as "association cortex" for complex higher order operations (Allman, 1990; Kaas, 1987; Pandya, Seltzer, & Barbas, 1988).

Sensory zones are the only means by which an organism can perceive the external world, and hence their task is to signal the different properties of objects in space. Thus, each modality is designed to respond only to particular stimuli and to detect only particular qualities of objects, and no matter how complex the sensory equipment, the nature of perception for all organisms is severely restricted because it is physically impossible for sensory receptors to pick up and signal all possible qualities of objects (I. C. Whitfield, 1982). This limitation in perceptual ability has led to the provocative hypothesis that a species' brain reflects the adaptive strategies of its ancestors in a given ecological zone. That is, within taxonomic groups "differences in the size of the brain and its parts should reflect major evolutionary trends in niche diversification" (Stephan, Baron, & Frahm, 1988, p. 1).

The Primate Niche and Neocortical Selection

Prosimian Radiation. The fossil record suggests that the primate order began in the Paleocene about 60 million years ago, having evolved from a line of long-snouted insectivores (Gingerich, 1990; R. D. Martin, 1990). All extant primates are believed to be descendants of arboreal ancestors, beginning with the Prosimii or lower primates. Although selection for land-based mammals favored highly specialized changes in body anatomy, tree-based early prosimians retained a generalized early mammal morphology. Instead, selection favored highly specialized enhancement of neocortical equipment with a heightening of the visual organ and a pruning of the olfactory organ. For example, selection for visual expansion is already conspicuous in the cranial anatomy of the 55-million-year-old *Tetonius homunculus*, a prosimian whose spherical skull is considered "remarkably advanced for its time [with] enlarged occipital and temporal lobes and reduced olfactory bulbs" (Radinsky, 1970, p. 209), suggesting "a visually, rather than olfactorily, oriented animal (K. D. Rose & Fleagle, 1987, p. 62). Other prosimian endocasts repeat this sensory trend (see Beard, Krishtalka, & Stucky, 1991; Jerison, 1990; Radinsky, 1970); moreover, postcranial hindlimb materials suggest that Eocene prosimians moved about by vertical clinging and leaping, a locomotor pattern common to extant prosimians. It is significant to note that this type of muscular movement would also require elaboration of visual, parietal, and motor cortex to enhance the precision of a grasping foot (Gidley, 1919; J. R. Napier & Walker, 1987; Walker, 1974, p. 376).

Anthropoid Radiation. Forty million years ago, in the late Eocene or early Oligocene epoch, generalized anthropoids (i.e., primitive monkey–ape forms) emerged in Africa (Simons, 1990; Tuttle, 1988). In cranial morphology, early simians reveal an expanded visual cortex and a further olfactory reduction over prosimians, indicating "an increased emphasis on vision and a decreased emphasis on smell" (Conroy, 1990; Radinsky, 1975, p. 156). This progressive shift from the olfactory organ to the visual organ involved much more than a transfer of sensory dominance; it radically altered primate perception from a modality that projects to the limbic system (a structure geared toward preservation and emotionally based responses) to one that projects to the neocortex (a structure primarily geared toward reasoning and intentional based responses). Thus, an emphasis on visually guided behavior would result in increased pressures to suppress emotional responses while promoting intentional responses to a complex and changing environment (Isaacson, 1982; MacLean, 1990).

The Primate Niche and Foraging Strategies

The diverse morphology of primate limb bones suggests that "locomotor experimentation" played a major role in the adaptive radiation of primates as they colonized new ecological zones (Lewis, 1974). Even early Eocene primates reveal an expansion of motor and parietal zones for haptic (or active touch) and proprioceptive (skin, muscles, and joint) sensations, seemingly to allow prosimians greater precision in balance and locomotor patterns in an arboreal zone (Hill, 1972; Walker, 1974). In many present-day prosimians this inchoate selection is reflected in a basic hand and foot locomotor pattern that is best suited for wrapping around wide, vertical tree trunks, with the hand used for grasping and the foot for propulsion.

In comparison, the Oligocene radiation of early generalized anthropoids (i.e., primitive monkeys and apes) was probably related to a niche shift onto the branches of trees, because primitive anthropoids show an expanded neocortex over prosimians in conjunction with skeletal changes for a coordinated hand and foot locomotion pattern (see von Bonin, 1952). Present-day monkeys reflect this basic quadrupedal anatomy by virtue of immobile shoulder joints, a small collarbone, a narrow rib cage, and limbs of similar length, all of which signal an original adaptation for "branch walking" using a tail for balance and the hindlimbs for propulsion (J. R. Napier & P. H. Napier, 1985; Tattersall, Delson, & van Couvering, 1988). In contrast, extant hominoids (apes and humans) are still morphologically equipped (despite secondary modifications) for climbing and below-branch "hand-traveling," made possible by virtue of a short and deep trunk, limbs of unequal length, lack of tail, mobile and specialized shoulders and specialized wrists and hands for greater flexibility and mobility (Hunt, 1991; Swartz, 1989).

Today the primate order is composed of nearly 200 species: 70% monkeys, 25% prosimians, and 5% hominoids (apes and humans). Ironically, the few hominoids of today are the descendants of a large adaptive radiation of ancestral hominoids who flourished in the early Miocene epoch about 20 million years ago, and who, today, can be grouped into the gibbon lesser apes or Hylobatidae; the Pongidae or Great Apes (chimpanzees, gorillas, and orangutans); and the Hominidae or humans. As the closest living relatives to humans, the Great Apes are always set apart from monkeys and lesser apes because of their large size, much bigger brains, and greatly augmented cognitive abilities.

In trying to understand the initial expansion of the hominoid neocortex, we can dismiss any notion that apes were favored with "more biological intelligence" in order to promote their reproductive fitness over Old World monkeys. Monkeys, in fact, are enormously successful primates whether viewed in terms of sheer numbers or species, whereas hominoids (except for humans) are viewed as a mere handful of species and from a selectionist perspective, "evolutionary failures" (Andrews, 1981). Yet, during the early Miocene period, apes were much more prolific than monkeys and occupied a broader variety of ecological zones. However, something altered this situation in the middle Miocene period, with the fossil record documenting an increasing monkey population and a decreasing hominoid population (Andrews, 1981; Tattersall et al., 1988). Even more intriguing is that during this replacement phase, when monkeys were taking over the former ape niches, hominoids (whose original postcranial materials indicate a quadrupedal walker) were undergoing unique changes for the specialized skeletal features that characterize apes and humans today (Andrews, 1981; Conroy, 1990; Tattersall et al., 1988; Temerin & Cant, 1983).

The fossil materials indicate that apes evolved the novel anatomical changes in order to exploit a peculiar, and most likely, marginal niche that required an unusual elaboration of the forelimbs for locomotion and for actual feeding. This adaptation to what was probably "terminal branch feeding" required a repertoire of novel movements for an arm-hanging adaptation (which should not be confused with gibbonlike ricochetal arm swinging, which was not part of the ancestral condition

(R. D. Martin, 1990). It first of all required (a) a strong finger flexion, if the hand is to suspend the body like hanging fruit; (b) a hand (rather than a foot) to propel the body through space; and (c) an extreme range of supination to rotate the body at about a half-circle. Selection, however, did much more: It seemingly favored the enhancement of motor area and visual-haptic coordination because a reliance on the forelimbs (without backing from the hindlimbs) would require increased cortical control over motor movements (Corruccini, Ciochon, & McHenry, 1975; Holloway, 1968). Unlike quadrupedal movement, which is a relatively stereotyped locomotor pattern, forelimb motion requires a much greater emphasis on individually learned navigational skills, especially for precise calculation of egocentric distance, requiring, in turn, the greater commitment to memory of learned secondary depth cues. Also the loss of the substantial support of four limbs and the dependence on the limited support of two limbs (without a tail for support) would optimize the tactile characteristics of the prehensile hands, especially for an increased sensitivity to roughness, slickness, vibrations, texture, temperature, and especially what lies under the surface of objects. Finally, the peculiar locomotor technique of having the arms raised high above the head in feeding, or hand-over-hand locomotion, would also foster increased tactual perception to process temporal sequential patterns for object recognition. Although a forelimb dominant creature would certainly rely on vision for guidance in locomotion, the visual would be deficient for laying hold of the structure of a tree-limb above the head once the prehensive hands are outside the range of vision. Moreover, there would be an increasing tendency for the haptic and visual to reorganize for coordinated action through multimodal rather than unimodal patterning, which was eventually to allow for the neurological capacity for language.

CORTICAL TRENDS IN PRESENT-DAY OLD WORLD HIGHER PRIMATES

The higher primate visual, auditory, and general somatic zones are lodged respectively in the occipital, temporal, and parietal lobes, and each is specialized to extract particular environmental features when activated by visual, acoustic, or tactile stimuli. From the admittedly narrow confines of a neurological perspective, the sensory zones then transmit and analyze this elementary information, after which it cascades through other cortical regions or association areas for more complex processing (see Mesulam, 1983; Pandya & Yeterian, 1985, for detailed discussion). The network relations that make complex cortical functions possible are well developed in present-day higher primates, with the primate neocortex itself viewed as "one of the hallmarks of mammalian brain evolution" (Jones, 1990, p. 31); a "strong progressive structure" that has steadily increased in primate evolution depending on the demands of the ecological niche (Mesulam, 1983; Stephan et al., 1988, p. 15).

Network Relations Among the Sensory Zones

Auditory Modality. The auditory zones in primates have seemingly undergone few changes during primate evolution, because despite different primate radiations, Old World monkeys, apes, and humans share a basic structural design (H. Heffner & R. Heffner, 1990; Kaas, 1987; Newman, 1988, p. 416). Above all, the primate auditory system is a specialized wide-ranging "early warning device" to discriminate and localize brief and abrupt environmental sounds, such as the thumps, chirps, snaps, pops, cracks, and thuds that suggest danger and predation (Masterton, 1992). Having been alerted, the visual system then normally attends to the object in space (Khanna & Tonndorf, 1978). All primates react to brief, sudden noise as if their source were animate; whereas continuous, periodic, or legato sounds are usually considered an inanimate source of sound or part of general background noise (Masterton, 1992; Masterton & I. Diamond, 1973, p. 431). From an evolutionary perspective, this function is so central to primate survival that in the words of Masterton and I. Diamond (1973), "it is virtually impossible to truncate the central auditory system in such a way as to make an animal incapable of responding to a brief sound" (p. 431). Apparently, following Stebbins (1965, p. 186), the hearing potential of all higher primates is about the same, and differences in auditory sensitivity among monkeys, apes, and humans are very small.

The primate auditory cortex is also essentially involved in distinguishing conspecific vocalizations, especially ones with communication significance (Brugge & Reale, 1985). Although poorly understood, the neural mechanisms for primate vocalizations are found in a number of different brain regions (Sutton & Jürgens, 1988). Although experiments have confirmed that primate calls are not entirely emotional or instinctual but have volitional components for voluntary and semantic signaling (Cheney & Seyfarth, 1990; Steklis, 1985), limbic cortex (especially the anterior cingulate gyrus) still retains control over vocal production in all nonhuman primates (Snowdon, 1990; Sutton & Jürgens, 1988). Humans also have vocalizations that can be laden with emotional content, but their auditory–vocal channel is under cortical control and adapted for voluntary, purposeful sounds. The difference between nonhuman and human primates is, perhaps, an important clue in tracing the evolution of language, especially spoken language.

The Haptic Modality. The perceptual processes of the somatosensory cortex involve a number of general somatic senses located in the skin, muscles, and joints, which transmit to the parietal lobe necessary information for fine sensorimotor coordination. For active haptic discrimination, Old World monkeys, apes, and humans are remarkably well endowed with prehensile hands (and feet) to actively explore the environment, along with a true opposable thumb for dexterity in grasping and manipulating objects. Unfortunately, few investigations have been carried out to discover how the sensitive pads on the primate fingertips process environmental information, although these pads have more sensitive receptors than most parts of the primate body (see Kaas & Pons, 1988; Taylor, Lederman, & R. H. Gibson, 1973). However, apes have been shown to have finer motor control and proprioception than monkeys (Holloway, 1968). Additionally, whereas monkeys have simple fingerprints, ape and human fingerprints evidence a shared intricate complexity of raised digital ridges pierced with sweat glands for a more sensitive touch and for a better grip on smooth surfaces (J. R. Napier & P. H. Napier, 1985).

In humans, although tactual perception is recognized as extremely complex, it is cast as a redundant or backup system for visual perception. However, Taylor et al. (1973) noted that "touch is old and intimate, and ill understood" (p. 252) with many largely latent powers, each with its own capacities and limitations. Curiously, most of the feature-extraction qualities of tactual perception are dormant in humans, unless the visual modality is incapable or deficient in some way for guiding activity. Under these conditions, by stringing together a succession of independent chunks of information, the tactile receptors create a pattern of the whole that allows for object recognition (as observed in blind individuals all the time). The haptic is employed also to enhance recognition of texture and what lies under the surface of objects, which the visual modality often cannot process alone (see Freides, 1974; Hampshire, 1975).

Visual Modality. In primates, the visual cortex is an elaborate structure in the occipital lobe, with a large expansion into the temporal lobe (Martin, 1990). Two distinctive features of the visual system in present-day monkeys, apes, and humans are: (a) stereoscopic vision, and (b) retina specialization for color vision and a finely tuned fovea. Most mammals have some binocular vision, but only in higher primates did an ability to distinguish objects as separated by air space undergo stereoscopic refinement, allowing for the precise coordination of the two eyes and the overlay of images (Campbell, 1986, p. 84; Ogle 1962a,b). In turn, this fostered the expansion of visual association zones to store visual memories on the distance and stability of objects in space over time. In addition, selection for color perception (which facilitated the detection of subtle light changes), and a fovea (which facilitated the detection of fine detail) evolved to complement stereoscopic vision. These complicated neurological changes equipped higher primates with the novel ability to "see" objects clearly in space.

Thus, although different sensory impressions will combine for perceptual demands, the visual sense in higher primates is overwhelmingly dominant for most spatial information. Moreover, in monkeys and apes, vision is not primary only for object recognition, but also for social communication, through gestures and body movements (Simonds, 1974, p. 36). In turn, the tactile and auditory modalities are complementary systems that fill in information about objects in space when visual processing is not possible or when the processing capacity of the visual modality is inadequate by itself. These extensive elaborations in visual equipment have assured that higher primates depend "almost entirely upon vision for orientation in space and for recognition of objects" (De Valois & G. Jacobs, 1971, p. 108).

In humans, research has confirmed the observation that vision acts as the major integrator of environmental stimuli and is overwhelmingly dominant in matters relating to object recognition (i.e., size, shape and spatial location; Freides, 1974; Posner, M. J. Nissen, & Klein, 1976; Rock, 1966; Warren & Pick, 1970). So powerful and dominating is the visual modality that it even influences the information pickup of the auditory and tactile sense. For example, in cases of intersensory conflict the visual system will determine what is perceived. In summarizing research on human visual dominance, Posner and associates (1976) concluded that "when information about an event was available from vision and from auditory or propioception, and when the visual information is adequate for responding, attention is directed to vision and that the visual modality may block information occurring in other modalities from awareness" (p. 170).

Cortical Association Areas

Besides primary sensory zones, other regions of cerebral cortex are extensively developed in higher primates, with strong evidence that these tissues regulate higher cognitive functions. Although these association areas are still poorly understood, they are normally identified on the basis of cellular makeup, connective patterns, and function, with their importance signified by the fact that they make up the bulk of neocortex in higher primates and almost 95% of human neocortex (P. McGeer, Eccles, & E. McGeer, 1987). To be elaborated on, elementary sensory input must pass through a complex network of intramodal linkages (i.e., adjacent intrinsic connections). In turn, these intramodal sensory areas project to more distant cortex, where sensory information is processed sequentially through cortico–cortical connections to even more distant cortical and limbic regions (Amaral & Price, 1984; Horel, 1988; Pandya et al., 1988). In higher primates, cortical sites have been isolated that function as connecting regions where sensory information converges. In particular, the inferior parietal lobe appears to be a "supermodal" processing area for cortico–cortical connections. For example, a recent study of several regions within the inferior parietal lobe of macaque monkeys *(Macaca)* revealed "a densely interconnected network serving a large number of brain regions" (Andersen, Asanuma, Essick, & Siegel, 1990, p. 66; Horel, 1988). In hominoids, a region within the inferior parietal lobe (i.e., the angular gyrus) contains multimodal sensory neurons and sits at the junction of the modality-specific somatic, visual, and auditory zones. Although small in apes compared to humans, this site is a "connecting station" for sensory convergence and (in addition to other sites) is believed to aid in direct cortical cross-modal associations (Dunaif-Hattis, 1984; Geschwind, 1965; Noback & Maskowitz, 1963). Early research on cortical associations supported the conclusion that nonlimbic intercortical associations among sense modalities were present in humans and absent in other animals (see

Burton & Ettlinger, 1960). This early finding, although incorrect, was then used to view language as a kind of cross-modal bridge that allowed direct associations among cortical senses. However, it is now clear that monkeys and apes can make both intramodal (e.g., visual–visual) and intermodal (e.g., visual–haptic) associations that bypass the limbic system (although sensory experience must eventually connect with limbic structures to be tagged with an affective label (Cowey & Weiskrantz, 1975; Davenport & Rogers, 1970; Ettlinger, 1973; Horel, 1988; P. McGeer et al., 1987). Thus, earlier conclusions had the causal arrow going the wrong way: language is not a precondition for cross-modal associations but rather, the capacity for cross-modal association is a pre-condition for language (Freides, 1974; Geschwind, 1965). Recently W. Whitfield (1985, p. 337) posed the question: What is the cortex for? On the basis of a series of experiments on auditory neocortex in higher mammals he concluded as follows:

> The function of auditory cortex and probably all sensory cortex is to group together those sets of diverse stimuli that have a common origin. It cannot be too strongly emphasized that this is entirely different from classification, indeed diametrically opposed to it. Classification on the basis of the presence or absence of a particular feature or property assists discrimination. *Recognition* requires an understanding that diverse sets of stimuli, which may have no feature in common "belong to" the same external source (the "object") (W. Whitfield, 1985, p. 345).

From the perspective that sensory cortex functions to detect "similarities among stimuli," great apes and humans have an elaborated "recognition system." For example, apes and prelanguage infants can perform cross-modal matching and transfer even when only photographs of objects are used (see Davenport, Rogers, & Russell, 1973; Ettlinger, 1973; Weiskrantz, 1977). In a recent experiment with "linguistically" trained common chimpanzees *(Pan troglodytes)* symbolic cross-modal transfer from visual–symbolic to haptic (and its reverse) was accomplished. Further, in a bonobo experiment (with *Pan paniscus),* the subject was able to match auditory–symbolic to visual–symbolic by attending to a speech sound and then correctly selecting the lexigram representing the spoken message (Savage-Rumbaugh, Sevcik, & Hopkins, 1988). Therefore, if we accept W. Whitfield's thesis that the mammalian sensory cortices evolved for such complex feature responses as "similarity detection," and apply it to the evolution of primates and the sophisticated sensory organs of Old World monkeys, apes, and humans, it is not difficult to see why, with the possession of roughly the same primary sensory equipment, their nervous systems respond to the same relational properties of physical stimuli for object recognition. Moreover, it is also not difficult to perceive why apes and humans who share some of the same homologous multimodal regions for sensory convergence, can transfer similar information across modalities for object recognition, even though it must first be broken down and repackaged in an acceptable form before it becomes functionally equivalent.

From this complex sensory foundation it is also understandable why African apes, with whom we share a close phyletic relationship and 98% of our DNA, should also share with humans the functional capacity to engage in symbolic representation. One neurological indication of this capacity may be the brain asymmetry found in anthropoid brains, especially a large cleft called the Sylvian fissure on the external surfaces of the cerebral hemispheres where the mean length on the left side is greater than on the right side. Although this anatomic asymmetry is characteristic of anthropoids, it is less pronounced in monkeys; only in apes and humans is there a further asymmetry in the height of the Sylvian point, suggesting a progressive trend in cortical complexity (Heilbroner & Holloway, 1989; LeMay, 1985; LeMay & Geschwind, 1975). What makes this asymmetry so intriguing is that areas along and near the Sylvian borders are involved in human language operations, including Broca and Wernicke's areas. Broca's area is located in the posterior inferior part of the frontal lobe, near the motor cortex. Apparently, it controls the muscles for speech production and speech fluency; it may also play a role in non-speech related functions (Bachman & Martin, 1991). Wernicke's region is located in the posterior temporal lobe near the auditory centers of the left hemisphere near primary and secondary auditory cortex, where speech perception has been localized (Seldon, 1985). Human sign-language research also confirms that these left hemisphere regions are also important for visual–gestural language functions (Haglund, Ojermann, Lettich, Bellugi, & Corina, 1993; Poizner, Bellugi, & Klima, 1990). These zones are generally accepted as central or "core" language centers, which are by definition both in theory and practice species-specific to humans.

Yet, the idea that language emerged as a "fixed entity" only in humans and without biological forerunners is inconsistent with evolutionary theory as well as the data on primates. It is well documented that the brains of Old World monkeys, apes, and humans are structured and built according to a common plan (Passingham, 1985; E. White, 1989). Further, a comparison of primate brain parts, moving from the insectivores through to prosimians, monkeys, apes, and then to humans demonstrates that "the neo(cortex) is by far the most progressive structure" (Stephan et al., 1988, p. 15). Thus, in a series of trends that themselves involved stages of functional differentiation, selection seemingly favored, in the evolution of primates, the successive elaboration of neocortical structures (Pandya et al., 1988).

In terms of cytoarchitectures, the aforementioned language centers have also been identified in higher primates (Dingwall, 1988). Broca's area, for instance, is functionally unique to humans, but association cortex cytoarchitectually homologous to Broca's area can be identified in macaque monkeys, although it lacks a vocalization function (Heilbroner & Holloway, 1989; Jürgens, 1974). The homologue of Wernicke's area has also been identified in macaques along with other structures that include the arcuate fasciculus (which connects Wernicke and Broca's areas). Although most experimental research of this type is restricted to monkeys, chimpanzees have been identified with auditory cortex that is homologous to that of humans (Newman, 1988). Great apes are also endowed with a much larger mass of cortex than monkeys and are known to have augmented multimodal regions, along with large auditory cortical fields. What seems clear is that the great apes are equipped with a biologically significant volume of cortical tissue for comprehending and producing "linguistic" signals when they are channeled through the visual–tactile modalities. The perceptual ability of bonobos *(Pan panisus)* provides even more compelling evidence that chimpanzees possess an auditory cortex that can recognize and process a linguistic code, a capacity that is ostensibly at odds with its own species-specific vocalizations. The question thus becomes: why did humans learn to talk?

THE HOMINID ADAPTIVE ZONE

Although the cerebral organization of language is still unknown, "large regions of the brain are connected to the sensory speech areas within a very few processing stages" with cerebral activities suggesting that multiple brain regions are involved in language processing (Seldon,

4. WAS SPEECH AN EVOLUTIONARY AFTERTHOUGH? 93

1985, p. 297), and that language itself involved stages that were "built up" over time (see Bachman & Martin, 1991). However, the focus here is only on why the hominid auditory modality became modified for speech production. Humans, of course, have the greatest neocortical elaboration, and available hominid endocasts document that after the pongid–hominid divergence (believed to be about 4 to 6 million years ago), the hominid brain tripled in size during a very brief period. Yet, new structures have not been discovered in the human brain (Gabow, 1977). Selection instead clearly favored the restructuring of size relationships, and more complex functional interactions between brain parts. Why was this so?

While the primate arboreal zone had favored strong selection pressures for elaboration and expansion of the visual and haptic organs for rational, voluntary responses, the primate vocal–auditory channel remained largely under limbic control. Thus, the first proto-hominids seeking adaptation to a terrestrial niche must have carried neurological attributes that had evolved for a forest adaptive zone. They possessed a large hominoid neocortex with voluntary control over visual and tactile responses, but with their vocal–auditory channel largely under limbic control. They possessed a hierarchy of the cortical sense modalities with vision dominant for object recognition. Moreover, anatomically, they had a series of generalized skeletal features. This hominoid legacy would have placed heavy constraints on the nature of adaptation to a new environmental zone, because as Stebbins (1969) emphasized, highly complex animals have an equally complex and precisely programmed pattern of gene and gene products that must be integrated with any new adaptive responses. Thus, proto-hominids were greatly circumscribed by the neurological and anatomic legacy acquired through 55 million years of primate evolution.

In considering, then, the selection pressures on early hominids for propositional speech, several points should be stressed: First, the evolution of hominids was influenced less by dramatic mutations than by extensions, elaboration, and alterations of the pongid biological heritage. Radical mutations would be too disruptive to these batteries of genes, as well as to their programmed sequences and relationships. As Fisher argued: "The probability that individual mutations will contribute to evolution is in inverse correlation to the intensity of their effect on the developing phenotype" (quoted in Stebbins, 1969, p. 104). Second, the neurological structure of proto-hominids was highly refined and placed severe restrictions on adaptation to the savanna niche. Third, brain size in hominids did not undergo real change until the rise of *Homo erectus* because the brains of the early Australopithecines remained in the pongid range for over 3 million years. Thus, there was a "hominid adaptive zone" long before explosive growth in the neocortex of ancestral hominids.

The selection pressures operating on early hominids cannot be discussed here (see Maryanski, 1993; Maryanski & Turner, 1992), but it is reasonable to hypothesize that the brain expansion was initiated only after the vocal–auditory channel became liberated from limbic control in interaction with the visual and haptic modalities. As has been long argued, savanna conditions favored bipedalism, which is assumed to have been crucial in changing the pharyngeal region to allow for a vocal tract that could produce a variety of acoustic sounds (Hill, 1972). This insight, however, has not been examined in sufficient detail, nor has it been systematically linked to a series of neurological changes occurring to the neocortex of hominids. Furthermore, it is argued here that it is in the selection pressures of the savanna as they shifted the integration of the sense modalities within and between the cortical and limbic systems that the origins of speech are to be uncovered.

The pivotal constraint in this alteration was visual dominance because proto-hominids were visual creatures with most information input received from and interpreted though the optical system and its interconnections. Moreover, as proto-hominids became bipedal, reliance on the visual modality intensified, because prehensile hands require physical contact with objects, leaving a hindlimb dominant creature heavily reliant on visual cues. This is probably the reason why the highly sophisticated haptic modality has so receded in importance as an organ to extract environmental stimuli for object recognition. In contrast, the auditory system still functioned as an early warning detection system breaking in automatically to alert the visual modality to attend to environmental stimuli. There can be little doubt, though, that such warnings only placed increased reliance on the visual system for appropriate behavioral responses in a predator-ridden open-country habitat. With proto-hominids lacking defensive weapons, it is understandable why selection favored the use of sophisticated neurological equipment to avoid predators by integrating, abstracting, and symbolically manipulating information. Those proto-hominids that could best abstract, generalize, and *visually* remember aspects of their environment were more likely to survive and reproduce. Moreover, because vocalizations remained largely under subcortical control, hominid calls were still primarily emotionally based responses. Early proto-hominids also may have had the bonobo's capability to pick up temporal sequences of acoustic stimuli through their auditory cortices, but they would have needed to channel their rational and intended *responses* to environmental phenomena through the visual and haptic modalities. This means that intended communication about the environment between group members also had to be channeled through these senses, and there can be no doubt that these were used by early proto-hominids for social communication and for the extraction of environmental stimuli.

Why, then, did the auditory–vocal channel become linked to the process of symbolization? The answer alone cannot be that bipedalism freed up the vocal tract for the speech process, because this explanation overlooks the fact that vocalizations themselves were largely under limbic control. Instead, from an auditory perspective, the cardinal evolutionary step was in placing the vocal apparatus under voluntary control. In the trees, an emotionally based and species-specific call system is highly advantageous because it can alert group members to danger in the relative safety of the forest canopy. Such is not the case in an open-country zone, in which a loud and emotional primate is soon a dead primate.

We can assume that these neuroanatomical changes evolved before human speech became possible. The initial growth of the brain in *Homo erectus* over the smallbrained Australopithecines may, in part, have been a reflection of neocortical expansion, with changes involving the "core speech areas," that is, the functional use of Broca's area and the expansion of Wernicke's area.

What, then, were the selection pressures for this rewiring of hominid neocortex? Also, why was speech developed rather than visual signs because vision is primary, the brain is conservative, and neurological change was necessary to release the vocal–auditory channel from dominant limbic control and, then, to reorganize the neocortex to integrate the auditory with the visual and tactile modalities? It is possible that visual–gestural languages did exist, because the language studies on African apes reveal how easily a proto-hominid could have handled a visual–gestural system. This system, however, has several disadvantages: (a) The recipient may not receive the message if it is preoccupied or in a state of reduced alertness; (b) the hands of a bipedal creature certainly carried weapons, food, babies, and other objects that would get in the way of gestural signing; and (c) the low-alerting nature of the visual system would require the auditory to break often in order to alert the animal to pay attention to a gestural sign.

All of these were disadvantages to a visual system of communication but, in trying to understand the selection pressures for human speech, the long-held assumption that needs for social communication caused language to first evolve should be rejected. Just as selection for visual–gestural signs or the capacity for speech perception (clearly documented in bonobos) occurred independently of any "need" for language, so also, the inherent capacity for acoustic representations occurred independently of selection for language.

Instead, all evidence regarding the evolution of the primate sense modalities suggests that the initial selection that placed the auditory–vocal channel under volutional or cortical control was related to its usefulness in the extraction of environmental stimuli. For most mammals, there is little protective refuge in an open-country zone, but most mammals are able to rely on their keen long-distance olfactory sense with its automatic alerting and lingering chemical cues that allow for the detection of predators and prey. The primate stereoscopic visual system is also an excellent long-distance sense for determining the distance of predators in space, but vision cannot always detect the presence of objects because it is often in reduced alertness or preoccupied, inefficient in low light situations, and nonfunctional in the dark. Vision is deficient as an early warning organ, and coupled with few built-in defense weapons (e.g., projecting canines, claws) and a greatly reduced olfactory organ, selection would operate to heighten the auditory modality to enhance perception (as does the haptic sense) where the visual system was deficient. Indeed, this analysis supports Jerison's (1973) thesis that voluntary acoustic sounds first evolved in hominids as a sensory tool to enhance the image construction capacity of an already sophisticated visual system.

Changes to the auditory organ, however, had to accommodate the fact that vision is dominant in primates. The auditory organ could not replace the visual organ for object recognition by evolving sonar or echolocation, because as Stebbins (1969) pointed out, "once a unit of action has been assembled at a lower level of the hierarchy of organization at higher levels, mutations that might interfere with the activity of this unit are so strongly disadvantageous that they are rejected at the cellular level and never appear in the adult individual in which they occur" (p. 105). Thus, vision would greatly restrict the nature of vocal-auditory changes, despite selection pressures for a heightened auditory organ. Modification could only come within the auditory system so as not to disrupt the prime function of the visual organ. Thus, where there were deficiencies of the optic system, selection pressures modified the auditory organ and integrated it with the haptic and visual systems. Thus by the time there was selection advantage in hominoid evolution for the use of vocal sounds for shared symbolic communication, much of the neurological work had already been done.

REFERENCES

Allman, J. (1990). Evolution of neocortex. In E. Jones & A. Peters (Eds.), *Cerebral cortex* (pp. 269-283). New York: Plenum.

Amaral, D. G., & Price, A. J. (1984). Amygdalo-cortical prosections in the monkey *(Macaca fasciularis). Journal of Comparative Neurology, 230,* 465–494.

Andersen, R. A., Asanuma, C., Essick, G., & Siegel, R. M. (1990). Cortico-cortical connections of anatomically and physiologically defined subdivisions within the interior parietal lobule. *Journal of Comparative Neurology, 296,* 65–113.

Andrews, P. (1981). Species diversity and diet in monkeys and apes during the miocene. In C. B. Stringer (Ed.), *Aspects of human evolution* (pp. 25–61). London: Taylor & Francis.

Bachman, D., & Martin, A. (1991). The cerebral organization of language. In A. Peters & E. Jones (Eds.), *Cerebral cortex.* (Vol. 9, pp. 213–255). New York: Plenum.

Beard, C., Krishtalka, L., & Stucky, R. (1991). First skulls of the early eocene primate shoshonius cooperi and the anthropoid–tarsier dichotomy. *Nature, 349,* 64–67.

Brugge, J., & Reale, R. (1985). Auditory cortex. In A. Peters & E. Jones (Eds.), *Cerebral cortex* (Vol. 4, pp. 229–266). New York: Plenum.

Burton, D., & Ettlinger, G. (1960). Cross-modal training in monkeys. *Nature, 186,* 1071–1072.

Campbell, B. (1986). *Human evolution.* New York: Aldine.

Cheney, D. L., & Seyfarth, R. (1990). *How monkeys see the world.* Chicago: University of Chicago Press.

Conroy, G. (1990). *Primate evolution.* New York: Norton.

Corruccini, R., Ciochon, R., & McHenry, H. (1975). Osteometric shape relationships in the wrist joint of some anthropoids. *Folia Primatologica, 24,* 250–274.

Cowey, A., & Weiskrantz L. (1975). Demonstration of cross-modal matching in rhesus monkeys, *macaca mulatta. Neuropsychologica, 13,* 117–120.

Davenport, R., & Rogers, C. (1970). Intermodal equivalence of stimuli in apes. *Science, 168,* 279–280.

Davenport, R. K., Rogers, C. M., & Russell, I. S. (1973). Cross-modal perception in apes. *Neuropsychologica, 11,* 21–28.

De Valois, R., & Jacobs, G. (1971). Vision. In A. Schrier & F. Slottnitz (Eds.), *Behavior of non-human primates* (pp. 107-157). New York: Academic Press.

Dingwall, W. (1988). The evolution of human communicative behavior. In F. Newmeyer (Ed.), *Language: Psychological and biological aspects* (Vol. III, pp. 274-313). Cambridge, England: Cambridge University Press.

Dunaif-Hattis, J. (1984). *Doubling the brain: On the evolution of brain lateralization and its implications for language.* New York: Peter Long.

Ettlinger, G. (1973). The transfer of information between sense-modalities: A neuropsychological review. In H. P. Zippel (Ed.), *Memory and transfer of information* (pp. 43-64). New York: Plenum.

Freides, D. (1974). Human information processing and sense modality: Cross-modal functions, information complexity, memory, and deficit. *Psychological Bulletin, 81,* 5, 284–310.

Gabow, S. (1977). Population structure and the rate of hominid evolution. *Journal of Human Evolution, 6,* 643–665.

Geschwind, N. (1965). Disconnection syndromes in animals and man. *Brain, XLXXXVIII,* 237–285.

Gidley, J. W. (1919). Significance of the divergence of the first digit in the primitive mammalian foot. *Journal of the Washington Academy of Science, 9,* 273–280.

Gingerich, P. (1990). African dawn for primates. *Nature, 346,* 411.

Haglund, M., Ojemann, G., Lettich, E., Bellugi, U., & Corina, D. (1993). Dissociation of cortical and single unit activity in spoken and signed languages. *Brain and Language, 44,* 19–27.

Hampshire, B. (1975). Tactile and visual reading. *New Outlook for the Blind, 69,* 145–154.

Hayes, C. (1952). *The ape in our house.* New York: Harper & Brothers.

Heffner, H., & Heffner, R. (1990). Role of primate auditory cortex in hearing. In W. Stebbins & M. Berkeley (Eds.), *Comparative perception VII* (pp. 279–310). New York: Wiley.

Heilbroner, P., & Holloway, R. (1989). Anatomical brain asymmetry in monkeys: Frontal, temporoparietal and limbic cortex in macaca. *American Journal of Physical Anthropology, 80,* 203–211.

Hill, J. (1972). On the evolutionary foundations of language. *American Anthropologist, 74,* 308–315.

Holloway, R. L. (1968). The evolution of the primate brain: Some aspects of quantitative relations. *Brain Research, 7,* 121–172.

Horel, J. (1988). Limbic neocortical interrelations. In H. Steklis & J. Erwin (Eds.), *Neurosciences* (Vol. 4, pp. 81–97). New York: Alan R. Liss.

Hunt, K. (1991). Positional behavior in the hominoidea. *International Journal of Primatology, 12,* 95–118.

Isaacson, R. (1982). *The limbic system.* New York: Plenum.

Jerison, H. (1973). *Evolution of the brain and intelligence.* New York: Academic Press.

Jerison, H.(1990). Fossil evidence on the evolution of the neocortex. In E. Jones & A. Peters (Eds.), *Cerebral cortex* (pp. 285–307). New York: Plenum.

Jones, E. (1990). Modulatory events in the development and evolution of primate neocortex. In E. Jones & A. Peters (Eds.), *Cerebral cortex* (pp. 311–362). New York: Plenum.

Jürgens, U. (1974). On the elicitability of vocalization from the cortical larynx area. *Brain Research, 81,* 564–566.

Kaas, J., & Pons, T. P. (1988). The somatosensory system of primates. In H. Steklis & J. Erwin (Eds.), *Neurosciences* (Vol. 4, pp. 421–468). New York: Alan R. Liss.

Kaas, J. (1987). The organization and evolution of neocortex. In S. Wise (Ed.), *Higher brain functions* (pp. 347-378). New York: Wiley.

Kellogg, W. N., & Kellogg, L. A. (1933). *The ape and the child.* New York: McGraw-Hill.

Khanna, S., & Tonndorf, J. (1978). Physical and physiological principles controlling auditory sensitivity in primates. In C. Noback (Ed.), *Sensory systems of primates* (pp. 23–52). New York: Plenum.

LeMay, M. (1985). Asymmetries of the brains and skulls of non-human primates. In St. Glick (Ed.), *Cerebral lateralization in non-human primates* (pp. 234-244). New York: Academic Press.

LeMay, M., & Geschwind, N. (1975). Hemispheric differences in the brains of great apes. *Behavior and Evolution, II,* 48–52.

Lewis, O. J. (1974). The wrist articulations of the anthropoidea. In F. A. Jenkins (Ed.), *Primate locomotion* (pp. 143–168). New York: Academic Press.

Lovilot, A., Tagifzouti, K., Simon, H., & Le Moal, M. (1989). Limbic system, basal ganglia and dopaminergic neurons. *Brain Behavior and Evolution, 33,* 157–161.

MacLean, P. D. (1990). *The triune brain in evolution.* New York: Plenum.
Martin, R. D. (1990). *Primate origins and evolution: A phylogenetic reconstruction.* London: Chapman & Hall.
Maryanski, A. R. (1993). The elementary forms of the first proto human society: An ecological social network approach. *Advances in Human Ecology, 2,* 215–241.
Maryanski, A. R., & Turner, J. H. (1992). *The social cage: Human nature and the evolution of society.* Stanford, CA: Stanford University Press.
Masterton, B. (1992). Role of the central auditory system in hearing: The new direction. *Trends in Neurosciences, 15,* 280–285.
Masterton, B., & Diamond, I. (1973). Hearing: Central neural mechanisms. In E. Carterette & M. Friedman (Eds.), *Handbook of perception, No. 3* (pp. 408–448). New York: Academic Press.
McGeer, P., Eccles, J., & McGeer, E. (1987). *Molecular neurobiology of the mammalian brain.* New York: Plenum.
Mesulam, M. M. (1983). The functional anatomy and hemispheric specialization for direct attention. *Trends in Neurosciences, 6,* 384–387.
Napier, J. R., & Napier, P. H. (1985). *The natural history of the primates.* Cambridge, MA: MIT Press.
Napier, J. R., & Walker, A. C. (1987). Vertical clinging and leaping: A newly recognized category of locomotion behavior of primates. In R. Ciochon & J. Fleagle (Eds.), *Primate evolution and human origin* (pp. 64–75). New York: Aldine de Gruyter.
Newman, J. (1988). Primate hearing mechanisms. In H. Steklis & J. Erwin (Eds.), *Neurosciences* (Vol. 4, pp. 469–499). New York: Alan R. Liss.
Noback, C., & Maskowitz, N. (1963). The primate nervous system: Functional and structural aspects in phylogeny. In J. Buettner-Janosch (Ed.), *Evolutionary and genetic biology of primates 1* (pp. 131–177). New York: Academic Press.
Ogle, K. (1962a). Objective and subjective space. In H. Davison (Ed.), *The eye* (pp. 215-217). New York: Academic Press.
Ogle, K. (1962b). Spatial localization through binocular vision. In H. Davison (Ed.), *The eye* (pp. 271-324). New York: Academic Press.
Pandya, D., Seltzer, B., & Barbas, H. (1988). Input-output organization of the primate cerebral cortex. In H. Steklis & J. Erwin (Eds.), *Neurosciences: Comparative primate biology* (Vol. 4, pp. 39–80). New York: Alan R. Liss.
Pandya, D., & Yeterian, E. H. (1985). Architecture and connections of cortical association areas. In A. Peters & E. Jones (Eds.), *Cerebral cortex* (Vol. 4, pp. 3–55). New York: Plenum.
Passingham, R. E. (1985). Rates of development in mammals including man. *Brain Behavior and Evolution, 26,* 167–175.

Poizner, H., Bellugi, U., & Klima, E. (1990). Biological foundations of language. *Annual Review of Neuroscience, 13*, 283–307.
Posner, M., Nissen, M. J., & Klein, R. (1976). Visual dominance: An information processing account of its origins and significance. *Psychological Review, 83*, 157–171.
Radinsky, L. B. (1970). The fossil evidence of prosimian brain evolution. In C. R. Noback & W. Montagna (Eds.), *Primate brain* (pp. 209–224). New York: Appleton-Century-Croft.
Radinsky, L. B. (1975). Primate brain evolution, *American Scientist, 63*, 656–663.
Rock, I. (1966). *The nature of perceptual adaptation.* New York: Basic Books.
Rose, K. D., & Fleagle, J. G. (1987). The second radiation-prosimians. In R. Ciochon & J. Fleagle (Eds.), *Primate evolution and human origin* (pp. 58–63). New York: Aldine de Gruyter.
Sapir, E. (1933). Language, *encyclopaedia of the social sciences.* New York: Macmillan.
Savage-Rumbaugh, S., Murphy, J., Sevcik, R., Brakke, K., Williams, S. L., & Rumbaugh, D. (1993). Language comprehension in the ape and child. *Monographs of the Society for Research in Child Development, 58*, (3–4).
Savage-Rumbaugh, S., Sevcik, R., & Hopkins, W. (1988). Symbolic cross-model transfer in two species. *Child Development, 59,* 617–625.
Seldon, H. L. (1985). The anatomy of speech perception: Human auditory cortex. In A. Peters & E. Jones (Eds.), *Cerebral cortex* (Vol. 4, pp. 273–320). New York: Plenum.
Simonds, P. (1974). *The social primates.* New York: Harper & Row.
Simons, E. (1990). Discovery of the oldest known anthropoidean skull from the paleogene of Egypt. *Science, 247,* 1567–1569.
Snowdon, C. (1990). Language capacities of non-human animals. *Yearbook of Physical Anthropology, 33,* 215–243.
Stebbins, L. (1965). *The basis of progressive evolution.* Chapel Hill: The University of North Carolina Press.
Stebbins, L. (1971). Hearing. In A. Schrier & F. Stollnitz (Eds.), *Behaviors of non-human primates* (pp. 160-192). New York: Academic Press.
Steklis, H. D. (1985). Primate communication, comparative neurology, and the origin of language re-examined. *Journal of Human Evolution, 14,* 157–173.
Stephan, H., Baron, G., & Frahm, H. (1988). Comparative size of brains and brain components. In H. Steklis & J. Erwin (Eds.), *Neurosciences* (Vol. 4, pp. 1–38). New York: Alan R. Liss.

Sutton, D., & Jürgens, U. (1988). Neural control of vocalization. In H. Steklis & J. Erwin (Eds.), *Neurosciences* (Vol. 4, pp. 625-648). New York: Alan Liss.

Swartz, S. (1989). Pendular mechanics and kinematics and energetics of brachiating locomotion. *International Journal of Primatology, 10,* 387–418.

Tattersall, I., Delson, E., & van Couvering, J. (1988). *Encyclopedia of human evolution and prehistory.* New York: Garland.

Taylor, M. M., Lederman, S. J., & Gibson, R. H. (1973). Tactual perception of texture. In E. Carterette & M. P. Friedman (Eds.), *Handbook of perception* (Vol. V, pp. 251-272). New York: Academic Press.

Temerin, A., & Cant, J. (1983). The evolutionary divergence of old world monkeys and apes. *The American Naturalist, 122,* 335–351.

Tuttle, R. (1988). What's new in African paleoanthropology? *Annual Review of Anthropology, 17,* 391–426.

von Bonin, G. (1952). Notes on cortical evolution. *AMA. Archives of Neurology and Psychiatry, 67,* 135–144.

Walker, A. C. (1974). Locomotor adaptations in past and present prosimian primates. In F. Jenkins, Jr. (Ed.), *Primate locomotion* (pp. 349–383). New York: Academic Press.

Warren, D., & Pick, H., Jr. (1970). Intermodality relations in localization in blind and sighted people. *Perception and Psychophysics, 8,* 430–432.

Weiskrantz, L. (1974). The interaction between occipital and temporal cortex in vision: An overview. In F. O. Schmitt & F. G. Worden (Eds.), *The neurosciences: Third study program* (pp. 189-204). Cambridge, MA: MIT Press.

White, E. (1989). *Cortical circuits: Synaptic organization of the cerebral cortex structure, function, and theory.* Boston: Birkhauser.

Whitfield, I. C. (1982). Coding in the auditory cortex. In W. D. Neff (Ed.), *Contributions to sensory physiology* (Vol. 6, pp. 159–178). New York: Academic Press.

Whitfield, W. (1985). The role of auditory cortex in behavior. In A. Peters & E. Jones (Eds.), *Cerebral cortex* (Vol. 4, pp. 329–348). New York: Plenum.

CHAPTER

5

PREFRONTAL CORTEX AND SYMBOL LEARNING: WHY A BRAIN CAPABLE OF LANGUAGE EVOLVED ONLY ONCE

Terrence W. Deacon
Boston University, Boston
Mailman Research Center, Belmont

Among the vast multitude of animal species, languagelike communication is the anomaly, not the rule. It is not just unusual or rare; it is essentially nonexistent except in one peculiar species: *Homo sapiens*, and I am not confining my definition of language to verbal communication or communication systems with exactly the grammatical structure that can be found in all human languages. I mean language in a generic sense: a mode of communication based upon symbolic reference and involving combinatorial rules that comprise a system for representing synthetic logical relationships among symbols. Under this definition, sign languages, mathematics, musical scores, and many rule-governed games might qualify as languagelike, but not bird songs, vervet monkey alarm calls, honeybee dances, or humpback whale songs (some animal communicative behaviors often cited as languagelike), because these nonhuman activities lack both symbolic and combinatorial function, although they resemble language in certain superficial features. No more than a minute vocabulary of meaningful units and two or three combinatorial rules are necessary to fulfill these criteria. A childlike five- or 10-word vocabulary and a grammar as simple as toddlers' two-word combinations would suffice. And yet, even under these loosened criteria, no other species on earth has evolved any form of communication that even remotely qualifies. This is an important, and little appreciated paradox, because it indicates that the complexity of language (e.g., the numbers of words and interdependent rules of grammar) is not the issue. Why are there no simple languages in the rest of the animal kingdom?

It is also not just a case of language not evolving in other species because there was no need. There is a fundamental difference in the potential for language. Thousands of years of living with domesticated animals and immersing them in human environments has not produced any well documented cases of pets who understand what is said, except in a very superficial ("rote learning") sense. In addition, three decades of intensive efforts to teach language to apes (and more recently to sea lions, dolphins, and a parrot) has shown that it takes almost heroic efforts and a careful choice of subjects and tasks to produce a modicum of symbolic understanding. Even these abilities are far more limited and ambiguous than first thought. At present, there is still considerable legitimate debate over the significance of the bits of languagelike behavior taught to nonhuman animals, and although I take a charitable view of many of these claims and do not doubt that given sufficient external support, a number of species might be able to develop some level of symbolic capacity, it is clear that spontaneous abilities to learn symbolic communication beyond rote-level associations (and thus not symbolic) are extremely limited outside our species.

Why did language evolve only once? Why is even a vastly simplified language so difficult for nonhuman species to acquire, whereas even an immensely complicated language appears easy for humans to acquire? I think we tend to gloss over the counterintuitive nature of these questions. Other species are capable of remarkably complex learning and cognitive analysis. Why can they not learn a very simplified language system? This apparent paradox strikes at the heart of what is generally the commonsense notion of the human–nonhuman difference: the assumption that it is the complexity of language that matters. This tacit belief is implicit in the two most common answers to these questions: (a) Humans have larger brains and are therefore smarter than other species; this makes them capable of using this much more complex form of communication. (b) Humans possess innate grammatical knowledge embodied in some unique human brain structure, and this makes learning the otherwise unlearnably complex rules of grammar and syntax largely unnecessary.

I have argued elsewhere that neither of these explanations offers anything more than a restatement of the question (Deacon, 1991). On the one hand, to argue that language requires more intelligence merely restates the fact that other species are not capable of learning language because of some unspecified cognitive limitation. It ignores both the peculiarity of many features of language and the multiple dimensions of cognitive processes that might be differentially involved in language abilities as compared to other cognitive processes. On the other hand, to argue that language can only be explained by postulating some uniquely human brain structure with a set of rules capable of specifying any language merely passes the buck to some hypothetical black box wherein the answer to all questions about language structure and human language abilities can be found. There is, though, a more serious criticism of these answers.

The force of both arguments is undermined when we stop trying to explain complicated modern languages and instead ask why simple languages do not occur in other species. If only a dozen or more words and a handful of grammatical rules were involved, a vast learning ability would be unnecessary, and if the rules for the grammar were not so many and so intricately interdependent, they would no longer seem unlearnable, and an innate universal grammar would be irrelevant. Both arguments answer a question that may have little to do with language origins. Language processing must place some unusually intense demands on neural computations that are not well supported in nonhuman brains. Otherwise, there would be many other species with languages. However, which neural computations are these, if they do not involve complex grammar or vocabulary?

A SIMPLE WORKING HYPOTHESIS: HUMAN BRAINS ARE ADAPTED TO LANGUAGE

Language is not just some superficial part of human thinking. We are not just apes who have dabbled with some special communication trick. Language is totally integrated into every aspect of human mental functioning. We are linguistic savants, lightning calculators of semantic and syntactic arithmetic, although people differ in linguistic abilities, it is a remarkable fact that only the most severely brain-damaged children fail to spontaneously develop some level of language competence. This rare and anomalous cognitive ability is thus one of the most robust and irrepressible characteristics of our species. This is hardly the mark of an evolutionary afterthought, of a function that arose secondary to general intelligence or tool use. Moreover, it shows none of the awkwardness, inflexibility, inefficiency, stereotypicality, or mismatch with other social and cognitive functions that might be expected of an ability that arose from natural selection by accident and without honing. The most obvious interpretation of these facts is that the human brain evolved with respect to language, not independent of it, and did not develop language abilities as secondary spin-offs of some other adaptation.

I suggest that the anatomical changes that make language so nearly effortless for modern humans arose as adaptations to 2 million years of cognitive demands imposed by languagelike communication. This does not require that modern language per se predated the changes in brain structure that facilitate it, only that some languagelike system of communicating was present throughout the major period of hominid brain evolution. The brains of transitional *australopithecines* and early hominines would have been no better suited to meet these demands than are the best nonhuman brains today. If forced, however, generation after generation, to accomplish a nearly impossible cognitive task, natural selection would have inevitably played a role to ease the burden and decrease the probability of failing.

Early forms of languagelike communication would have recruited brain structures that evolved previously for other functions. Their overlap with these novel cognitive tasks would have been incidental, but all other brain structures would have been even less well suited. Ultimately, though, those brain structures most impacted by these new computational burdens would be subject to the most intense effects of natural selection. This is an important hint. The effects of this adaptational process ought to have produced some of the most marked deviations of human brain structure from what is found in a typical primate brain. Reversing this logic, we would predict that those brain structures that are most deviant in human brains offer the best indices of the peculiarities of language processing demands.

ONTOGENETIC CONSTRAINTS ON HUMAN BRAIN EVOLUTION

The most salient comparative feature of the human brain is its comparatively large size. The majority of claims about what is different about the human brain focus on this one trait. Although the change in human brain size must feature prominently in any theory of human brain evolution, it is not necessarily the case that brain size, itself, is the trait that needs to be explained. Large human brain size almost certainly is not a simple trait with simple consequences (e.g., increased intelligence), although many theories tacitly assume that it is. Bigger brains are not just bigger, they are inevitably different.

Although assessing the anatomical differences between human and nonhuman brains might seem to be a simple matter, it is far from a trivial project. The large size of the human brain makes comparisons with other species' brains problematic. Larger brains have different proportions among their parts than do smaller brains, so determining which of the myriad of differences between brains are significant requires more than directly comparing structures, measurements, or lists of connections. The key to this problem is that the relative sizes of different brain structures are highly correlated. This pattern of correlated size changes is not surprising, given the systemic interconnectedness of different brain regions and the variety of ways that developing brains dynamically match cell populations and connection patterns in interdependent structures. Although comparative anatomists have labored for a century to produce data on surfaces, volumes and neuronal population counts for the various brain structures in humans and other primates, only recently have we begun to understand the details of the embryonic mechanisms that determine these structural differences.

Remarkably, one can predict the size of most large forebrain structures in primate brains on the basis of brain size alone. However, in the case of the human brain, this predictability breaks down in complex and interesting ways. Within each major "organ" of the brain, such as the cerebral cortex or thalamus, there are numerous structural and functional subdivisions. Many of these cortical areas, nuclei, and subdivisions diverge from primate predictions to varying degrees. This has given anatomists the impression that individual brain structures can grow and evolve in a piecemeal mosaic fashion. Many researchers have consequently theorized about independent adaptational functions for each of these apparent differences, but are these changes independent, or are many or all of these deviations superficial expressions of some more global underlying cause? We can begin to distinguish between these possibilities by analyzing the developmental mechanisms that are most likely to affect them.

Although quantitative data comparing the growth of embryonic structures in human and nonhuman primate brains are unavailable, one can gain a fair picture of the human deviations by comparing adult brain structures in groups that correspond to the major embryological growth fields. During development, the sizes of brain structures are determined hierarchically as the brain differentiates from major structural components into progressively smaller subdivisions. Extrapolating back from structural components that correspond to some of the earliest structural divisions to be formed, some large-scale patterns can be discerned. There appear to be two broad moieties of embryonic brain regions in humans that are out of proportion with respect to each other. The cerebral and cerebellar cortices as well as the tectum are apparently larger than would be expected compared with most remaining brain structures including the diencephalon, basal ganglia, brain stem, and spinal cord, along with many other structures. However, within either of these two groupings of structures, the components seem well proportioned with respect to each other (Deacon, 1984, 1988, 1990). In general, the enlarged structures are all cortical-like surface structures located roughly on the anterior dorsal surface of the brain, and the comparatively smaller structures are all nuclear structures located ventrally and in the interior of the brain. The different structures that scale according to the same pattern are not associated by common connectivity or by common function, and represent all levels of the brain and nearly the entire range of sensorimotor modalities. They are, however, associated by position and by similarities of their laminated cell architectures.

What then are the causes of this unprecedented break in the typical primate growth allometry of these early appearing brain regions? The mechanisms determining numbers of cell divisions, and thus target cell numbers, are as yet unknown. There are, however, some clues of a correlational nature. The comparatively enlarged and nonenlarged structures within the human brain divide roughly along suggestive embryonic lines. The embryonic neural tube is initially divided into dorsal and ventral halves by a tiny sulcus along each side of its interior wall, the sulcus limitans. This marks a developmental boundary that is respected by generative events all along the neuraxis. The three major divisions of the brain that are comparatively enlarged in humans are located on the dorsal anterior surface of the neural tube above this dorsal-ventral dividing line. The nonenlarged structures derive from the ventral half.

Recently, breakthroughs in developmental genetics have provided further clues to the significance of this pattern. Using in situ hybridization to discover when and where in the embryonic body selected genes are activated, it has become possible to map the sequence of genetic events that initially establish many of the major divisions of brain structures. Those that appear to play the crucial roles in initially partitioning the relatively undifferentiated neural tube into major brain regions produce proteins that bind to DNA and probably serve to regulate expression for suites of other genes. These "homeotic" genes, named for the whole-body segment modifications that often result from mutations affecting them, are highly conserved in all animals and are the initial determinants of cell lineage groups and cell fates. The expression domains of these homeotic genes appear to be essential for specifying the extent of progenitor cell regions that will become distinct brain structures. Although knowledge is still very incomplete concerning their functions in the developing brain and the patterning of their expression, the regions of enlarged and unenlarged cell populations in human brains appear to respect some of these boundaries, suggesting that the proportional differences might be traceable to changes in the expression of certain homeotic genes. It is particularly relevant that the division between the dorsal enlarged and ventral unenlarged structures of the telencephalon follows the gene expression boundary respected by many genes. More work is needed with human and primate embryos in order to test this apparent gene–allometry correlation, and to determine at what stage mitotic differences between these regions begin to be evident. Nevertheless, a shift in cell proliferation patterns at an early stage in neuraxis development could be sufficient to produce a subsequent systematic restructuring of circuitry in human brains as they mature.

In order to trace the consequences of such an early quantitative change in brain development, it must be recognized that most of the information ultimately employed to build a functioning brain does not derive from genetic sources. It is rather the result of cell–cell interactions that incorporate spatial and, eventually, experiential information into the differentiation process (Deacon, 1990; Purves, 1988; Purves & Lichtman, 1985). This slight alteration in proportions of cells in human embryogenesis likely produces a cascade of other developmental consequences (see Fig. 5.1). These ensue because the patterns of axonal connections between structures are determined by competitive processes among developing axons. Because of this, we should expect that differences in numbers of projections from various areas competing for the same targets will be biased in favor of projections from larger structures.

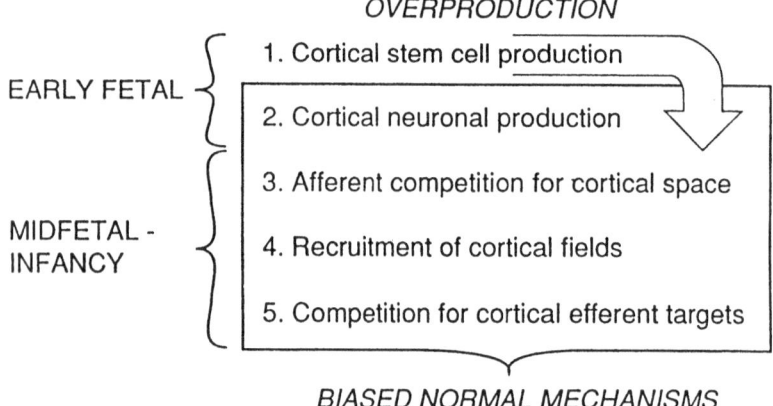

Fig. 5.1. List of the proposed sequence of embryological events that determine the unique proportions and connectional relationships of human brain structures.

The effects of cell-proliferation allometry appear to be particularly important for the development of connections of the cerebral cortex. For example, projections from peripheral organs like the eye and the tactile sensory system normally recruit target populations of neurons within the thalamus and cortex that are appropriate for the number of afferent inputs they supply. This has been demonstrated by many experiments that manipulate numbers and patterns of peripheral inputs during early life. This sort of developmental displacement of some projections by others has been demonstrated by a number of experiments in which these relationships are directly manipulated (an example is shown in Fig. 5.2). Extrapolating this effect to the human brain–body relationship suggests an interesting possibility. Because the human body is only a fraction as large as one that would normally carry a brain the size of the human brain, recruitment of central neuronal populations

5. PREFRONTAL CORTEX AND SYMBOL LEARNING　　　　111

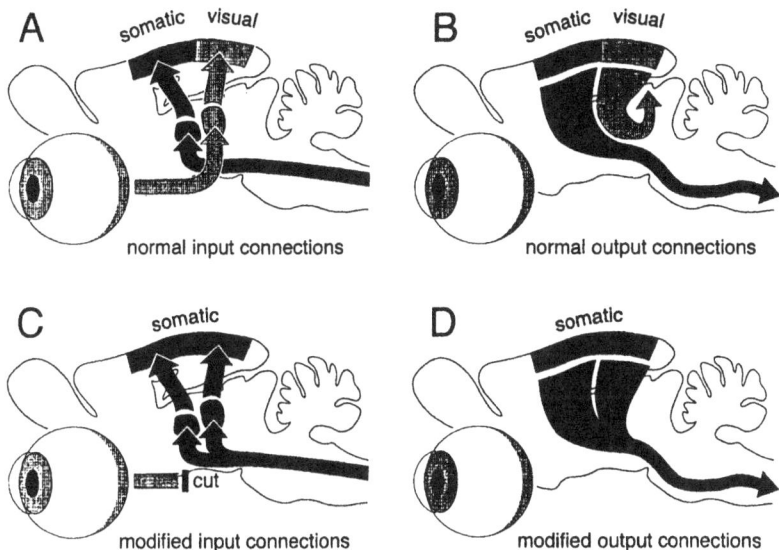

Fig. 5.2. Graphic depiction of an experiment described by O'Leary (1992) in which visual and somatic cortex and their projection systems are modified by prenatal elimination of visual inputs. A. Normal visual and somatic sensory input pathways to the thalamus and from the thalamus to the cortex. The visual pathways are shown in lighter gray, and the somatic pathways are shown in darker gray. B. Normal cortical output pathways into the spinal cord (somatic) and tectum (visual). Although in early stages of development both visual and somatic cortical outputs project to both tectal and spinal targets in an undifferentiated pattern, during later development the tectal connections of somatic cortex and the spinal connections of visual cortex are competitively eliminated. C. Cutting the projections from the retina eliminates the visual inputs that would ordinarily have recruited space in the lateral geniculate nucleus of the thalamus, and instead allows other afferent projections (e.g., ascending somatic projections) to recruit this abandoned target, thereby expanding the cortical representation of somatic responses. D. The alteration of thalamic inputs and cortical fields in C. produces a different pattern of cortical outputs as well, due to the loss of fetal tectal connections and retention of spinal connections for both cortical regions. Thus, one sensory system replaces the other.

should be significantly reduced with respect to the size of the brain. This is exemplified by the allometric relationships exhibited in the human visual pathways. Both the lateral geniculate nucleus, which receives primary inputs from the retina, and area 17 of the cerebral cortex, which receives lateral geniculate projections, are significantly smaller than would be predicted in a typical primate brain that reached human proportions. This follows inevitably from the fact that a brain of this size would actually be expected only in an ape of immense proportions, and this ape would have had much larger eyes and retinas than we have. However, with input and output systems recruiting less synaptic "space" than expected, some other systems must stand to benefit in their recruitment. In contrast, those thalamic nuclei and cortical areas that receive predominantly central originating projections, especially from enlarged structures, are not similarly constrained and appear to inherit the cortical space that is not taken up by the comparatively reduced sensory and motor maps. One region of the brain appears to have benefitted most from this bias in favor of central versus peripheral projections: the prefrontal cortex. According to extrapolations derived from two different data sources (Deacon, 1984; 1988), prefrontal cortex is at least twice the size that would be predicted in an ape brain of this size (see Fig. 5.3).

The brain is not simply a collection of independently functioning anatomical modules, but a network. Many prior theories describing how brains evolved can be characterized as mosaic theories, suggesting that new brain structures were progressively added to old ones during evolution. This view, however, has become untenable in the face of recent embryological data indicating that cortical areas do not develop from an intrinsic protomap, but rather reflect a dynamic differentiation process, partly determined by geometric patterns of input and output connections and partly by the competitive elimination of nonspecific

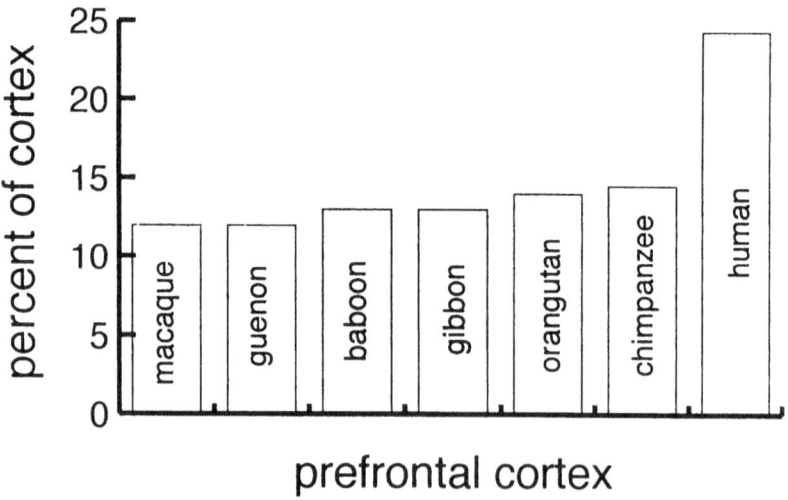

Fig. 5.3. One of many quantitative analyses (see Deacon, 1984, 1988 for others) that shows prefrontal enlargement in humans with respect to various monkeys and apes. Data are graphed by percentage of cortical surface area (as reported in Blinkov & Glezer, 1968).

connections. Cell production within the cerebral cortex precedes differentiation of its functional subdivisions, such as the prefrontal cortex. As a result, determination of which cells are destined to become prefrontal cells is a matter of dividing up a fixed total surface. Thus, the enlargement of the prefrontal cortex indirectly results from the convergence of a number of systemic developmental processes, not the addition of extra neurons to this part of the brain (Deacon, 1990b).

Owing to the magnitude of this difference, expansion of the prefrontal lobes during human evolution has been noticed by brain evolution researchers since the late 19th century. (Although there have been studies purporting to show that prefrontal lobes are not comparatively enlarged, each has suffered either from errors in correcting for allometric trends or from problems of confounding different cortical regions in different species.) The differences between previous views about prefrontal enlargement and the approach taken here derive from the two misunderstandings about brain evolution that have motivated this embryonic approach: the tendency to view it as a mosaic enlargement of an isolated "organ" of the brain and a predisposition to interpret it in terms of increased cognitive power of the prefrontal lobes. Not only must we view the enlargement in systemic terms, but we must understand the functional consequence in these terms as well. We must address these two formidable problems before we can hope to understand the significance of an enlarged prefrontal cortex. First, we need to consider the plausible mechanisms by which brain structure size differences could influence brain function. Second, we must sort through the considerable disagreement about the nature of prefrontal functions.

Irrespective of the developmental mechanisms that produced it, prefrontal enlargement and its correlated connectional effects clearly stand out as the most extensive differences distinguishing human brains from other primate brains. This major restructuring is our best clue concerning what is unique about human brains and their overall function, as well as the best source of information about the kind of cognitive demands that drove human brain evolution in the first place. We are reluctantly forced to try to make some sense of these two most enigmatic problems in one.

OVERVIEW OF PREFRONTAL ANATOMY AND CONNECTIVITY

Just as prefrontal expansion can be understood only as a function of dynamic systemic interactions between many brain structures during development, so its structural and functional consequences also require an understanding of systemic consequences of changes in size. Its comparative enlargement with respect to the majority of other brain structures in cortex and elsewhere is a consequence of the developmental competitive advantage that its afferents have over other types of cortical projections, which include a very wide range of other cortical areas, including all sensory and motor modalities, and numerous subcortical regions. Of particular interest are the widespread cortical connections with nearly every modality of cortex. In an anatomical sense it stands between sensorimotor cortical areas and limbic cortex. Given its very large size compared to the sizes of its targets, it can be expected to occupy a far greater proportion of available synapses in these structures during development than do other structures that send competing afferents to these targets. Consequently, compared with more typical primate and mammal brains, prefrontal information processing will likely play a more dominating role in nearly every facet of sensory, motor, and arousal processes in humans. Irrespective of whether this structure has more capacity in some information-processing sense because of its size, it simply has more "votes" in whatever is going on in those regions of the brain to which it projects. In general terms, human information processing should be biased by an excessive reliance on and guidance by the kinds of manipulations that prefrontal circuits impose on the information they process. We humans should therefore exhibit a "cognitive style" that sets us apart from other species, a pattern of organizing perceptions, actions, and learning that is peculiarly "front-heavy" so to speak, but how can this be described in neuropsychological terms?

Although during development the prefrontal region is probably carved out as a single projection field, in the mature brain the prefrontal cortex is not a single homogeneous structure with a single function. As a result there is a danger of overgeneralizing from studies based on one prefrontal area to the whole prefrontal region. Different prefrontal regions receive diversely different cortical inputs and outputs that provide hints concerning their functional differences. Many regions receive inputs from specific sensory or motor modalities, and others receive converging inputs from more than one modality. No prefrontal area, however, receives direct input from primary sensory or motor cortices. One reason the prefrontal region remains to some extent mysterious is that its "map" structure is difficult to discern. Unlike the cortical topography of most sensory areas, positions within prefrontal regions do not seem to correlate with the peripheral topography of any sensory receptor surface, nor is there a clear map of motor topography. One hint concerning the sort of "mapping" of functions within the prefrontal regions, however, comes from studies of visual attention and the subcortical structures that underlie it. Goldman-Rakic (1987) and her colleagues demonstrated that one portion of the prefrontal cortex in monkeys (the dorsal lateral prefrontal region or principalis region, named for its location surrounding the principal sulcus) is organized according to the direction of attention-driven eye movements with respect to the center of gaze. Damage to some sector of this region can selectively block the ability to learn to produce or inhibit directed eye movements in a particular direction or in response to cues in a particular direction. Not surprisingly this subregion of the prefrontal cortex is located adjacent to a region known as the frontal (motor) eye field, which directs eye movement. The eye-movement–attentional features of this region of the prefrontal cortex are consistent with its input–output association with the deep layers of the superior colliculus (a midbrain structure associated with visual orienting). This same sector of prefrontal cortex also shares extensive corticocortical connections with temporal and parietal visual areas (Barbas & Mesulam, 1981). Dorsally and ventrally adjacent to this zone are regions that are reciprocally connected to auditory and multimodal auditory–somatic cortical areas of the temporal lobe (Barbas & Mesulam, 1981; Deacon, 1992; Pandya & Barnes, 1987). These regions likely also send projections to other collicular regions where there is auditory representation (in the deep layers of the superior colliculus and the inferior colliculus). These areas may be expected to "map" auditory orienting processes in ways analogous to the way in which the principalis cortex "maps" visual orienting. It is less easy to find map correlations for orbital and medial regions of the prefrontal cortex. These have predominantly limbic and adjacent prefrontal cortical connections and output pathways that include structures more associated with visceral and arousal functions than with sensorimotor functions.

The function of the lateral divisions of prefrontal cortex must be understood partly in terms of attentional mechanisms, both with respect to collicular systems and to cortical systems to which they project outputs, whereas the function of orbital and medial divisions of prefrontal cortex must, in contrast, be more involved with arousal, visceral, and autonomic functions. These two systems are not only structurally interconnected, but are probably functionally interdependent as well. Arousal, orienting, and attending are all part of the same process of shifting motivation to regulate adaptive responses to changing conditions. The lateral divisions may provide a substrate for intentionally overriding collicular orienting reflexes, using orienting information as cues for working memory about alternative stimuli or to select among many sensory configurations for further sensory analysis. The orbital and medial divisions may provide correlated shifts in arousal and autonomic readiness both to support shifts in attention and to inhibit the tendency for new stimuli to command attentional arousal.

FAMILY RESEMBLANCES BETWEEN PREFRONTAL FUNCTIONS

Is there then a common theme? Is there something that all of these prefrontal cortical regions do similarly? This is no simple question. In fact, it remains one of the more debated questions in neuropsychology (for in-depth reviews see Fuster, 1980; Perecman, 1987; Stuss & Benson, 1986). It is a difficult question because the explanation cannot be tied directly to any sensory or motor function. When prefrontal areas are damaged, there are no specific sensory or motor problems. Surgeons who performed prefrontal lobotomies earlier in this century used to note that it did not reduce the IQs of their patients. Consequences of prefrontal damage show up only in certain rather specific sorts of learning contexts. Nevertheless, these can be extensive and ultimately debilitating. Moreover, there is not just one type of prefrontal deficit, but variants that approximately correspond to distinct prefrontal subdivisions. Because the various prefrontal areas are connected to different cortical and subcortical structures, they produce slightly different types of impairments when they are damaged. Not only are there numerous competing theories attempting to explain individual types of prefrontal impairments, but there also is no account of the family resemblances

5. PREFRONTAL CORTEX AND SYMBOL LEARNING

that link the many different deficits associated with different prefrontal subareas.

I start by taking a global overview of prefrontal functions, not by treating the prefrontal cortex as homogeneous, but rather by searching among prefrontal areas, connections, and deficits for common themes and family resemblances. I am encouraged that there are some common threads because of the global similarities in connectional architecture that link these areas with the rest of the brain. I suspect that, like the numerous subareas of the visual cortical system, the different prefrontal regions share a common computational problem, but have broken it up into dissociable subtasks in large brains, perhaps separated according to modality differences.

Let me begin by sampling a variety of interesting tasks affected by damage to the prefrontal cortex in monkeys. Fig. 5.4 provides a schematic depiction of a number of learning tasks that have specific association with distinct prefrontal subdivisions. Beginning with the classical prefrontal task identified by Jacobsen (1936) many decades ago, Fig. 5.4a depicts the delayed response or delayed alternation task. In this task a food object is placed in a covered container as the monkey watches. Then the monkey is distracted for a few seconds, often by pulling down a blind, and finally is allowed to retrieve the food object by uncovering it. This is no problem, on a succeeding trial, the hidden food object is placed in the alternative container, again in full view. Now, however, after the delay period, rather than looking in the new hiding place, the prefrontal-damaged monkey again tends to look in the place where he found food before, not where he saw it being hidden. (This is similar to the hidden object problems demonstrated in young children by Piaget [1952].) Some have explained this as a problem with short-term memory. The monkey might be unable to use information from a past trial to influence its choice in a future trial. A simple memory problem, however, would tend to produce random performance. In general, the animal's perseveration indicates that it does remember the previous successful trial, all too well, it would seem. Apparently it either cannot inhibit the tendency to return to where it won the reward the last time or it cannot subordinate this previously stored information to the new problem. Historically, interpreters of prefrontal deficits have split evenly over whether they interpret it in terms of memory or in terms of response inhibition. However, before taking sides we should consider a few additional examples.

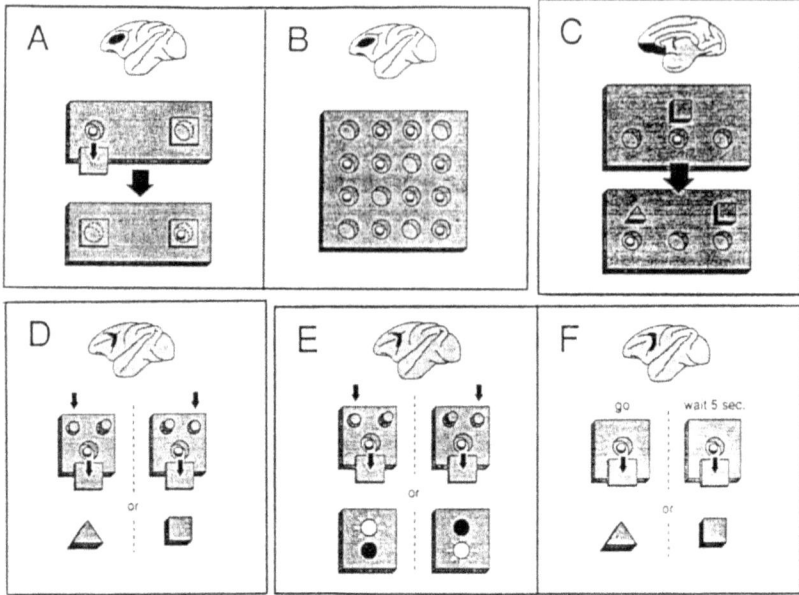

Fig. 5.4. Diagrammatic depiction of six different cognitive deficits shown in monkeys with frontal lobe damage to different subregions. A. Delayed response (delayed alternation) task associated with dorsal lateral prefrontal damage (Jacobson, 1936). B. Self-ordered sampling task associated with dorsal lateral prefrontal damage (simplified from Passingham, 1985) C. Delayed nonmatch to sample task associated with ventral medial prefrontal damage (Mishkin & Manning, 1978). D. and E. Conditional association tasks (spatial versus nonspatial cues, respectively) associated with periarcuate prefrontal damage (Petrides, 1982, 1985). F. Go–no-go task associated with periarcuate premotor damage (Petrides, 1986).

Another more sophisticated version of the same task has been investigated by Passingham (1985; see Fig. 5.4b). It offers some insight into how this task might have real-world adaptive consequences. As in the simple delayed response experiment, food is placed in food wells while the monkey watches (although the observation is not a necessary factor), but in contrast to the simpler task, the food this time is hidden in all or many of a large number of wells. No delay is necessary. The monkey must simply sample its way through the wells to retrieve all the food objects. Monkeys with efficient sampling strategies will not tend to sample the same wells twice. Once food has been located in one place and taken, there is no reason to go back and check it out. Prefrontal-damaged monkeys, however, fail to efficiently sample. They perseverate by returning more often to previously sampled wells and failing to sample others. Again, it is not clear whether one should consider this forgetfulness or failure to inhibit repetition of past responses. The

5. PREFRONTAL CORTEX AND SYMBOL LEARNING 119

practical significance of such an ability is clear, however. This is precisely the sort of problem that might be faced by an animal foraging in many different places. Once all of the food has been eaten in one place, it makes no sense to go back looking for more later, even if the food tasted particularly good there.

Turning now to medial frontal damage, we find a slightly different kind of deficit. Monkeys with medial prefrontal damage succeed at the hidden object-type tasks, but they fail at tasks in which the shift in food location is cued by a shift in stimulus as well. Fig. 5.4c depicts this sort of task. The food object is hidden, and unlike the situation presented by the hidden object task, the location is cued by some stimulus. After the monkey succeeds at this task, the food object is rehidden, and the hiding place is marked by a new stimulus, with the previous stimulus now marking no food. Thus the monkey must learn that the food will always be hidden where the new stimulus of the two is placed. Medial prefrontal damage appears to preferentially affect this kind of learning but not delayed response, delayed alternation, nor sampling tasks that are sensitive to dorsal lateral prefrontal damage.

Compare this to tasks sensitive to lesions of posterior lateral prefrontal regions. These tasks have a multipart form. Figures 5.4d and 5.4e provide examples of these tasks. Common to these tasks is a dependency between two classes of cues or between alternative cues and behavior options. In Fig. 5.4d one cue stimulus indicates that the food is hidden in the lighted well, whereas the alternative cue indicates that the food is hidden in the unlighted one. The pattern is "if X then Z, if Y then not Z." It is a conditional relationship in which one stimulus indicates the relationship between another stimulus and the position of the food. In Fig. 5.4e there is a similar dependency relationship, but this time between a stimulus pattern and a choice of buttons that open the food well. In contrast to the previous task, there is no spatial difference in food position, but as in the last task, there is a conditional relationship in which the stimulus indicates which of two alternatives is associated with the food. Depending on the stimulus presented, the monkey has to reverse its expectation about the association between the reward and some behavioral option.

These tasks are all different, and yet they share a number of common features. Even though they all involve some apparent inability to inhibit responding, this may be secondary. Prefrontal-damaged animals do not show a problem with simple go–no-go tasks that require withholding a response, as in Fig. 5.4f. In this sort of task the presentation of one of two different stimuli indicate whether an immediate response or the same response delayed for just a few seconds will produce a reward. Animals who have difficulty suppressing a response will be unable to learn such tasks because they will fail at the no-go task. Prefrontal damage generally does not produce significant impairment on simple go-no-go tasks. This difficulty is demonstrated by premotor lesions, which additionally produce problems with motor sequences and skilled movements.

One might also argue that all of these tasks involve holding information in mind although not acting on it, a function that some have called working memory. The deficit pattern is not simply a failure of short-term memory, however, because the perseverative failures are themselves the best indications of acting on the basis of prior information. In fact, information in short-term memory seems to inappropriately dominate the tendency to respond. What must be held in mind in these tasks is not just prior information, but information about the applicability of that information in a different context. One of the most salient common feature of these tasks sensitive to prefrontal lesions is that they all, in some way or other, involve shifting between alternatives or opposites, alternating place from trial to trial, shifting from one stimulus to a new one, or from one pair-wise association to another depending on the presence of different cues. Tasks sensitive to prefrontal damage thus all involve short-term memory, attention, suppression of responses, and context sensitivity, but they all have one other important feature in common. Each involves a kind of negation relationship between stimuli or stimulus–behavior relationships. They all have to do with using information about something one has just done or seen against itself, so to speak, to inhibit the tendency to follow up that correlation and, instead, shift attention and direct action to alternative associations. Precisely because one association works in one context or trial it is specifically excluded in the next trial, or under different stimulus conditions. An implicit "not" must be generated to learn these tasks, not just an inhibition.

Similar deficits are well known in human patients (Kolb & Whishaw, 1990; Stuss & Benson, 1986), even though associations between specific tasks and different prefrontal subareas are not worked out as well in humans. For example, human prefrontal patients often fail at card-sorting tasks that require them to change sorting criteria.

5. PREFRONTAL CORTEX AND SYMBOL LEARNING

They also tend to have trouble generating lists of word. In trying to generate word lists according to some criterion or instruction, they hardly get past the first few names of things before getting stuck or repeating items already named. These two skills are formally similar to conditional association and sampling tasks, respectively.

In addition, prefrontal patients also often have difficulty learning mazes based on success–failure feedback, making plans and spontaneously organizing behavior sequences, and with tasks that require taking another perspective (allocentric vs. egocentric). Analogous to using a mirror, thinking in allocentric terms requires a systematic reversal of response tendencies. In general, tasks that require convergence on a single solution are minimally impacted, but those that require generating or sampling a variety of alternatives are. This capacity has been called "divergent thinking" by Guilford (1967), and may explain why prefrontal damage does not appear to have a major effect on paper-and-pencil IQ tests. Like the logic shared by tasks sensitive to different frontal lobe defects in monkeys, the many human frontal lobe signs also crucially involve difficulties in using information negatively. Prefrontal patients show a generalized tendency to be controlled by immediate and simple correlative relationships between stimuli and rewards, which essentially blocks the ability to entertain higher order associative relationships because of the inability to subordinate one set of associations to another.

These insights about prefrontal functions, although far from solving the riddle of the prefrontal lobes, may offer sufficient information for understanding the significance of the remarkable expansion of this structure in human evolution. They do, however, beg this question: What crucial adaptation demanded such a premium on the ability to learn complex conditional and negational relationships?

THE SYMBOL ACQUISITION PROBLEM

If prefrontal expansion, and, by implication the increasing influence of its functions over other cognitive and sensorimotor processes, is both a consequence and a cause of human cognitive evolution, then it is reasonable to suspect that its functions ought to provide insight into our most divergent cognitive ability—language. It does not follow that prefrontal cortex is the locus of language functions, the repository for grammatical knowledge, or the basis for increased intelligence. I think it is none of these. Rather, I believe it addresses a learning problem that lies at the heart of language: the problem of the missing simple languages. I suggest that we have been looking at the wrong level of the phenomenon for answers. Other animals' brains are not just abysmal at performing the computations required for analyzing the grammatical relationships between symbols; they cannot even be tested adequately, because they are unable to perform the necessary computations for learning even a simple symbolic reference system. In other words, I think that it is not grammar that is holding other species back. It is something much more basic and more subtle: symbolic reference.

What is so hard about learning symbolic reference? Why should symbolic associations be different from other associations? One possibility is that they might involve more complicated stimuli. For example, there might be more details to remember or fewer clues to help one learn the associations. Another possibility is that one may need to learn many more associations for any of them to be useful. For example, in language it seems necessary to combine words into sentences for them to be usable. Isolated words have meaning only in special kinds of utterances such as commands, naming objects, or identifying people. However, there is a third possibility that I wish to explore: The possibility that symbolic associations are different in more fundamental ways from other kinds of associations, different in response to situations that nonhuman brains are poorly equipped to handle and that human brains have become specialized to overcome.

This begs an old and stubbornly resistant philosophical question: What is special about the way we represent and understand meanings in language? This question refers to the essential difference we recognize when distinguishing understanding from mere rote learning. I argue that there is a crucial difference that distinguishes symbolic associations from other forms of learned associations, but that we tend to ignore this difference because we usually find the transition between nonsymbolic associations and symbol learning so effortless. The tacit assumption is that word reference is essentially learned in the same way as are other associations. The commonsense idea is that a symbolic association is formed when we learn to pair a sound or inscription with something else in the world. The idea or concept of the thing associated with the sign constitutes the symbolic link. According to this view, the association between a word and what it represents is not essentially distin-

5. PREFRONTAL CORTEX AND SYMBOL LEARNING 123

guished from the kind of association made by an animal in a Skinner box when it learns that there is a correlation between a red light and the availability of food. The conditioned stimulus takes on referential power in this process: It represents something about the state of the apparatus for the animal. It is, technically, an index of a change in state of the Skinner box. When the light is off, there is no food available, but when it is illuminated, food is available. When the light is off, no action the rat can perform will induce the apparatus to deliver the food, but when it is illuminated, the rat can perform a particular associated behavior (e.g., pressing a bar), and food will be delivered. Although common sense suggests that word meaning is more complicated than this and that conditioned association is somehow more mechanical and nonsemantic, it has been curiously difficult to find a clear exposition of the difference between them in either the psychological or philosophical literature.

The development of stimulus generalization or learning sets has also been compared to symbol learning, but these are also not sufficient to explain the difference between symbolic and nonsymbolic associations. A similarity is often suggested because terms for things usually name classes of things rather than individual things. Transference of learning from stimulus to stimulus or from context to context occurs as a natural incidental consequence of learning. This is the case because there is always some ambiguity as to the essential parameters of events that are antecedent to the conditions the subject is seeking to reproduce and because the learning process is essentially a statistical estimate of the sufficient stimulus. Thus, to the extent that other stimuli or stimulus contexts are physically similar in some respect to the implicit subsample used for training, they are also incidentally learned. Although this may be formally represented in psychological models as though the subject has learned rules for identifying associative relationships, the generalization effect is not so much the result of listed criteria as it is a failure to distinguish, a tendency to gloss over differences. Transference of learning can be broadened by training that purposely varies stimulus and response conditions along certain parameters. This kind of generalization is still essentially based on one-to-one pairings of stimuli, but what constitutes a stimulus is ambiguous in certain dimensions.

Simple conditioned stimuli are ultimately symptomatic or indexical of the stimuli with which they have become associated. Stimuli linked by learned association are acquired because of their contiguity or coincidence in space or time, by the fact that they habitually "go together" in some way or other. In the same way that the presence of a fever indicates other disease conditions are also probable, or that smoke indicates combustion, the conditioned stimulus is a signal to the subject in the present state that the device or the experimenter will likely provide the associated reward. The stimulus is evidence of this change in state. To distinguish this sort of associative relationship from others, particularly symbolic associations, I identify it as indexical association.

Understanding the difference between this sort of learned association and symbolic association is fundamental to my argument, so I digress slightly from the brain–language problem to deal with this most ensnaring philosophical problem. Given the history of failures to solve the conundrums it poses, I hope the reader will be charitable if in this short exposition I do not fully plumb the depths of the problem. I do hope that at least the skeleton of the approach becomes clear. The answer I propose can be paraphrased by saying that symbols are essentially about indexical associations, not about objects directly.

Take, as a starting point, words and objects. The source of the problem in understanding the difference between the symbolic and nonsymbolic relationships involved is that terms for objects can be paired with things in a way that superficially resembles conditioned association. However, by virtue of the fact that words also represent relationships to other words (think of the way a dictionary works), this pairing is far from the whole story. It is actually by virtue of this sort of dual reference to objects and to other words (or at least to other semantic alternatives) that a word conveys the information necessary for picking out objects of reference. Unlike a colored light in a Skinner box, a word does not refer to some thing or condition by virtue of habitually being associated with it (in fact, the physical association between a word and an appropriate object of reference can be quite rare or even an impossibility), but rather by virtue of carving out a kind of logical space. Words superimpose pragmatic logical boundaries on the physical continuities and discontinuities found among real stimuli and events. This is what provides the power of symbolic relationships: By virtue of the possible combinatorial interrelationships between symbols, there can be an exponential growth of reference with each new added element.

5. PREFRONTAL CORTEX AND SYMBOL LEARNING

Even without struggling with the philosophical subtleties of this relationship, we can immediately see its significance for learning. The learning problem associated with symbolic reference is a consequence of the fact that what determines the pairing between a symbol (such as a word) and some object or event is not their probability of co-occurrence, but rather some complex function of the relationship that the symbol has to other symbols. Learning is, at its base, a function of the probability of correlations between things, from the synaptic level to the behavioral level. Past correlations tend to predict future correlations, and so provide a powerful, if simple, recipe for adaptation. To comprehend a symbolic reference, however, you must selectively ignore certain habitual associations and correlations between symbols as stimuli and their objects of reference as stimuli, and focus instead on the relationships between different symbols and the way these modify the probabilities of symbol–object co-occurrence. This is a troublesome shift of focus. The correlations between symbols and objects are merely the clues for determining the more crucial relationships between the symbols themselves, and these clues are not highly correlated. Let me offer an extended example to help demonstrate this problem.

One of the most insightful examples of the difference between conditioned associations and symbolic associations is offered by a set of experiments that attempted to test symbolic abilities in chimpanzees. This study was directed by Sue Savage-Rumbaugh and Duane Rumbaugh at the Yerkes Primate Center (Rumbaugh & Rumbaugh 1978; Savage-Rumbaugh, Rumbaugh, Smith, & Lawson, 1980). The chimps in this study were taught to use a special computer keyboard made up of lexigrams—geometric drawings on large keys. Although previous experiments had shown that chimps have the ability to learn a large number of paired associations between lexigrams (and, in fact, other kinds of symbol-tokens) and objects or activities, some problems arose when they were required to use these in simple combinatorial relationships. To test the chimps' symbolic understanding of the lexigrams, they were trained to chain lexigram pairs in a simple verb–noun relationship (e.g., a sequence glossed as meaning "give," which caused a dispenser to deliver a solid food, and "banana" to get a banana). There were initially only two "verb" lexigrams and four food or drink lexigrams to choose from, and each pair had to be separately taught. But after successful training of each pairing, the chimps were presented with all of the options they had learned independently and were required to choose the combination that was most appropriate on the basis of food availability or preference. Curiously, this task was not implicit from their previous training, evidenced by the fact that some chimps tended to stereotypically repeat only the most recent single learned combination, whereas others chained all of the options together, irrespective of the intended meanings and what they knew about the situation. Thus, they had learned the individual associations but had failed to learn the system of relationships of which these correlations were a part. Although the logic of the combinatorial relationships between lexigrams was implicit in the particular combinations that the chimps learned, the converse exclusive relationships had not been learned. Although implicit for those of us who treat them symbolically from the start, the combinatorial rules of combination and exclusion that underlie the symbolic use of these lexigrams was vastly underdetermined by the training experience.

It is not immediately obvious exactly how much exclusionary information is implicit, but it turns out to be quite a lot. Think about it from the naive chimpanzee perspective for a moment. Even with this ultrasimple symbol system with six lexigrams and a two-lexigram combinatorial grammar, the chimpanzee is faced with the possibility of sorting among 720 possible ordered sequences ($6*5*4*3*2*1$) or 64 possible ordered pairs. The training has offered only 4 prototype examples, in isolation. Although each chimp may begin with many null hypotheses about what works, these are unlikely to be in the form of rules about allowed and disallowed combinations, but rather about possible numbers of lexigrams that must be pressed, their positions on the board, and their colors or shape cues that might be associated with a reward object.

Recognizing this limitation, the experimenters embarked on a rather interesting course of training. They set out to explicitly train the chimps which cues were irrelevant and which combinations were not meaningful. This poses an interesting problem that every pet trainer faces. You cannot train what not to do unless the animal first produces the disallowed behavior and it can be immediately punished or at least explicitly not rewarded. Accordingly, first the chimps had to be trained to produce the incorrect association (e.g., mistaking keyboard position as the relevant variable) and then be explicitly not rewarded for that particular association. By a complex hierarchic training design involving thousands of trials, it was possible to systematically exclude all inappropriate associative and combinatorial possibilities, leaving the animals able to produce the correct lexigram strings essentially every time. Remarkably, after this training regimen, when a new food item and new lexigram was introduced, some of the chimps were able to respond correctly the first time or with only a few errors instead of hundreds as before. What had happened to produce this difference? How had this process helped the chimps graduate from what we would recognize as rote learning to what we would call an understanding of the meaning of the lexigrams?

What the animals had learned was not only an association between lexigrams and objects or events. They had learned a set of logical relationships between the lexigrams defined by exclusion and inclusion. More important, these lexigram–lexigram relationships formed a complete system in which each possible relationship of adjacency, substitutability, or opposition was defined. In fact, the chimps had to learn that the relationship of a lexigram to an object is a function of the rela-

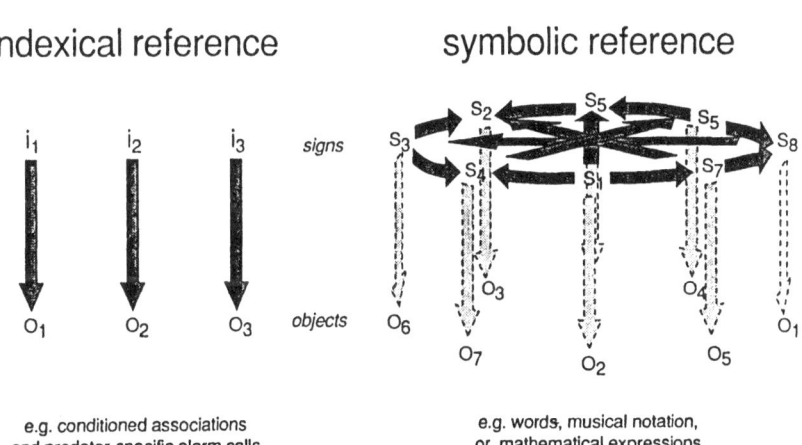

Fig. 5.5. Schematic depiction of the difference between indexical reference, as might be created by correlative-associative learning, and symbolic reference. Simple associative links between sign stimuli and objects are one-to-one and essentially independent of one another (indicated by dark arrows in the left figure), except insofar as the stimulus parameters might overlap. Correlation between sign stimulus and object is the basis for indexical reference relationships. Symbolic reference is based primarily upon the system of combinatorial inclusion–exclusion relationships between stimulus signs (symbols) and the way these pick out categorical boundaries of classes of indexical associations (indicated by dark solid arrows connecting symbols). Although indexical links still exist between objects and symbols that represent them, these are entirely secondary to symbol–symbol relationships, and are no longer a function of correlation and co-occurrence (indicated by light gray dashed arrows).

tionship it has to other lexigrams, not a simple function of the correlated appearance of both lexigram and object. Reference is determined indirectly. This subordination of associative relationships to combinatorial relationships between symbols is schematically depicted in Fig. 5.5. Indexical associations are one-to-one, and the indexical reference is achieved as a function of the correlations between some token (i.e., the sign stimulus) and some object (shown as a solid arrow).

In contrast, the system of token-token interrelationships, such as those between lexigrams or words (shown as solid arrows interconnecting symbols), is essentially independent of their indexical functions. Tokens indicate one another in the sense that their presence or position in a communicative activity influences the admissibility or nonadmissibility of others. This, however, is a purely conventional token–token indexicality because it constitutes a closed group of "pointing" relationships (i.e., determines reference to objects collectively as a function of relative position within this token–token reference system). Symbolic reference emerges from the hierarchic relationship between these levels of indexicality. Although the indexical reference of symbol–tokens to objects is maintained, it is no longer determined by a simple correlational relationship between sign and object. The subordination of indexical reference to the lexigram–lexigram relationship, however, makes a new kind of generalization possible: logical generalization, as opposed to stimulus generalization. This is what made the no-trial-learning of new lexigram–object relationships possible for Sherman and Austin, the chimps that succeeded in this task..

The system of lexigram–lexigram interrelationships is a source of implicit knowledge about how novel lexigrams must be incorporated. Adding a new food lexigram, then, does not require the chimp to learn the correlative association from scratch each time. The referential relationship is no longer a function of lexigram–food co-occurrence, but rather a function of the relationship this new lexigram has with the system of other lexigrams. There is a shift in analysis from relationships among stimuli to relationships among lexigrams as logical operators. A new food or drink lexigram must fit into a predetermined slot in this system of relationships. There are only a few possible alternatives to sample, and none require the chimps to assess the probability of paired lexigram-food occurrence because lexigrams need no longer be treated as indices of food availability. As with words, the probability of co-occurrences may be quite low. In a real sense the lexigrams are

5. PREFRONTAL CORTEX AND SYMBOL LEARNING 129

the chimps' ability to extrapolate to new lexigram–food relationships is a way of demonstrating whether or not they have learned this logical-categorical generalization. It is a crucial defining feature of symbolic reference.

The experimenters provided a further, and in some ways more dramatic, demonstration of the difference between the rote learning of lexigram–object correlations and symbolic learning by comparing the performance of the two symboling apes, Sherman and Austin, to a previous subject, Lana, who had been trained with the same lexigram system but not in the same systematic fashion. Lana had learned a much larger corpus of lexigram–object associations, though, by simple paired associations. All three chimps were able to learn a task that required sorting food items together in one pan and food items together in another. (Lana learned in far fewer trials than Sherman and Austin.) After this, when presented with new foods or tools the apes were able to generalize from their prior behavior to sort these new items appropriately as well. This is essentially a test of stimulus generalization, although it is based on some rather abstract qualities of the test items (e.g., edibility). A second task, though, in which the chimps had to associate each of the same food items with a single lexigram for "food" and the same tool items with a single lexigram for "tool," provided different results. This task clearly distinguished the symboling chimps from Lana. Even though all three chimps were able to learn the new associations (this took as many trials to learn as did the original training), when asked to generalize the referential scope of these lexigrams to two new foods and two new tools, only Sherman and Austin were able to do so essentially without errors. Lana not only failed to add the new items as referents of the lexigrams, but also became unsettled by the errors, and in successive testing ignored what she had previously learned. She treated these new trials as independent from the preceding trials, and essentially assumed that she needed to learn the new associations from scratch.

Sherman and Austin, as a result of their experience with a previous symbol system, had recruited the individual lexigram–object associations they had acquired by rote, and used them to create two new symbolic categories that superseded the individual associations. It took hundreds or thousands of trials to learn the first simple one-to-many associations, because there was no systemic relationship in the chimps' small existing lexigram set into which a general reference for "food" and "tool" would fit. Once the chimps had established the new symbolic relationship, though, it was easily expandable. Because of this, they generalized to new associations, not by stimulus features, but by what amounted to semantic features. They were eventually able to fully integrate these categories with their existing system by learning associations between these two lexigrams and other lexigrams, eventually associating lexigrams of individual food items directly with the lexigram for food. Although it typically took hundreds, even thousands of trials for the chimps to acquire a new rote association, once a systemic relationship was established, new items could be added essentially without any trial and error. This difference translated into more than a hundredfold increase in learning efficiency and supplies a key to understanding the apparent leap in human intelligence as compared to other species. Increased intelligence does not produce symbols; instead, symbols increase effective intelligence. The power of the symbolic step in this learning process derives from the fact that the chimps essentially knew something that they had never explicitly learned. Implicit knowledge is an inevitable spontaneous product of symbolic representation. This fact plays a critical role in many facets of language acquisition often attributed to innate foreknowledge.

I have chosen to recount this "ape-language" study, not because it portrays any particularly advanced abilities in chimpanzees, nor because I think it is somehow representative, but because of the clarity with which it portrays the special nature of symbol learning, and because it provides an example of the hierarchic relationship between symbolic and indexical (simple correlative) referential relationships. Symbolic referential relationships are constituted of relationships among indexical referential relationships. Indexical associations are necessary stepping stones to symbolic reference, but must ultimately be overcome and ignored for symbolic reference to work.

The temporal–spatial correlations between the sign stimulus and object do not mean what they predict (i.e., that one is causally related to the other). To learn symbolic associations, the apparent causal implications of correlative associations must be ignored, and associated causal expectations must be suppressed to serve the search for a higher order relationship between the sign stimuli irrespective of their causal correlations with other objects. This higher order relationship is not determined by any physical properties of the sign stimuli. It is a logical relationship defined by allowed and disallowed combinations. Before symbolic reference is possible, one must first learn many nonsymbolic associative relationships that are, in effect, only symptoms of a higher order symbol system. The association between a sign stimulus and an object must be understood, not as pointing to that object, but as pointing to the place that this associative relationship occupies in a system of other associative relationships, and by virtue of which it is identified.

The problem with symbol systems, then, is that there is both a lot of learning and unlearning that must take place before even a single symbolic relationship is available. Symbols cannot be acquired one at a time the way other learned associations are, except after a reference symbol system is established. A logically complete system of relationships among the set of symbols must be learned before the symbolic association between any one symbol and an object can be thereby determined. The learning step occurs prior to recognizing the symbolic function, and this function only emerges from a system; it is not vested in any individual sign–object pairing. For this reason it is hard to get started. To learn the first symbolic relationship requires holding a lot of potential combinations in mind at once in order to discover how any one fits in with the others. Even with a very small set of symbols, the number of possible combinations is so vast that sorting out which combinations work and which do not requires sampling and remembering a large number of possibilities. Moreover, rote memory of which combinations worked in which situations may work against the need to decompose the combinatorial relationships in order to discover the underlying rules of logical exclusion and inclusion that they encode. The problem with learning to reproduce symbolic material by rote (i.e., learned as indexical associations such as learning to reproduce a mathematical calculation by memory) is that the information is not generalizable, except with respect to perceptual parameters of the stimuli. It is the essence of symbolic associations that their reference is determined by general rules, logical relationships that have application across all possible combinations in the system.

THE CONTRIBUTION OF THE PREFRONTAL CORTEX TO SYMBOL LEARNING

This difference between associative learning and symbol learning has some interesting consequences so far as the evolution of intelligence and language are concerned. The ability to acquire learned associations between stimuli enables an animal to more efficiently and flexibly adapt to the cause–effect contingencies of a complex changing environment. The ability to learn quickly to discern and predict the most highly correlated spatial–temporal relationships among events is a powerful strategy for internalizing the structure of the world around us. It is, however, a poor strategy for learning symbolic relationships.

In fact, it is probably the case that an ability to rapidly discover and memorize the simple correlative relationships among stimuli would interfere with the discovery of abstract rules of logical combination among these same stimuli that could be the basis for symbolization. Because the probability of correlating a symbol with a given object depends entirely on which other symbols it precedes, follows, or co-occurs with, the statistics of correlation provide a poor predictor of the relationship across all possible occurrences. Furthermore, the smarter the learning device, brain, or otherwise, the quicker it will tend to jump to such conclusions, because it will discover the subtle differences in the weightings of statistical associations more quickly. The faster the statistical weighting of correlations is discovered, the faster the learning process will proceed. Such a statistical best guess, however, must ignore any large-scale distributed logic that might be exhibited combinatorially, yet this is precisely what is needed to build a symbolic system. In short, increased intelligence defined in this way would likely be counterproductive to symbolic learning.

This is the reason why the evolution of the human brain is explicitly not well described as the evolution of increased intelligence. Building a smarter brain is not sufficient to get over the threshold separating simple associative learning abilities and symbolic learning abilities. In fact it makes the threshold higher. It may also partially explain why children, with their somewhat limited learning rates and memory spans, may be so much better than adults at learning symbolic systems from scratch. Their intelligence does not get in their way, so to speak.

What then took human brains over this hump? I suggest that this is the significance of prefrontal cortex enlargement and the expansion of its projection systems. It is not because we have a smarter prefrontal cortex, but rather because the prefrontal system has become much more involved in the activities of all other brain systems. Maslow once quipped that if the only tool you have is a hammer, you will tend to treat everything like a nail. This offers an analogy I would apply to this prefrontal change. The prefrontal propensity to inhibit the tendency to act on simple correlative stimulus relationships and instead sample possible higher order sequential or hierarchic associations has come to dominate the human learning process more than in any other species. In simple terms, much more control of the brain is vested in the prefrontal cortex in human brains. The way the parietal cortex handles tactile and movement information, the way the auditory cortex handles sound information, and the way the visual cortex handles visual information is now much more constrained by prefrontal activity than in other species.

The contributions of prefrontal areas to learning all involve, in one way or another, the analysis of higher order associative relationships. More specifically, judging from the effects of damage to prefrontal regions, they are necessary for learning associative relationships in which one association is in some way subordinated to another. These mental computations address the most critical learning problem faced during symbol acquisition. The more complicated the combinatorial relationships or the more easily confused the correlated relationships, the more prefrontal systems are taxed. This is clearly demonstrated by cerebral blood flow and PET imaging studies of the metabolic correlates of different cognitive tasks in human subjects. Complex sorting problems and difficult word-association tasks have been shown to particularly activate prefrontal metabolism (see also Deacon, 1991, on language tasks). There is also indirect evidence that task difficulty determines how much prefrontal cortex gets recruited to the task. Electrical stimulation studies of awake neurosurgery patients has shown that patients with lower verbal IQs tend to have larger regions of prefrontal cortex susceptible to disruption of language tasks (Ojemann, 1979).

BRAIN–LANGUAGE COEVOLUTION

Expansion of the prefrontal cortex and its projection fields in human evolution can be interpreted in the context of these special learning problems. It is not clear whether we should interpret prefrontal expansion as an enhancement of these classes of mental computations or merely as a predisposition to treat most learning contexts as involving combinatorial and conditional relationships. Either interpretation would contribute significantly to symbol learning, possibly at some cost in terms of simple associative learning. However we interpret this difference, it cannot be doubted that such a major change in brain structure reflects some rather special learning demands faced by our ancestors, but by no other species. It can hardly be a coincidence that the most salient difference in human brain structure and the most salient difference in human cognitive abilities converge on the same learning problem. The magnitude of prefrontal enlargement and the nearly 2-million-year time course of this evolutionary change suggest that these capabilities were under powerful selection for a considerable period during hominid evolution.

This may also provide an explanation for the failure of languagelike (symbolic) communication to evolve in all but one species. A simple improvement of such things as learning rates or memory capacity cannot account for the transition to symbolic communication that took place in hominid evolution. One cannot extrapolate some general tendency toward more complex communication or higher intelligence and arrive at language evolution because the cognitive requirements for efficient associative learning conflict in many ways with those that would enhance symbol learning. Selection for the one would tend to be countered by selection for the other. The transition from associative forms of learning and communication to symbolic forms requires the crossing of a high threshold in terms of learning costs. The organism must invest immense learning effort into acquiring associative relationships that make no sense until the whole system of interdependent associations is sorted out. In other words, for a long time in this process nothing useful can come of it. Only after a complete group (in the mathematical sense) of interdefined symbols is assembled can any one of them be used symbolically. Until then, their indexical associations will be useful in only a limited set of stereotypic contexts. To approach most learning problems with the expectations and biases that would aid symbol learning would be very inefficient for most species.

The time course of brain–language coevolution can be estimated unambiguously because of the way this difference in brain structure correlates with features that can be discerned from fossils. Prefrontal enlargement and the enlargement of its projection fields is determined systemically by competitive processes during development that are reflected in global brain parameters, specifically the relationship between brain and body size. The size of the cortical region recruited by the medial dorsal and anterior thalamic nuclei (that project to prefrontal cortex in adult brains) is a function of competition with thalamic projections associated with peripheral sensory and motor systems. Consequently, the relative size of the brain with respect to the body (which correlates with the size of peripheral organs and their projections) should be an accurate index of the proportions of cortical areas, including the size of the prefrontal cortex. As hominid brains first began to significantly enlarge with respect to body size approximately 2 million years ago, they were not merely increasing in brain size, but in the proportion of prefrontal cortex and the proportion of prefrontal projections into target fields that in other brains would be occupied with other sensory, motor, or limbic projections.

Hominid brain expansion can therefore be used as an index of the change in its internal structure and for the degree of functional change associated with incremental prefrontal expansion. The increase in brain size traced from *Homo habilis* to *Homo sapiens* therefore is a symptom of prolonged selection favoring an alternative learning strategy. Almost certainly this reflects an increasing need for combinatorial and hierarchic learning, even at the expense of more basic correlative learning strategies. These hominids were not getting smarter in any simple sense. They were likely getting dumber in terms of correlative–associative learning that is so critical for solving problems posed by physical or social circumstances.

The cognitive abilities favored and enhanced by this evolutionary trend, however, were the sine qua non of symbol acquisition. Even learning the simplest symbolic relationships places heavy demands on these particular cognitive abilities. Attention to higher order distributed associations and away from those based on temporal–spatial correlations tends to render these other forms of associative learning somewhat less efficient. It is difficult to imagine what other practical domain could benefit from such a shift in learning style. No other species evolved this ability because incremental change in learning abilities that would enhance symbol acquisition would be counterproductive to learning in the absence of symbolic communication. It is hard to imagine, then, that anything other than the significant advantages of symbolic communication (in whatever form) could account for selection pressures that would drive such an unusual course of brain evolution. Some simple symbolic communication must, therefore, have preceded and driven hominid brain evolution, not followed it.

This theory of brain–language coevolution forces us to entirely rethink hominid origins. The restructuring of the hominid brain was not sudden, nor was it merely a quantitative expansion. It took place incrementally (although I leave it to paleontologists to quibble about the number and size of the increments, it is at least certain that it was not a one- or two-step process) over the course of approximately 1.5 million years beginning approximately 2 million years ago with the species *Homo habilis*. The impetus behind this restructuring of the brain appears to have been the unusual nature of the cognitive demands imposed by symbolic communication, not some generalized demand on intellectual capacity. Selection for prefrontal expansion derives from the incredible demands that symbol learning places on combinatorial and hierarchic learning processes.

This neurological adaptation does not directly account for the evolution of complex grammar, and offers no support for the idea of a modular innate universal grammar. If anything, it suggests that the evolution of grammatical systems is, at most, a secondary issue. To the extent that symbolic associations are inherently and irreducibly combinatorial and hierarchic, any adaptation that increases the facility for producing and analysing such relationships will contribute to the ability to become skilled at handling the sorts of computations that syntactic processes require. The human facility for constructing and analyzing complex sequential and hierarchic relationships may also offer some insight into other related abilities and predispositions nascent in human brains, from art and music to mathematics and game playing. It shows humans to be peculiarly unique among species, not just for their language abilities, but for their odd style of thinking and learning.

REFERENCES

Barbas, H., & Mesulam, M.-M. (1981). Organization of afferent input to subdivisions of area 8 of the rhesus monkey. *Journal of Comparative Neurology, 200,* 407–431.

Blinkov, S., & Glezer, I. (1968). *The human brain in figures and tables.* New York: Plenum.

Deacon, T. W. (1984). *Connections of the inferior periarcuate area in the brain of Macaca fascicularis. An experimental and comparative investigation of language circuitry and its evolution.* Unpublished doctoral dissertation, Harvard University, Cambridge, MA.

Deacon, T. W. (1988). Human brain evolution: II. Embryology and brain allometry. In H. Jerison & I. Jerison (Eds.), *Intelligence and evolutionary biology* (pp. 383–415). Berlin: Springer-Verlag.

Deacon, T. W. (1990a). Fallacies of progression in theories of brains size evolution. *International Journal of Primatology*,

Deacon, T. W. (1990b). Rethinking mammalian brain evolution. *American Zoologist, 30,* 629–705.

Deacon, T. W. (1992). Brain-language co-evolution. In J. A. Hawkins (Ed.), *The evolution of human languages* (pp. 49-88). Redwood City, CA: Addison-Wesley.

Fuster, J. (1980). The prefrontal cortex: Anatomy, physiology and neuropsychology of the frontal lobe. New York: Raven.

Goldman-Rakic, P. R. (1987). Circuitry of the primate prefrontal cortex and regulation of behavior by representational memory. *Handbook of Physiology,* 373–418.

Guilford, J. (1967). *The nature of human intelligence.* New York: McGraw-Hill.

Jacobsen, C. (1936). Studies of cerebral function in primates. *Comparative Psychology Monographs, 13,* 1–68.

Kolb, B., & Whishaw, I. (1990), *Fundamentals of human neuropsychology.* 3rd ed. New York: Freeman.

Linden, R. (1990). Control of neuronal survival by anomalous targets in the developing brain. *Journal of Comparative Neurology, 294,* 594–606.

Mishkin, M., & Manning, F. (1978). Nonspatial memory after selective prefrontal lesions in monkeys. *Brain Research, 143,* 313–323.

Ojemann, G. A. (1979). Individual variability in cortical localization of language. *Journal of Neurosurgery, 50,* 164–9.

O'Leary, D. (1992). Development of connectional diversity and specificity in the mammalian brain by the pruning of collateral projections. *Current Opinions in Neurobiology, 2,* 70–77.

Pandya, D., & Barnes, C. (1987). Architecture and connections of the frontal lobe. In E. Perecman (Ed.), *The frontal lobes revisited* (pp. 41–72). New York: IRBN Press.

Passingham, R. E. (1985). Memory of monkeys *(Macaca mulatta)* with lesions in prefrontal cortex. *Behavioral Neuroscience, 99,* 3–21.

Perecman, E. (Ed.) (1987). *The frontal lobes revisited.* New York: The IRBN Press.

Petrides, M. (1982). Motor conditional associative learning after selective prefrontal lesions in the monkey. *Behavioral and Brain Research, 5,* 407–413.

Petrides, M. (1985). Deficits in nonspatial conditional associative learning after periarcuate lesions in monkey. *Behavioral and Brain Research, 16,* 95–101.

Petrides, M. (1986). The effect of periarcuate lesions in the monkey on the performance of symmetrically and asymmetrically reinforced visual and auditory go, no-go tasks. *Journal of Neuroscience, 6,* 2054–2063.

Piaget, J. (1952). *The origins of intelligence in children.* New York: International Universities Press.

Purves, D. (1988). *Body and brain. A trophic theory of neural connections.* Cambridge, MA: Harvard University Press.

Purves, D., & Lichtman, J. (1985). *Principles of neural development.* Sunderland, MA: Sinauer Associates.

Savage-Rumbaugh, E. S., & Rumbaugh, D. M. (1978). Symbolization, language and chimpanzees: A theoretical reevaluation based on initial language acquisition processes in four young *Pan troglodytes. Brain and Language, 6,* 265–273.

Savage-Rumbaugh, E. S., Rumbaugh, D. M., Smith, S. T., & Lawson, J. (1980). Reference: The linguistic essential. *Science, 210,* 922–925.

Stuss, D. T., & Benson, D. F. (1986). *The frontal lobes.* New York: Raven.

PART III

ONTOGENESIS OF LANGUAGE

CHAPTER

6

ORIGINS OF COMMUNICATION IN INFANCY

Marc H. Bornstein
National Institute of Child Health and Human Development, Bethesda

During the first fortnight he often started on hearing any sudden sound, and blinked his eyes. [...] The noise of crying [...] is of course uttered in an instinctive manner, but serves to show that there is suffering. After a time the sound differs according to the cause, such as hunger or pain. [...] When 46 days old, he first made little noises without any meaning to please himself, and these soon became varied. When five and a half months old, he uttered an articulate sound "da" but without any meaning attached to it. When a little over a year old, he used gestures to explain his wishes. [...] At exactly the age of a year, he made the great step of inventing a word for food, namely, mum, *but what led him to it I did not discover. [...] Before he was a year old, he understood intonations and gestures, as well as several words and short sentences. He understood one word, namely, his nurse's name, exactly five months before he invented his first word* mum; *and this is what might have been expected, as we know that the lower animals easily learn to understand spoken words.*

—From *A Biographical Sketch of an Infant*
by Charles Darwin (1877)

In the first months of life, infants coo and babble; by their 24th month, toddlers can speak some grammatically correct sentences. In the first months, infants respond to the human voice; by their 24th month, toddlers comprehend the meaning of some prepositions. Language acquisition lies at the nexus of impressive accomplishments in the perceptual, cognitive, and social spheres of development. Human language is also a multivariate matter of study, because it simultaneously involves sounds, semantics, and syntax, each of which has both productive and receptive constituents.

Consider a toddler's task in understanding mother's meaning when she says simply:

Yourteddyislyingonthecouchsweetie.

The child must simultaneously segregate the sound stream into individual word forms and comprehend the meaning of each, in part at least, by decomposing the grammatical structure linking the word forms. (Sometimes Sweetie may actually even get the teddy.) Therefore, no matter how complex, abstract, and formidable the language, the cognitively immature infant rapidly and effortlessly becomes facile in both understanding and speaking. This chapter addresses the most vexing question, *How?*

Some theoreticians have argued that language learning proceeds strictly on the basis of the child's experiences. In the 4th century, St. Augustine wrote that children learn language by imitating their elders, and just 16 centuries later Skinner (1957) argued that children learn language, as they do any system of behavioral contingencies, through reinforcement. In contrast, other theorists have asserted that a child's first language could be built only on innate biological processes (e.g., Bickerton, 1990; Chomsky, 1965; Jakobson, 1968; Lenneberg, 1967). However, language is surely too rich, unique, and complex a system for the infant simply to *learn,* just as it is too rich, unique, and complex a system for the newborn simply to *know.* One observer of the historical give-and-take between these nurture and nature views concerning the origins of language dubbed this "the debate between the impossible and the miraculous." Indeed, the tension between biology and culture in language acquisition is so compelling, and so confounding, that in 1866 the Linguistic Society of Paris banned its discussion!

In this chapter, I review some early ontogenetic aspects of language acquisition. I describe select recent research on how infants develop from nonverbal individualists into interactive conversationalists, willing and able to articulate their cares, needs, desires, and dreams to others. I do not attempt to be comprehensive; that would be impossible at this stage in the development of language studies. Rather, my more modest goal is to impart a flavor of contemporary excitement about the origins of communication in infancy. As background, I start with a brief description of norms and individual variation in early language acquisition, then turn to discuss how infants' experiences complement their capacities by channeling the development of communication toward increasingly effective interactions and integration into the social world. Next, I take up production and comprehension in two important and basic systems of language: Perception and production of speech sounds and the way children begin to acquire referential forms.

Infants are surprisingly prepared in each of these realms, possessing both the motivation and the competencies to ensure that they quickly become full linguistic participants. Infants are also afforded every opportunity by their environment to succeed. In short, the initial acquisition of language reflects competencies that are a part of a child just as much as it reveals the child's early and rich exposure to a target language. The origins of communication in infancy are active and constructive and inextricably embedded in the larger context of adult–infant social interaction. Consequently, there exists plenty of opportunity for the play of biology as well as culture in the early ontogeny of language.

NORMS AND INDIVIDUAL VARIATION IN EARLY LANGUAGE DEVELOPMENT

There exist a strong normative tradition in the field of developmental psycholinguistics, a popularity of description, and a fundamental and important distinction between production and comprehension. These characteristics serve to reinforce the fact that there are many powerful and regular biological contributions to language growth. J. F. Miller and R. S. Chapman (1981) documented a significant and strong relation between chronological age and mean length of utterance (MLU) in a sample of middle-class children 17 to 59 months of age conversing with their mothers during free play. They found that MLU increases at an average rate of 1 to 2 morphemes per year. Indeed, in their data and those of others, the relation between age and MLU during the critical ages of 2 and 3 years is essentially linear (Scarborough, Weikoff, & R. Davidson, 1986).

The nomothetic approach, however, masks a central everyday consideration of individual variation (e.g., Goldfield & Snow, 1989; Thal & E. A. Bates, 1990). Respect for individual variation also helps in addressing questions about the origins and development of language. Children of the same age vary dramatically on nearly every index of language development, and individual differences in children's language, as well as their sources of variation, occupy a central position in the study of language development. The classic illustration of individual variation was provided by R. Brown (1973), who traced speech development in Adam, Eve, and Sarah. All three children achieved common goals, and growth rates were nearly equivalent among them. However, Eve started on the road to language production considerably earlier than did Adam or Sarah, making the same progress from 19 to 27 months that Adam and Sarah made from 26 to 42 months. For example, Eve used an average of three morphemes per utterance at about 2 years of age, whereas Adam and Sarah did not do so until approximately the age of 3, a third of their lifetimes later. At 13 months, some toddlers comprehend 10 words, others 75; and some produce no words, others 27. At 20 months, individual toddlers range from fewer than 10 to more than 400 words in their productive vocabularies. There is also a fair amount of consistency in children: 13-month productive vocabulary size predicts 20-month productive vocabulary size, as well as 20-month grammar and pragmatic diversity in child speech (Tamis-LeMonda & Bornstein, 1990, 1991).

This work exemplifies a quantitative approach to the study of individual variation. Other investigators have attempted to capture qualitative differences in young children's speech. At one end of a hypothesized continuum are "referential" children, whose early vocabularies are marked by a high proportion of object labels and whose speech is organized around information. At the other end of the continuum are "expressive" children, whose early vocabularies comprise relatively more pronouns and action words, and whose speech is marked by social formulae and routines intended to communicate feelings and desires (see E. A. Bates, Bretherton, & L. Snyder, 1988). Most children, of course, present a more balanced picture of referential and expressive speech, and differences between them are therefore a matter of degree (Bretherton, McNew, L. Snyder, & E. A. Bates, 1983; Peters, 1983).

Individual variation in language probably has several sources. As might be expected, one school of developmental psycholinguists has argued that biology and maturation are primary. Another school has suggested that aspects of the language environment promote these distinctions. Mothers who refer to and describe objects, and who request and reinforce names for things, tend to have infants of the referential strand, whereas mothers who refer to persons, and who use their speech to regulate behavior, tend to have expressive children. Still another school has argued that lexical differences among children are predicted by unique combinations of children and their caregivers (Goldfield, 1987): Referential children use objects to elicit maternal attention and have mothers who describe and label objects, whereas expressive children and their mothers rank low on these measures. In short, theoreticians have offered nature, nurture, and transactional explanations to account for individual variation in language development.

SYNCHRONY IN SPEECH

Infants obviously come very far very fast in acquiring the complex symbolic system known as language. In the task of learning the different constituents of language, the child is neither ill-equipped nor alone. Adult and infant alike are geared to the "infant" developing into the "conversant." In this section, I discuss a few basic, but sophisticated mechanics and processes that infants and their caregivers bring to initial communication, including infant-directed speech, turn taking, and dynamic sensitivity. These examples begin to illustrate a certain parent–infant synchrony—interaction, adjustment, and accommodation in communicative transaction—all of which appear to promote early language development.

Infant-Directed Speech

People normally repackage language aimed at infants to match presumed or evaluated infant capacities. As is well known, mothers, fathers, caregivers, and even older children adopt a special dialect when addressing infants, called *infant-directed speech*. Many characteristics of infant-directed speech have been identified (for a review, see Bornstein & Lamb, 1992), and they include prosodic features (higher pitch, greater range of frequencies, more varied and exaggerated intonation), simplicity features (shorter utterances, slower tempo, longer pauses between phrases, fewer embedded clauses, fewer auxiliaries), redundancy features (more repetition over shorter amounts of time, more immediate repetition); lexical features (special forms such as "mama"), and even content features (restriction of topics to the child's world). Importantly, infant-directed speech appears to be intuitive, nonconscious, and essentially universal.[1] Fernald et al. (1989) analyzed the fundamental frequency (as well as utterance duration and pause duration) of mothers' and fathers' naturalistic speech to preverbal infants, respectively, in French, Italian, German, Japanese, British English, and American English. They found cross-language consistency in patterns of prosodic modification in infant-directed versus adult-directed speech. Mothers and fathers alike use higher minimum, mean, and maximum fundamental frequency and a greater variability in fundamental frequency when they address infants (and they also use shorter utterances and longer pauses). When communicating with their infants, deaf mothers modify their sign language in some similar ways (Erting, Prezioso, & Hynes, 1990).

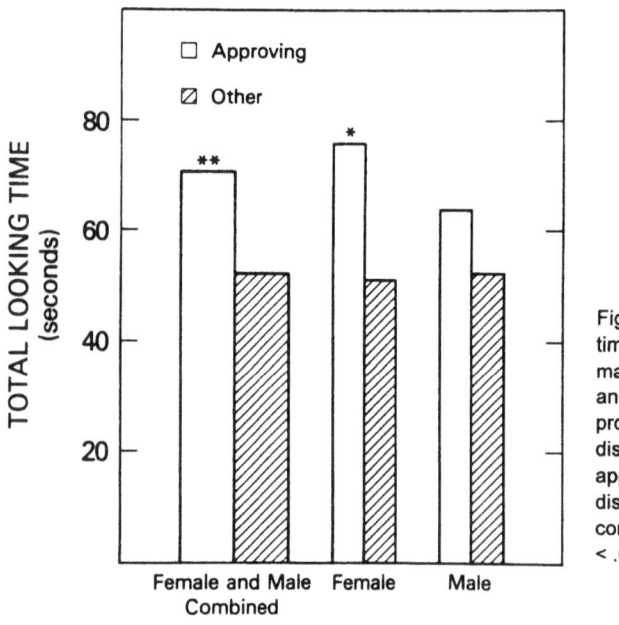

Fig. 6.1. Total looking time (sec) to female and male combined, female, and male naturally approving versus naturally disapproving, reverse-approving, and reverse-disapproving melodic contours ($* p < .05$; $** p < .01$).

---

[1]Although not without exception; see, for example, Ratner and Pye (1984) on Quiche Mayan mothers.

Infant-directed speech is thought to serve several purposes: to elicit attention, modulate arousal and communicate affect, and facilitate language comprehension. With regard to eliciting attention, infants respond more to their own mothers' voice when she is speaking this so-called "motherese" (e.g., Fernald, 1985; Fernald & Kuhl, 1987; Glenn & Cunningham, 1983). In an experimental study, H. Papoušek, M. Papoušek, and I found that visual attention in 4-month-olds is influenced by melodic patterns prototypic of "naturally approving" and "naturally disapproving" infant-directed speech, independent of linguistic and other contextual information (M. Papoušek, Bornstein, Nuzzo, H. Papoušek, & Symmes, 1990). Fig. 6.1 shows that approving contours recruited infant looking as compared to disapproving and control contours. These data suggest that individual melodic prototypes can function as a kind of didactic caregiving message for infants.

The prosody of infant-directed speech also appears to regulate infant arousal level and communicate affect to the infant. For example, H. Papoušek and M. Papoušek (1991) have found that certain intonation contours in mothers' speech to their babies recur with greater-than-chance regularity in particular types of interactions, and these regularities are found in a wide variety of languages, including American English, German, and Mandarin Chinese. Mothers use rising pitch contours to engage infant attention and to elicit an infant response, bell-shaped contours to maintain infant attention, and falling contours to soothe a distressed infant.

Finally, the prosodic modifications of infant-directed speech facilitate processing and comprehension on the part of the infant. Exaggerated prosody is thought to help infants track and parse the speech stream, as well as to provide acoustic cues to the syntactic structure of linguistic messages (Hirsh-Pasek et al., 1987; Morgan, 1986; Peters, 1983). For example, infants discriminate among sounds embedded in multisyllabic sequences better in infant-directed speech than in adult-directed speech (Karzon, 1985).

Turn Taking

Adults conversing with one another tend to match certain temporal factors in their speech, and turn taking is fundamental to the structure of adult dialogue. Turn taking in mother-infant exchange is common, too, with roots deep in initial interactions, as Kaye (1982) observed during mother–newborn feeding. Several authors have closely analyzed the temporal mechanics of speech between mothers and babies (Jasnow & Feldstein, 1986). Dyads typically engage in alternating vocalizations to a significantly greater degree than they do in simultaneous vocalizations. Others, too, including Stern (1977), have observed that patterns of mother–infant vocal exchange are structurally similar to patterns that typify adult conversation, although they differ in timing: The initiating vocalizations of mothers and babies are followed by suppression of vocalization, thereby opening the door for the partner to "join in."

K. Bloom (1988; K. Bloom, Russell, & Wassenberg, 1987) studied the effects of such turn taking in mother–infant conversation on subsequent infant vocalization. In one experiment, one group of 3-month-olds experienced conversational turn taking, and another experienced random responsiveness on the part of an adult. Infant vocalizations were then counted and categorized as either speechlike or nonspeechlike. When adults maintained a prototypic conversational give-and-take pattern, infants produced a relatively higher ratio of speechlike to nonspeechlike sounds. In a second experiment, adult responsiveness consisted of conversational turn taking or responsiveness using nonverbal vocalizations, smiling, and touching the infant's abdomen. Again, turn taking facilitated a speak–listen pattern of vocalizing by the infant, but this time, in the absence of a verbal component of the adult's response, turn taking did not facilitate infant production of speechlike sounds. These experiments together show that infants who participate in normal "conversation" vocalize more as if they are "really talking" and that what adults say to 3-month-olds influences what those infants are likely to reply in return.

Dynamic Sensitivity

Finally, parental speech adjustments are dynamically sensitive to infants' changing capacities. Generally, prosodic modifications diminish during infancy—observation shows reductions in infant-directed speech and increases in the use of adult conversational tones, even between 2 and 5 months after birth (Fig. 6.2)—and semantic and syntactic modifications constantly match toddlers' newly developing linguistic competencies (Bornstein & Tamis-LeMonda, 1990). In this way, parents create and maintain appropriate vocal environments for cognitively developing infants.

6. ORIGINS OF COMMUNICATION IN INFANCY

Indeed, parents are sensitive both to infant age and to infant competence. (Of course, the two are often confounded.) On the basis of the organization of several factors in a given mother's language, Bellinger

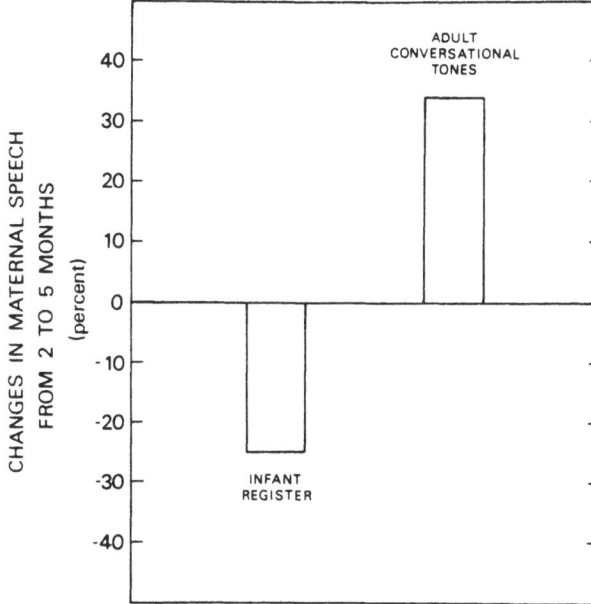

Fig. 6.2. Changes in mothers' use of infant-directed speech and adult-directed speech as their infants age from 2 to 5 months.

(1980) found it possible to predict the exact chronological age of her child, and McLaughlin, D. White, McDevitt, and Raskin (1983) found that the mean length of mothers' utterances systematically matches the mean length of their 1½- to 3½-year-olds' utterances.

In summary, the language system starts at a certain basal level of sophistication and consistently progresses to greater levels of accomplishment; its growth in turn signals the social environment to alter input to accord with its changing level. A corollary of this view is that a single kind of input may affect development differently at different times, perhaps because the changing system interprets and utilizes even constant input differently at different times. Thus, early in life the intonations of infant-directed maternal speech may maintain attention or modulate arousal, whereas at later points they may communicate affect, help to identify mother, or facilitate speech perception.

SPEAKING AND UNDERSTANDING SPEECH

The auditory stimuli that specify speech involve a complex interplay of frequencies and intensities of sound waves arrayed over time (G. A. Miller, 1981). On hearing a stimulus, the infant's tasks are to decode the complex vibratory pattern that the sound projects onto the auditory apparatus and to reconstruct it into a psychologically meaningful pattern. In speaking, the infant must determine what will go into the array and then articulate it. How do babies begin to accomplish these tasks? In this section of the chapter, I focus on first aspects of speech sound perception and production.

Speech Sound Perception

Broca (1824–1880) identified a region of forebrain in the left hemisphere specifically associated with the production of language, and Wernicke (1848–1905) identified a corresponding region toward the rear of the left hemisphere associated with the comprehension of language (Springer & Deutsch, 1985). Concomitantly, Witelson (1985) showed that the size of key anatomical structures in the auditory association area of the left hemisphere measure proportionately as great in the fetal, neonatal, and infant brain as in the adult brain. Further, D. L. Molfese and V. J. Molfese (1979, 1980, 1985, 1992) provided concordant electrophysiological evidence regarding hemispheric specialization for speech in newborn (and preterm) infants. They presented syllables, words, and mechanical sounds to infants and observed that the evoked response to speech stimuli was larger over the left temporal region than over the right, and that the evoked response to mechanical sounds was larger over the right temporal region than over the left. Provocatively, they also found that the disparity of hemispheric response in infancy predicted the children's level of language skill assessed on the McCarthy Scales at 3 years. There appear, therefore, to be at least some identifiable neurological bases for language acquisition in infants.

The auditory system is quite well developed before birth, and infants appear to possess innate perceptual propensities and capacities, however primitive, that aid language learning. Even in the womb, fetuses might process more than mere bits of sound and pieces of language (DeCasper & Fifer, 1980; Spence & DeCasper, 1984); newborns hear, orient to, and distinguish sounds (Aslin, Pisoni, & Jusczyk, 1983;

Schneider & Trehub, 1985), and babies seem especially primed to perceive and to appreciate sounds in the dynamic form and range of human speech (Trehub & Chang, 1977).

Consider, however, the seemingly impossible task of segmenting the speech stream, knowing where one word ends and the next begins, for example, *before* knowing any words or even what a word is. Imagine then having to do so for different speakers speaking in different contexts. As the following series of experiments illustrates, some infant competencies appear to have evolved to address these problems, namely segmenting sounds, matching sounds and sights, and recognizing particular speech.

It was once argued that, because sounds vary so much from one language to another, meaningful distinctions among sounds must be shaped by experience. Cross-language research now confirms that, although many sounds are possible, languages tend to use only relatively small numbers of distinct and meaningful sounds in their speech. Some Polynesian languages use as few as 15 such phonemes, for example, whereas some European and Asian languages use as many as 75; English uses about 40. Significantly, some phonemes may be distinguished universally, and they tend to be represented in the perceptual capacities of young babies. Specifically, infants perceive "categories" of some speech phononemes such as place of articulation or voice-onset time (Bornstein, 1979, 1987; Eimas, 1975). It appears that the sounds of speech are not experienced as a Jamesian "blooming, buzzing confusion" by the infant, but instead, even near the beginning of life, many sounds are naturally partitioned into smaller (and presumably more intelligible and more easily grasped) categories. These speech sounds are certainly not invested with meaning in infancy, even if they are quickly discriminated by babies as psychological units. Apparently, the auditory system is structured in a way that promotes the grouping together of select sounds, without the requirement of extensive linguistic experience (Bornstein, 1987). However, research has also shown that experience may induce speech sound categories quickly (Lasky, Syrdal-Lasky, & Klein, 1975; Streeter, 1976), and that experience is critical to maintaining these same perceptual discriminations (Werker, 1994).

The baby's knowledge of how speech sounds work in context is also much more advanced than was once believed. In adults, certain mouth movements (e.g., opening) are naturally correlated with certain sound characteristics (e.g., loudness) but not others (e.g., softness). Infants, too, appear to possess the ability to match particular sounds with face forms articulating those sounds (Kuhl & Meltzoff, 1982). Infants only 5 months of age who were presented with the choice of looking at either of two films, while a particular sound synchronous with one was presented at the midline, matched their looking patterns to corresponding sounds.

Infants also appear able to identify particular speakers on the basis of very little experience. DeCasper and Fifer (1980) tape recorded mothers reading Dr. Seuss' (1937) *And To Think That I Saw It On Mulberry Street;* then they made the infant's own mother's voice, or the voice of another mother, available to the newborn to hear if the baby sucked on a pacifier. Babies who participated were all less than 3 days of age at testing, and could only have been exposed postnatally to their own mothers' voices for 12 hours. These newborns not only discriminated their mothers' voices from those of female strangers, but they reportedly "worked" (i.e., sucked more) to produce their own mothers' voices in preference to the voice of the other females. These results suggest that prenatal, or only very brief postnatal, experience influences babies' auditory perceptions and performance. The question of which one was resolved in a follow-up study. Spence and DeCasper (1984) found that newborns prefer stories that their mothers had read to them *in utero* over stories that were new. That is, *prenatal* auditory experience could determine *postnatal* preference.

These several lines of research illustrate the ingenuity and energy of researchers and human infants alike in analyzing speech. The research tells us that, either natively or on the basis of very little experience, young babies partition the speech stream, coordinate correspondences between eye and ear, and recognize the source of speech. These capabilities and others yet to be discovered, no matter how advanced in and of themselves, certainly do not represent infants as fully sophisticated listeners. However, each capability provides infants with some advantage, ensuring that they begin the task of deciphering language from a less than naive starting point.

Speech Sound Production

Most investigators agree that all infants traverse stages in early verbal development—from a prelinguistic to a one-word to a multiphoneme stage—with transitions in between. Two early manifestations of infant

6. ORIGINS OF COMMUNICATION IN INFANCY

prelinguistic vocalizations are crying and babbling. Speech production is one of the most complex human action patterns (Lieberman, 1991), and the origins of regularity in early speech production constitute one of several convergences of biology and culture in language development.

The infant's cry is a very revealing kind of vocalization. On the basis of cry characteristics, it is possible to differentiate among a variety of developmental states (Lester & Boukydis, 1985). Few adults can deny or disregard a baby's cry; it compels us to respond, and the nearly universal response is to be nurturant in some way. In observations of home-based naturalistic interactions of mother–infant dyads in New York City, Paris, and Tokyo, my colleagues and I evaluated different categories of maternal responsiveness in relation to prominent categories of infant activity, including infants' distress vocalizations. Mothers in all three locales responded to infant distress vocalizing most often by being nurturant (Bornstein et al., 1992). Indeed, mothers even exhibit automatic autonomic responsiveness to their infants' hunger cries.

Although babies' cries inform parents about their state, babbling is a first significant sign of infants' nondistress communications. Babbling represents a deceptively simple development, but there is more to infants' babbling than first meets the ear. Perhaps babbling assumes heightened significance because it comprises infants' first structured vocalizations, sounds like fun, and fills the eerie void between silence or crying so common to early infancy on the one hand and the advent of the toddler's first intelligible words on the other.

Relations between the development of early babbling and first speech are obscure. Some have argued that the two are separate periods of vocal production, the earlier one random and ephemeral, and the later one fixed and structured (e.g., Jakobson, 1968). Others have pointed out, however, that both periods rest on the same innately programmed articulatory mechanisms, that the two are linked by virtue of the fact that they share the same fundamental speech sounds, and that babbling production continues to coexist with the child's first words (e.g., Boysson-Bardies & Vihman, 1991; J. L. Locke, 1983; Oller, 1980; Vihman & R. Miller, 1988). In babbling, there are frequent repetitions of the same syllable or syllable sound, and this practice makes perfect in the sounds, syllables, and sequences of syllables that eventually comprise the child's full-blown speech. Oller (1980) defined *canonical syllables* as the first units of child speech to exhibit the timing characteristics of adult consonant and vowel production. These typically appear at about 8 months in normal-hearing infants whichever the ambient language. Children usually also draw their early lexicon from the phonetic repertoire established in the course of babbling.

Sound production in newborns is constrained by the anatomy of the oral cavity and by respiratory patterns (Laver, 1980; Lester & Boukydis, 1992). The vocal tracts of adults and infants differ (Kent & Murray, 1982), and these differences have profound effects on articulation, imitation, and learning speech. Although babbling was once thought to encompass nearly all the basic sounds found in all languages, anatomical constraints may promote a particular developmental scheme for speech sound production. Such constraints on prespeech capacities might even foretell the composition of first words. Early babbling is thus rooted in anatomical biases and ease of motor control common to all children. Vihman (1991) studied infants' and toddlers' vocalizations in four language communities: Japanese, French, Swedish, and English. A very small number of syllables accounted for half of those produced in all of these groups, and the two highest-use syllables, the dental /da/ and bilabial /ba/, were used by all.

This observation may presage a charming and telling cultural consequence. The highest probability syllabic combinations in infant speech, based on a theory of consonant–vowel contrasts, tend to be those that connote important meanings very early in life. Cross-cultural linguistic research shows that, of four logically possible first sound combinations involving front and back consonant and vowel pairs, /pa/-like, /da/-like, and /ma/-like sounds, that is front-consonant back-vowel pairs, are used as parental kin terms in 57% of 1,072 languages studied, whereas only 25% would be expected by chance (Murdock, 1959). Could it be that parents have adopted as generic labels for themselves, sounds from their own infants' earliest, anatomically determined vocal repertoires?

Babbling may be the product of an amodal brain-based language capacity under maturational control. Petitto and Marentette (1991) observed manual babbling in deaf infants 10 to 16 months of age exposed to sign languages from birth. On the basis of a comparison with babbling in hearing infants, they concluded that experience with speech per se is not critical to the emergence of such babbling. Rather, similarities in manual and vocal babbling indicate that babbling is a more abstract and generalized communicative capacity.

Early vocal babbling appears, therefore, to emerge naturally and to be anatomically constrained, different kinds of linguistic experience also appear to influence the ontogeny of babbling. Every child uses two sources of perceptual information when beginning to speak: feedback from his or her own speech and from the speech of others. This is at base a constructivist point of view. Therefore, deaf infants' babbles can be expected to fall behind those of hearing infants (Gilbert, 1982; Oller, 1980; Stoel-Gammon, 1988; Stoel-Gammon & Otomo, 1986). Oller and Eilers (1988) recorded babbling longitudinally in normal hearing and handicapped deaf infants. Normal-hearing babies entered the canonical babbling stage between 6 and 10 months of age, whereas the range for deaf babies was 11 to 25 months. Hearing-impaired infants also produced fewer consonant types, showed a decrease in types over time, and they used a lower proportion of multisyllabic utterances, whereas normal-hearing babies showed a larger number of consonant types, increased in such types over time, and increased in proportion of multisyllabic utterances. Deaf infants almost never learn to speak normally. It would appear from these studies, therefore, that auditory input is necessary for the normal and timely development of the range of adultlike syllables.

In addition, some components of early babbling are positively influenced by local auditory input. Clearly, infants born into different language communities rapidly grow up to speak different languages. Boysson-Bardies, Sagart, and Durand (1984) recorded pure samples of babbling among 6-, 8-, and 10-month-old babies from Paris, Tunis or Algiers, and Hong Kong. (French, Arabic, and Cantonese differ from one another in voice quality, stress, and proportion of consonantal to vocalic sounds among other things.) The researchers then asked French monolingual adult judges—both experienced phoneticians and lay people—to identify which babbling samples came from French babies. The phoneticians could correctly identify the country of origin in 6-month-olds' "speech"; both the trained and lay groups correctly identified the patrimony of 8- and 10-month-olds. (Analysis of the speech samples revealed that intonation in pitch and intensity contours cued the adults' perceptions.) Because the language the infant hears is the only conceivable cause of such an effect, it is highly likely that speech in infants as young as 6 months of age has already been influenced by their language environment. In short, the environment swiftly and surely channels early speech development toward the adult target language, therefore, (reciprocally) very young infants must be extraordinarily sensitive to particular auditory experiences.

In the cross-cultural study of responsiveness referred to earlier, Japanese, French, and U.S. American mothers were observed to respond to their infants' nondistress vocalizations most often by imitating and thereby promoting speech (Bornstein et al., 1992); as we learned from K. Bloom's work, conversational turn taking promotes infant vocalization. Reciprocally, social deprivation appears to suppress infant vocalization. Infants reared in orphanages during the first 6 months of life (earlier in this century) typically produced fewer different types of vowels and consonants, and also were observed to vocalize vowels and consonants less frequently than did infants reared in normal intact families (Brodbeck & Irwin, 1946).

In summary, infants' earliest sensitivities to sound and their earliest vocal expressions give evidence of strong biological (anatomical and maturational) influences. Very soon, however, both perception and production of sound become subject to the linguistic environments provided by parent, home, and culture.

I now turn to consider a second system of early language development and the biological and cultural forces that help to transform infants' initial verbalizations and perceptions into meaning.

REFERENCE

How do children learn reference, and what factors help to account for differences in the origins and development in this critical sphere language acquisition? Theorists of different schools have offered opposing answers to this question. Not surprising, nativists have been there to champion straightforward physical and biological accounts. Suggesting that early reference relates to maturation and growth, the Emperor Constantine (280?–337) in the 4th century opined that infants could only form words when their teeth had erupted. Centuries later, Gesell (1945) and Lenneberg (1967) wrote that early verbal production and comprehension turn on growth and maturation of brain structures.

When mother points to a teddy lying on the couch and says to her young infant, "Your teddy is lying on the couch, Sweetie," the mother is simultaneously pointing to an object, location, texture, degree of attractiveness—to an infinite set of properties. The child needs to figure out what new words mean, to make word–concept associations. As philosophers have argued, this is an *inductive* task in which the available evidence by itself is virtually always too impoverished to eliminate all but the one correct hypothesis about what it is exactly to which a word form applies (Quine, 1960). Moreover, infants, who as a group suffer known and severe cognitive limitations, are the ones who must solve the problem.

Does new-word understanding depend on general hypothesis testing? An experiential account in answering this question would be impossibly time consuming, and could not be applied to all word learning anyway (Chomsky, 1965). It has been argued, rather, that infants possess capacities for "fast mapping" complex semantic properties (E. Clark, 1988; Markman, 1987, 1989; Waxman & Gelman, 1986). When the child is told, "Your...teddy...is...lying...on...the...couch," what is communicated minimally is that "teddy" (a) is a word unit, (b) refers to one object, (c) contrasts with "couch," and (d) is not an adjective or verb. That is, several so-called *constraints* or biases have been posited to help children rule out alternative hypotheses of word meaning, direct them to focus on more likely hypotheses and thereby facilitate the development of word–world relations, or encourage them in doing both. An example of such a constraint is the "whole-object" assumption (Markman & Hutchinson, 1984). Under this argument, it is thought that when an adult points to an object and labels it, the child first perceives the novel label as referring to a whole object, and not to its parts, substance, or other properties (although it could very well refer also to these other things). Another much studied constraint is "mutual exclusivity," the assumption that a given object has only one label (Markman, 1989; Merriman & Bowman, 1989). Suppose Sweetie already knows that a teddy is a teddy when mother points and says, "Your teddy is lying on the couch." The mutual exclusivity bias suggests to the child that "couch" cannot apply to teddy and therefore has to apply to something else in the vicinity of the teddy. In this way, Sweetie learns the new word "couch" incidentally through mutual exclusivity and, of course, that the word applies to another whole object, the couch.

Most words that the language-learning child hears are novel, but children are credited with a set of constraints or early biases that guide their hypotheses about the meanings of novel words. These constraints are conceived as natural, as default assumptions in language acquisition, in that the child possesses and automatically uses them in the absence of information to the contrary. In essence, such constraints provide the child with a head-start in problem solving what words in the language might mean.

TABLE 6.1

Representative Predictive Correlations from Habituation in Infancy

	AGE	r
Bayley Scale Score [a]	12 months	.46
Productive Vocabulary [b]	12 months	.52
Bates Language Comprehension [c]	13 months	.35
Belsky Play Competence [d]	13 months	.36
Representational Competence [e]	13 months	.57
Reynell Language Score [f]	24 months	.55
Wechsler Test Score [g]	48 months	.54

[a] Bayley Scales of Infant Development (Bayley, 1969).
[b] Maternal estimate (Bornstein & Ruddy, 1984).
[c] Maternal Language Interview (E. A. Bates, Bretherton, & L. Snyder, 1988).
[d] Manual for the Assessment of Performance, Competence, and Executive Capacity in Infant Play (Belsky & Most, 1981; Belsky, Hrncir, & Vondra, 1983).
[e] Latent variable of language comprehension (c) and play sophistication (d) (Tamis-LeMonda & Bornstein, 1989).
[f] Reynell Developmental Language Scales (Reynell, 1981).
[g] Wechsler Preschool and Primary Scale of Intelligence (Wechsler, 1963).

Of course, infants also bring active cognitions to the task of acquiring language. Habituation is the decrement in attention that infants show to a repeated or continuously available stimulus (Bornstein, 1985a). Habituation is construed as (at least in part) the analog in adults of encoding, construction, and comparison with some kind of internal representation

(Bornstein, 1985a, 1989). Table 6.1 displays representative data from several longitudinal studies conducted in my laboratory linking measures of habituation in the first 6 months of life with various language (and cognitive) outcome measures evaluated between 1 and 4 years of age in the same children. Efficiency of habituation in infancy predicts at 1 year: language production and comprehension, play sophistication (level of pretense), and representational competence (a latent variable constructed of unique overlapping variance in language comprehension and play sophistication); at 2 years verbal competence; and at 4 years: full-scale intelligence-test performance (which is highly verbal). These stability correlations have a mean of about .50.

When we stop to consider the tasks implied in reference—the isolation of a person, property, object, or event in the environment and the association of a particular sound thereto—it is difficult to accept the notion that biological maturation, natural biases, or even information-processing capacities, alone or combined, account for semantic development. Central nervous system function may be a necessary condition, but it does not seem to be sufficient: Experiences must play a significant role. The simplist model suggests that the development of naming might be determined (at least to some degree) by what naming children hear. In 1690, the English empiricist philosopher John Locke (1632–1704) wrote in *An Essay Concerning Human Understanding*: "to make [children] understand what the names of simple ideas or substances stand for, people ordinarily show them the thing whereof they would have them have the idea; and then repeat to them the name that stands for it" (Book III, Chapter IX, 9, p. 108).

Moreover, research shows that mothers' single-word utterances are just those that appear earliest in their children's vocabularies (R. S. Chapman, 1981; Nelson, 1973). I found that mothers' didactic engagements and labeling predict their 1-year-olds' language competencies (Bornstein, 1985b).

Of course, interpreting the direction of influence is always uncertain in concurrent correlation. It could be that maternal speech influences child speech, or that children who understand or use nouns earlier, for example, promote the use of nouns by their mothers. However, studies utilizing experimental designs, statistical techniques, and strategies for demonstrating specific links between select inputs and particular language acquisitions have increasingly bolstered the assertion that specific parental activities, or other aspects of the environment, have significant roles to play in the growth of specific infant verbal skills (Belsky, Goode, & Most, 1980; Bornstein, 1985b; Lucariello, 1987; S. L. Olson, J. E. Bates, & Bayles, 1986; Tamis-LeMonda & Bornstein, 1989; Wachs & Chan, 1986). For example, mothers' use of infant-directed speech at 2 months uniquely predicts the frequency of their infants' nondistress vocalizations at 5 months, over and above the infants' own vocal contribution from 2 to 5 months and the mothers' use of infant-directed speech at 5 months (Bornstein & Tamis-LeMonda, 1990). Labels have nearly a .5 probability of being the loudest word in the speech of mothers showing toys to their 1-year-olds, and relative loudness could easily help cue infants to map new words onto referent objects (Messer, 1981). Mothers' speech to infants also consistently positions key words at points of perceptual prominence in the speech stream, notably on exaggerated fundamental frequency peaks in utterance-final position, whereas in speech to adults the use of a prosodic emphasis is more variable (Fernald & Mazzie, 1991).

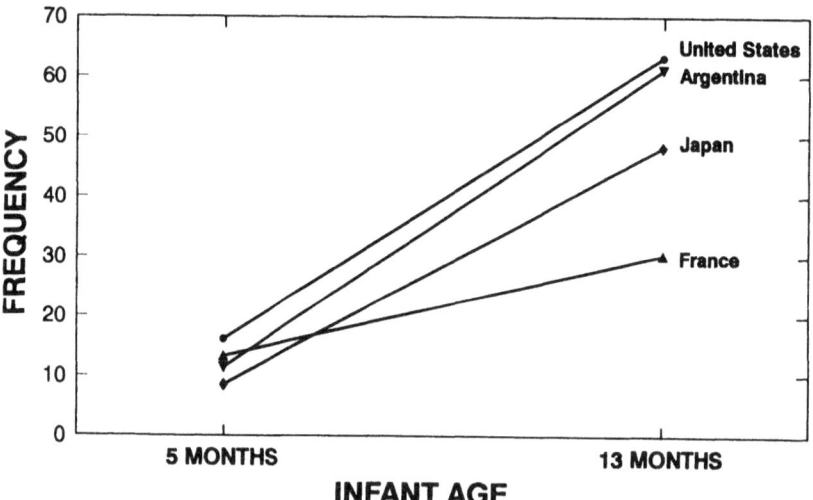

Fig. 6.3. Reference to the environment in maternal speech to infants of 5 and 13 months in Argentina, France, Japan, and the United States.

Mothers often and naturally refer to persons, objects, activities, or events in the environment verbally by describing, labeling, or asking about the qualities of the referent (e.g., "That's a spoon," or "What color is the truck?"). Baldwin and Markman (1989) showed infants from two age groups (10–14 and 17–20 months) pairs of unfamiliar toys in two situations: a pointing-alone condition and a labeling-and-pointing condition. During a play session later, infants looked longer at target toys that had been labeled than at those that had not. That is, language labeling increased infants' attention to objects beyond the time that the labeling itself actually occurred, and language per se maintained infant attention to objects over and above pointing. This form of referential language is also reputedly associated with vocabulary expansion during early development (R. S. Chapman, 1981; Furrow, Nelson, & Benedict, 1979; Goldfield, 1987; Newport, H. Gleitman & L. R. Gleitman, 1977).

Mothers are nearly universally prone to use such reference in speech to their babies.[2] As Fig. 6.3 shows, Argentine, French, Japanese, and U.S. American mothers alike tend to use more and more reference—about their infants, themselves, and the environment—as their infants grow from the prelingual age of 5 months to the beginning verbal age of 13 months (Bornstein et al., 1992). Over the second half of the first year of life (i.e., as infants begin to achieve verbal and other competencies), mothers appear to expect that their infants need and can process more information about themselves, about mother, and about surroundings. Thus, as infants achieve sophisticated levels of motor exploration and cognitive comprehension, their mothers increasingly orient and prepare them for the world outside the dyad. In this way, too, mothers and infants demonstrate that they are partners in communicating, coordinated with one another verbally and nonverbally with respect to topic.

Many parenting characteristics (quality of attachment, involvement, and control style) have been implicated in predicting early language competence in children (Bee et al., 1982; Belsky, Goode, & Most, 1980; Bornstein, 1985b; R. H. Bradley, Caldwell, & Elardo, 1979; Carew, 1980; Grolnick, Frodi, & Bridges, 1984; Matas, Arend, & Sroufe, 1978; S. L. Olson, Bayles, & J. E. Bates, 1986; Slade, 1987a, 1987b; Sorce & Emde, 1981; Tamis-LeMonda & Bornstein, 1989; Wachs & Gruen, 1982). For example, S. L. Olson, J. E. Bates, and Bayles (1984) found with 6-month-olds that mothers' affectionate touching, rocking, holding, and smiling significantly predicted a composite measure of cognitive–language competence in the same children at 2 years. In a series of prospective longitudinal studies, I analyzed influences of selected maternal activities on the growth of early produc-

---

[2]Although again not without exception; see Schieffelin (1986, 1990) on Kaluli mothers.

tive and receptive vocabulary as well as on later verbal intelligence (Bornstein, 1985b, 1989). For example, Tamis-LeMonda and I measured infant habituation at 5 months in relation to language comprehension (and play sophistication) at 13 months. We also assessed mothers' didactics at the two ages. We then used structural equation modeling to examine the unique contributions of infant habituation and maternal interaction to toddler language and cognitive abilities. Fig. 6.4 shows the relevant model; three sets of results in it are noteworthy.

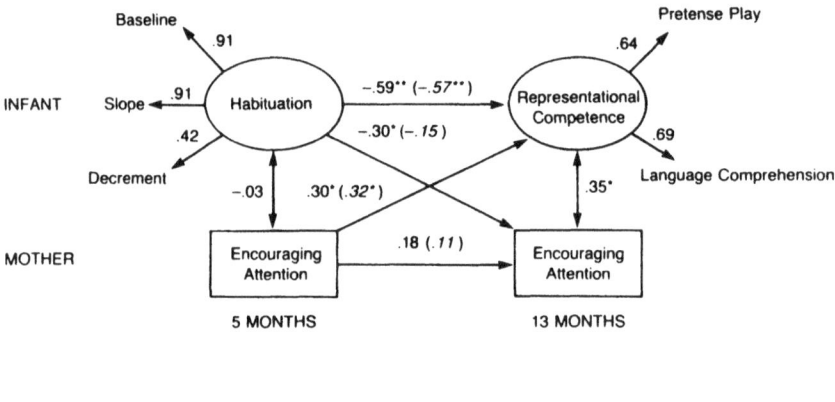

Goodness-of-Fit Index = .90 (adjusted .72)
χ^2 (10) = 13.33, p = .21

*p < .05
**p < .01

Fig. 6.4. Infant habituation and maternal encouragement of attention at 5 months in relation to maternal encouragement of attention and toddler representational competence at 13 months.

First, a latent variable of habituation at 5 months (constructed of the three indicator variables: baseline, slope, and decrement) significantly predicted language comprehension, play sophistication, and (as shown) the latent variable of representational competence (constructed of the two indicator variables: language comprehension and play sophistication) at 13 months. Note that habituation predicted thus *after* the influences of both 5- and 13-month maternal encouraging attention were partialled (indicated by the italicized correlation). This finding, controlled for the role of experience, reveals a direct tie between early infant information-processing skills and later language (and cognitive) performance.

The second result is that maternal didactics at 5 months (encouraging attention, labeling, etc.) independently predicted the same longitudinal outcome. Importantly, we have determined that these same maternal didactic activities possess predictive relevance for developing language competence in a non-Western culture (Bornstein, Miyake, Azuma, Tamis-LeMonda, & Toda, 1990). Japanese mothers, who more often encourage their 5-month-olds didactically, have children who score higher on the Japanese version of the Peabody Picture Vocabulary Test when they reach 2½ years of age.

As a final result, babies tend to influence their mothers' didactic activities over time. This finding reflects a second class of "infant effects" in communicative development: Beyond stability of infant contribution (one class of "infant effect"), the infant can influence his or her own development *indirectly* by influencing parents or other caregivers. In a later embellishment of this design with older infants, we evaluated maternal didactic and social interactions in the home in relation to toddler language skills at 13 months. The influence of maternal didactic activities related conditionally to maternal social activities and to the role of the child in the interaction (Vibbert & Bornstein, 1989). In predictions of children's noun comprehension, for example, when mothers exerted a high degree of control over didactic exchanges (i.e., when mothers initiated and maintained object-centered interactions more than did their toddlers), the children showed virtually linear gains in language skill to the degree that their mothers also engaged in social activities. However, when toddlers had more control of didactic exchange (i.e., when toddlers initiated and maintained object-centered interactions more than their mothers), maternal social input was unassociated with language growth.

Beyond interaction, components of the child's physical environment are acknowledged to influence communicative development directly. Wachs and Chan (1986) observed that parents who provide their child with new toys and changes in room decorations are also more likely to name objects for the child. However, the physical parameters of the environment also exert an influence on child language acquisition in and of themselves, and not simply as a function of parental naming.

Clearly, neither nativist nor empiricist accounts alone tell a complete story about early referential development. Together, each has something to say. Behavior genetic designs confirm biological and experimental contributions to the growth of communicative competencies of infants. The Colorado Adoption Project, for example, studying rates of early communicative development, unearthed significant associations between adoptees and their biological parents as well as adoptees and their adoptive parents (Hardy-Brown, 1983; Hardy-Brown & Plomin, 1985; Hardy-Brown, Plomin, & DeFries, 1981; Plomin & DeFries, 1985; see, too, Ho, 1987; R. J. Rose et al., 1980; Scarr & Weinberg, 1983). Genetic influences are manifest by individual differences in infant communicative performance, and the effects of shared experience between adoptees and their adoptive parents are evident in the effects of imitation of infant vocalization and in contingent vocal responsiveness to infant vocalization.

Once the child attains one-word speech, word learning proceeds rapidly. If lexical size estimates are at all accurate, the average 3-year-old possesses a vocabulary of 3,000 words. Therefore, between approximately 12 and 36 months, children acquire 4 new words per day on the average. In so doing, children demonstrate perceptual attentiveness, exploratory venturesomeness, and mental absorptiveness, even as they and their experiences vary so enormously.

CONCLUSIONS

Infancy translates literally to mean "incapable of speech," yet infancy is, paradoxically, the point of departure for understanding cultural and biological forces bound up in early language development. Infancy is also a time of great achievements in language learning. Because the adult endpoint of language acquisition is so complex and variable, as Peter Brueghel's 1563 depiction of the *Tower of Babel* reminds us, many have argued that specific sounds, semantics, and syntax, indeed the act of communicating, must all be learned. On the same grounds, however, others have argued that the intricate and multifaceted edifice of language could not but be constructed on inborn propensities and abilities.

The question of child natural language development has been asked with surprising frequency in history, and by a surprising group of individuals from Pharaohs to phoneticians. James I of England (1566–1625) is reputed to have posed the question and a way to address it. Long interested in the Bible—his is the "King James" version—James sought to identify the original language of Adam and Eve, and to do so, he conceived of a unique experiment. He proposed to place two infants on an otherwise uninhabited island in the care of a deaf–mute nurse. James thought to observe *if* the two would spontaneously develop speech and *what* characteristics their natural language would have.

(Although this study probably was within his power, King James seems never to have conducted it.) Some would predict that linguistic structures develop spontaneously, others that they could only reflect worldly experience—the heart of the debate between "the impossible and the miraculous."

In this chapter on origins of communication in infancy, I have only scratched the surface topography in a very rich field, and have only addressed sound and semantics, skirting syntax, pragmatics, and other topics entirely; clearly, there exist many treasures still to be unearthed. On the one hand, in the space of about 2 years, infants master at least the rudiments of language without explicit instruction and without noticeable effort. Children everywhere seem to get on the same road to achieve basic linguistic proficiency, and they travel at more or less the same rate down that road, largely (although not wholly) independent of their general intelligence, the language community in which they are reared, and the amount of tuition they receive. On the other hand, all manifestations of the language system seem to be constructed or transformed by specific experiences: Toddlers learn only the particular language (and even the idiosyncratic dialect) to which they are exposed, and individual experiences are regularly associated with individual differences in language competencies. Thus, language acquisition appears to be both rigid and flexible; it assures desired outcomes even in the face of environmental instability, while at the same time encouraging flexibility in response to environmental diversity.

The child brings neurological networks, perceptual prerequisites, and cognitive competencies to language learning, as well as experience with meaning, maybe intent, and the dialogic nature of protolinguistic social interactions. Young babies signal adults in many special ways, from crying and babbling to gesturing, smiling, and looking, that together promote the purpose of communicating. In addition, language growth is fostered in a medium of fine-tuned accommodation that coexists between caregiver and child; most adults go out of their way to help even not knowing it. These features characterize the all-important transaction that serves the origins of communication. Despite seeming barriers to normal everyday interchanges that nature has erected between caregivers and their newborns, together parent and child actively strive impressively, and regularly succeed, in fostering communicative competence in children.

ACKNOWLEDGMENTS

This chapter summarizes selected aspects of my research, and portions of the text have appeared in previous scientific publications cited in the references.

REFERENCES

Aslin, R. N., Pisoni, D. B., & Jusczyk, P. W. (1983). Auditory development and speech perception in infancy. In M. M. Haith & J. J. Campos (Eds.), *Infancy and the biology of development* (pp. 573–687). Also in P. Mussen (Gen. Ed.), *Handbook of child psychology, Vol. 2.* New York: Wiley.

Baldwin, D. A., & Markman, E. M. (1989). Establishing word-object relations: A first step. *Child Development, 60,* 381–398.

Bates, E. A., Bretherton, I., & Snyder, L. (1988). *From first words to grammar.* New York: Cambridge University Press.

Bayley, N. (1969). *Bayley scales of infant development.* New York: The Psychological Corp.

Bee, H. L., Barnard, K. E., Eyres, S. J., Gray, C. A., Hammond, M. A., Spietz, A. L., Snyder, C., & Clark, B. (1982). Prediction of IQ and language skill from perinatal status, child performance, family characteristics, and mother–infant interaction. *Child Development, 53,* 1134–1156..

Bellinger, D. (1980). Consistency in the pattern of change in mother's speech: Some discriminant analyses. *Journal of Child Language, 7,* 469–487.

Belsky, J., Goode, M. K., & Most, R. K. (1980). Maternal stimulation and infant exploratory competence: Cross-sectional, correlational, and experimental analyses. *Child Development, 51,* 1163–1178.

Belsky, J., Hrncir, E., & Vondra, J. (1983). *Manual for the assessment of performance, competence, and executive capacity in infant play.* Unpublished manuscript, The Pennsylvania State University, University Press.

Belsky, J., & Most, R. K. (1981). From exploration to play: A cross-sectional study of infant free play behavior. *Developmental Psychology, 17,* 630–639.

Bickerton, D. (1990). *Language and species.* Chicago: University of Chicago Press.

Bloom, K. (1988). Quality of adult vocalizations affects the quality of infant vocalizations. *Journal of Child Language, 15,* 469–480.

Bloom, K., Russell, A., & Wassenberg, K. (1987). Turn taking affects the quality of infant vocalizations. *Journal of Child Language, 14,* 211–227.

Bornstein, M. H. (1979). Perceptual development: Stability and change in feature perception. In M. H. Bornstein & W. Kessen (Eds.), *Psychological development from infancy: Image to intention* (pp. 37–81). Hillsdale, NJ: Lawrence Erlbaum Associates.

Bornstein, M. H. (1985a). Habituation of attention as a measure of visual information processing in human infants: Summary, systematization, and synthesis. In G. Gottlieb & N. A. Krasnegor (Eds.), *Measurement of audition and vision in the first year of postnatal life: A methodological overview* (pp. 253–300). Norwood, NJ: Ablex.

Bornstein, M. H. (1985b). How infant and mother jointly contribute to developing cognitive competence in the child. *Proceedings of the National Academy of Sciences U.S.A., 82,* 7470–7473.

Bornstein, M. H. (1987). Perceptual categories in vision and audition. In S. Harnad (Ed.), *Categorical perception* (pp. 287–300). New York: Cambridge University Press.

Bornstein, M. H. (1989). Stability in early mental development: From attention and information processing in infancy to language and cognition in childhood. In M. H. Bornstein & N. A. Krasnegor (Eds.), *Stability and continuity in mental development: Behavioral and biological perspectives* (pp. 147–170). Hillsdale, NJ: Lawrence Erlbaum Associates.

Bornstein, M. H., & Lamb, M. E. (1992). *Development in infancy.* New York: McGraw-Hill.

Bornstein, M. H., Miyake, K., Azuma, H., Tamis-LeMonda, C. S., & Toda, S. (1990). Responsiveness in Japanese mothers: Consequences and characteristics. *Annual Report of the Research and Clinical Center for Child Development,* University of Hokkaido, Sapporo, Japan.

Bornstein, M. H., & Ruddy, M. (1984). Infant attention and maternal stimulation: Prediction of cognitive and linguistic development in singletons and twins. In H. Bouma & D. Bouwhuis (Eds.), *Attention and performance X* (pp. 433–445). Hillsdale: NJ: Lawrence Erlbaum Associates.

Bornstein, M. H., & Tamis-LeMonda, C. S. (1990). Activities and interactions of mothers and their firstborn infants in the first six months of life: Covariation, stability, continuity, correspondence, and prediction. *Child Development, 61,* 1206–1217.

Bornstein, M. H., Tamis-LeMonda, C. S., Tal, J., Ludemann, P., Toda, S., Rahn, C. W., Pêcheux, M. G., Azumi, H., & Vardi, D. (1992). Maternal responsiveness to infants in three societies: The United States, France, and Japan. *Child Development, 63,* 808–821.

Bradley, R. H., Caldwell, B. M., & Elardo, R. (1979). Home environment and cognitive development in the first 2 years: A crosslagged panel analysis. *Developmental Psychology, 15,* 246–250.

Bretherton, I., McNew, S., Snyder, L., & Bates, E. A. (1983). Individual differences at 20 months: Analytic and holistic strategies in language acquisition. *Journal of Child Language, 10,* 293–320.

Brodbeck, A. J., & Irwin, D. L. (1946). The speech behavior of infants without families. *Child Development, 17,* 145–156.

Brown, R. (1973). *A first language: The early stages.* London: George Allen.

Carew, J. V. (1980). Experience and the development of intelligence in young children at home and in day care. *Monographs of the Society for Research in Child Development, 45* (67, Serial No. 187).

Chapman, R. S. (1981). Mother–child interaction in the second year of life: Its role in language development. In R. Schiefelbusch & D. Bricker (Eds.), *Early language: acquisition and intervention* (pp. 201–250). Baltimore, MD: University Park Press.

Chomsky, N. (1965). *Aspects of the theory of syntax.* Cambridge, MA: MIT Press.

Clark, E. (1988). On the logic of contrast. *Journal of Child Language, 15,* 317–335.

Darwin, C. R. (1877). A biographical sketch of an infant. *Mind, 2,* 286–294.

de Boysson-Bardies, B., Sagart, L., & Durand, C. (1984). Discernible differences in the babbling of infants according to target language. *Journal of Child Language, 11,* 1–15.

de Boysson-Bardies, B., & Vihman, M. M. (1991). Adaptation to language: Evidence from babbling and first words in four languages. *Language, 67,* 297–319.

DeCasper, A. J., & Fifer, W. P. (1980). Of human bonding: Newborns prefer their mothers' voices. *Science, 208,* 1174–1176.

Eimas, P. D. (1975). Speech perception in early infancy. In L. B. Cohen & P. Salapatek (Eds.), *Infant perception: From sensation to cognition (Vol. 2,* pp. 193–231). New York: Academic Press.

Erting, C. J., Prezioso, C., & Hynes, M. O. (1990). The interactional context of deaf mother- infant communication. In V. Volterra & C. Erting (Eds.), *From gesture to language in hearing and deaf children* (pp. 97–106). Berlin: Springer.

Fernald, A. (1985). Four-month-old infants prefer to listen to motherese. *Infant Behavior and Development, 8,* 181–182.

Fernald, A., & Kuhl, P. K. (1987). Acoustic determinants of infant preference for motherese speech. *Infant Behavior and Development, 10,* 279–293.

Fernald, A., & Mazzie, C. (1991). Prosody and focus in speech to infants and adults. *Developmental Psychology, 17,* 209–221.

Fernald, A., Taeschner, T., Dunn, J., Papoušek, M., Boysson-Bardies, B., & Fukui, I. (1989). A cross-language study of prosodic modifications in mothers' and fathers' speech to preverbal infants. *Journal of Child Language, 16,* 477–501.

Furrow, D., Nelson, K. E., & Benedict, H. (1979). Mothers' speech to children and syntactic development: Some simple relationships. *Journal of Child Language, 6,* 423–442.

Gesell, A. (1945). *The embryology of behavior.* New York: Harper & Row.

Gilbert, J. H. V. (1982). Babbling and deaf children: A commentary on Lenneberg et al. (1965) and Lenneberg (1967). *Journal of Child Language, 9,* 511–515.

Glenn, S. M., & Cunningham, C. C. (1983). What do babies listen to most? A developmental study of auditory preferences in non-handicapped infants and infants with Down's syndrome. *Developmental Psychology, 19,* 332–337.

Goldfield, B. A. (1987). The contributions of child and caregiver to referential and expressive language. *Applied Psycholinguistics, 8,* 267–280.

Goldfield, B. A., & Snow, C. E. (1989). Individual differences in language acquisition. In J. B. Gleason (Ed.), *The development of language* (pp. 303–325). Columbus, OH: Merrill.

Grolnick, W., Frodi, A., & Bridges, L. (1984). Maternal control style and the mastery motivation of one-year-olds. *Infant Mental Health Journal, 5,* 72–82.

Hardy-Brown, K. (1983). Universals in individual differences: Disentangling two approaches to the study of language acquisition. *Developmental Psychology, 19,* 610–624.

Hardy-Brown, K., & Plomin, R. (1985). Infant communicative development: Evidence from adoptive and biological families for genetic and environmental influences on rate differences. *Developmental Psychology, 21,* 378–385.

Hardy-Brown, K., Plomin, R., & DeFries, J. C. (1981). Genetic and environmental influences on rate of communicative development in the first year of life. *Developmental Psychology, 17,* 704–717.

Hirsh-Pasek, K., Nelson, K. E., Jusczyk, P. W., Cassidy, K. W., Druss, B., & Kennedy, L. (1987). Clauses are perceptual units for young infants. *Cognition, 26,* 269–286.

Ho, H. Z. (1987). Interaction of early caregiving environment and infant developmental state in predicting subsequent cognitive performance. *British Journal of Developmental Psychology, 5,* 183–191.

Jakobson, R. (1968). *Child language, aphasia and phonological universals.* New York: Humanities Press.

Jasnow, M., & Feldstein, S. (1986). Adult-like temporal characteristics of mother-infant vocal interactions. *Child Development, 57,* 754–761.

Karzon, R. G. (1985). Discrimination of polysyllabic sequences by one- to four-month-old infants. *Journal of Experimental Child Psychology, 39,* 326–342.

Kaye, K. (1982). *The mental and social life of babies.* Brighton, UK: Harvester Press.

Kent, R. D., & Murray, A. D. (1982). Acoustic features of infant vocalic utterances at 3, 6, and 9 months. *Journal of the Acoustical Society of America, 72,* 353–365.

Kuhl, P. K., & Meltzoff, A. N. (1982). The bimodal perception of speech in infancy. *Science, 218,* 1138–1140.

Lasky, R. E., Syrdal-Lasky, A., & Klein, R. E. (1975). VOT discrimination by four to six and a half month old infants from Spanish environments. *Journal of Experimental Child Psychology, 20,* 215–225.

Laver, J. (1980). *The phonetic description of voice quality.* Cambridge, UK: Cambridge University Press.

Lenneberg, E. H. (1967). *The biological foundations of language.* New York: Wiley.

Lester, B. M., & Boukydis, C. F. Z. (Eds.) (1985). *Infant crying: Theoretical research perspectives.* New York: Plenum.

Lester, B. M., & Boukydis, C. F. Z. (1992). No language but a cry. In H. Papoušek, U. Jürgens, & M. Papoušek (Eds.), *Nonverbal vocal communication: Comparative and developmental approaches* (pp. 145–173). Cambridge, UK: Cambridge University Press.

Lieberman, P. (1991). *Uniquely human: The evolution of speech, thought, and selfless behavior.* Cambridge: Harvard University Press.

Locke, J. (1690/1959). *An essay concerning human understanding.* New York: Dover.

Locke, J. L. (1983). *Phonological acquisition and change.* New York: Academic Press.

Lucariello, J. (1987). Spinning fantasy: Theme, structure and knowledge base. *Child Development, 58,* 434–442.

Markman, E. M. (1987). How children constrain possible meanings of words. In U. Neisser (Ed.), *Ecological and intellectual factors in categorization* (pp. 255–287). Cambridge, MA: Cambridge University Press.

Markman, E. M. (1989). *Categorization in children: Problems of induction.* Cambridge, MA: MIT Press, Bradford Books.

Markman, E. M., & Hutchinson, J. E. (1984). Children's sensitivity to constraints on word meaning: Taxonomic vs. thematic relations. *Cognitive Psychology, 16,* 1–27.

Matas, L., Arend, R., & Sroufe, L. A. (1978). Continuity of adaptation in the second year: The relationship between quality of attachment and later competence. *Child Development, 49,* 547–556.

McLaughlin, B., White, D., McDevitt, T., & Raskin, R. (1983). Mothers' and fathers' speech to their young children: Similar or different? *Journal of Child Language, 10,* 245–252.

Merriman, W. E., & Bowman, L. L. (1989). The mutual exclusivity bias in children's word learning. *Monographs for the Society for Research in Child Development, 54,* Serial No. 220.

Messer, D. J. (1981). The identification of names in maternal speech to infants. *Journal of Psycholinguistic Research, 10,* 69–77.

Miller, G. A. (1981). *Language and speech.* New York: Freeman.

Miller, J. F., & Chapman, R. S. (1981). The relation between age and mean length of utterance in morphemes. *Journal of Speech and Hearing Research, 24,* 154–161.

Molfese, D. L. (1992). The use of auditory evoked responses recorded from newborn infants to predict language skills. In M. Tramontana & S. Hooper (Eds.), *Advances in child neuropsychology* (pp. 1–23). New York: Springer.

Molfese, D. L., & Molfese, V. J. (1979). Hemisphere and stimulus differences as reflected in cortical responses of newborn infants to speech stimuli. *Developmental Psychology, 15,* 505–511.

Molfese, D. L., & Molfese, V. J. (1980). Cortical responses of preterm infants to phonetic and nonphonetic speech stimuli. *Developmental Psychology, 16,* 574–581.

Molfese, D. L., & Molfese, V. J. (1985). Electrophysiological indices of auditory discrimination in newborn infants: The bases for predicting later language development. *Infant Behavior and Development, 8,* 197–211.

Morgan, J. L. (1986). *From simple input to complex grammar.* Cambridge, MA: MIT Press.

Murdock, G. P. (1959). Cross-language parallels in parental kin terms. *Anthropological Linguistics, 1,* 1–5.

Nelson, K. E. (1973). Some evidence for the cognitive primacy of categorization and its functional basis. *Merrill-Palmer Quarterly, 19,* 21–39.

Newport, E. L., Gleitman, H., & Gleitman, L. R. (1977). Mother, I'd rather do it myself: Some effects and non-effects of maternal speech style. In C. E. Snow & C. A. Ferguson (Eds.), *Talking to children: Language input and acquisition* (pp. 109–149). Cambridge, England: Cambridge University Press.

Oller, D. K. (1980). The emergence of sounds of speech in infancy. In G. Yeni-Komshian, J. F. Kavanaugh, & C. A. Ferguson (Eds.), *Child phonology* (Vol. 1, pp. 93–112). New York: Academic Press.

Oller, D. K., & Eilers, R. E. (1988). The role of audition in infant babbling. *Child Development, 59,* 441–449.

Olson, S. L., Bates, J. E., & Bayles, K. (1984). Mother-infant interaction and the development of individual differences in children's cognitive competence. *Developmental Psychology, 20,* 166–179.

Olson, S. L., Bayles, K., & Bates, J. E. (1986). Mother-child interaction and children's speech progress: A longitudinal study of the first two years. *Merrill-Palmer Quarterly, 32,* 1–20.

Papoušek, M., Bornstein, M. H., Nuzzo, C., Papoušek, H., & Symmes, D. (1990). Infant responses to prototypical melodic contours in parental speech. *Infant Behavior and Development, 13,* 539–545.

Papoušek, H., & Papoušek, M. (1991). Innate and cultural guidance of infants' integrative competencies: China, the United States, and Germany. In M. H. Bornstein (Ed.), *Cultural approaches to parenting* (pp. 23–44). Hillsdale, NJ: Lawrence Erlbaum Associates.

Peters, A. M. (1983). *The units of language acquisition.* Cambridge, UK: Cambridge University Press.

Petitto, L. A., & Marentette, P. F. (1991). Babbling in the manual mode: Evidence for the ontogeny of language. *Science, 251,* 1493–1496.

Plomin, R., & DeFries, J. C. (1985). *The origins of individual differences in infancy: The Colorado adoption project.* New York: Academic Press.

Quine, W.V.O. (1960). *Word and object.* Cambridge, MA: MIT Press.

Ratner, N. B., & Pye, C. (1984). Higher pitch in BT is not universal: Acoustic evidence from Quiche Mayan. *Journal of Child Language, 11,* 512–522.

Reynell, J. (1981). *Reynell developmental language scales* (revised). Windsor, UK: NFER-NELSON.

Rose, R. J., Boughman, J. A., Corey, L. A., Nance, W. E., Christian, J. C., & Kang, K. W. (1980). Data from kinships of monozygotic twins indicate maternal effects on verbal intelligence. *Nature, 283,* 375–377.

Scarborough, H., Wyckoff, J., & Davidson, R. (1986). A reconsideration of the relation between age and mean utterance length. *Journal of Speech and Hearing Research, 29,* 394–399.

Scarr, S., & Weinberg, F. A. (1983). The Minnesota adoption studies: Genetic differences and malleability. *Child Development, 54,* 260–268.

Schieffelin, B. B. (1986). *The acquisition of Kaluli.* Hillsdale, NJ: Lawrence Erlbaum Associates.

Schieffelin, B. B. (1990). *The give and take of everyday life: Language socialization of Kaluli children.* Cambridge, UK: Cambridge University Press.

Schneider, B., & Trehub, S. E. (1985). Infant auditory psychophysics: An overview. In G. Gottlieb & N. A. Krasnegor (Eds.), *Measurement of audition and vision in the first year of postnatal life* (pp. 113–126). Norwood, NJ: Ablex.

Seuss, D. (1937). *And to think that I saw it on Mulberry Street.* New York: Vanguard Press.

Skinner, B. F. (1957). *Verbal behavior.* New York: Appleton.
Slade, A. (1987a). A longitudinal study of maternal involvement and symbolic play during the toddler period. *Child Development, 58,* 367–375.
Slade, A. (1987b). Quality of attachment and early symbolic play. *Developmental Psychology, 23,* 78–85.
Sorce, J., & Emde, R. N. (1981). Mother's presence is not enough: The effect of emotional availability on infant exploration. *Developmental Psychology, 17,* 737–745.
Spence, A. J., & De Casper, A. J. (1984). *Human fetuses perceive maternal speech.* Paper presented to the International Conference on Infant Studies, New York, April 5–8.
Springer, S. P., & Deutsch, G. (1985). *Left brain, right brain.* San Francisco, CA: Freeman.
Stern, D. N. (1977). *The first relationship: Infant and mother.* London: Fontana.
Stoel-Gammon, C. (1988). Prelinguistic vocalizations of hearing-impaired and normally hearing subjects: A comparison of consonantal inventories. *Journal of Speech and Hearing Disorders, 53,* 302–315.
Stoel-Gammon, C., & Otomo, K. (1986). Babbling development of hearing-impaired and normally hearing subjects. *Journal of Speech and Hearing Disorders, 51,* 33–41.
Streeter, L. A. (1976). Language perception of 2-month-old infants shows effects of both innate mechanisms and experience. *Nature, 259,* 39–41.
Tamis-LeMonda, C. S., & Bornstein, M. H. (1989). Habituation and maternal encouragement of attention in infancy as predictors of toddler language, play, and representational competence. *Child Development, 60,* 738–751.
Tamis-LeMonda, C. S., & Bornstein, M. H. (1990). Language, play, and attention at one year. *Infant Behavior and Development, 13,* 85–98.
Tamis-LeMonda, C. S., & Bornstein, M. H. (1991). Individual variation, correspondence, stability, and change in mother and toddler play. *Infant Behavior and Development, 14,* 143–162.
Thal, D., & Bates, E. A. (1990). Continuity and variation in early language development. In J. Colombo & J. Fagen (Eds.), *Individual differences in infancy: Reliability, stability, prediction* (pp. 359–383). Hillsdale, NJ: Lawrence Erlbaum Associates.
Trehub, S. E., & Chang, H. (1977). Speech as reinforcing stimulation for infants. *Developmental Psychology, 13,* 121–124.
Vibbert, M., & Bornstein, M. H. (1989). Specific associations between domains of mother-child interaction and toddler referential language and pretense play. *Infant Behavior and Development, 12,* 163–184.

Vihman, M. M. (1991). Early syllables and the construction of phonology. In C. A. Ferguson, L. Menn, & C. Stoel-Gammon (Eds.), *Phonological development: Models, research, implications* (pp. 393–422). Hillsdale, NJ: Lawrence Erlbaum Associates.

Vihman, M. M., & Miller, R. (1988). Words and babble at the threshold of language acquisition. In M. D. Smith & J. L. Locke (Eds.), *The emergent lexicon* (pp. 151–183). New York: Academic Press.

Wachs, T. D., & Chan, A. (1986). Specificity of environmental action, as seen in environmental correlates of infants' communication performance. *Child Development, 57,* 1464–1474.

Wachs, T. D., & Gruen, G. E. (1982). *Early experience and human development.* New York: Plenum.

Waxman, S. R., & Gelman, R. (1986). Preschoolers' use of superordinate relations in classification and language. *Cognitive Development, 1,* 139–156.

Wechsler, D. (1963). *Wechsler preschool and primary scale of intelligence.* New York: The Psychological Corporation.

Werker, J. F. (1994). Cross-language speech perception: Developmental change does not involve loss. In J. Goodman & H. Nusbaum (Eds.), *The development of speech perception: The transition from speech sounds to spoken words* (pp. 93–120). Cambridge, MA: MIT Press.

Witelson, S. F. (1985). On hemisphere specialization and cerebral plasticity from birth: Mark II. In C. T. Best (Ed.), *Hemisphere function and collaboration in the child* (pp. 33–85). New York: Academic Press.

CHAPTER

7

THE TEMPORAL ORGANIZATION OF LANGUAGE: DEVELOPMENTAL AND NEUROPSYCHOLOGICAL ASPECTS

Angela D. Friederici

Max-Planck-Institute of Cognitive Neuroscience, Leipzig

The language faculty, no doubt, is the very faculty that characterizes the human species. The evolution of this faculty has been described as a coevolutionary process of neurological adaptations and changes in language use (Deacon, 1992). We do not know what these changes in language use during the early phylogenesis of the language faculty may have been. What appears, however, to be a central characteristic of *language use* is the fact that spoken language is produced and perceived as a *sequence in time*.

One of the critical features of language use, then, is its dependency on time. The use of the different linguistic units (phonemes, syllables, words, and phrases) must follow a strict temporal organization in normal speech production (Levelt et al., 1991; Schriefers, Meyer, & Levelt, 1990) and also in auditory language comprehension (Friederici, 1985; Marslen-Wilson & Tyler, 1980). If the temporal structure of language is critical for adult language use, then it may also be crucial in the ontogenesis of language use as well. Only a few studies, however, have investigated this issue developmentally, but the available studies suggest that this may indeed be the case (Friederici, 1983b; but see Tyler, 1984; Tyler & Marslen-Wilson, 1981). Moreover, assuming that the actual sequencing and temporal organization of different linguistic units is in the core of the overt language faculty, it is likely that this temporal aspect has found its reflection in a particular neural system subserving it.

In this chapter I try to specify these claims, presenting evidence for the hypothesis that (a) syntactic processes are fast, automatic and informationally encapsulated in the adult language user, that (b) these processes only gradually gain their modular status during development, and that (c) these highly time-dependent language processes are subserved by a distinct neural system, possibly the anterior parts of the left hemisphere.

THE TEMPORAL STRUCTURE OF LEXICAL ACCESS IN THE ADULT LISTENER

The ability to process language in comprehension and production is ultimately tied to a successful lexical access which at a phrase level includes access, to content words as well as to function words. The access to content words, its temporal structure, and the influence of preceding context have been the subject of numerous studies (for reviews see Seidenberg & Tanenhaus, 1986; Simpson, 1984; Tanenhaus & Lucas, 1987; Tyler & K. H. Frauenfelder, 1987). Access to those elements that carry structural information, such as function words and bound grammatical morphemes, has been investigated in only a few studies (Friederici, 1985; Swinney, Zurif, & Cutler, 1980). These elements, however, are critical when it comes to producing or comprehending an utterance beyond the scope of single words.

Function words and bound morphemes are the structural building blocks for any phrase, because they mark the phrase boundaries and other syntactic relationships. In contrast to content words, which make up a large *open class*, functional elements are restricted in number and thus are a *closed class*. Functional elements also differ from content words in that they are of a high frequency of occurrence. All this may effectuate that these elements, in particular, are processed in a fast and automatic way. Fast access to these elements and the structural infor-

7. TEMPORAL ORGANIZATION OF LANGUAGE

mation they carry may, in turn, allow early structuring of the language input. The hypothesis was proposed that language parsing is supported by a special access device whose particular function is to guarantee fast access to those elements that mainly carry structural information, that is, the closed-class elements (D. C. Bradley, Garrett, & Zurif, 1980).

A number of experiments were conducted in different laboratories to provide evidence for this interesting claim. However, most researchers were not very successful in establishing the predicted processing difference between the open and closed classes in lexical decision experiments (e.g., Gordon & Caramazza, 1983; Segui, Mehler, U. Frauenfelder, & Morton, 1982). One of the reasons for this may have been the fact that in all of these studies, open- and closed-class words were presented in word lists and never in sentences. It appears, however, that function words can only serve their structuring function once they appear in sentential or phrasal context.

In searching for a differential processing pattern for open- and closed-class words, we conducted a series of experiments in which open- and/or closed-class words were presented in sentence context (Friederici, 1985; Friederici & Kilborn, 1989; Friederici, Wessels, Emmorey, & Bellugi, 1992). In one of these experiments, processing of open-class words and the processing of closed-class words were compared directly (Friederici, 1985). The critical open- and closed-class targets appeared in sentences, each given always as the second sentence in a sentence pair. This second sentence was preceded by a context sentence that either was or was not semantically related to the second sentence. Sentence pairs were presented auditorily, and subjects were asked to monitor for critical targets specified prior to the presentation of each sentence pair. Targets were one- and two-syllable words of each class (for experimental details, see Friederici, 1985).

On the basis of the special retrieval hypothesis for closed-class elements, it was predicted that for normal adult subjects closed-class elements should be accessed faster than open-class elements. Under the assumption that processing of closed-class elements is highly automatic and informationally encapsulated, monitoring of closed class elements was expected to be uninfluenced by variations of the semantic context of a given sentence. The results confirmed the predictions. Closed-class words were processed faster than open-class words. Moreover, the processing of open-class words, but not processing of closed-class words, was affected by semantic context. Semantically related contexts quickened the recognition of open-class words compared to an unrelated context.

From this it was concluded that normal adults process elements of the closed class in a fast, automatic, and informationally encapsulated way. A further condition of this experiment included prepositional forms in either a referential function (locative prepositions) or a structural function (obligatory prepositions) and led to a specification of this conclusion. The data indicated that fast and informationally encapsulated access was restricted to those closed-class elements that mainly carry structural information, and therefore was a function of the information to be processed rather than a function of word class.

Thus, it appears that there is a special access to the structural information encoded in closed-class elements that functions in a modular fashion. This access device seems to meet some critical criteria Fodor (1983) listed as necessary conditions for cognitive modules: They are fast, and work in an informationally encapsulated way. In addition to these two criteria, Fodor named two other major criteria for cognitive modules: They have a fixed neural basis, and are genetically determined.

To evaluate whether the functioning of the closed-class access device can be related to a particular brain system, an additional experiment was conducted with two aphasic groups consisting of patients who suffered from circumscribed brain lesions. The patients of one group were classified as agrammatic Broca's aphasics who had brain lesions in the anterior part of the left hemisphere. The other aphasic group consisted of patients classified as Wernicke's patients who had lesions in the posterior part of the left hemisphere. Broca's aphasia, characterized clinically by agrammatic speech output, seemed to be a condition in which to observe a selective breakdown of the fast access device for closed-class words. The monitoring experiment described previously was conducted with patients of both aphasic groups (Friederici, 1983a).

Agrammatic Broca patients showed a performance pattern that was clearly different from that of normal adults in that they demonstrated extremely long monitoring times for the function words compared to the open-class words. They were similar to normal adults, in that a semantic context effect was found for the processing of content words, but not of function words. Wernicke patients, in contrast, showed a pattern most similar to that of normal adults with faster reaction times for function words compared to content words, although their overall reaction times were longer than in normal adults. Interestingly, Broca aphasics were quite able to detect function words correctly, except that their reaction to these words was increased by about 200 ms compared to closed-class words.

This breakdown in the temporal coordination of lexical access to closed-class elements and to open-class elements gave rise to a characterization of Broca's aphasia in terms of a deficit in the temporal domain of language use (Friederici, 1988; Hagoort, 1989). The deficit was defined as a specific delay in the activation and use of structural information encoded in closed-class elements (Friederici & Kilborn, 1989).

The finding that this processing deficit is particularly linked to patients with lesions in the left anterior cortical areas raises the possibility that these areas are involved in the temporal organization of language. Before we turn to this hypothesis in more detail by evaluating neuroanatomical and neurophysiological evidence I briefly present some developmental data that seem to suggest that this automatic language processing device is not established in early childhood, but only develops as the brain matures.

TEMPORAL CHARACTERISTICS OF LEXICAL ACCESS TO OPEN- AND CLOSED-CLASS WORDS IN CHILDREN

In considering the relation of brain maturation and language development, the empirical data are very sparse. A review of the literature on aphasia during childhood reveals that young children up to the age of 9 to 10 years do not seem to show the same relation between brain lesion and behavioral pattern normally seen in adults (Basso & Scarpa, 1990; Paquier & Van Dongen, 1991; Van Hout & Lyon, 1986; Visch-Brinck & Van de Sandt-Koenderman, 1984; for a review, see Friederici, 1994). In young children lesions in the posterior parts of the left hemisphere do not cause a fluent paragrammatic production behavior typically seen in adults with lesions in the Wernicke's area. This could be taken as an indication that the automatic procedures, by which syntactic information is processed online, are not available during early language acquisition, but only develop on the basis of already acquired syntactic knowledge.

In order to study this hypothesis children of different age groups were tested using the word monitoring paradigm described before (Friederici, 1983a). Wording in the sentences was adapted for children, but the structure of the sentence remained comparable to that of the adult study. Children were trained to monitor for content words and function words while listening to the sentences.

Children of six different age groups participated in the study. Their mean ages were 5.3, 7.3, 8.3, 8.8, 9.7, and 11.7 years. Younger children (5.3, 7.3, and 8.3 years old) showed longer monitoring times for closed-class than for open-class words. Most interestingly, there was a clear semantic context effect for monitoring of both open- and of closed-class words. At the age of 8.8 years, monitoring for closed-class words was as fast as monitoring for open class-words. However, there was still an effect of semantic context for both word classes. At the ages of 9 to 11 years, finally, monitoring for closed-class words was faster than monitoring for open-class words, and the processing of closed-class words was independent from the semantic variable. Thus, at this age children provide a behavioral pattern similar to that of normal adults.

These findings seem to indicate that the fast and autonomously working access device for the closed-class words, as seen in the adult listener, only develops slowly over the years. Although the child is perfectly able to use syntactic knowledge when constructing and understanding sentences, say at the ages of 7 to 8 years, it appears that children at these ages do not use the mechanism to process syntactic information during language perception in the same fast and automatic way adults do. The influence of semantic aspects on children's processing of closed-class elements can be seen as a further hint that children at a younger age do not rely on a highly autonomous mechanism for the processing of structural information. Their processing of structural information is influenced by incongruous semantic information.

The neurophysiological data available with respect to the processing of open- and closed-class elements during development suggest a correlation between the behavioral changes and changes in the involvement of different cortical areas. A recent event-related brain potential study (Holcomb, Coffey, & Neville, 1994) indicates that the development toward this special autonomously working retrieval mechanism for closed-class words seen in the adults, may be connected to a functional reorganization of the language supporting brain systems. Holcomb et al. (1994) found that adult reading of open-class words was correlated with maximal brain activation over the posterior parts of the left hemisphere, whereas their reading of function words was correlated with major activation over the anterior parts. Children up to the age of 10 years, however, showed a different pattern. Major brain activation was seen over the posterior part of the left hemisphere for both open-class and closed-class word reading.

Thus, it seems likely that anterior parts of the left hemisphere are particularly involved in the automatic syntactic processes seen in adults, and that these only establish their functions during development.

THE BRAIN-PROCESSES RESPONSIBLE FOR THE TEMPORAL ORGANIZATION OF LANGUAGE

On the basis of the data presented so far, the hypothesis may be formulated that, in the adult brain, Broca's and adjacent areas subserve the fast and automatic syntactic processes. Lieberman (1984) already proposed that the brain mechanisms regulating the sequence of complex motor control necessary for human speech are the basis for syntactic processing. Greenfield (1991) supported this view in specifying a part of the prefrontal cortex just superior and anterior to Broca's area, namely Brodmann's area 46, to be relevant for the hierarchical organization of elements in general, and for language in particular. Deacon (1989, 1992) using neuroanatomical evidence specified four particular areas in the anterior parts of the left hemisphere and their function with respect to language. He argued that there is no single specialized language area subserving a single function defined with respect to Broca's aphasia, but rather four adjacent, functionally distinct areas in the ventral-frontal region of the left hemisphere. Grammatical functions are attributed to a ventral prefrontal area located just in front of the premotor cortex. Neuroanatomically this area is directly connected with the dorsal-prefrontal cortex and Wernicke's area. These connections are viewed to subserve the temporal organization of language behavior in both production and comprehension.

Electrical stimulation studies (Ojemann & Mateer, 1979), as well as PET and regional blood flow studies (Ingvar, 1983), partly support this functional brain map. I now present neurophysiological evidence from event-related potential studies (ERP) that agrees with the hypothesis that left anterior areas may be particularly involved in fast syntactic processes during comprehension.

Electrophysiological studies of cognition (Kutas & Van Petten, 1988; Picton & Stuss, 1984) have shown that the event-related brain potentials registered during language comprehension differ as a function of a sentence's semantic adequacy. For example, when comparing the waveforms of a correct and semantically incorrect sentence, one usually observes a negativity of about 400 ms after the occurrence of a semantic anomaly in a sentence. This negativity widely distributed over the posterior parts of both hemispheres has been called N400. For syntactic violations no such unitary correlate has been identified so far. Different working groups (Garnsey, Tanenhaus, & R. M. Chapman, 1989; Hagoort, C. Brown, & Groothusen, 1994; Neville, Nicol, Barss, Forster, & Garrett, 1991; Osterhout & Holcomb, 1992) have found different patterns correlated with various types of syntactic violations. In most of these studies, however, the topography of these patterns was not discussed extensively (but see Neville, Nicol, Barss, Forster, & Garrett, 1991).

In two experiments we investigated the event-related brain activity of normal adult language users while they were reading and while they were listening to sentences. In one of the experiments, we explored the processing of syntactic knowledge encoded in open-class items (Rösler, Friederici, Pütz, & Hahne, 1993). The sentence material consisted of a sentence ending in a verb form (past participle), which made up a correct sentence or violated either the verb's selectional restrictions (semantic aspects) or its subcategorization requirements (syntactic aspects). In this study we found a negative event-related potential component present around 400 ms for the processing of both the semantic and the syntactic aspects encoded in the verb, although their topographical distribution differed. We observed a classical N400 pattern for the semantic anomaly, but a particular asymmetry in the negativity over left Broca's area and left frontal electrodes compared to the corresponding sites in the right hemisphere for the syntactic anomaly. This asymmetry was interpreted to reflect the processing of syntactic information (i.e., subcategorization information) encoded in open class elements.

In the second experiment, which may be even more relevant for the issue discussed here, we investigated the processing of purely structurally encoded syntactic information (Friederici, Pfeifer, & Hahne, 1993). In this experiment, which used connected speech as stimulus material, subjects were required to listen to sentences followed by a probe word. The subjects' task was to decide whether the probe word had appeared in the prior sentence or not. Sentences used in this experiment (a) were correct (e.g., Der Präsident wurde begrüßt/The president was greeted), (b) contained a selectional restriction violation (e.g., Der Honig wurde ermordet/The honey was murdered), or (c) contained a violation of the phrase structure (e.g., Die Kirche wurde am geschlossen/The church was on closed). In this latter sentence type the presence of the preposition requires the continuation of a prepositional phrase (i.e., the preposition "am/on") must be followed by a noun phrase. Instead, the subjects heard the past participle form of a verb which, in German, obligatorily stands in clause final position.

For the semantic condition we expected a N400 wave in the event-related brain potential. Given what we said about the fast and automatic processing of syntactic information in the adult listener, we expected a special correlate for these processes to manifest earlier than any correlate for semantic processes because the detection of a semantic violation, but not of a structural violation, requires the full access to the lexical entry. Detection of the syntactic violation in the present sentence type (c) requires only the recognition of the word's syntactic category, a piece of information that may be accessed and used much faster than other types of information encoded in lexical elements (Frazier, 1990; Frazier & Rayner, 1982).

Event-related brain potentials recorded from seven electrodes (Fz, Cz, Pz, "Broca left," "Wernicke left", "Broca right," "Wernicke right,") and averaged over sixteen subjects supported the predictions. For the semantic condition, we observed the classical N400 waveform (i.e., a negativity starting at 400 ms after the onset of the critical word with its maxima at central electrodes and with a posterior distribution). The ERP results for the structural violations showed an early negativity peaking between 180 and 200 ms at the anterior frontal electrodes and more pronounced over the left hemisphere than over the right hemisphere. This early negativity was followed by a N400-like negativity most pronounced over the midline. Although we must be cautious in drawing strong topological conclusions from a study in which only seven electrodes were used, there appears to be an asymmetry for the early negativity with a maximum over the electrodes placed over Broca's left and frontal areas correlated only with violations of the phrase structure.

The present findings, as well as those of Neville et al. (1991) are in agreement with the hypothesis that Broca's area and adjacent prefrontal areas in the left hemisphere or both subserve the fast and automatic syntactic processes. However, the spatial resolution of the present recordings does not allow us to draw topographical conclusions firm enough to meet the specific predications made by the functional map proposed by Deacon (1992).

The assumption that Broca's and adjacent areas (and projections to or from them) are responsible for the temporal organization of grammatical information rather than representing grammatical knowledge itself is, however, supported by the finding that patients with damage to Broca's area who demonstrate a deficit in the temporal organization of language are able to judge the grammaticality of a sentence (Huber, Cholewa, Wilbertz, & Friederici, 1990; Linebarger, Schwarz, & Saffran, 1983; Wulfeck, 1987). In contrast, patients with lesions in the Wernicke area are not able to perform reliably on grammaticality judgment tasks (Blumstein, Milberg, Dworetzky, Rosen, & Gershberg, 1991; Huber et al., 1990), but look similar to normals in some online perception tasks such as in the word monitoring task or priming tasks (Friederici, 1983a). In these latter patients the intact Broca's anterior areas may still support some of the automated syntactic processes, whereas conscious access to grammatical knowledge is impaired due to lesions in the Wernicke area.

CONCLUSIONS

The reported studies focusing on temporal aspects of language processing allow a number of conclusions. On the one hand, the discussed data indicate that syntactic processes are highly automatic and informationally encapsulated in the normal adult. On the other hand, the data show that these processes only gradually gain their modular status during development. The data also suggest that this developmental change in the behavior may be accompanied by a functional reorganization of the cortex. Moreover, they support the specific hypothesis that Broca's and adjacent areas subserve these automatic, temporally constrained syntactic processes.

ACKNOWLEDGMENT

This research was supported by the Alfried Krupp von Bohlen und Halbach-Stiftung.

REFERENCES

Basso, A., & Scarpa, M. T. (1990). Traumatic aphasia in children and adults: A comparison of clinical features and evolution. *Cortex, 26,* 501–514.
Blumstein, S. E., Milberg, W. P., Dworetzky, B., Rosen, A., & Gershberg, F. (1991). Syntactic priming effects in aphasia: An investigation of local syntactic dependencies. *Brain and Language, 40,* 393–421.
Bradley, D. C., Garrett, M. F., & Zurif, E. B. (1980). Syntactic deficits in Broca's aphasia. In D. Caplan (Ed.), *Biological studies of mental processes* (pp. 269-286). Cambridge, MA: MIT Press.
Deacon, T. W. (1989). The neural circuitry underlying primate calls and human language. *Human Evolution, 4,* 367–401.
Deacon, T. W. (1992). Brain-language coevolution. In J. A. Hawkins & M. Gell-Mann (Eds.), *The evolution of human languages. Proceedings of the workshop on the evolution of human languages* (pp. 49–83). Santa Fe, CA: Addison-Wesley.
Fodor, J. A. (1983). *The modularity of mind: An essay on faculty psychology.* Cambridge, MA: MIT Press.
Frazier, L. (1990). Exploring the architecture of the language-processing system. In G. T. M. Altmann (Ed.), *Cognitive models of speech processing. Psycholinguistic and computational perspectives* (pp. 409–533). Cambridge, MA: MIT Press.
Frazier, L., & Rayner, K. (1982). Making and correcting errors during sentence comprehension: Eye movements in the analysis of structurally ambiguous sentences. *Cognitive Psychology, 14,* 178–210.
Friederici, A. D. (1983a). Aphasics' perception of words in sentential context: Some real-time processing evidence. *Neuropsychologia, 21,* 351–358.
Friederici, A. D. (1983b). Children's sensitivity to function words during sentence comprehension. *Linguistics, 21,* 717–739.
Friederici, A. D. (1985). Levels of processing and vocabulary types: Evidence from on-line comprehension in normals and agrammatics. *Cognition, 19,* 133–166.
Friederici, A. D. (1988). Agrammatic comprehension: Picture of a computational mismatch. *Aphasiology, 2,* 279–284.

Friederici, A. D. (1994). Funktionale Organisation und Reorganisation der Sprache während der Sprachentwicklung: Eine Hypothese. *Neurolinguistik, 8,* 41–55.

Friederici, A. D., & Kilborn, K. (1989). Temporal constraints on language processing: Syntactic priming in Broca's aphasia. *Journal of Cognitive Neuroscience, 1,* 262–272.

Friederici, A. D., Pfeifer, E., & Hahne, A. (1993). Event-related brain potentials during natural speech processing: Effects of semantic, morphological and syntactic violations. *Cognitive Brain Research, 1,* 183–192.

Friederici, A. D., Wessels, J., Emmorey, K., & Bellugi, U. (1992). Sensitivity of inflectional morphology in aphasia: A real-time processing perspective. *Brain and Language, 43,* 747–763.

Garnsey, S. M., Tanenhaus, M. K., & Chapman, R. M. (1989). Evoked potentials and the study of sentence comprehension. *Journal of Psycholinguistic Research, 18,* 51–60.

Greenfield, P. M. (1991). Language, tools and brain: The ontogeny and phylogeny of hierarchically organized sequential behavior. *Behavioral and Brain Sciences, 14,* 531–595.

Gordon, B., & Caramazza, A. (1983). Closed and open class lexical access in agrammatic and fluent aphasia. *Brain and Language, 19,* 335–345.

Hagoort, P. (1989). Decay of syntactic information in language comprehension of agrammatic aphasia. *Journal of Clinical and Experimental Neuropsychology, 11,* 357.

Hagoort, P., Brown, C., & Groothusen, J. (1994). The syntactic positive shift as an ERP-measure of syntactic processing. *Language and Cognitive Processes, 8,* 439–483.

Holcomb, P. J., Coffey, S. A., & Neville, H. J. (1994). Visual and auditory sentence processing: A developmental analysis using event-related brain potentials. *Developmental Neuropsychology, 8,* 203–241.

Huber, W., Cholewa, J., Wilbertz, A., & Friederici, A. D. (1990). What the eyes reveal about grammaticality judgment in aphasia. *28th Annual Meeting of the Academy of Aphasia,* October 1990. Baltimore, USA

Ingvar, D. H. (1983). Serial aspects of language and speech related to prefrontal cortical activity: A selective review. *Human Neurobiology, 2,* 177–189.

Kutas, M., & van Petten, C. (1988). Event-related potential studies of language. In P. K. Ackles, J. R. Jennings, & M. G. H. Coles (Eds.), *Advances in psychophysiolog* (Vol. 3, pp. 139–184). Greenwich: JAI Press.

Levelt, W. J. M., Schriefers, H., Vorberg, D., Meyer, A., Pechmann, T., & Havinga, J. (1991). The time course of lexical access in language production: A study of picture naming. *Psychological Review, 98,* 122–142.

Lieberman, P. (1984). *The biology and evolution of language.* Cambridge, MA: Harvard University Press.

Linebarger, M. C., Schwarz, M., & Saffran, E. M. (1983). Sensitivity to grammatical structure in so-called agrammatic aphasia. *Cognition, 13,* 361–392.

Marslen-Wilson, W. D., & Tyler, L. K. (1980). The temporal structure of spoken language understanding. *Cognition, 8,* 1–71.

Neville, H. J., Nicol, J., Barss, A., Forster, K., & Garrett, M. F. (1991). Syntactically based sentence processing classes: Evidence from event-related brain potentials. *Journal of Cognitive Neuroscience, 3,* 155–170.

Ojemann, G. A., & Mateer, C. (1979). Human language cortex: Localization of memory, syntax, and sequential motor-phoneme identification systems. *Science, 205,* 1401–1403.

Osterhout, U., & Holcomb, P. J. (1992). Event-related brain potentials elicited by syntactic anomaly. *Journal of Memory and Language, 31,* 785–804.

Paquier, P., & Van Dongen, H. R. (1991). Two contrasting cases of fluent aphasia in children. *Aphasiology, 5,* 235–245.

Picton, T. W., & Stuss, D. T. (1984). Event-related potentials in the study of speech and language: A critical review. In D. N. Caplan, A. R. Lecours, & A. M. Smith (Eds.), *Biological perspectives on language* (pp. 303-360). Cambridge, MA: MIT Press.

Rösler, F., Friederici, A. D., Pütz, P., & Hahne, A. (1993). Event-related brain potentials while encountering semantic and syntactic constraint violations. *Journal of Cognitive Neuroscience, 5,* 345–362.

Schriefers, H., Meyer, A. S., & Levelt, W. J. M. (1990). Exploring the time course of lexical access in language production: Picture-word interference studies. *Journal of Memory and Language, 29,* 86–102.

Segui, J., Mehler, J., Frauenfelder, U., & Morton, J. (1982). Word frequency effect and lexical access. *Neuropsychologia, 20,* 615–627.

Seidenberg, M. S., & Tanenhaus, M. K. (1986). Modularity and lexical access. In I. Gopnik (Ed.), *From models to modules: Proceedings of the McGill Cognitive Science Workshops* (pp. 135-157). Norwood, NJ: Ablex Press.

Simpson, G. B. (1984). Lexical ambiguity and its role in models of word recognition. *Psychological Bulletin, 96,* 316–340.

Swinney, D. A., Zurif, E. B., & Cutler, A. (1980). Effects of sentential stress and word class upon comprehension in Broca's aphasics. *Brain and Language, 10,* 132–144.

Tanenhaus, M. K., & Lucas, M .M. (1987). Context effects in lexical processing. *Cognition, 25,* 213–234.

Tyler, L. K. (1984). Integration of information during language comprehension: A developmental study. *Papers and Reports on Child Language Development, Stanford, 23,* 125–134.

Tyler, L. K., & Frauenfelder, K. H. (1987). The process of spoken word recognition: An introduction. *Cognition, 25,* 1–20.

Tyler, L. K., & Marslen-Wilson, W. D. (1981). Children's processing of spoken language. *Journal of Verbal Learning and Verbal Behavior, 20,* 400–416.

Van Hout, A., & Lyon, G. (1986). Wernicke's aphasia in a 10-year-old boy. *Brain and Language, 29,* 268–285.

Visch-Brinck, E. G., & Van de Sandt-Koenderman, M. (1984). The occurrence of paraphasias in the spontaneous speech of children with an acquired aphasia. *Brain and Language, 23,* 258–271.

Wulfeck, B. (1987). Grammaticality judgments and sentence comprehension in agrammatic aphasia. *Journal of Speech and Hearing Research, 31,* 72–81.

PART

IV

ENVIRONMENT AND CULTURE AS SHAPING FORCES

CHAPTER

8

GENETIC HISTORIES AND PATTERNS OF LINGUISTIC CHANGE

Alberto Piazza
University of Torino, Italy

Reconstruction of human history by genetic data is a kind of exercise whose value is being increasingly challenged by methods and evidence from other disciplines. When I submit the methods and the results our genetic studies can provide to an audience of nonbiologists, for example, scholars of history or scholars of linguistics, the most frequent question I am asked is, "What are *our* studies going to gain from *your* studies?" In other words, how could one discipline benefit from the results of another? In the following review, I try to give some answers to this question. In a study by Cavalli-Sforza, Piazza, Menozzi, and Mountain (1988), the spread of anatomically modern man was reconstructed on the basis of genetic, archaeological, and linguistic evidence: The main message was that the three sciences reflect a common, underlying history, the history of our past still frozen in the genes of modern populations. What can be considered something more than a suggestion requires us to dig deeper into the history of populations. As a geneticist, I introduced the expression *genetic histories* (Piazza, Cappello, Olivetti, & Rendine, 1988b) to point out the historical interpretation of genetic data collected from extant populations, the methodological approach based on the assumption that, if we find many genes today showing the same geographical frequency patterns, this may be due to the noncoincidental history of our species. Because biological evolution cannot be tested by reproducible experiments as in the so-called exact sciences, our effort has been directed to find support from fossil data or from such "cultural fossils" as lexical substrata, toponyms, and so forth, left exposed by languages in their process of change.

In this contribution, I present some analogies between linguistically and genetically homogeneous geographical areas in Europe as examples of actual cases in which genetics and linguistics supply complementary and corroborating information (see also Cavalli-Sforza, Menozzi, & Piazza, 1994).

THE BASQUES, A GENETIC RELIC

My first example is a population still speaking a non-Indo-European language, the Basque population. From a methodological point of view, I selected this population because their linguistic isolation is indisputable, and I hoped they could show what supplementary information genetic data can supply. What genetic relations do the Basques have with their surrounding modern populations, all of them Indo-European speakers?

Almost half a century ago, it was suggested (Bosch-Gimpera, 1943) that the Basques are the descendants of populations who lived in Western Europe during the late Paleolithic period. Their withdrawal to the area of the Pyrenees, probably caused by different waves of invasion, left the Basques untouched by the Eastern European invasions of the Iron Age. If the language of the Basques is any testimony to their ethnic genealogy (linguistic records show that they had no or few contacts with the Celts and Iberians), another matter could be their biological features as compared to other European populations. In his study of the geographic distribution of Rh blood groups, Mourant (1948) pointed out that, as originally observed by Etcheverry (1947), the Rh negative gene, which is found almost exclusively in Europe, has its highest frequency among the Basques. Mourant hypothesized that modern Basques may consist of a Paleolithic population with an extremely high Rh negative gene, which later mixed with people from the Mediterranean. Thirty years later, Cavalli-Sforza and coworkers (Ammermann &

8. PATTERNS OF LINGUISTIC CHANGE

Cavalli-Sforza, 1984; Bertranpetit & Cavalli-Sforza, 1991) suggested that the immigrants might have been the Neolithic farmers who came from the Near East, and whose descendants today have an Rh negative gene with very low frequency.

Blood types detected by immunological techniques, electrophoretic variants reflecting variations in electrophoretic mobility of enzymes or proteins, and anthropometric traits such as morphological measurements, skin and hair color, and body shape are the major source of data for measuring variations in extant human populations. Blood types and electrophoretic variants are genetically controlled markers; that is, their transmission from one generation to the next and their distribution in different populations can be predicted by probabilistic laws. These are usually expressed in terms of quantities called *gene frequencies*. A *gene* is a segment of DNA in an individual's chromosome that controls the expression of a genetic trait (i.e., a blood type), and the frequencies of their variants in a population (called *alleles*) define the gene (or allele) frequencies. They usually vary in different populations and over time, within the same population.

Data were obtained for a total of 15 genetic systems and 65 alleles (Piazza, Cappello, Olivetti, & Rendine, 1988a). The alleles are variants of the same genetic system (or *locus*), and the frequencies of each of them are called gene or allele frequencies. A subsample taken from the very large data bank forming the basis of our book (Cavalli-Sforza, Menozzi, & Piazza, 1994) served to supply a substantial set of gene frequency data for the populations given in Table 8.1. The gene frequencies considered for our analysis are averages over all samples included in our database with a specific population name, geographical area, and linguistic group. Names in capital letters (last column) refer to populations, whereas names in lower-case letters refer to geographical areas where the samples of the specified linguistic group were drawn. Sample sizes are not given in Table 8.1 because they vary, depending on the genetic systems. Moreover, sample sizes of fewer than 100 individuals were ignored.

TABLE 8.1

Populations and Samples

Population	Linguistic group	Samples
Basque	Non-Indo-European	France, Spain
France Central	Indo-European	
France North	"	
France Béarn	"	
France Catalogne	"	
France Corse	"	
Spain	"	
Italy Sardinia	"	
Italy Liguria	"	
Italy	"	
Italy other regions	"	
England	"	
Greece	"	
Europe North	"	BELGIUM, DENMARK, THE NETHERLANDS, ICELAND, IRELAND, NORWAY, SCOTLAND, SWEDEN, WALES
Europe Central	"	AUSTRIA, CZECH REPUBLIC, GERMANY, POLAND, RUSSIA, SWITZERLAND
Africa North	Afro-Asiatic	Algeria, Egypt, Libya, Morocco, Tunisia
Africa East	"	Djibouti, Ethiopia, Kenya, Somalia, Sudan
Near East	"	Iraq, Iran, Jordan, Kuwait, Lebanon, Saudi Arabia, Syria, Yemen
Turkic	Altaic	Altai, DOLGAN, TURK, TURKOMAN, TUVAN, UZBEK, YAKUT
Caucasian	Caucasian	Caucasus, Dagestan, Georgia

8. PATTERNS OF LINGUISTIC CHANGE

TABLE 8.2
Genetic Distances Between Basques and Some Selected Populations

Population	Genetic Distance (×10,000)
France Béarn	70
Spain	102
France Catalogne	107
France Central	113
England	132
France North	153
Italy	157
Europe Central	163
Italy Liguria	173
Europe North	180
Greece	194
France Corse	224
Caucasian	241
Near East	242
Italy Sardinia	312
Africa North	355

TABLE 8.3
Genetic Distances and Times of Possible Admixtures of Basques With Relevant Populations

Population	Distance	Years B.P.
France Béarn	100	2,000
Spain	146	3,000
France Catalogne	153	3,100
Caucasian	344	6,800
Near East	346	6,900
Italy Sardinia	446	8,900

One approach in studying the genetic differentiation of populations has made use of genetic distance coefficients between population pairs. Without going into detail regarding the literature and the controversy generated by it, the genetic distance can be simply defined as a measure of similarity between two populations. Originally proposed by Cavalli-Sforza and Edwards (1964, 1967) nearly 30 years ago, this parameter is a useful tool for interpreting genetic differences whenever we are aware of the (genetic) assumptions on which it is based. From the many formulations of this measure in the literature, we adopted the coancestry coefficient proposed by Reynolds, Weir, and Cockerham (1983) as the most reliable in the common case of samples of different sizes. This measure of genetic distance applies specifically to short-term evolution, and whenever the divergence between populations sharing a common ancestral population may be regarded as being due mainly to genetic drift, it is proportional to the time of divergence. An example of the calculation is displayed in Table 8.2, in which the genetic distances between Basques and the populations of Table 8.1 are shown.

The sample from France-Béarn shows the greatest genetic similarity with the Basques. This is not unexpected if one thinks of French Gascogne as the geographical area where the Vascon ethnic group could have been the last to have differentiated from the Basques. Toponymy provides evidence that the Basque language was in the past more widespread in the southwest of France (Ruffié & Bernard, 1974). Evidence from not yet published genetic analyses of the French provinces supports an impressive analogy between gene frequency and dialect geographical distribution in France. Particularly the Béarn region shows clear genetic differences when compared with other French regions.

Gene flow of European origin can reasonably be excluded in the Basques. However, a percentage of Basque genes seems to be shared with Sardinian ancestors. Their origin is unknown, but archaeology shows the settlement of Sardinia as being very old, and DNA mitochondrial data (Di Rienzo & Wilson, 1991) show Sardinians and Middle Easterners to have common ancestors. Our genetic analyses offer linguists the following information:

1. On the basis of a hypothetical "Pyrenean" population originally settled in a large area including the homonymous mountains, we can postulate that the genetic differentiation of modern Basques from the

8. PATTERNS OF LINGUISTIC CHANGE

neighboring Béarn sample occurred, at the latest, during the Romanization period, about 2,000 years B.P.

2. On the assumption that genetic distances are proportional to the times when populations separated (which is strictly valid only if genetic drift is a major cause of differentiation), we can rewrite Table 8.2 in Table 8.3 in which the times of differentiations are calculated from the genetic distances by setting the time of differentiation between Basques and the French from Béarn at 2,000 years B.P. By comparing Table 8.3 with sufficiently known historical dates, it seems plausible that genetic differentiation of Basques from European samples occurred before the Celtic invasion (2,600 years B.P.).

3. If Basques share a common ancestry with Caucasian populations, the corresponding modern samples (including Sardinia, whose Eastern component is documented) show hypothetical separation times before the introduction of farming (ca. 6,000–5,500 years ago). This genetic evidence supports the idea that the Basques are the descendants of a Paleolithic population. The linguistic evidence of possible Caucasian substrata (Trombetti, 1926) could reflect a common genetic origin with populations that might have occurred at the latest before the Neolithic introduction of agriculture.

PRE-ROMAN GENETIC AND LINGUISTIC SUBSTRATA

The population name Basque itself has an interesting history. The Basques call themselves *Euskaldunak*: The term *Basque* derives from *Vascos*, a Spanish word. If one studies the geographical distribution of the place names ending with the suffix *asc*, one will find a large region where such place names are significantly represented, from the southwest of France to the Po delta in Italy. The number of place names whose origin is documented in historical records before 1850 is 262 (Riva, 1964), and there is a general agreement among linguists in associating this suffix with a Pre-Indo-European *Ligurian* substratum. Note that place names are generally very conservative, being notoriously resistant to ethnic stratification. Conquerors may impose a language on the population, but usually they can only modify the place names without changing them entirely. The presence of these place names in the Alpine region between Italy and the Swiss Italian-speaking region, but excluding the region north of the Po, is also interesting. The linguistic

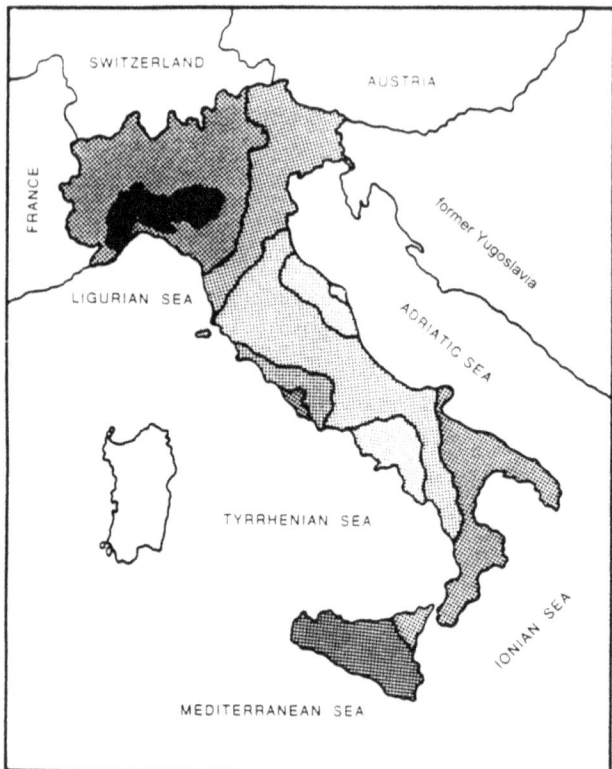

Fig. 8.1. Synthetic geographic map of the 3rd principal component values grouped in 8 classes and calculated from 34 gene frequencies in Italy. It conveys 14% of the original genetic variation (from Piazza et al., 1988b).

interpretation of this kind of geographical distribution—one linguistically homogeneous area surrounded by two marginal areas with the same characteristics—was proposed by the followers of the Italian school at the beginning of this century, and is known as "linguistic geography." The leading figure was G. I. Ascoli, but the names of Bartoli, Merlo, Ribezzo, Trombetti, and Terracini were also influential, and it is very unfortunate that their work has not been translated into a non-Italian language. One of the so-called Bartoli rules says that if a central area is linguistically homogeneous and surrounded by marginal areas that are linguistically different from the central one, but equal among themselves, the languages of the marginal areas are nearly always older than that of the central area. In other words, the peripheral areas are more resistant to linguistic change than the central one. The place names of Ligurian origin seem to confirm this rule because their distribution surrounds a region of Celtic superstratum that eliminated any Pre-Indo-European relics, but, of course each historical reconstruction has to be documented in some way, possibly by archaeological records.

8. PATTERNS OF LINGUISTIC CHANGE

One way to check whether a geographical area known to be linguistically homogeneous was settled by an ethnic group that left very few records is to look for the genes of their potential ancestors in that geographical area.

Fig. 8.1 shows what genetics can contribute to the study of genetic histories. It is a synthetic map of the information contained in the gene frequency distribution in Italy today (Piazza, Cappello, Olivetti, & Rendine, 1988b): It represents 14% of the total genetic variability present in Italy. Differences in shading correspond to differences in 34 genes considered globally. It clearly discriminates the modern descendants of the Ligurians (most intensely shaded area) from the rest of Italy. Claimed to be among the most ancient ethnic groups of western Europe, the Ligurians' original domain far exceeded the confines of the modern region bearing their name. As yet unpublished results obtained by using a higher number (65) of gene frequencies supplemented by detailed anthropometric measurements done at the beginning of our century (Livi, 1896–1905) confirm the peculiar genetic identity of the Ligurians: They seem to belong to a Mediterranean cluster of populations having some genetic similarity with Iberian (including the Basques) and Near Eastern populations.

This map of Italian gene frequencies also shows the opposite (least intense shading) pole indicating the discrimination in a cultural area whose inscriptions, among the oldest in Italy (perhaps 7th century B.C.), are linguistically grouped under the name of East Italic (Pulgram, 1958). From the archaeological point of view, the local culture is called *Picene–Adriatic*, and until the Iron Age is characterized by homogeneous burial sites indicating inhumation, whereas neighboring regions had changed to incineration of the bodies (Prosdocimi, 1978). This has led some scholars to think that the inhabitants of this region (Picenes) were among the most ancient non-Latinian settlers in Italy (Italici) in historical times (Devoto, 1967; Duhn, 1924). Their sample size at the beginning of the third century B.C. was estimated to be around 250,000 (Beloch, 1886).

Although the non-Indo-European nature of the Ligurian language has been a subject of debate because of the very small number of glosses dating back to at least before the Celts occupied most of the Po valley in the early 6th century B.C. (Prosdocimi, 1978; Whatmough, 1937), nobody doubts the non-Indo-European origin of the Etruscans (Pallottino, 1978), and a natural question is whether in the blood of today's Tuscan inhabitants we are able to recognize the fingerprints of their ancestors' genes.

Fig. 8.2. Synthetic geographic map of the 2nd principal component values grouped in 8 classes and calculated from 34 gene frequencies in Italy. It conveys 20% of the original genetic variation (from Piazza et al., 1988b).

Fig. 8.2, which considers about 20% of the total genetic variation in Italy, shows a strikingly dark area that is almost exactly congruent with the area once formed by Etruscan cities. Is it a mere coincidence? Apart from the number of genetic samples that must be increased to supply more definitive results, I think we are faced with the same problem regarding the Tuscan dialect. Its area is well defined by a number of phonetic and lexical isoglosses, but nobody claims that it is a non-Indo-European or a pre-Roman language. Quite the reverse, it was adopted and is considered the "true" Italian language. It happened that the transition from Etruscan to Latin was so difficult, and the innovation so remarkable, that the process of a nearly complete language substitution produced deep, unconscious reactions by the speakers, and it is these reactions to innovation that can be detected as fossils in the language substratum of their descendants. The more different the languages of the conquerors and their conquered populations, the more recognizable

8. PATTERNS OF LINGUISTIC CHANGE

these fossils are. Genetics can be of considerable help in recognizing such fossils and possibly the population in which they originated for at least two reasons. First, the transmission of genes is a much slower process than the transmission of a cultural trait as a linguistic item; therefore, genes keep their identity for a longer time. The second important reason relates to the fact that the transmission of genetic traits is highly dependent on population size. Whereas it is perfectly legitimate to suppose that a few people can impose their language on large populations—as the Romans did—and spread it over a large region, it is much more difficult to think of the same process in genetic terms. Some well-organized people might subdue a whole population, but asking them to spread their genes within it would really be too demanding! It is our hypothesis that the Romans subdued the Etruscan inhabitants, but not entirely their genes, so that a part of their probable descendants have preserved them.

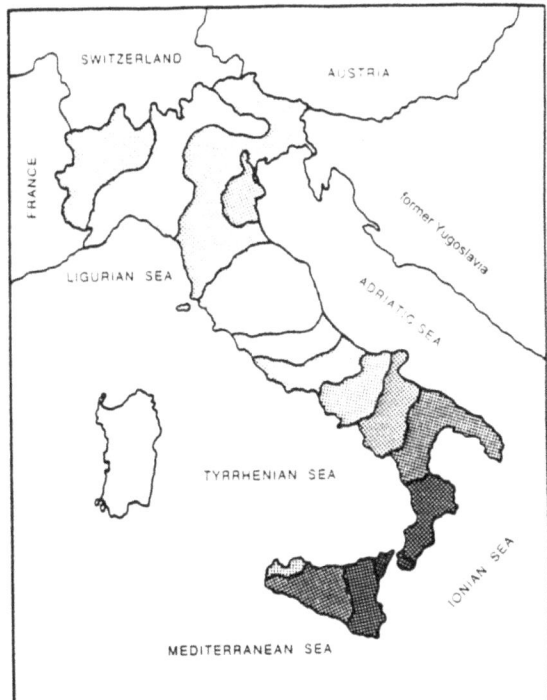

Fig. 8.3. Synthetic geographic map of the 1st principal component values grouped in 8 classes and calculated from 34 gene frequencies in Italy. It conveys 30% of the original genetic variation (from Piazza et al., 1988b).

So far, our studies seem to show that the non-Indo-European roots of Italy are not only detectable, but also are the only ones. This, however, is clearly not true. In fact our genetic analysis of Italy shows that the synthetic map accounting for the highest percentage of the total genetic variation (about 30% compared with 20% and 15% of the above Ligurian and Etruscan non-Indo-European maps) is due to a clear gradient from north to south (Fig. 8.3), a differentiation that we interpreted as having originated from the Greek colonization in historical times (8th–9th century B.C., Bérard, 1957). The hypothesis is supported by the remarkable demographic development of the Greek colonies in southern Italy. Called *Magna Graecia,* its population probably surpassed the Greek population of the motherland. Greek was spoken there until the 12th century, and a proportion of surnames are still Greek, showing a distribution very similar to the gradient of the map.

Clearly, the use of a language by a population is a cultural trait that cannot be imposed, even by politically powerful people, without a substantial impact on the genetic structure of the population itself. However, when this cultural trait is associated with a specific genetic identity, then language and population may be shown to share a common origin. In the case of Italy, we characterize the pre-Roman period as that of the main settlement and migration of peoples that determined the present pattern of genetic differentiation. Such early timing is less surprising than it might at first appear. In fact, it has been shown that the genetic structure of the present European populations is likely to be the result of the expansion of Neolithic farmers from the Near East 10,000 years ago (Ammerman & Cavalli-Sforza, 1984; Menozzi, Piazza, & Cavalli-Sforza, 1978).

THE ORIGIN OF EARLY INDO-EUROPEAN SPEAKERS

According to Renfrew (1987), Indo-European languages were first spoken by Neolithic migrants from Anatolia (Turkey), who established the first European farming communities in Greece about 6,500 years B.C. From Greece they diffused their economy and their language to the rest of Europe by population growth and expansion, sustained by their superior food production techniques, a mechanism we originally suggested for the movement of farmers (Menozzi, Piazza, & Cavalli-Sforza, 1978). The Anatolian origin caused much discussion among linguists. Whereas some of them agreed that Proto-Indo-Europeans may have originated either in Anatolia (Dolgopolsky, 1988) or in Transcaucasia (Gamkrelidze & Ivanov, 1990), most accepted the "Kurgan"

8. PATTERNS OF LINGUISTIC CHANGE

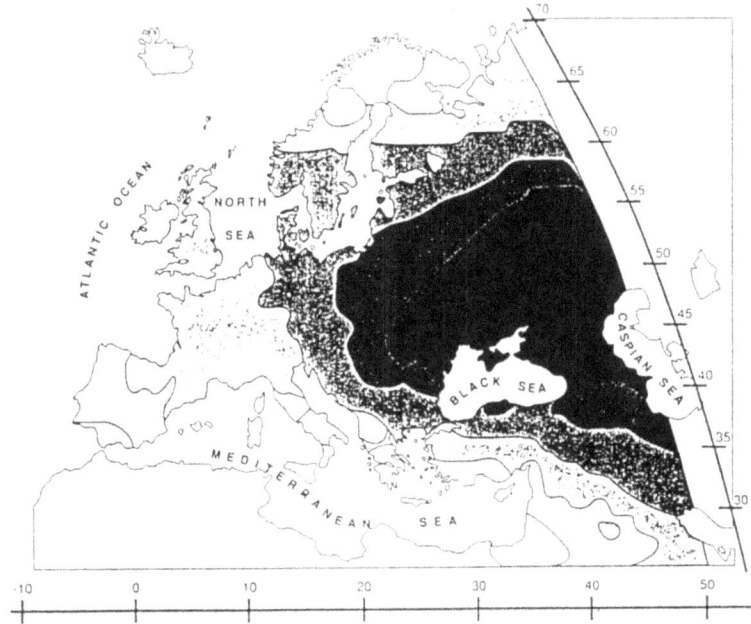

Fig. 8.4. Synthetic map of the 3rd principal component values grouped in 8 classes and calculated from 95 gene frequencies in Europe. It represents 10.6% of the original genetic variation.

theory by Gimbutas (1991), who viewed the original speakers of Proto-Indo-European as moving sometime between 4,300 and 2,800 (calibrated) years B.C. from the southern steppes of Russia (between the Black and the Caspian seas, where the so-called *Kurgan culture* has been first documented) and spreading westward to the British Isles as well as eastward and southwest. In comparing the reconstructed cultural vocabulary of the Proto-Indo-Europeans with the archaeological and environmental record, Mallory (1989) reviewed a series of inconsistencies with an Anatolian and Greek origin going back to 9,000–10,000 B.P. Some further criticisms on the linguistic side are detailed in Jasanoff (1988). The lack of archaeological evidence of domesticated horses in Anatolia before the 4th millennium B.C. (in Greece before the 3rd) and the adoption of horseback riding by the Bell Beaker people in central Europe, including Spain in the second half of the 3rd millennium B.C. (Mallory, 1969), are among the arguments (J. M. Diamond, 1992) making a Proto-Indo-European homeland in Anatolia or Greece hard to prove. A more comprehensive genetic picture of Europe is presented by our analysis of the European fraction of a new (and to our

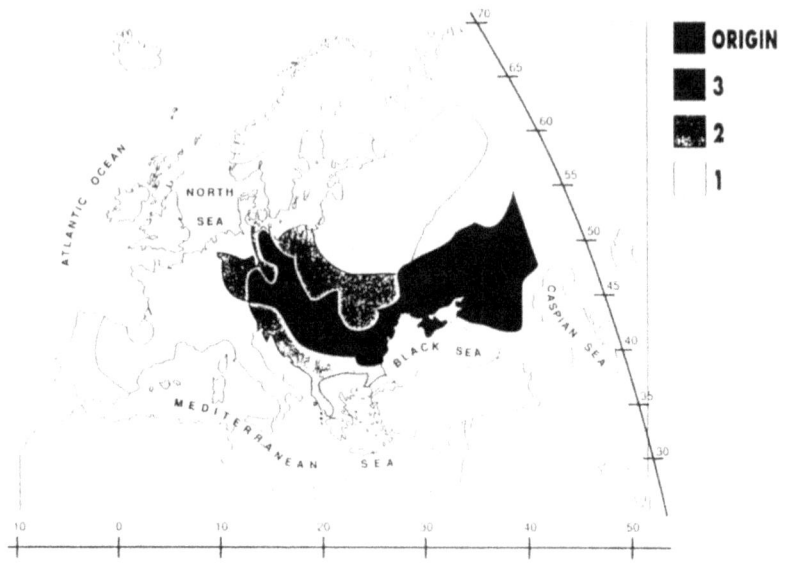

Fig. 8.5. The shaded areas show the origin of Kurgan influence in Lower Volga-Don steppes and the distribution of Kurgan Waves numbers 1, 2, and 3 sites, as described in Gimbutas (1991), and as drawn in Fig. 2B of Sokal et al. (1992). The different shades numbered 1, 2, or 3 outline regions that received one, two, or three of the Kurgan waves. Thus area 2 received waves 1 and 2, or 1 and 3, or 2 and 3, etc. (Piazza et al., 1995).

knowledge the most complete) collection of available population gene frequency data (Piazza et al., 1995).

The geographic map of the first principal component scores (PC1), when compared to the previous analysis with fewer data (Menozzi et al., 1978), agrees to a greater extent with the archaeological information: Congruence between the gene frequency gradient and archaeological dates of the first arrival of Neolithic farmers has been tested by correlating archaeological dates and PC1 interpolated at the same geographical locations. As gene frequencies and dates of the first arrival of Neolithic farmers are both spatially autocorrelated processes, the statistical significance of the correlation coefficient has to be properly modified if we want to test the null hypothesis of the two processes being spatially autocorrelated. We applied the method proposed by Clifford, Richardson, and Hémon (1989), based on the evaluation of an effective sample size that takes into account the spatial structure. We obtained a correlation $r = 0.906$, which was tested by the Student statistics $t = 3.911$ with 3 and 351 degrees of freedom ($p < 0.05$).

8. PATTERNS OF LINGUISTIC CHANGE

The map of Fig. 8.4, which conveys 10.6% of the total genetic variation in Europe, shows the contour plot of the gene frequency third principal component scores (PC3). The impressive analogy of the significant gradient displayed in Fig. 8.4 with a map showing the origin and diffusion of the Kurgan culture (Fig. 8.5) developed by pastoral nomads of the Eurasian steppes starting around 4,300 B.C. (calibrated years), is worth considering, given the suggested connection between this culture and migrations of Indo-European speakers (Gimbutas, 1991).

Statistical significance testing for an association between the Kurgan model and PC3 is not easy to perform, mainly because the dating of the spatial diffusion by the Kurgan culture is not as detailed as that collected for early Neolithic farmers in Europe. Gimbutas's work (1991) identifies the area of origin of Kurgan people and the extension of their three waves of diffusion in Europe, but the dynamics of the process and its precise dating are confused by the infiltration of other cultures into the same geographical areas. We are therefore limited to testing how different geographical areas (the area of the Kurgan people's origin and the regions of Europe that received either none, one, two or three of the Kurgan waves described by Gimbutas; see Fig. 8.5) are correlated with the PC3 scores of Fig. 8.4. We performed the analysis in the following way: We associated score 4 to the area of origin of the Kurgan people, and the scores 3, 2, 1, 0 to the geographical areas of Europe receiving respectively three, two, one, and none of the Kurgan waves, the idea being that the Kurgan acculturation is stronger the higher the number of invasions. We then simply correlated these scores with the PC3 scores over the 2,382 points representing the geographical map and used the Clifford et al. (1989) approach to take into account the interdependence (autocorrelation) of these sample units. We obtained a significant value of $r = 0.538$; $t = 2.217$ ($p < 0.05$).

This suggests an expansion from the steppes between the Black and Caspian seas. Renfrew (1987) raised the question of the cultural advantage that might have allowed the invaders and their descendants to establish their language over such a wide area. Recent archaeological evidence of horseback riding at the Sredny Stog site of Dereivka around 4,000 B.C. (Antony & D. R. Brown, 1991) suggests that the spread of Proto-Indo-European speakers might have received an initial boost, not from the process of riding alone, but rather from the addition of riding to the preexisting agriculture and herding (J. M. Diamond, 1991). The invention of the wheel (the archaeological record in the same geographical area of vehicles is around 3,300 B.C.) probably provided further economic and military advantages that accelerated the expansion of Indo-European speakers to most of Europe.

It is well known that hypotheses on the geographical origin of a language are difficult to prove or disprove. The problem is complicated by the possibility that the group of Indo-European speakers might have undergone several expansions at different times and places. Our genetic data show that a Proto-European speaker's possible homeland in the Kurgan region is not incompatible with an Anatolian origin. Both may be correct, the Kurgan origin being subsequent and secondary to the spread of agriculture to the steppes. If, however, a "secondary products revolution" (Sherratt, 1981) developed in the late Neolithic period, then words for yoke, plough, wool, and so on, all ascribed to a Proto-Indo-European language, would weaken the hypothesis of an association between earliest Neolithic and Indo-Europeans. Recently, Sokal, Oden, and Thomson (1992) undertook a direct study of the correlations between genetic and linguistic expansions postulated by Renfrew and Gimbutas and obtained negative results for both. They calculated partial correlations between frequencies of single genes and possible routes of expansions with geographical distances kept constant. Our method is entirely different from theirs and has produced different conclusions, even though we also took into account a possible confusing effect of a space autocorrelation. The utility of our method for separating different expansions has been validated in previous simulations (Rendine, Piazza, & Cavalli-Sforza, 1986). The reason for the discrepancy between the two approaches requires further investigations.

Barbujani and Sokal (1990) found a correlation between linguistic and genetic boundaries in Europe. In the majority of cases (22 out of 33), there were also physical barriers that may be the cause of both genetic and linguistic boundaries. In nine other cases, there were only linguistic and genetic boundaries, no physical ones; three of these (northern Finland vs. Sweden, Finland vs. Kola peninsula, Hungary vs. Austria) separate Uralic from the Indo-European languages. It remains to be established whether in some of these cases linguistic boundaries have generated or enhanced genetic boundaries, or if both are the consequence of political, cultural, and social boundaries (as in the case of Lapps and non-Lapps) that have played a role similar to that of physical barriers.

8. PATTERNS OF LINGUISTIC CHANGE

Our results suggest that much of the demographic history and prehistory of Europe can be enlightened by studying its human population genetics. This knowledge may contribute to archaeology, history, and linguistics, and the joint study from all of these perspectives will be especially illuminating because modern molecular techniques have raised the analysis of genetic variation to an unprecedented degree of sophistication.

A DIRECT ANALYSIS OF LINGUISTIC AND GENETIC STRUCTURES IN SARDINIA

The genetic analyses shown so far constitute indirect approaches. Genetic gradients are correlated qualitatively or quantitatively with known linguistic areas usually defined by lexical or phonetic isoglosses (Barbujani & Sokal, 1990; Piazza et al., 1988b; Sokal, 1988) or, on a world scale, by linguistic macrophyla (Cavalli-Sforza, Piazza, Menozzi, & Mountain, 1988). In a review, Barbujani (1991) was able to list 15 papers in which genetic and linguistic differences were subjected to correlation measurement. These range from no correlation to a value of .70, but the only study in Europe using the percentage of *cognates* (lexical items with the same meaning and the same root) from a reference list of meanings as a measure of linguistic distance is our study of Sardinia (Piazza, unpublished).

The cultural isolation of Sardinia is a well-known fact given the many linguistic maps that show such isolation. One example is the geographical distribution of the word *blind* in Romance Europe. Not only is the common occurrence of a higher differentiation in Italy apparent, but two terms are pre-Roman relics: *zurpu*, in Sardinia, of Mediterranean origin, and *borgno*, in an area that includes Piemont, western Liguria, and the Franco-Provençal region of France. All other words are of Romance origin. By applying Bartoli's rule given before, the type *orbu* (from the Latin *orbus*—"derived of," implying *lumine*—light) replaced the Latin original classical type *caecus*, today only present in central Italy, Corse and Iberia. In France, there is *aveugle*, which probably derives from the Latin *orbus ab oculis*, afterward shortened and modified to *aveugle* (from *ab oculis*).

The genetic isolation of Sardinia from the rest of Europe is also well-known. Many genes (and the common Rhesus type among them) have frequencies completely different not only from those in Italy, but also from those in Europe. Some genes show affinities with Near Eastern populations, whereas some other genes, although far fewer, show affinities with the Basques, as if a very old, pre-Neolithic, Mediterranian substratum had played a significant role in the differentiation of the Sardinian people. This scenario differs, however, from that of the Greek origin. The differentiation of Sardinia is difficult to date, but at any rate, it goes back at least to pre-Roman settlement.

In addition to Sardinia's being culturally and genetically different from the rest of Europe, its internal cultural and genetic structures are also extremely differentiated. A linguistic atlas of Sardinia (a sample is described in Terracini & Franceschi, 1964) made it possible to compile a detailed geographical distribution of lexical types. About 3,000 glosses were collected from 38 sites but, regrettably, left unpublished. This invaluable treasure has been made available to us for screening in order to match the genetic data.

Three different and independent sources of data have been analyzed: (a) linguistic data in the form of a list of the most conservative 200 lexical items distributed over 22 areas of Sardinia, with the fraction of different glosses associated with the same meanings (cognates) for any pair of geographical areas taken as a measure of their lexical differentiation; (b) isonimy data from the exhaustive collection of 180,836 surnames supplied by the telephone directories in Sardinia; they can be considered as genes transmitted by the male Y chromosome; and (c) genetic data, a total of 42 genes provided by all published and unpublished reports on Sardinian gene frequencies available to us. Lexical, isonimy, and genetic differentiation have been compared by computing appropriate similarity or distance estimates for the same 22 geographical areas.

In condensing the genetic history of Sardinia into the map of its gene frequencies globally, the most remarkable finding is the clear discrimination between the "archaic" areas, which are all clustered together, and those where Phoenician and Carthaginian colonizers are known to have settled. In a collaborative work with Contini (Contini, Griffo, Rendine, & Piazza, 1989), we showed a striking analogy between our genetic images and the geographic distribution of the place names in -ai, -ei, -ui, -oi, and in the oxytone forms believed to be of pre-Roman origin (Terracini, 1927).

8. PATTERNS OF LINGUISTIC CHANGE

Another interesting result was obtained by quantitative analysis of the correlations between the linguistic, isonymy, and genetic sources of data. Geographical distances were also considered. Lexical differentiation is most strongly correlated with isonymy (92%) and, in decreasing order, with genetics (80%) and geography (72%). Isonymy is more strongly correlated with genetics (75%) than with geography (59%). The smallest correlation is between isonymy and geographical distance (59%).

The lack of relevant archaeological records in Sardinia prevents the dating of prehistoric migrations, or the ascertaining of their dimension. Linguistic toponymy records are the only source of information useful for screening the different ethnic stratifications of prehistoric times. A possible synchrony of genetic and linguistic clocks can help in dating those stratifications by the use of language substrata as evolutionary fossils. Again, one of the main messages from our analyses of Sardinia is that the genetic and linguistic structures of contemporary populations still reflect the history of our distant past as if it had been frozen for centuries.

WHAT TO DO?

In the reconstruction of the genetic histories, we found that the voices of remote ancestors echo more loudly than do the voices of more recent ones. Italy, for instance, has been divided into genetically distinct areas on the basis of the frequency of blood groups (but on a European and on a global scale, there is not much difference). These blood groups concur to a great extent with the history of Italy's cities and regions: The genes of the present inhabitants still show strong affinities with those of their supposed prehistoric ancestors, just as substrata of their ancient and mostly extinct speech are found in the dialects of modern Italy. Where this kind of study is heading depends on our interdisciplinary efforts. To a biologist who studies human evolution, the notion that conservative linguistic elements might still link extant populations is clearly challenging. The contribution of archaelogists is well defined, but what can geneticists and linguists achieve together?

One possible answer is given by Table 8.4, in which the *Linguistic Atlases of Europe* are listed by countries. These contain a wealth of information, the results of many years of painstaking, often obscure, work. My experience is that only from the common analysis of real data can students of different disciplines benefit from each other. Problems such as the sampling of linguistic and genetic types are important for both geneticists and linguists. They depend on what the scientists' purpose is. Generally speaking, I have found that scholars in linguistics are more inclined to study the history of a single linguistic item, be it a lexeme, a phoneme or a morpheme. On the contrary, scholars of population biology are more interested in the study of biological types on a global, multivariate basis.

TABLE 8.4

Linguistic Atlases of Europe

Country	Author(s)	Acronym	Maps	Points
Germany	Wenker, Wreder			0
Wallonia	Haust	ALW	374	350
Iberia	Navarro Tomas	ALPI	75	500
Cataluna	Griera	ALC	1,000	101
France	Gilliéron, Edmond	ALF	1,920	101
	Dauzat (regional)	NALF	1,200	1,917
Italy, SSw	Jaberg, Jud	ALS	2,000	354
Italy	Bartoli, Pellis, Terracini	ALI	2,800	1,000
Corse	Gilliéron, Edmond	ALCO	799	44
	Bottiglioni	ALEIC	2,001	49
Rumania	Weigand	WLAD	67	652
	Puscariu, Pop, Petrovici	ALRI	600	385
Europe	Alinei	ALE	in preparation	

I conclude with an example taken from my field experience working with a linguistics expert on Sardinian dialects. When I first proposed to study the geographical distribution of the island's dialects, the linguists I contacted looked at me as though I were rather foolish. They were very kind, however, in showing me parts of the still unpublished *Linguistic Atlas of Sardinia*. At the time, nobody was working on it. It took me and my collaborators 3 years of work to screen the 3,000 morphemes collected in 32 sample points and computerize them. When I went back to the linguists with the first results, they were a little suspicious but interested. One of them said, "I spent most of my life studying the word *head* in the Indo-European languages. What can *you* tell me about it?" The researcher had made a telling point: I found it difficult to explain how much more meaningful the analysis of language types is if it is done at a multivariate level. Only when we sit down to discuss what specific information could be shared by our different disciplines, and which analysis could be carried out to our reciprocal advantage, can such an effort reach our common purpose: giving the silent voices of our past a chance to be heard.

REFERENCES

Ammerman, A. J., & Cavalli-Sforza, L. L. (1984). *Neolithic transition and the genetics of populations in Europe.* Princeton, NJ: Princeton University Press.

Antony, D. W., & Brown, D. R. (1991). The origin of horseback riding. *Antiquity, 65,* 22–38.

Barbujani, G. (1991). What do languages tell us about human microevolution? *Trends in Ecology and Evolution, 39,* 151–156.

Barbujani, G., & Sokal, R. R. (1990). Zones of sharp genetic change in Europe are also linguistic boundaries. *Proceedings of the National Academy of Sciences, 87,* 1816–1819.

Beloch, J. (1886). *Die Bevölkerung der griechisch-römischen Welt (Human settlements in the Greek-roman world).* Leipzig, Germany: Duncker and Humblot.

Bérard, J. (1957). *La colonisation grecque de l'Italie méridionale et de la Sicile dans l'antiquité (The Greek colonisation of Southern Italy and Sicily in the past).* Paris: Presses Universitaires de France.

Bertranpetit, J., & Cavalli-Sforza, L. L. (1991). A genetic reconstruction of the history of the population of the Iberian peninsula. *Annals of Human Genetics, 55,* 51–67.

Bosch-Gimpera, A. (1943). El problema de los origines vascos (The problem of Basque origins). *Eusko-Jakintza, 3,* 39.

Cavalli-Sforza, L. L., & Edwards, A. W. (1964). Analysis of human evolution. *Proceedings of the XI International Congress of Genetics, 3,* 923–933.

Cavalli-Sforza, L. L., & Edwards, A. W. (1967). Phylogenetic analysis. Models and estimation procedures. *American Journal of Human Genetics, 19,* 223–257.
Cavalli-Sforza, L. L., Menozzi, P., & Piazza, A. (1994). *The history and geography of human genes.* Princeton, NJ: Princeton University Press.
Cavalli-Sforza, L. L., Piazza, A., Menozzi, P., & Mountain, J. (1988). Reconstruction of human evolution: Bringing together genetic, archaeological, and linguistic data. *Proceedings of the National Academy of Sciences, 85,* 6002–6006.
Clifford, P., Richardson, S., & Hémon, D. (1989). Assessing the significance of the correlation between two spatial processes. *Biometrics, 45,* 123–134.
Contini, M., Cappello, N., Griffo, R., Rendine, S., & Piazza, A. (1989). Géolinguistique et géogénétique: Une démarche interdisciplinaire (Geolinguistics and geogenetics: An interdisciplinary approach). *Géolinguistique, 4,* 129–197.
Devoto, G. (1967). *Gli antichi italici (The old Italics).* Firenze, Italy: Vallecchi.
Diamond, J. M. (1991). The earliest horsemen. *Nature, 350,* 275-276.
Diamond, J. M. (1992). *The third chimpanzee: The evolution and future of the human animal.* New York: Harper
Di Rienzo, A., & Wilson, A. C. (1991). Branching pattern in the evolutionary tree for human mitochondrial DNA. *Proceedings of the National Academy of Sciences USA, 88,* 1597–1601.
Dolgopolsky, A. B. (1988). The Indo-European homeland and lexical contacts of proto-Indo-European with other languages. *Mediterranean Language Review, 3,* 7–31.
Duhn, F. (1924). *Italische Gräberkunde (The Italic heritage).* Heidelberg, Germany: Winters Universitätsbuchhandlung.
Etcheverry, R. (1947). El factor Rh en personas de ascendencia ibérica e italica residentes en la Argentina (The Rh-factor in individuals of Iberian and Italian ancestry who live in Argentina). *Sem. méd., Buenos Aires, 2,* 500 (1–8).
Gimbutas, M. (1991). *The civilization of the Goddess: The world of old Europe.* San Francisco: Harper.
Gamkrelidze, T. V., & Ivanov, V. V. (1990). The early history of Indo-European languages. *Scientific American, 262,* 82–89.
Jasanoff, J. H. (1988). Review of the book by Renfrew (1987), see below. *Language, 64,* 800–802.
Livi, R. (1896-1905). *Antropometria militare (;oöotary anthropometry).* Rome: Giornale del Regio Esercito.
Mallory, J. P. (1989). *In search of the Indo-Europeans: Language, archaeology and myth.* London: Thames & Hudson.

Menozzi, P., Piazza, A., & Cavalli-Sforza, L. L. (1978). Synthetic maps of human gene frequencies in Europeans. *Science, 201,* 786–792.
Mourant, A. E. (1948). Basque blood groups. *Nature, 162,* 27.
Pallottino, M. (1978). *The Etruscans.* New York: Penguin.
Piazza, A., Cappello, N., Olivetti, E., & Rendine, S. (1988a). The Basques in Europe: A genetic analysis. *Munibe Antropologia-Arqueologia, 6,* 168–176.
Piazza, A., Cappello, N., Olivetti, E., & Rendine, S. (1988b). A genetic history of Italy. *Annals of Human Genetics, 52,* 203–213.
Piazza, A., Rendine, S., Minch, E., Menozzi, P., Mountain J. & Cavalli-Sforza, L.L. (1995). Genetics and the origin of European languages. *Proceedings of the National Academy of Sciences USA, 92,* 5836–5840.
Prosdocimi, A. L. (Ed.). (1978). Lingue e dialetti dell'Antica Italia (Tongues and dialects in Old Italy). *Popoli e Civiltà dell' Antica Italia, 6.* Rome: Biblioteca di Storia Patria.
Pulgram, E. (1958). *The tongues of Italy.* Cambridge, MA: Harvard University Press.
Rendine, S., Piazza, A., Cavalli-Sforza, L. L. (1986). Simulation and separation by principal components of multiple demic expansions in Europe. *The American Naturalist, 128,* 681–806.
Renfrew, C. (1987). *Archaeology and language: The puzzle of Indo-European origins.* New York: Cambridge University Press.
Reynolds, J., Weir, B. S., & Cockerham, C. C. (1983). Estimation of the co-ancestry coefficient. Basis for a short-term genetic distance. *Genetics, 105,* 767–779.
Riva, P. (1964). *Ricerche sul suffisso "-asco" (Investigations on the "-asco" suffix).* Torino, Italy: Frossasco.
Ruffié, J., & Bernard, J. (1974). Peuplement du Sud-Ouest Européen. Les relations entre la biologie et la culture (Human settlements of South-Western Europe. The relations between biology and culture). *Cahiers d'Anthropologie et d'Ecologie Humaine, II,* 3.
Schule, W. (1969). Glockenbecher und Hauspferde. In J. Boessneck (Ed.), *Archaeologisch-biologische Zusammenarbeit in der Vor- und Frühgeschichtsforschung* (pp. 88–93). Wiesbaden, Germany.
Sherratt, A. (1981). Plough and pastoralism: Aspects of the secondary products revolution. In I. I. Hodder, G. Isaac, & N. Hammond. (Eds.), *Pattern of the past: Studies in honour of David Clarke* (pp. 261–305). Cambridge, England: Cambridge University Press.
Sokal, R. R. (1988). Genetic, geographic, and linguistic distances in Europe. *Proceedings of the National Academy of Sciences, 85,* 1722–1726.
Sokal, R. R., Oden, N. L., & Thomson, B. A. (1992). Origins of the Indo-Europeans: Genetic evidence. *Proceedings of the National Academy of Sciences, 89,* 7669–7673.

Terracini, B. (1927). Osservazioni sugli strati più antichi della toponomastica sarda (Some observations on the older substrata of Sardinian toponimy). Reprinted in *Pagine e appunti di linguistica storica*. Firenze, Italy: Le Monnier.

Terracini, B., & Franceschi, T. (1964). *Saggio di un atlante linguistico della Sardegna* (Essay of a lingustic atlas of Sardinia). Torino, Italy: Stamperia Editoriale Rattero.

Trombetti, A. (1926). *Le origini della lingua Basca* (The origins of the Basque language). Bologna, Italy: Forni.

Whatmough, J. (1937). *The foundation of Roman Italy*. London: Methuen.

CHAPTER

9

ORALITY, LITERACY, AND COGNITIVE MODELING

Eckart Scheerer
University of Oldenburg, Germany

That which is reasonable in us saw that it was necessary to impose words on things but the words could not be heard by absent people. So reason gave birth to letters that divided the words into vowels, semivowels and mute sounds.
—Aurelius Augustinus (A.D. 386)

In order for there to be speech, first the tongue must strike the air and if there were no letters, the meaning of a word would be difficult to establish.
—Severinus Boethius (ca. A.D. 500)

In his contribution to this volume, Bechtel argues for the importance of "external symbols such as sounds and inscriptions" in language use. He also speculates that "even in private thinking we are using symbols as if they were external." In this chapter, the points made by Bechtel are generally endorsed, but with one important qualification. In mentioning some differences between "sounds" and "inscriptions," Bechtel treats the two as equivalent with respect to their symbolic function. In contrast to this, I show that formal symbol manipulation presupposes the existence of written notational systems, both linguistic and extralinguistic.

I aim to establish a link between two interdisciplinary ventures that up until now have made no contact: cognitive science on the one hand

and the study of literacy on the other hand. Two interrelated theses will be defended: (a) The "symbolic" level of mental functioning is not a property of the human cognitive system or of the human brain considered in isolation, but can only be understood as a consequence of the historical emergence of written language and other permanent notational systems; (b) "Primary" oral language (i.e., language historically antedating the "invention" of writing and ontogenetically the acquisition of written language) and the mental processes underlying it are not symbolic in the sense of the symbol-processing paradigm, but subsymbolic in the sense of the connectionist, or network modeling, approach.

Because notational systems are cultural products, the two theses imply that important aspects of linguistic and cognitive function are culturally and historically conditioned and cannot be explained by natural evolution alone. Once it is understood that emergent properties often arise from the interaction between entities (see Bechtel, chap. 3, this volume, for details), there is nothing mysterious about the idea that the level at which linguistic and cognitive functions need to be analyzed is not the individual mind (or brain), but its interaction with is physical, social, and cultural environment.

The most provocative aspect of the present treatment is my insistence on a fundamental dichotomy between spoken and written language. Therefore, the first section in this chapter provides some conceptual clarifications and a sketch of the empirical data supporting the dichotomy. In the second section, the perspectives of the symbol paradigm and of connectionism on internal representation are examined, and it is concluded that symbol processing captures the properties of written language and connectionism properties of spoken language. The third section deals with the objection that the effects of literacy are metacognitive only and defends the thesis that literacy has a "symbolizing" effect on linguistic and cognitive processes. The fourth section discusses ape language studies and some data from paleoanthropology to show that permanent, external symbols are a necessary precondition for the emergence of internal symbols. In the fifth section, I use the historical development of writing systems as an illustrative case to show how symbols may be grounded in the discovery of invariances on the basis of covariation among sequences of events.

9. ORALITY, LITERACY, AND COGNITIVE MODELING

ORALITY AND LITERACY

Conceptual Issues: Primary Orality and Typographic Literacy

What follows is a brief outline of the various meanings attached to conceptual pairs: spoken and written language, orality and literacy. We begin with spoken–written language.

First, spoken and written language is defined in terms of sensory modalities for perceiving it and motor systems for producing it. Audition and vision, speaking and writing differ in significant aspects that, taken together, constitute different media of communication. *Verba volant, scripta manent:* Spoken words are volatile, written words are permanent. Audition is temporal and vision is spatial. Written language is conveyed by discrete signals, whereas spoken language is transmitted as a continuous signal flow. Consequently, written utterances are physically segmentable; that is, they can be "taken apart" and "put together again" by overt motor acts, whereas spoken utterances must be segmented mentally, by covert acts. The physical segmentability of written language is its most basic property, enabling us to manipulate (i.e., to lay hands on) the symbols of which it consists.

The second comparison is semiotic and focuses on the referential function and the "grain size" of symbol systems. The standard conception is that writing represents speech, speech represents thought, and only thought represents "things." Contrasted with this is the more recent concept of an (at least partial) autonomy of written language as a semiotic system that may "bypass" speech, or at least represent aspects of language other than speech. Prima vista, direct semiotics is most plausible in the case of logographic writing systems, whereas phonographic writing systems (syllabaries and alphabets) seem to be tied to derivative, speech-mediated semiotic function. However, type of writing system and direct versus indirect semiotics are not related to each other in a one-to-one fashion. Phonographic writing systems code certain aspects of semantics, syntax and pragmatics independently of spoken language, and logographic writing tends to incorporate clues to pronunciation. Thus, the differences among writing systems relate to the degree of transparency versus opacity and level of integration at which semiotic dimensions are expressed. Nevertheless, the (fully developed) alphabet is the only writing system in which written symbols and speech sounds are mapped onto each other.

Third, written and spoken language differ in communicative function. Prior to the invention of electromagnetic means of transmitting and recording speech, oral communication required the presence of speaker and listener in the same spatially and temporally circumscribed setting, which was limited by the carrying range of sound waves and by the necessity of "online" production and reception. Written language does not operate under these immediacy constraints. It is communication at a distance, in space as well as in time.

'Spoken–written language' represents descriptive concepts, whereas 'orality–literacy' refers to the external and internal preconditions and consequences of spoken and written language and, in virtue of this, are dispositional concepts.

A first meaning presupposes the existence of a fully developed practice of writing in a given language and investigates formal, mostly stylistic, contrasts between oral and literate mode(s) of linguistic processes and their cognitive presuppositions. The typical catchword is that there are different "registers" for "using" a given language. Because it is possible to speak in a "written language register" and to write in a "spoken language register," the "registers" can be disconnected from the medial, semiotic, and communicative properties of speaking and writing. This opens the way for transmitting literate language via the speaking–hearing "channel;" and it forces us to dissociate the "registers" from the spoken–written language concept and to subsume them under the notion of oral versus literate types of discourse (Biber, 1988).

A second orality–literacy contrast refers to languages, societies, and cultures and is defined in terms of the absence or presence of a writing system for a given language and of writing–reading as a mode of communication in a given society or culture. Conceptually, the distinction is easy to apply: A language for which no writing system exists is oral, and a society–culture in which writing is unknown is oral. The facts are more complicated. Many cultures have developed sectoral or functionally restricted types of literacy: Only certain professional specialists or privileged classes are literate, or writing is used only for certain purposes and not for others for which it might be used. Even *prima facie* oral cultures may be exposed to literate modes of discourse by contact with modern communication media (and in earlier times, with traders, missionaries, etc.). It may be doubted whether exclusively oral cultures exist at all under present conditions.

A third meaning of "literacy" refers to individuals and their degree of mastery of written language. Its opposite is "illiteracy," not "orality." Illiteracy is not a unitary concept. We must distinguish between absolute, functional (reading and writing had been acquired but are no longer used), and partial illiteracy (reading, but not writing, is historically widespread). Moreover, even absolute illiterates are often exposed to formal properties of literate discourse by listening to the media, having written texts being read to them, and so forth. Consequently, generalized cognitive effects of illiteracy are not likely to be found in illiterate members of literate societies. Still, to an absolute illiterate the medial, semiotic, and communicative properties of written language are not accessible and we can expect some effects of this.

When contrasting orality and literacy, I refer to the extreme corners of the conceptual grid defining orality–literacy (i.e., primary orality and typographic literacy). In line with Ong (1967), "primary orality" is used to denote a linguistic–cultural state and its reflection in the individual person who has made no contact whatever with written language and literate discourse. "Typographic literacy" refers to a state of unrestricted literacy encompassing an entire culture, owing to the universal presence of printed (i.e., standardized) materials and to an educational system in which school attendance is obligatory for everybody.

Although we are witnessing a degree of secondary reoralization (i.e., phone calls replace letters; radio and TV replace books; etc.), modern industrialized societies and their modal members are characterized by typographic literacy. Primary orality is largely a historical phenomenon. Initially, literacy research was mainly concerned with the type of diachronic, epochal contrast emphasized here. For that reason, relevant authorities on primary orality and on the effects of literacy are the pioneers of the field, such as Walter J. Ong, Albert Lord, and Jack Goody.

SOME PROPERTIES OF PRIMARY ORALITY

No Access to Speech Sounds. Objectively, as a signal stream, and subjectively, in phenomenal experience, spoken language is a continuous flow of events from which context-free elements are lacking. This contrasts with the letters of an alphabetic script, which are arranged like pearls on a string in which the shapes of individual letters do not depend on the shapes of their neighbors. The spatial and linear arrangement of written language permits manipulations that cannot be done in the world of (primary) oral language. Whereas it is easy to write down the letters of a word in reverse order, spoken words cannot be treated in that fashion. Furthermore, the very notion of a reversible sequence of elementary language units is due to the spatialization involved in the introduction of (alphabetic) writing (Ong, 1967).

The oral language user does not hear speech sounds (phonemes), because these are abstract units that are phenomenally not represented and become accessible only as a result of the user being exposed to an alphabetic script. Oral segmentation is sensitive to first-order parameters such as sound pressure and fundamental frequency (phenomenal loudness and pitch), whose time-dependent variation constitutes prosody, rhythm, and melody. In addition, phonotactic regularities are used for locating the boundaries of syllables, which are prosodic units (potential loci of stress) and seem to constitute the basic units of speech perception in the primary oral mode. The psychological reality of syllables at the level of primary orality is evidenced by the structure of oral poetry, which is based on counting syllables and arranging them into stress, tonal, and length patterns (meters).

Oral poetry (Lord, 1960) also gives clues to the acoustic parameters available to oral listeners. Rhyming, in the strict sense, is not present. Instead, the oral poet exploits acoustical similarities occurring either in the "body" ("unclean rhymes") or in the "onset" of syllables ("assonances"). Exact matching of speech sounds is not required. Oral listeners are sensitive to some kind of acoustic similarity metric, which enables them to go one step deeper than the syllable, but not all the way down to phonemes.

Experimental studies on adult illiterates confirm the conclusions drawn from the properties of oral poetry. Illiterates display some deficits in tasks requiring the segmentation of spoken language (Morais, 1987). These deficits are especially marked in two types of task: deletion of initial consonants from words and progressive segmentation of a spoken utterance in its components. Illiterates are not unable to perform progressive segmentation, but they typically stop with syllables. Many of them simply cannot delete initial plosive consonants, which is understandable because these have no existence outside of context. Their ability to generate and recognize rhymes is much better than their segmentation abilities. The segmentation deficit is linguistic, not general.

9. ORALITY, LITERACY, AND COGNITIVE MODELING

Illiterates are as good as literates in deleting initial tones from melodies, and Bertelson, de Gelder, Tfouni, and Morais (1989) have reported that the speech segmentation deficit was present even in an illiterate community leader who had excellent communicative skills.

The speech segmentation abilities of prereading children are similar to those of adult illiterates. The central role of phonological awareness in reading acquisition is now hardly ever contested (R. K. Wagner & Torgesen, 1987), and the relevant results, such as the inability to delete initial consonants, are quite robust. The smallest natural speech unit for prereading children is again the syllable, which may be further divided into onset and "rime" (i.e., body and coda; Treiman, 1983).

Awareness of speech sounds depends on exposure to an alphabetic or at least a phonographic script. Chinese who have learned pinjin (Chinese written in the Latin alphabet) have far superior speech–sound segmentation abilities (in Chinese) than Chinese who have learned the traditional hanzi only (Read, Zhang, & Ding, 1986). Chinese residing in the Netherlands develop speech–sound segmentation abilities for Dutch only if they have taken courses in reading and writing Dutch (De Gelder, Vroomen, & Bertelson, 1993). In contrast, Japanese children acquire speech–sound segmentation skills (though later than American children), even when they are not trained in the alphabetic transliteration of Japanese (Mann, 1986). Japanese *kana* are a transparent phonographic syllabary, whereas Chinese *hanzi* at best give clues to pronunciation.

Normally, speech–sound awareness comes about concurrently with and as a result of reading instruction, but some children develop it prior to formal reading instruction. In favor of access to speech sounds not mediated by written language, we might cite the language games children love to play in virtually all, including preliterate, cultures. Language games may in fact promote speech–sound awareness. Among preschool children the ability to recite nursery rhymes is associated with individual differences in phonemic awareness (McLean, Bryant, & Bradely, 1987), and training programs that do not employ written language have been quite effective in promoting it (Lundberg, 1991). However, such findings do not invalidate the thesis that speech sounds are not accessible under conditions of primary orality. Many language games draw on abilities (e.g., exploiting assonances) that are present at that stage, but do not presuppose access to speech sounds. Others that do are derivative from written language (e.g., Pig Latin). To that extent they are illustrations of (synchronic) orality based on (diachronic) literacy. Examples of that sort abound, but often are not recognized as such: Anagrams, palindromes, acrostychs can all be done orally, and yet they cannot and do not exist in preliterate cultures.

Coordinative, Nonpropositional, Formulaic Structure. The structure of oral discourse is coordinative and additive, whereas literate discourse has subordinative, hierarchical structure. One might argue that this is just a matter of literary genres or of "registers"; and from a synchronic viewpoint, this is true. Diachronically, though, things are different. The early stages of language (both in history and in ontogeny) are characterized by a pragmatic, presyntactic mode of discourse, which, inter alia, has the following properties: Topic-comment word order, concatenation, use of intonation for marking the topic—comment structure, and zero anaphora. "Syntacticization" is the result of an evolutionary process contingent on large-scale sociocultural change from the "society of intimates" to the "society of strangers"; the apex of this process is the "written register of human language" (Givón, 1979, p. 307). Most languages spoken in preliterate, small societies prefer loose, coordinated constructions over condensed, syntacticized constructions. Even today there are apparently languages where subordination does not exist, and these are exclusively found in "preindustrial, illiterate societies" (Givón, 1979, p. 298).

To demonstrate a causal effect of writing on the emergence of syntactic structure, we need to compare one and the same language in both the oral and literate states. Because the process of syntacticization is likely to be slow and our knowledge of language history is based on written records, relevant evidence is difficult to obtain. Nevertheless, there are a few examples. During 100 years of literary tradition, the language of the Inuit has developed syntactic subordination devices that originally were lacking (Kalmár, 1985). In Old English homilies (an oral genre recorded in a newly written language) the order in which grammatical cases occur in sentences was entirely dependent on the speaker's communicative intentions; no autonomous, arbitrary syntactic rules are needed to account for the regularities inherent in the ordering of cases (García, 1979).

Language is propositional when the meaning of complex representations is decomposable into the context-free meaning of its constituents. Many oral utterances violate this requirement. They express a single nondecomposable thought. Moreover, formally permissible lexical, semantic, and syntactic modifications do not produce another meaning, but annihilate the thought expressed by the utterance. Prototypes of such nonpropositional utterances are proverbs and, at the subsentential level, idioms. Many proverbs are ungrammatical under the generative account, but could be accommodated in a grammar recognizing multiple coexistent sentence patterns (Norrick, 1985). Idioms are also an anomaly for generative grammar and from that perspective are taken to be "frozen" patterns (Frazer, 1970).

However, perhaps "living" language has arisen from "defrosting" an inventory of idiomatic patterns by exploring similarity relations between them. If so, primary oral language would be non-propositional in toto. Aphasiology provides some evidence, if we accept the principle that residual language functions among aphasics reflect phlyo- and ontogenetically old strata of language development.

Consider Broca's aphasia first. According to Friederici (chap. 7, this volume), Broca aphasics suffer from a deautomatization of grammatical processing. Givón (1979) interprets syntactic discourse as an automatic processing strategy. In terms of his theory, Broca aphasics fall back to the effortful, slow, and hesitating production that characterizes presyntactic, pragmatic discourse. Because Broca aphasics are still able to appraise the grammaticality of utterances, and their "telegraphic" speech often honors syntax, they cannot be said to operate at an exclusively nonpropositional level.

Things are different, however, in the case of global aphasia. Hughlings Jackson (1874) had already described their problems in his days as due to the loss of an ability to "propositionize" (i.e., to string together words to express ideas). Nevertheless, aphasics retain the ability to produce some largely emotive and recurrent utterances called "automatic" by Jackson on account of their involuntary character. The existence of speech residuals among otherwise speechless patients has always been recognized by aphasiologists. Espir and F. Rose (1970) called them "nonintellectual speech" and classified them into emotional utterances, songs and poems, serial speech, and social gestures of speech. Van Lancker (1987) redefined the Jacksonian dichotomy into a propositional–nonpropositional dimension. In propositional utterances, "the meaning follows from an analysis of the meaning of the component parts of the utterance." Nonpropositional utterances "have a meaning that flows from the utterance as a whole" (Van Lancker, 1987, p. 55).

Van Lancker made a good case that nonpropositional speech is the specific linguistic function of the right hemisphere and in part may be subcortically mediated, whereas "ortholinguistic structure" (making possible propositional language) is mediated by the left hemisphere. From a synchronic perspective, Van Lancker argued in favor of a "separate but equal" role of propositional and nonpropositional language. Diachronically, she tends to consider nonpropositional language as the more archaic form.

The history of language provides qualified evidence that primary oral language was nonpropositional—qualified because the evidence comes from poetry rather than from ordinary language. Ever since Parry's (1928/1971) work on the traditional epithet in Homer, oral poetry has been recognized as being largely composed of formulae. A formula is "an expression regularly used, under the same metrical conditions, to express an essential idea" (Parry, 1928/1971, p. 13). The archetype of a formula is the combination "epitheton + proper name," but formulae can be structurally more complicated. Oral compositions are formulaic to an astonishing degree; among 50 verses of *Beowulf*, Magoun (1953) found only 15 that had no doubles in the corpus of Anglo-Saxon poetry. Formulae are not absolutely rigid, but allow a certain degree of variation which, however, is constrained by metric exigencies and must leave their meaning intact.

Against the objection that poetry is not prose and that the latter might be nonformulaic, it should be mentioned that the earliest specimens of prose in Greek, the writings of the pre-Socratic philosophers, still share some characteristics of oral poetry in that the free use of linguistic means is often constrained by rhythmical considerations. In early Near Eastern prose, including the Bible, the *parallelismus membrorum*, the pairwise arrangement of clauses according to their meaning, is a pervasive phenomenon that also imposes constraints on full generativity of linguistic expression. Apart from their mnemonic value, these phenomena testify to the cognitive effort needed for the production of texts on the background of cultures still predominantly deploying language in the presyntactic–pragmatic mode.

"Natural," Situation-Dependent Semantics. Speech as well as phonographic writing are arbitrary in that (apart from isolated cases of onomatopoetics) they bear no similarity to their referents. This is a commonplace of modern thought, formulated already by Aristotle. Yet, the view that word meanings are conventional and arbitrary is a product

of writing culture suggesting that written or printed, but not spoken, words may be mere labels (Ong, 1982). The belief that words are related by nature to their referents stands at the beginning of human thinking about language, as witnessed by the Biblical narrative of Adam knowing the correct names of animals and by the pre-Socratic philosophers whose natural, even onomatopoetic etymologies were attacked by Plato. Here again, ontogeny mirrors history. Children up to the age of 5 tend not to differentiate between words and their referents. Preschoolers treat questions about words as questions about things: "Pencil" is a word "because it writes," and "train" is a word "because there are lots of carriages" (Papandropoulou & Sinclair, 1974, p. 244). Strictly speaking, because children do not act in the same way towards words as toward their referents, they are confusing words and their concepts, but all the same, (spoken) word and meaning cannot be separated. At the ages of 5 to 7, words begin to have an autonomous reality, though by no means among all children (Markman, 1976), and some beginning readers do not differentiate between the properties of written words and their referents; long words must denote bigger things than brief words do. Confusion between words and referents sometimes persists among adults, especially in people with a low literacy level (Hamilton & D. Barton, 1983).

Even though all languages of the world seem to have a term for "word," preliterate cultures have a different concept of a word than do literate cultures. The oral concept of a word refers to any meaningful utterance of almost any length, a generalization abstracted by Lord (1960) from the study of oral poetry as practiced in literate culture, but even more valid for truly preliterate cultures. Consider the metalinguistic vocabulary of the Eipo, neolithic horticulturalists in Western Irian that have little contact with written culture (Heeschen, 1978). The Eipo have one word glossed as "sound, utterance, word, speech, and language," but none referring to smaller linguistic units, except a word for "proper name," which they also use in reference to telling stories, singing songs, and so forth. Although they use a word originally denoting "kernel" for the meaning of "name" (as against the name itself), "no real opposition between the concept and the acoustic form is [thereby] established" (p. 161).

Because the preliterate and the literate perspectives on the concept of a word are so different, the word is not the best level at which to analyze the semantics of oral language. Nevertheless, most of the relevant studies have been concerned with word meanings, and under that caveat they are consonant with a view that sees preliterate thinking as being tied to the immediate life-world (*Lebenswelt*) of individuals. Concerning the meaning of concrete nouns as used by preschool children, the "functional core" hypothesis (Nelson, 1974) covers most of the evidence. The knowledge revealed by preschoolers' use of concrete nouns refers to appearances, uses, actions, and locations, whereas logical relations such as super- and subordination are absent (Anglin, 1985). As revealed by Luria's (1976) classical studies, the thought of adult members of a preliterate culture has the same characteristics. The illiterate Usbek peasants classified nouns according to the function of their referents in concrete, work-related situations. They refused to define words (because they are known to everybody) and were not able (or at least unwilling) to draw inferences concerning cognitively or geographically remote facts, all of which could be done by those of their peers that had acquired reading and writing. In sum, the proximity versus distance polarity that characterizes spoken versus written language has a parallel in the mental models employed by members of oral versus literate cultures.

Reconstructive and Interactive Memory. In the history of experimental research on memory, it has become customary to distinguish between the Ebbinghaus tradition (rote memorization of meaningless syllables) and the Bartlett tradition (reconstructive and schematizing recall of stories). From the present-day cognitive perspective, the two traditions scheme is evaluative: The Ebbinghaus tradition is bad, and the Bartlett tradition is good. Yet they reflect two equally justifiable perspectives on memory. Literate memory is the domain of the Ebbinghaus tradition and oral memory is the domain of the Bartlett tradition. Extended verbatim recall, the Ebbinghaus method is possible only when supported by written texts (Hunter, 1985). In contrast, Bartlett's serial recall method, based on orally transmitted stories and inspired by Bartlett's anthropological background, brings to light some features of memory functioning when no written records are available.

Our best information about oral memory under real-life conditions comes from Lord's (1960) studies on the composers and performers of Yugoslavian heroic–epic poetry. They learned their craft in a kind of apprenticeship. Their songs were massively formulaic and based on a limited stock of fixed-character descriptions, settings, and events. They

9. ORALITY, LITERACY, AND COGNITIVE MODELING

were convinced that they were able to produce verbatim repetitions of the same song, but recordings revealed that the repetitions were by no means identical. When performing, the singers reconstructed their songs from their traditional repertoire and relied on interaction with their audience. Their metrical formulae, which were set into a melodic pattern rendered not only vocally but also on a monochord instrument played by themselves, helped them not to loose the thread of their poem. Their audiences did not expect anything new; the well-known formulae and thematic units were recognized through a pattern-matching process, and this was the foremost source of satisfaction in the singers' performances.

Although it is generally accepted that oral memory usually functions in the reconstructive and socially interactive way just outlined, there has been some debate concerning the nonexistence of lengthy verbatim recall among preliterate societies (Finnegan, 1977). However, as conceded by Finnegan (1988), the presumed counterexamples from the South Pacific may have been mediated by literate practices. Another counterexample (Goody, 1987) is the century-long verbatim transmission of the Rigveda, which are assumed to have been recited in chorus by the Brahmans who had a deep mistrust in writing or may not even have had a writing system. It seems that the chorus-recital technique would have provided a type of social control of memory that normally is exerted by written language. The nonexistence of writing in the classical Veda period has been doubted, however. If it were, in fact, orally composed and transmitted, the Vedic literature is an anomaly that has no known parallels in history.

ORALITY–LITERACY AND CONNECTIONISM–SYMBOL PROCESSING

Approaches to Internal Representation

Bechtel (chap. 3, this volume) provides a general description of the symbol-processing paradigm and a detailed examination of some connectionist models of language processing. My presentation of the symbol processing versus connectionism controversy is therefore restricted to those topics relevant to the comparison with the orality–literacy dichotomy. The focus is on the concept of internal representation. I use the concept in the widest possible sense, referring to any internal state of a system that can be given some semantic interpretation. Defined that broadly, the concept of internal representation is applicable to both types of modeling approaches, which in the following are designated by N (for "network") and S (for "symbolic") representations.

Context-Free, Discrete Symbols Versus Context-Dependent Continuous Subsymbols. According to the symbol-processing approach, symbols have the following properties. They are discrete (digital) classes of local system states drawn from a finite inventory of such states. "Digital" as used here is a functional term not necessarily implying that the physical states themselves must be discrete, but if they are, in fact, continuous, then any intermediate value must be assignable to one symbol only within the defined inventory. They are context-free in a formal or syntactic sense. That is, once a physical state has been assigned to a symbolic category, its processing depends on its form only (i.e., on those properties that define it as a symbol). Context effects are not excluded, but they operate at the level of symbols and not at the level of physical states instantiating them. Discrete and context-free states become symbols only by virtue of some semantic interpretation. At least a subset of symbols—those that are primitive, (i.e., not defined in terms of or derived from other symbols—must have a context-free semantic interpretation (i.e., their reference or meaning do not depend on the (symbolic) context in which they occur).

In the most popular variants of N models, the processing units arranged in layers such that at least one layer is "hidden" (i.e., not in direct contact with the system environment). Momentarily active representations reside in the activation vector over the hidden units, whereas stored representations are instantiated by the connection weights. The latter are continuously modified via the learning procedure, and this means that one and the same stimulus will produce different activation patterns in the course of learning. The internal states of N systems, even if semantically interpretable, do not function as symbols in the sense of the symbol-processing approach. They are realized by continuous variables, and digitization would serve no useful purpose within a network, except for communication with the system environment. The activation vector across the hidden units is not only affected by the stimulus being presented, but depends on the entire stimulus domain, the learning procedure, and the sequence in which the stimuli are presented. There is nothing like a context-free form of N representations, and the same applies to their semantics. The connect-

9. ORALITY, LITERACY, AND COGNITIVE MODELING

ivity pattern obtaining at the learning asymptote reflects the regularities inherent in the stimulus domain, and single stimuli are not represented absolutely, but only relative to the background of these regularities.

N representations are subsymbolic, because the activation of single units in N systems "correspond to the constituents of the symbols used in the symbol paradigm" (Smolensky, 1988, p. 3). The "constituents" stand in a nonlinear, nonadditive relation to the symbols. A one-to-one symbolic redescription of the constituents must be excluded in order for them to qualify as subsymbols.

Structured Versus Holistic Representation. Under the symbol paradigm, most representations consist of more than one symbol; under the neural network paradigm, they are reflected in the activation of more than one unit. The relation between complex representations and their components is usually described by the dichotomy "local versus distributed," but this applies to their physical instantiation. For the referential relation between representations and their objects or domains, the relevant dichotomy is "structured vs. holistic" (Scheerer, 1993a). In structured representations, the components of the representation refer to components of its object, whereas in holistic representation there is no referential relation at the level of components.

In the symbol paradigm, structured representations are not just a subclass of representations, but the only ones that are acceptable. It is required that the meaning of complex representations be computationally derivable from the meaning of their components, in which "computational" refers to the application of syntactic rules without regard for the content of the representational components on which they operate. This is one of the core assumptions of Fodor's (1976) "Language of Thought" theory.

The internal structure of N representations cannot be exploited by syntactic transformation rules, because N systems do not operate under such rules. N systems typically develop holistic representations. A minimum requirement for representational states is that they must display some correspondence or at least correlation with what they are supposed to represent. How is this requirement met for holistic representations? The answer must not be sought in a single activation vector, but in the set of activation vectors produced by a set of stimuli. If such sets are analyzed by multivariate methods, the units fall into clusters that are related to properties of the stimulus domain or its mapping onto output units (Gorman & Sejnowski, 1988; Sejnowski & Rosenberg,

1987). The similarity relations among activations vectors preserve the similarity relations among stimuli (i.e., activation vectors represent according to the principle of secondary isomorphism; Shepard & Chipman, 1970).

Internal Versus External Semantics. Here we ask at which locus the meaning of representational states originates: Does it arise within the system itself (internal semantics) or outside of the system (external semantics)?

In computer programs, the meaning of constants and variables is determined by their syntax alone, and thus their semantics is completely internal. Some variables will refer to states of the system environment, but the latter must be made known to the program through interfaces, and once they have been assigned values, their further processing is driven by the syntax of the program alone. Regarding the nonartifical mind as seen by the symbol paradigm, the same picture is drawn by the principle of methodological solipsism (Fodor, 1981). It states that mental processes are causally affected by the form of the representations alone, such that every difference in content must be mirrored in some formal difference. The content of a representation cannot be changed without also changing its form. Representations get their contents by a psychophysical process extrinsic to the cognitive system. The primacy of their form implies that in any other conceivable environment, the system would operate in the same way that it does in its factual environment.

In N systems, the potential semantics of system states is constrained by the choice of network architectures and learning procedures. Within this constraint, though, the actual semantics of network states is dependent on the system environment, which is external. Their meaning cannot be established by considering the network alone, independent of its environment, and changing the environment will of necessity change the semantics of a network operating in it.

Passive Versus Active Representation. Here we are concerned with the conditions under which stored representations are activated and with the modus operandi of the activated, occurrent representations. An occurrent representation is passive when it is recalled in the same form as some stored representation, and when it requires some process operating on it in order to have some causal power within the system. In active representations, the occurrent representation is not necessarily isomorphic with some stored representation, and its causal powers derive from the sole fact of its being activated, without any additional process operating on it.

S representations are passive. As long as they are not needed, they reside in some storage medium where they wait to be called on; and although their use may modify them, the mere process of recalling them does not. Even when activated, S representations are causally inert unless some rule-governed process operates on them. N representations are active. The activation pattern of the hidden units is not a mere replica of the connection strengths instantiating stored network representations, but depends on a number of additional factors, always including the input activation conveyed via the connections and, optionally, the previous activation state of the hidden units. Once hidden units are activated, their activation is relayed to those units with which they are connected. Thus, the mere presence of an activation vector ensures that it exerts a causal influence.

FOUR PARALLELS

The most fundamental parallel pertains to the concept of formal symbols (i.e., discrete, context-free events connected and transformed by means of formal rules and functioning as carriers of internally determined meaning). This concept is not applicable to spoken language in the state of primary orality, although it is self-evident that it applies to written language. The spoken–written language pair refers to the actual physical signals by which linguistic utterances are instantiated, and thus it seems to externalize a dichotomy that the connectionism–symbol processing pair asserts with respect to the internal functioning of the cognitive system. I hope to show that the actual causal sequence proceeds in the opposite direction: The network versus symbols dichotomy and its subject matter (the two modes of cognitive functioning denoted by it) results from the internalization of two types of external signal systems as embodied in spoken versus written language.

Structured–Holistic Representation. At the stage of primary orality, listeners do not have access to a discrete, irreducible inventory of speech sounds. At least from the first-person perspective, spoken language is represented in a way that fails to meet the requirements of an S representation: Complex representations cannot be decomposed into recombinable elementary symbols. The closest primary-oral approximation to the concept of a component of S representations is the syllable. But even this is not defined in a context-free fashion; although syllabification is often possible, the boundaries between syllables are unstable. In sum, spoken language seems to be more akin to an N representation, with the proviso that unstructured representations may be put into a mapping relation with their domains via the principle of secondary isomorphism. The sensitivity of primary-oral listeners to auditory similarities shows that this precondition is fulfilled.

Propositional–Nonpropositional Language. In arguing that primary oral language is nonpropositional, it is not implied that the primary-oral speaker does not have the means to find new linguistic utterances for new experiences. Except for the earliest stages of linguistic development, this would be an absurdity. It is implied, however, that the creativity of primary oral language is not mediated by formal-combinatorial grammar and syntax. It is now generally accepted that N systems display limited or weak compositionality, as opposed to the strong compositionality maintained by symbol-processing approaches and most forcefully by the "language of thought" theory. The structure of primary oral language is more akin to weak than to strong compositionality.

Internal–External Meaning. In a famous thought experiment, Searle (1980) imagined someone shut up in a room who has access to an unlimited supply of written materials in Chinese, including dictionaries and grammars, and learns to form all kinds of correct expressions in Chinese, but who, according to Searle, does not understand the very same expressions he or she is using correctly. One thought experiment is worth another. Let us therefore imagine speakers of a language who do not understand each other in the (complete) dark because the deictical lexemes of their spoken language require the presence of visible objects in order to be understood. The thought experiment is meant to illustrate that two types of meaning (one internal, based on the linguistic system itself; the other external, depending on the physical and social environment) stand in an intuitively plausible relation to the written–spoken language dichotomy. To the extent that it is accurate to impute internal semantics to symbol systems and external semantics to network systems, a viable parallel between spoken language and N representation and written language and S representation has again been suggested.

Passive–Active Mode. If we concede that extended verbatim recall is possible for written texts only, and that the relevant ability needs a literate culture for its development, then we cannot fail to notice the similarity of the underlying memory representation to the typical mode of existence of S representations, which "sit there," awaiting their retrieval in the same form in which they were stored. Oral memory shares with N representations properties such as inherent instability across repetitions, existence only when activated, and activation according to the pattern recognition and pattern completion modes.

TWO OBJECTIONS

Do these parallels allow the conclusion that the symbol paradigm is not applicable to primary oral language and the mentality corresponding to it? Two objections may be made against the validity of this claim.

The Metacognitive Objection

The first objection maintains that the effects of literacy do not pertain to the objective structure of cognitive processes, but rather to the subject's awareness of them. Most researchers in the field subscribe to this view. The segmentation deficits of illiterates and of prereaders are typically reported under the heading of "phonological awareness" or even "metaphonological awareness." The general idea is that reading and nonreading subjects have the same phonological representations, but compared to readers nonreading subjects are less aware, or differently aware, of them. According to D. R. Olson (1991), literacy is best seen as a metalinguistic activity. This, however, does not imply that literacy, once attained, cannot exert a top-down influence on the linguistic representations to which it refers. More generally, metacognition would be useless if it were causally inert with respect to cognition. In the spirit of this principle, let us look for evidence that the representations underlying speech perception and production are in fact modified by the acquisition of written language.

For this to happen, speech representations must be modifiable in principle. There is now a growing consensus, based on word production and perception studies, that the segmental structure of spoken language is not there from the start, but undergoes a development extending until the early school age. A child's first words are not represented as a sequence of independent phonemes, but holistically as a pattern of (subsymbolic) features such as articulatory routines or gestures. As the lexicon expands, the scope of representation narrows down to sublexical levels, beginning with the syllable. However, the holistic–featural representation still persists at the syllabic level, and the restriction of the representational scope to the phonemic level is not fully achieved until the age of 7. These changes in the underlying representations mirror the developmental trends in phonological awareness (Fowler, 1991). Consequently, the speech awareness of prereading children should not be described as imperfect knowledge of phonological representations, but as perfect knowledge of nonphonological representations.

An important manifestation of the global developmental trend is the different role of the syllable between adults and preschool children, as inferred from speech errors and speech games (Berg, 1992). In the adult, the syllable has a hierarchical structure and provides a frame for the serial arrangement of phonemes. When speech sounds are erroneously transposed, their within-syllable position remains the same, and reversals and transpositions of entire syllables are extremely rare. In contrast to this, speech games of children are based on the syllable as an unanalyzed unit.

If preschoolers do not have a phonologically organized representation of speech, this should show up in their spontaneous spellings; and this is actually what happens. The creative spellings of kindergarteners are predominantly phonetic. That is, they are based on articulatory and acoustical features, and from the child's perspective, they arise from the expectation that what sounds similar should be spelled similar (Read, 1986). The resulting spellings often come into conflict with standard morphophonological accounts. The different spoken realizations of the English plural morpheme and the past tense morpheme are, as a rule, spelled differently. Independent of morphology, allophones are not recognized as such. In German the two phones [χ] and [ç] are both allophonic; their distribution is complementary, and they are both spelled with the digraph <ch>. Yet spontaneous spellers use different letters for them (see Scheerer-Neumann, 1988, for an example). Such nonstandard, phonetically based spellings often persist in the early school years. Once the standard spelling is acquired, many people are no longer able to discriminate the phonetic features to which preschoolers are sensitive, and in the case of homographs, they hear and produce different sounds where phonologically there are no differences.

Evidence relevant for a cognitive, as opposed to a metacognitive, interpretation of literacy should also come from neuropsychology. In about 95% of people phonemic abilities are controlled by the left hemisphere, but the contribution of literacy to left-hemisphere dominance for phonemic speech remains controversial. If we accept, for the sake of argument, the thesis that the hierarchically ordered, serial structure of speech results from the acquisition of an alphabetic script, then we can deduce some empirically testable conclusions from it.

Compared to literates, illiterates should display diffuse, bilateral cortical localization of language, which means that the right hemisphere should contribute more strongly to speech perception and production. We should therefore expect a higher incidence of crossed aphasia (aphasia resulting from right-hemisphere damage in dextrals) in illiterates than in literates. A study by Cameron, Currier, and Hearer (1971) seemed to support this prediction, but the better-controlled study by A. R. Damasio, Castro-Caldas, Grosso, and Ferro (1976) did not find evidence for a contribution of literacy to the "brain specialization for language." The current textbook opinion (Hamsher, 1991) is that illiterates' "hemispheric specialization for language for the most part do[es] not appear to differ from those of literate individuals" (p. 352). Nevertheless, the case for a different pattern of brain specialization in illiterates is not entirely closed. Two well-controlled studies have revealed some subtle differences between literates and illiterates. H. Damasio, A. R. Damasio, Castro-Caldas, and Hamsher (1979) found that in listening to dichotically presented word pairs differing in the initial phoneme, only literates showed the usual right-ear superiority whereas "dysliterates" showed a left-ear advantage. Lecour and Parente (1991), in corroborating that there was no difference in the incidence of overall crossed aphasia between literates and illiterates, found that in a picture-naming task illiterates with a stroke to the right hemisphere differed from healthy illiterate controls on a paraphasia, but not on a word-finding score.

If exposure to an alphabetic script (rather than to written language per se) facilitates the specialization of the left hemisphere for language, then we should expect the incidence of crossed aphasia to be higher among people using a logographic script. Hu, Qiou, and Zhong (1990) found the incidence of crossed aphasics to be 15% among dextral stroke patients of Han (Chinese) nationality, as compared to the 2% rate quoted in most European publications. Uigurs und Kazakhs living in the same area, but using a script based on the Arabic alphabet, had an incidence of crossed aphasia nearer to the European figure. Among the Han, only 2% were classified as Wernicke's aphasics, but 67% as Broca aphasics, a figure out of proportion to anything known from the Western literature.

Perhaps Wernicke's aphasia is a "cultural artifact" resulting from the use of an alphabetic (or at least a phonographic) writing system. Two facts support this somewhat bold conjecture. First, virtually every Wernicke aphasic suffers from problems in phoneme discrimination, to such an extent that Luria (1966) felt justified in renaming Wernicke aphasia as "afferent phonemic aphasia" (see also Blumstein, 1973). Second, the incidence of Wernicke aphasia in childhood is very low. Not long ago, the textbook opinion was that fluent (Wernicke, *posterior*) aphasia is never seen before the age of 10 years (Aram, 1991). Some younger cases have now been documented, but the clinical impression remains that all childhood aphasias below the age of 7 are of the nonfluent type (Friederici, personal communication). Again, the magical age of 7 years, which in all Western countries happens to coincide with the acquisition of the "alphabetic principle"!

Why is childhood aphasia almost always of the Broca type? Agrammatism, a prominent feature of Broca aphasia, results from deautomatization, rather than from absolute loss of grammatical knowledge. If automatized grammatical processing is a product of written language, then preliterate children should behave like Broca aphasics, even when not braindamaged. There is, in fact, some evidence for this (Friederici, chap. 7, this volume), and at first sight childhood aphasia, because it is of the Broca type, seems to be just an exacerbation of a normal developmental state. However, one additional factor may be involved. In order to translate automatically grammatical structures into phonologically organized speech sounds, Broca's area must rely on phonemic input provided by Wernicke's area. If this interpretation is correct, then childhood aphasia of the typical Broca variety should result not only from anterior, but also from posterior, lesions. This is actually the case, and there is even a slight trend toward greater deficits following posterior left lesions (Aram, 1991, p. 443). Even though the classical view that early childhood aphasia results equally often from left- and from right-hemisphere lesions is no longer tenable (Woods & Teuber, 1978), intrahemispheric specialization still seems to undergo developmental differentiation, eventually resulting in a segregration of the functions subserved by Broca and Wernicke's areas.

Received wisdom denies that this segregation is driven by alphabetically organized written language, but there is some evidence that aphasic children suffer from a lack of phonological awareness. Aram, Ekelman, and Whitaker (1987) reported that left-lesioned children made more errors in a word-finding task in response to phonemic cues than did right-lesioned children. In contrast, Woods and Carey (1979) found no hemispheric difference in tasks requiring rhyming and the completion of nursery rhymes. This pattern is similar to the relevant abilities of adult illiterates, who are able to rhyme but are poor at recognizing the identity of initial sounds in words. Among children who have recovered from aphasia, spelling problems are likely to persist, sometimes even permanently (Aram, 1991).

In summary, by requiring an analytic, phonemic approach to speech, and thus symbolizing spoken language, alphabetic writing arguably has a double, interhemispheric and intrahemispheric effect on brain organization for language: left-lateralization and functional segregation between anterior and posterior language areas. The available evidence at best points to a facilitative effect and is compatible with the view that lateralization and functional segregation would have occurred in any case. However, this is because we do not have the right kind of evidence. We need thorough ethnoneuropsychological studies of brain organization for language among the members of the few remaining preliterate cultures, and more systematic neuropsychological research on the effects that use of a nonphonographic writing system has on the cerebral control of speech perception and production.

The Deep Theory Objection

The second objection claims that the symbol-processing theory, like generative phonology and grammar, is a deep theory trying to explain empirical phenomena by means of theoretical constructs that need not be observable at the surface level of the to-be-explained empirical domain. Even if it were the case that surface representations are holistic, context-sensitive and so on, this would not preclude the effect to explain these properties via interactions occurring among the elements of an inventory of context-free deep-structure symbols.

This objection had some force as long as there was no explanatory alternative to the deep theories of language and cognition. Once nonsymbolic explanatory accounts of surface-level linguistic and cognitive processes are, in principle, available, the symbol-processing theory cannot be defended any more on the grounds that it is "the only game in town." The postulate that there are context-free internal symbol systems must be justified on independent grounds. What is needed, then, is a theoretical account of symbol genesis, but if we maintain that the language of thought functions like a computer program, it is useless to ask how symbols have arisen in the first place. The symbols are a product of the human designer or programmer, a process that has no parallel in natural history. The programming-language view of cognitive functioning also permits us to situate the symbol-processing theory with respect to the orality–literacy dimension. Computer programs are written in some programming language. This is not a metaphor, but must be taken literally. Even if it were possible to program a computer via spoken commands and to receive spoken output from the machine, the program would still be represented in the form of written language, because, like any external script, it works with context-free, discrete, spatially ordered symbols. The language of computers is inherently written language, and artificial intelligence (provided it exists) instantiates not *oratio mentalis* (the spoken language of the mind), but *scriptura mentis*, that is, mind (or brain) writing (Sokolowski, 1988).

The written-language explanatory background is especially evident in the case of standard grammatical theory, which is studded with expressions that make sense only if they are applied to written language: "rewrite rules," "left movement", "right movement," "left- and right-branching structures," and a veritable bonanza of spatialized temporal relations. The oddity of these expressions becomes obvious only if they are applied to languages with right-to-left writing systems; then suddenly we get an inkling that "left" and "right" are standard metaphorical expressions applied to temporal ordering (Hawkins & Carter, 1988, p. 312). A more revealing insight would reveal that the entire apparatus

9. ORALITY, LITERACY, AND COGNITIVE MODELING 235

of rewriting, left and right moving, branching, embedding, and so forth. simply is not applicable to primary oral language.

The theory of segmental phonology arguably has arisen from importing the alphabet into the auditory structure of speech (Aronoff, 1992). If so, then theory has repeated a process that occurs in the individual language user as a result of exposure to an alphabetic writing system.

In general, theories positing the formal manipulation of internal symbols are best conceived as a kind of scientific metacognition, as conceptually reconstructed access to cognitive processes. As such, they need not be based on introspection. Rather, like metacognition in general, they derive from observing one's own behavior and its effects on the physical and social environment. If so, then the theory that thinking is formal symbol manipulation must have arisen after the practice of formal symbol manipulation had found sufficiently wide social dissemination to be considered as a general phenomenon rather than a special case. Intellectual history shows this to be true. The relevant historical process was quite protracted and found completion only in the early modern period. Key events were the final acceptance of Arabic numerical notation, the replacement of the abacus by paper-and-pencil, "algoristic" arithmetics, the widespread dissemination of printing, and the switch from early-medieval "neumes" to modern musical notation (see Scheerer, 1993b, for more details.) It is no coincidence that the first philosopher to identify thinking with formal, content-free symbol manipulation was Leibniz, who himself had constructed one of the first mechanical calculators (Krämer, 1991).

THE HISTORICAL GENESIS OF GRAPHIC SYMBOLS

"Artificial" Symbol Acquisition

Why must there be symbols in a cognitive system's environment for the system to develop a symbolic level of functioning? Natural cognition is instantiated by living systems, and such systems, considered in isolation and separated from their environment, do not dispose of symbols. So far, no physiological level of functioning has been found that on its own, as a proper, natural function would develop formally manipulated, content-free symbols. Neither is there an anatomical structure specifically predisposed for symbol production. If the living brain is to be compared to a computer, then the comparison must be to an analog machine, an immense network of networks, and all symbols must be implemented by networks. If N systems are to emulate combinatorial S systems, then their environmental domain must itself be combinatorial. It follows that organisms, which in their own ecological niche did not develop symbols, may acquire symbols, provided they are confronted with external S systems and their utilization.

In their natural habitat, chimpanzees did not develop spoken language. Nevertheless, they have been taught to understand and use some symbols. The most successful attempts in that direction have been made by use of lexigrams (i.e., permament, noniconic visual symbols). Chimpanzees do use some symbolic gestures spontaneously (Parker & K. R. Gibson, 1979). Thus, teaching sign language to them seems more natural and actually was done in several projects. Chimpanzees instructed in a simplified version of American Sign Language acquired an extensive vocabulary of signs, often used the signs on their own initiative, sometimes forming sequences of more than 5 signs. Nevertheless, it has been doubted that their signing behavior was truly linguistic. They were prone to interrupt their teachers and, in general, did not honor "conversational rules"; as a result, their utterances were mostly imitations or other responses to the prior signing of their teachers and lacked the productivity and systematicity that presumably is a defining property of natural language (Terrace, Petito, Sanders, & Bever, 1980). Even though it has been suspected that lexigrams, too, have served as discriminative stimuli supporting imitative or stereotyped response sequences, it has now been established that apes taught with lexigrams have gained insight into their symbolic function and use them spontaneously and productively in diversified contexts (Savage-Rumbaugh, 1986, 1990).

So far, the symbol-using abilities of apes under different training procedures (sign language versus lexigrams) have not been subjected to a comparative empirical test. The scientific community is interested in linguistic capacities of apes *per se* and tends to discuss the various training approaches from a technical or methodological standpoint only. Both types of training may have been successful in building up protolinguistic capacities in apes, albeit of a different kind: Signing apes have learned oral protolanguage and lexigram-trained apes have acquired written protolanguage. Although it is received via the visual channel, sign language shares many properties of spoken language. Gestural signs are produced in a continuous stream, their shapes are influenced by context, and new symbols can be formed by blending already-acquired symbols. These properties explain both the strengths and the weaknesses of sign-language use by apes. On the strong side, the apes are able to create new sign gestures, to produce sign blends and more transparent sign compounds, and to use analogs of intonation in the auditory domain by varying, in a quite literal sense, illocutionary force (Patterson, 1980). On the weak side, breaking up a stream of signs into individual signs and emancipating sign use from immediate context is difficult, if not impossible. The iconicity of many signs and the existence of a phylogenetic background of natural sign-gestures may also be impediments for decontextualization. Gestures have some properties that are different from spoken language. For instance, apes can and do sometimes produce two signs at a time, and their impolite behavior in conversation may reflect a medial property of sign language (signing does not interrupt the signing of others in the way that speaking interrupts the speaking of others). With these provisos, signing apes arguably operate at an incipient stage of the pragmatic, presyntactic level that is typical for primary oral language.

The basic advantage of lexigrams may well be that they partake of the medial and semiotic properties of written language: permanence, discrete inventory of symbols, and spatial position of signs separable from the temporal sequence of signing. To be freely combined and recombined, symbols must be physically segmentable, which, at the chimpanzee level, seems to require that they can be manipulated in a literal sense.

In itself, access to physically manipulable symbols does not guarantee formal symbol manipulation. Among the "literate" apes, form and semantic content are not factored out, and the way the apes treat the symbols depends on both their semantic content and their pragmatic function. Nevertheless, they may operate at an incipient level of formal symbol utilization defined by decontextualization and arbitrariness. Chimpanzees acquire symbols when their human caretakers use the symbols for marking everyday routines. The routines need not be performed at once, but can also be merely planned (Bechtel 1990; Savage-Rumbaugh, 1990). Routines consist of components that can be inserted into other routines. If every component is separately marked, components occurring in more than one routine will be marked by symbols occurring in more than one sequence or spatial arrangement. When the chimpanzees recognize that symbols used in different contexts are the same and have the same referents, and when they use one and the same symbol in different contexts, their symbol use can be said to have reached a first stage of decontextualization, even though they do not use them totally outside of context. The symbols are also arbitrary, in that they are not iconic with respect to the routines and the chimpanzees do not confuse them with their referents, i.e., the actions marked by them.

Although symbol acquisition by chimpanzees under human control is a laborious process that must be tightly structured by the trainers, the pygmee chimpanzee, Kanzi, has acquired the use of symbols in a much less effortful way, by watching the (not very successful) symbol-manipulation attempts of his mother. Among Kanzi's many achievements, the most fascinating is his ability to understand spoken utterances not exceeding a certain length, something that so far has not occurred among other "educated" chimpanzees. If it could be safely established that this achievement was contingent on his use of lexigrams, then a causal role of written language in the segmentation of spoken language would be demonstrated.

Glossogenesis and Grammatogenesis

The acquisition of symbols by chimpanzees is clearly artifical, induced by their human trainers. For man, however, we must not only explain how symbols are acquired, but also how they came into being in the first place. My scenario bears some similarity to the picture drawn by Greenfield (1991), but diverges from hers in an important point.

Greenfield sees the phylogenetic roots of symbolic processes in the production and use of tools. In nonhuman primates, the cortical control of the motor skills needed for the production and use of tools is located in an area homologous to Broca's area in humans. Tool use requires motor acts with a combinatorial-sequential, and at higher stages, a hierarchical structure. Across the primates, the requisite structures display a phylogenetic developmental trend that has parallels in human ontogeny, both linguistically and cognitively. This allows the conclusion that the combinatorial, sequential and hierarchic structure (presumably) typical of human language has inherited the anatomical location and cognitive structures underlying tool use in nonhuman primates.

9. ORALITY, LITERACY, AND COGNITIVE MODELING 239

The Greenfield scenario takes as its *explanandum* the traditional, grammatico-phonological view of language. In line with this perspective, the "grain size" of the combinatorially structured (proto-)language that Greenfield envisaged is at the level of speech sounds as structured by grammar, to be described by morphophonology. This is not plausible. The linguistic equivalents of objects in tool use are not phonemes or grammatical categories, but words (or other meaningful utterances) and their relation to other words (or meaningful utterances) (Tomasello, 1991). Direct comparisons between modern languages and prelinguistic preadaptations may not be appropriate. To Greenfield, once language has evolved from proto-language it already has grammatical structure. However, in all probability, grammar is itself a product of intralinguistic development, arising from an initial word-order-based syntax via the transformation of words into grammatical morphemes (Givón, 1979). Greenfield also neglected to observe the difference between the hierarchical, spatial schemata used to elucidate the phrase structure of sentences and the spatial arrangements of objects in tool use. The former are only in the mind (even worse, of the linguist, not necessarily of the language user); the latter are "out there" and if mentally represented, the representation is in a visuospatial format. Tool use should be considered not only in its motor aspects, but also in terms of the visual properties defining tools and their objects.

Tools have some properties that qualify them as preadaptations for the emergence of visual symbolism and ultimately of written language. Their use implies a certain degree of decontextualization. When natural objects are used as tools, the object is taken out of its original context and inserted into another context. When apes make tools, they do it for their own immediate benefit only; they do not store them for later use, nor do they adapt them for use by other apes. Tool-use traditions may emerge at that level, as documented among chimpanzees living in the wild. The use of tools is learned via "apprenticeship," through observation and imitation. Techniques of tool production among early hominids have remained virtually the same for 1 million of years, indicating that they may have been transmitted in this procedural, nonverbal way. A profound change occurred at the middle–late stone age transition, 50,000 to 30,000 years ago. We now witness the mass production of standardized and specialized tools, coming in regional styles (industries). Standardized tools have no parallel anywhere in the animal kingdom, and it is generally agreed that their production is an important marker for the emergence of *homo sapiens*.

According to one interpretation, (Mellars, 1989; R. White, 1989a), stone-age "industries" presuppose planning and language. Others (Dibble, 1989) think that the standardization is an artifact of the classification method, and that the tool types are a function of available materials and technologies. Thus, they do not presuppose the capacity for linguistic categorization and standardized tool making could still be transmitted in the nonlinguistic apprenticeship mode (Wynn, 1991). The two approaches may capture two stages in tool production, however. Network modeling has taught us that goals need not be explicitly represented in order for goal-directed behavior to occur. Perhaps tool types have developed through a process of multiple simultaneous constraint satisfaction. Once attractors have emerged in the weight-state space of a network, they serve as prototypes for the categorization of new input vectors. Categorization may have been the result of an unplanned process, of a network settling into an optimal solution, but it would have been economical not to repeat that process after stable prototypes had formed themselves. This could be achieved by having a representation of the prototype available before beginning work on the next tool. The representation originally may have been an optimally shaped tool itself, and the ability to refer to such a concrete model in its absence would have conferred an evolutionary advantage. In summary, sensorimotor categorization must have preceded linguistic categorization, but the latter (either vocal or gestural) is likely to have assisted in the stabilization and spatiotemporal dissemination of tool types and the associated production processes.

Many artifacts remaining from the middle–upper paleolithic transition period are not tools, but objects for decorating one's own body, such as beads and pendants made of bones rather than stones and also standardized to a considerable extent. Their production must have been organized in a sequence of steps such as piercing, grinding, and polishing (R. White, 1989a). Body ornaments often bear representational designs, with a social meaning; some were made from materials that were not locally available and were procured by an early form of trade. R. White (1989b) concludes (a) that a creative revolution marked by the emergence of visual thinking occurred in the upper palaeolithic shift and (b) that the revolution was contingent on language-as-we-know-it (i.e., speech). Although conclusion (a) is correct, conclusion (b) does

9. ORALITY, LITERACY, AND COGNITIVE MODELING

not necessarily follow, at least not if stated in unidirectional fashion, because it must be asked how awareness of the symbolic, representational function of spoken language could have arisen in prehistory in which there was not yet a community of language users providing that function for today's children. The emergence of visual–representational capacities is clearly documented, and the relevant insight may have been derived from the exercise of these capacities (Noble & Davidson, 1991). We should envisage the possibility that visual thinking has acted back on spoken language, in the specific sense of facilitating referent–object separation. Perhaps, after all, oral language never was exclusively oral!

Although they were relatively decontextualized, standardized, representational, and imbued with socially constituted meaning, palaeolithic ornaments and other art objects cannot be considered as proto-writing. They are, however, prewriting in that writing ultimately draws on abilities first manifested in the earliest practices of graphic and pictorial representation.

Under the present approach, graphic symbols reflect proto-writing when they are conventionalized, standardized and are used for transmitting and preserving information in the absence of both the source and the referential objects of that information. (Beads, etc., are not proto-writing because the social display for which they are meant works only in conjunction with their bearer; stone-age cave paintings are not proto-writing because they are not standardized.) Proto-writing is negatively defined by the absence of a systematic relationship between the symbol inventory and its referential domain. Whenever we have a holistic system of conventionalized graphic representation, then we are dealing with proto-writing. Thus defined, instances of proto-writing are potter's marks and seals, but also semasiographic writing in which one compact thought is expressed by a combination of graphic symbols, as well as pictographic writing so long as the individual icons are not arranged in a way that reflects their temporal sequence in a narrative.

Writing in the wide sense is defined by the existence of a systematic mapping relation between the representational system and its referential domain; it presupposes structured representation, although not necessarily of a combinatorial nature. Writing in the strict sense is subordinated to language. A conceptually straightforward criterion for distinguishing the two is that understanding a piece of writing in the strict sense presupposes knowledge of the language to which it stands in a mapping relation, whereas such knowledge is not required for understanding written symbols in the wide sense.

Did writing historically emerge at once in its language-subordinated form, or was there a period of nonlinguistic writing in the wide sense? The data favor the second alternative. The practice of writing, when it first emerged among the Sumerians, was intended to document economical and administrative transactions. This could have been done by means of language-subordinated writing, but, as a matter of fact, it was not. The administrative texts resulting from this utilization of writing display the following two remarkable properties (H. J. Nissen, Damerow, & Englund, 1991, p. 70, my translation): (a) "The meaning of the symbols was determined by production, distribution, and administrative processes, and was not the same as the corresponding concepts of the language," and (b) "the symbols were not arranged according to linguistic–syntactic criteria, but the format of the tables, representing some economical transaction, determined where each symbol had to go." That is, the administrative texts were instances of writing in the large sense, and their historical priority shows that linguistically subordinated writing was a secondary development, probably motivated by the potentialities discovered to be inherent in nonlinguistic writing. Writing was not invented as a means to represent linguistic structure.

FROM EVENT STREAM TO SYMBOL CHAINS

Invariance Extraction Through Covariance Detection

Theories that derive phonologically organized language from the structure of action need to explain the emergence of a discrete symbol inventory from the continuous flow of acoustical signals or articulatory events characterizing spoken language. Action, considered in isolation, cannot do the job because it is itself continuous. Only actions that interact with objects acquire sequential and hierarchical structure. This is the reason why tool use is so important, but the segmentation it provides ends at the level of words or other meaningful units.

Taken in isolation, event streams can be segmented if discontinuities are signaled by strong perceptual cues. Prosodic and phonotactic cues are effective, as shown by recent work on infant speech perception. In the absence of such cues, segmentation on the basis of a single

9. ORALITY, LITERACY, AND COGNITIVE MODELING 243

sequence seems impossible. This is acknowledged by the motor theory of speech perception according to which "speech perception is constrained by tacit knowledge of what a vocal tract does when it makes linguistically significant gestures" (Repp & Liberman, 1987, p. 98). Thus, covariance between the acoustical and the articulatory streams is necessary, but owing to coarticulation effects, the articulatory stream often provides weak segmentation cues only and is itself context dependent. Therefore, the emergence of context-free symbols still is not guaranteed. The conventional, arbitrary segmentation of an event stream requires covariance with an event sequence that already is physically or perceptually segmented.

In order to be discovered, covariances need not be deterministic; probabilistic correlations are sufficient. Connectionist models are able to bring to light invisible, nonlinear and context-sensitive correlations. The grain size of subsymbolic representations in N systems is not constant, but varies according to systems dynamics, the objectively existing covariances, and the learning procedure. Coherently activated groups of fine-grained subsymbols may be combined into one more coarse-grained subsymbol. The reverse is also possible if a distributed representation scheme is used: A coarse-grained subsymbol may be resolved into more fine-grained subsymbols. Consistent covariance results in the network adapting deterministic, rulelike behavior, and this emergent rulelike coding can be applied to new inputs without further learning (Van Orden, Pennington, & Stone, 1990).

In principle, it must be possible to symbolize invariances that can be extracted by connectionist models; otherwise, grapheme–phoneme correspondence rules could never have been formulated. However, the problem is not yet solved by state-of-the-art connectionist modeling. Although activation vectors over hidden units in connectionist visual word recognition have been reduced to grapheme–phoneme correspondences, so far this has been done outside of the models themselves by applying multivariate methods to sets of activation vectors (Sejnowski & Rosenberg, 1987). Assuming that the problem can be solved, the following spiral-like evolution of N and S representations may be envisaged: extraction of invariances from covariant event sequences, segmentation and symbolizing of output information, utilization of the symbolized event sequence to discover covariance with another event sequence, symbolization, invariance extraction, and so forth. In the course of this process, the grain size of the subsymbols and the symbols corresponding to them may change in any direction. A single direction of evolution (e.g., from coarse-grained subsymbol to fine-grained or vice versa) is not prescribed in advance.

How Script and Sound Came Together

The spiral-like evolution of symbolization accounts for the main trends in the development of writing: the successive appearance of logographic, syllabic, and alphabetic writing. In reducing the history of writing to these three stages, it is not implied that the alphabet is the unavoidable endpoint of a teleologically predetermined sequence. Many writing systems have not reached the alphabetic stage, and they are not inferior on that account. There is at least one historical example for the abandonment of an already existing syllabary in favor of a logographic system (the Hittites; see Davies, 1986). Under certain conditions discussed in the following, scripts can also start at the syllabic stage. Despite such complications, history does not provide a single example in which an alphabetic writing system was invented from the scratch, that is, without any previous knowledge of writing (in the strict sense). The alphabet was only invented once in history.

In Sumerian, the earliest written language, the reliance on an established practice of writing in the wide sense is historically well documented. Already existing visual–symbolic representations were put to linguistic use, a process that was facilitated by the oligosyllabic structure of the Sumerian language. Wherever scripts have been invented in the first place, this has occurred for languages whose words and morphemes or both are one syllable long (Daniels, 1992). The perceptual salience of syllables makes it possible to discover their covariation with written symbols.

According to Ehlich (1983), the earliest stage of writing was characterized by sound-meaning-writing unity; that is, writing was the visualization of linguistic relations (including their semantic relations). The unitary stage of writing was a successful solution to certain problems of information storage and transmission in Sumerian society, but it generated new problems. Some of these were raised by the internal structure of the linguistic signal (consisting of both sound and meaning), others by the inability to represent operational units of language. In Ehlich's treatment of how these problems were solved, primacy is given to spoken language as the motor of development. The covariance

9. ORALITY, LITERACY, AND COGNITIVE MODELING

detection hypothesis suggests a more active participation of written symbols.

The first problem is posed by the fact that there are fewer graphic signs than meanings that need to be encoded by them. If meaning is taken as part of the (spoken-language) signal, writing can do little to change it. A different picture emerges, though, when we take an extralinguistic, cognitive perspective on meaning. Then meaning will become the third partner in a covariance detection scheme, and graphic signs will have a chance to impose structure on conceptual meanings that spoken language expresses in a nontransparent fashion. Two ways of expanding the semantic power of logograms are possible: assigning new meanings to existing logograms or introducing new logograms.

The first operates in a manner typical for N systems, that is, by diffusely spreading activation that leads from one concept to another, associatively related concept. The Sumerian sign for "mouth" stands also for "speak"; the sign for "star" also denotes "heaven" and "god." The auditory forms of the spoken words have nothing in common.

The second way relies on an elementary analysis of semantic constituents. New signs are formed by combining existing signs such that the meaning of the compound can be derived from the meaning of its components. Thus, mouth + water = drink, mouth + bread = eat, and so forth. A related, though later, development consists of introducing semantically classifying (unpronounced) signs or sign components (cuneiform and Egyptian "determinatives," Chinese "signifiers") that partition the universe of written discourse into semantic domains. In both cases, writing makes explicit semantic structures that are not overtly expressed in the surface structure of spoken language.

Originally the Sumerians wrote root morphemes only. The Sumerian language was agglutinative and had grammatical affixes for marking number, case, and so forth. These were not written in the administrative texts, but when the first literary, continuous texts were recorded, the scribes had to find a way to represent them graphically. Their solution was the rebus principle: An existing sign stood for a word that sounded like the operational language unit they wanted to write. For instance, the plural affix ME was written with a sign denoting a word ME, meaning "tongue" (Driver, 1976).

Two questionable assumptions are typically made in explaining this achievement: (a) Elements such as grammatical morphemes and particles were difficult to write because the logograms were derived from pictograms making them suitable only for representing concrete concepts. Given the tradition of using nonpictographic, essentially abstract symbols in the proto-writing and writing of number concepts, it is difficult to believe that the idea of a noniconic sign was totally alien to the early scribes; (b) the Sumerian scribes were intuitive grammarians who, on the basis of spoken language alone, recognized grammatical affixes as such. It is not necessary to make this assumption. The oligosyllabic structure of their language may have helped the scribes to parse affixed words into their syllabic components, but parsing words into syllables is not the same as doing a morphemic analysis, even if most morphemes are syllabic and for these the outcome is the same. The decomposition of plural forms, case forms, and so forth into root morpheme + affix can be explained without recourse to grammatical analysis if there is indeed a written sign available that covaries with a spoken unit that is acoustically identical or at least similar to the affix.

Let us assume a network consisting of an acoustically driven input layer, two output layers (one visual, the other semantic), and at least one hidden layer. Because all number and case forms of a spoken word belong to one and the same, rather narrow, semantic domain, it is reasonable to let them be connected initially to one and the same semantic output representation. As long as there is no auditory–visual covariance, the hidden activation vectors corresponding to the auditory input vectors will be very similar to each other, and they will not represent the structure of the auditory input. However, when the auditory inputs differ on components that are mapped onto different visual output representations, then the hidden activation vector will contain the information necessary to activate different semantic representations within a domain. Thus, it will implicity represent the auditory–semantic relations inherent in the relevant domain (see Hinton & Shallice, 1991 for the emergence of visual–semantic interactions in a network architecture similar to that proposed here). To convert this to an explicit representation, we need to extract from the compound activation vector the separate contributions of the auditory-visual mappings. This is not an easy task because these contributions will not add up in a linear fashion. However, in principle the problem can be solved by adopting sophisticated schemes such as Smolensky's (1990) tensor–product representation.

When time-ordered phenomena are modeled by a network, they are not represented in a serial string, but as a simultaneous vector in which time-related information is implicitly represented via transitional probabilities and other local context markers. It follows that the spatial structure of a visual output vector will not preserve the temporal structure of an auditory input vector. We therefore predict that in the initial stages of writing, graphic symbols will not be arranged in a way that uniquely maps the temporal sequence of speech production. Rather, graphic symbols will be locally connected (e.g., by adjacency in any direction) in a way that is independent of the general direction of writing, which, as a result, will correspond more to the sequence of thought than to the sequence of words. This, precisely, is observed in all early forms of logographic writing (not only in administrative but also in literary texts), and Egyptian hieroglyphic writing never completely emerged from this state (Jensen, 1970). An exclusively glossogenic account of the origin of writing cannot explain the locally autonomous arrangement of graphic symbols. The linearization of writing (i.e., its subordination under the temporal sequence of speech) depends on the symbolization of speech that historically was imported from written language via the covariance-detection mechanism.

The rebus principle was applied not only to grammatical affixes, but also to the writing of proper names, loan words, and foreign expressions. These applications paved the way to phonographically syllabic writing, but did not result in a purely phonographic system of writing. The Sumerians and Egyptians, although the former were able to represent vowels and the latter consonants, never switched to complete phonography, not even on a syllabic basis. Even when an already existing writing system is adapted for writing another language, logographic writing is never completely abandoned. The importation and adaptation of logographic writing systems usually results in even more complicated combinations of logography and phonography, as witnessed by Akkadian in the ancient Near East and of course by Japanese. Pure phonography is always the result of deliberate invention or planning in which an existing inventory of graphic signs, but not the writing system itself, is pressed into service for writing a previously unwritten language. The prototypical case is the invention of writing by members of oral cultures who came into contact with missionaries, observed their literate practices and the graphic symbols used by them, but did not understand the language of the missionaries. The best example is Sequoyah's invention of the Cherokee script (see Daniels, 1992, for a brief survey of others). In such cases the inventor starts with a logographic conception of writing and perhaps even devises a logographic script, but then abandons the idea as impracticable and switches to a syllabary, especially if the structure of his own language is well adapted to syllabic writing.

In summary, logographic writing is conservative, and witnessing the writing of a language one does not understand is the only way to break away from it. According to the present view, both phenomena have the same cause: the presence versus absence of a semantic motivation of graphic sign use. Again, if we assume an auditory input vector connected via at least one hidden layer to semantic as well as visual output layers, and if the semantic and the visual output layers are not perfectly correlated, then the hidden units will convey semantic as well as visual information. The number of simple, unanalyzable logograms is bound to be smaller than the number of word meanings. The correlation, therefore, will never be perfect, and if separable components are lacking on both the visual and the semantic sides, the compound activation vector will not be analyzable in the way that it is analyzable in the root morpheme + bound morpheme case. We never get rid of the semantics associated with those graphic signs that lack separate graphic–acoustic associations for their parts, although we can still treat such unanalyzed graphic signs by the rebus principle. This is what happened when the Akkadians took over the Sumerian system; one and the same Sumerian symbol could be used as a logogram and as a rebus sign standing for either a Sumerian or an Akkadian syllable (Jensen, 1970.). In contrast, if we borrow graphic signs from a language we do not understand, then they do not carry their own meaning, and we can choose them as arbitrary symbols for those auditory units that are easily segmentable (i.e., syllables). Pure phonography is especially likely to emerge when the borrowed graphic signs are noniconic. A test case is Sequoyah's syllabary, whose shapes were fashioned after the example of Latin letters, and which is purely phonographic, as compared to various scripts of non-Chinese languages in China fashioned after the Chinese example, which are predominantly phonographic, but retain many logographic elements (see Jensen, 1970).

The earliest surviving alphabet (the Ugarit script) was written in cuneiform characters and denotes the consonants of a Semitic language. To the present day, the practice of writing only consonants has been preserved in all Semitic languages. Even though it is not contested that the concept of consonantal writing was made possible by the structure of Semitic languages, linguists are not unanimous as to whether the resulting writing system is alphabetic or syllabic. Gelb (1963) claimed that prior to the introduction of vowel diacritics, Semitic writing was syllabic, but this claim has been rejected by most modern historians of writing in favor of an incomplete alphabet. If we distinguish between the formal description of the writing system and the psychological processes underlying its invention, then Gelb's view may still be valid for the latter if it is taken to mean that segmental (phonemic) awareness was not needed in order to develop a defective (consonantal) alphabet.

In the Semitic languages, most root morphemes are three-consonant "skeletons," and grammatical and word-formation functions are fulfilled by inherent or affixed vowels. As a result, each consonant skeleton denotes an entire semantic field, and only shades of meaning within that field are signaled by the vowels. Thus, in Arabic everything connected with writing is expressed by the consonant skeleton "ktb." If a linguistic corpus of that sort were submitted to a network classifier, each consonant skeleton would form an attractor into whose basin all of its variants would fall. Because vowels never differentiate between basic meanings, however, they would not show up in the internal representation. To write the vowels would have been a more sophisticated achievement than not to write them. If the inventors of the Semitic scripts had operated in a nonwriting environment, they would have ended up with a logographic system. In the multilingual environment of Palestine and Syria, though, they had access to various languages written in scripts that already had developed a strong syllabic–phonographic component, among them one with a consonant–vowel (CV) system (Daniels, 1992). Given that in a consonant-skeleton language the multidimensional similarity space resulting from speech–meaning covariance must have been structured along consonantal dimensions, the existing CV system would have been reduced to a C + any vowel system, because the V portion would have served no discriminative function. Syllable-closing consonants were probably isolated via phonotactic cues (Daniels, 1992). In Hebrew and some other Semitic writing systems, syllable-final consonants are indicated by a special letter (the schwa sign in Hebrew). This is to be expected if the consonant letters initially denoted C + any vowel syllables.

Some historians of writing emphasize the acrophonic principle, which posits the ability of the early scribes to isolate the beginning sounds of words and syllables or both and mark them by graphic signs.

The idea is most often invoked for explaining the traditional names of the letters of the alphabet. Aleph, beth, gimel, and so on are supposed at the beginning to have been logographic signs. After performing consonant deletion, the alphabetic script inventors would have used the logographic signs for denoting the initial consonants of their spoken forms. This explanation is totally incompatible with everything we know about how speech segmentation works when an alphabetic script is not available. The names of the letters still have to be explained, but it is sufficient to assume that the early scribes were able to discern the similarity between words beginning with the same syllable, and accordingly, for teaching and memorization purposes, picked out one prototype for each similarity group, much as we today use "telephone alphabets" (Gelb, 1963).

Although the letter names were not involved in the invention of the alphabetic principle, they were instrumental in the evolution of the system of consonant signs into the complete alphabet known to us from our own script. According to a well-invented anecdote, a Phoenician literate trader explained to his illiterate Greek partner about writing and started with the aleph, beginning as it does with a glottal stop. The Greek, not able to produce a glottal stop, went away with the idea that the name was aleph without the glottal stop. The details of the story are inaccurate (Faber, 1992), but the principle behind it is correct. Apart from some later developments within Greek itself, the Greek vowel signs were derived from Semitic consonant signs indicating sounds not occurring in the Greek language, then followed by vowels present in Greek. These consonants were deleted (not by conscious phonemic segmentation, but through contact between languages with different sound patterns) and the vowel signs remained, supported and maintained by Greek language in which the basic semantic contrasts are expressed through vowel, and not only through consonant, contrasts. The earliest Greek orthographies were by no means phonologically perfect. Thus, one must inevitably concur with Faber's (1992) conclusion that phomenic segmentation arose as an epiphenomenon of alphabetic writing. The chicken-and-egg problem has been solved: Phonemic segmentation depends on the alphabet, not the other way around.

ACKNOWLEDGMENT

The preparation of this chapter was supported by the Deutsche Forschungsgemeinschaft, DFG Grant Ro 481/11-1.

REFERENCES

Anglin, J. M. (1985). The child's expressible knowledge of word concepts: What preschoolers can say about the meanings of some nouns and verbs. In K. E. Nelson (Ed.), *Children's language* (Vol. 5, p. 72–128). Hillsdale, NJ: Lawrence Erlbaum Associates.
Aram, D. M. (1991). Acquired aphasia in children. In M. T. Sarno (Ed.), *Acquired aphasia* (2nd ed., pp. 425–454). New York: Academic Press.
Aram, D. M., Ekelman, B. L., & Whitaker, H. L. (1987). Lexical retrieval in left and right lesioned children. *Brain and Language, 31,* 61–87.
Aronoff, M. (1992). Segmentalism in linguistics: The alphabetic basis of phonological theory. In P. Downing, & S. D. Lima (Eds.), *The linguistics of literacy* (pp. 71–82). Amsterdam: Benjamins.
Bechtel, W. (1990). Multiple levels of inquiry in cognitive science. *Psychological Research, 52,* 271–181.
Berg, T. (1992). Umrisse einer psycholinguistischen Theorie der Silbe. In P. Eisenberg, K. H. Ramers, & H. Vater (Eds.), *Silbenphonologie des Deutschen* (pp. 45–99). Tübingen, Germany: Narr.
Bertelson, P., de Gelder, B., Tfouni, L. V., & Morais, J. (1989). Metaphonological abilities of adult illiterates: New evidence for heterogeneity. *European Journal of Cognitive Psychology, 1,* 239–250.
Biber, D. (1988). *Variation across speech and writing.* Cambridge, UK: Cambridge University Press.
Blumstein, S. E. (1973). *A phonological investigation of aphasic speech.* The Hague, Netherlands: Mouton.
Cameron, R. F., Currier, R. D., & Hearer, A. F. (1971). Aphasia and literacy. *British Journal of Disorders of Communication, 6,* 161–163.
Damasio, A. R., Castro-Caldas, A., Grosso, J. T., & Ferro, J. M. (1976). Brain specialization for language does not depend on literacy. *Archives of Neurology, 33,* 300–301.
Damasio, H., Damasio, A. R., Castro-Caldas, A., & Hamsher, K. (1979). Reversal of ear advantage for phonetically similar words in illiterates. *Journal of Clinical Neuropsychology, 1,* 331–338.
Daniels, P. T. (1992). The syllabic origin of writing and the segmental origin of the alphabet. In P. Downing & S. D. Lima (Eds.), *The linguistics of literacy* (pp. 83–110). Amsterdam: Benjamins.

Davies, A. M. (1986). Forms of writing in the ancient mediterranean world. In G. Baumann (Ed.), *The written word: Literacy in transition* (pp. 51–78). Oxford, UK: Clarendon Press.

De Gelder, B., Vroomen, J., & Bertelson, P. (1993). The effects of alphabetic reading competence on language representation in bilingual Chinese subjects. *Psychological Research, 55,* (4), 315–321.

Dibble, H. L. (1989). The implications of stone tool types for the presence of language during the lower and middle paleolithic. In P. Mellars & C. Stringer (Eds.), *The human revolution* (pp. 415–432). Edinburgh: University of Edinburgh Press.

Driver, G. R. (1976). *Semitic writing: From pictograph to alphabet.* London: Oxford University Press.

Ehlich, K. (1983). Development of writing as social problem solving. In F. Coulmas & K. Ehlich (Eds.), *Writing in focus* (pp. 99–130). Berlin: Mouton.

Espir, L., & Rose, F. (1970). *The basic neurology of speech.* Oxford, UK: Blackwell.

Faber, A. (1992). Phonemic segmentation as epiphenomenon: Evidence from the history of alphabetic writing. In P. Downing & S. D. Lima (Eds.), *The linguistics of literacy* (pp. 111–134). Amsterdam: Benjamins.

Finnegan, R. (1977). *Oral poetry.* Cambridge, UK: Cambridge University Press.

Finnegan, R. (1988). *Literacy and orality: Studies in the technology of communication.* Oxford, UK: Blackwell.

Fodor, J. A. (1976). *The language of thought.* Hassocks, UK: Harvester.

Fodor, J. A. (1981). Methodological solipsism considered as a research strategy in cognitive psychology. *Behavioral and Brain Sciences, 3,* 63–110.

Fowler, A. E. (1991). How early phonological development might set the stage for phoneme awareness. In S. A. Brady & D. P. Shankweiler (Eds.), *Phonological processes in literacy* (pp. 91–118). Hillsdale, NJ: Lawrence Erlbaum Associates.

Frazer, B. (1970). Idioms within a transformational grammar. *Foundations of Language, 6,* 22–42.

García, E. C. (1979). Discourse without syntax. In T. Givón (Ed.), *Syntax and semantics, 12: Discourse and syntax* (pp. 23–50). New York: Academic Press.

Gelb, I. J. (1963). *A study of writing* (rev. ed.). Chicago: University of Chicago Press.

Givón, T. (1979). *On understanding grammar.* New York: Academic Press.

Goody, J. (1987). *The interface between the written and the oral.* Cambridge, UK: Cambridge University Press.

9. ORALITY, LITERACY, AND COGNITIVE MODELING 253

Gorman, R. P., & Sejnowski, T. J. (1988). Analysis of hidden units in a layered network trained to classify sonar targets. *Neural Networks, 1,* 75–89.

Greenfield, P. M. (1991). Language, tools and brain: The ontogeny and phylogeny of hierarchically organized sequential behavior. *Behavioral and Brain Sciences, 14,* 531–596.

Hamilton, M., & Barton, D. (1983). A word is a word: Metalinguistic skills in adults of varying literacy levels. *Journal of Pragmatics, 7,* 581–594.

Hamsher, K. (1991). Intelligence and aphasia. In M. T. Sarno (Ed.), *Acquired aphasia* (2nd ed., pp. 339–372). New York: Academic Press.

Hawkins, J. A., & Carter, A. (1988). Psycholinguistic factors in morphological asymmetry. In J. A. Hawkins (Ed.), *Explaining language universals* (pp. 280–317). Oxford, UK: Blackwell.

Heeschen, V. (1978). The metalinguistic vocabulary of a speech community in the highlands of Irian Jaya (West New Guinea). In A. Sinclair, R. J. Jarvella, & W. J. M. Levelt (Eds.), *The child's conception of language* (pp. 155–190). Berlin: Springer.

Hinton, G. E., & Shallice, T. (1991). Lesioning an attractor network: Investigations of acquired dyslexia. *Psychological Review, 98,* 74–95.

Hu, Y.-H., Qiou, Y.-G., & Zhong, G.-Q. (1990). Crossed aphasia in Chinese: A survey. *Brain and Language, 39,* 347–356.

Hunter, I. M. L. (1985). Lengthy verbatim recall: The role of text. In A. W. Ellis (Ed.), *Progress in the psychology of language* (Vol. 1, pp. 207–236). Hillsdale, NJ: Lawrence Erlbaum Associates.

Jackson, H. J. (1915). On the nature of the duality of the brain. *Brain, 38,* 80–103. (Original work published 1874.)

Jensen, H. (1970). *Sign, symbol and script* (transl. from the 3rd German ed.). London: Allan & Unwin.

Kalmár, I. (1985). Are there really no primitive languages? In D. R. Olson, N. Torrance, & A. Hildyard (Eds.), *Literacy, language and learning: The nature and consequences of reading and writing* (pp. 148–166). Cambridge, UK: Cambridge University Press.

Krämer, S. (1991). *Berechenbare Vernunft. Rationalismus und Kalkül im 17. Jahrhundert. [Computable reason. Rationality and computation in the 17th century.]* Berlin: De Gruyter.

Lecour, A. R., & Parente, M. A. (1991). A neurological point of view on social alexia. In D. R. Olson, & N. Torrance (Eds.), *Literacy and orality* (pp. 236–250). Cambridge, UK: Cambridge University Press.

Lord, A. B. (1960). *The singer of tales.* Cambridge, MA: Harvard University Press.

Lundberg, I. (1991). Phonemic awareness can be developed without reading instruction. In S. A. Brady & D. P. Shankweiler (Eds.), *Phonological processes in literacy* (pp. 47–54). Hillsdale, NJ: Lawrence Erlbaum Associates.

Luria, A. R. (1966). *Higher cortical functions in man.* New York: Basic Books.

Luria, A. R. (1976). *Cognitive development: Its cultural and social foundations.* Cambridge, MA: Harvard University Press.

Magoun, F. P., jr. (1953). Oral-formulaic character of Anglo-Saxon narrative poetry. *Speculum, 28,* 446–467.

Mann, V. A. (1986). Phonological awareness: The role of reading experience. *Cognition, 24,* 65–92.

Markman, E. M. (1976). Children's difficulty with word-referent differentiation. *Child Development, 47,* 742–749.

McLean, M., Bryant, P., & Bradley, L. (1987). Rhymes, nursery rhymes, and reading in early childhood. *Merrill-Palmer Quarterly, 33,* 266–281.

Mellars, P. (1989). Technological changes at the middle-upper palaeolithic transition. Economic, social, and cognitive perspectives. In P. Mellars & C. Stringer (Eds.), *The human revolution* (pp. 338–365). Edinburgh: University of Edinburgh Press.

Morais, J. (1987). Phonetic awareness and reading acquisition. *Psychological Research, 49,* 147–152.

Nelson, K. E. (1974). Concept, word, and sentence: Interrelations in acquisition and development. *Psychological Review, 81,* 267–285.

Nissen, H. J., Damerow, P., & Englund, R. K. (1991). *Frühe Schrift und Techniken der Wirtschaftsverwaltung im alten Vorderen Orient. [Early writing and technologies of economic administration in the ancient Near East.]* Bad Salzdethfurt, Germany: Franzbecker.

Nittrouer, S., Studdert-Kennedy, M., & McGowan, R. S. (1989). The emergence of phonetic segments: Evidence from the spectral structure of fricative-vowel syllables spoken by children and adults. *Journal of Speech and Hearing Research, 32,* 120–132.

Noble, W., & Davidson, I. (1991). Evolving remembrances of times—past and future. *Behavioral and Brain Sciences, 14,* 572.

Norrick, R. M. (1985). *How proverbs mean: Semantic studies in English proverbs.* Berlin: Mouton.

Olson, D. R. (1991). Literacy as metalinguistic activity. In D. R. Olson & N. Torrance (Eds.), *Literacy and orality* (pp. 251–270). Cambridge, UK: Cambridge University Press.

Ong, W. J. (1967). *The presence of the word.* New Haven, CT: Yale University Press.

Ong, W. J. (1982). *Orality and literacy: The technologizing of the word.* London: Methuen.

Papandropoulou, I., & Sinclair, H. (1974). What is a word? *Human Development, 17,* 241-258.
Parker, S. T., & Gibson, K. R. (1979). A developmental model of the evolution of language and intelligence in early hominids. *Behavioral and Brain Sciences, 2,* 367-408.
Parry, M. (1971). L'epithète traditionelle dans Homère. Translated in *The making of Homeric verse: The collected papers of Milman Parry.* Oxford: Clarendon Press. (Original work published 1928.)
Patterson, F. G. (1980). Innovative uses of language by a gorilla: A case study. In K. E. Nelson (Ed.), *Children's language* (Vol. 2, pp. 497-561). Hillsdale, NJ: Lawrence Erlbaum Associates.
Read, C. (1986). *Children's creative spelling.* London: Routledge & Kegan Paul.
Read, C., Zhang, Y.-F., & Ding, B. Q. (1986). The ability to manipulate speech sound depends on knowing alphabetic writing. *Cognition, 24,* 31-44.
Repp, B. H., & Liberman, A. M. (1987). Phonetic category boundaries are flexible. In S. Harnad (Ed.), *Categorical perception* (pp. 89-112). Cambridge, UK: Cambridge University Press.
Savage-Rumbaugh, E. S. (1986). *Ape language: From conditioned response to symbol.* New York: Academic Press.
Savage-Rumbaugh, E. S. (1990). Language as a cause-effect communication system. *Philosophical Psychology, 1,* 55-76.
Scheerer, E. (1993a). Mentale Repräsentation in interdisziplinärer Perspektive (Mental representations in interdisciplinary perspective). *Zeitschrift für Psychologie, 201,* 136-166.
Scheerer, E. (1993b). *Orality and literacy: Implications for the modeling of cognitive processes* (Rep. No. 13). Universität Oldenburg, Institut für Kognitionsforschung.
Scheerer-Neumann, G. (1988). Die Entwicklung von Spontanschreibungen (The development of spontaneous writing). *Germanistische Linguistik, 93-94,* 27-58.
Searle, J. R. (1980). Minds, brains, and programs. *Behavioral and Brain Sciences, 3,* 417-457.
Sejnowski, T. J., & Rosenberg, C. R. (1987). Parallel networks that learn to pronounce English text. *Complex Systems 1,* 145-168.
Shepard, R. N., & Chipman, S. (1970). Second-order isomorphism of internal representations. *Cognitive Psychology, 1,* 1-17.
Smolensky, P. (1988). On the proper treatment of connectionism. *Behavioral and Brain Sciences, 11,* 1-74.
Smolensky, P. (1990). Tensor product variable binding and the representation of symbolic structures in connectionist systems. *Artificial Intelligence, 46,* 159-216.

Sokolowski, R. (1988). Natural and artificial intelligence. In S. R. Graubard (Ed.), *The artificial intelligence debate: False starts, real foundations* (pp. 45-64). Cambridge, MA: MIT Press.

Terrace, H. S., Petitto, L. A., Sanders, R. J., & Bever, T. G. (1980). On the grammatical capacity of apes. In K. E. Nelson (Ed.), *Children's language* (Vol. 2, pp. 371–495). Hillsdale, NJ: Lawrence Erlbaum Associates.

Tomasello, M. (1991). Objects are analogous to words, not phonemes and grammatical categories. *Behavioral and Brain Sciences, 14*, 575–576.

Treiman, R. (1983). The structure of spoken syllables: Evidence from novel word games. *Cognition, 15*, 49–74.

Van Lancker, D. (1987). Non-propositional speech: Neurolinguistic studies. In A. W. Ellis (Ed.), *Progress in the psychology of language* (Vol. 3, pp. 49–118). Hillsdale, NJ: Lawrence Erlbaum Associates.

Van Orden, G. C., Pennington, B. F., & Stone, G. O. (1990). Word identification in reading and the promise of subsymbolic psycholinguistics. *Psychological Review, 97*, 488–522.

Wagner, R. K., & Torgesen, J. K. (1987). The nature of phonological processing and its causal role in reading acquisition. *Psychological Bulletin, 101*, 192–212.

White, R. (1989a). Visual thinking in the ice age. *Scientific American, 261*(1), 74–81.

White, R. (1989b). Production complexity and standardizing in early Aurignacian bead and pendant manufacture In P. Mellars & C. Stringer (Eds.), *The human revolution* (pp. 366–390). Edinburgh: Edinburgh University Press.

Woods, B. T., & Carey, S. (1979). Language deficits after apparent clinical recovery from childhood aphasias. *Annals of Neurology, 6(5)*, 405–409.

Woods, B. T., & Teuber, H.-L. (1978). Changing patterns of childhood aphasia. *Annals of Neurology, 3*, 273–280.

Wynn, T. (1991). The comparative simplicity of tool-use and its implications for human evolution. *Behavioral and Brain Sciences, 14*, 576–577.

In Place of a Conclusion

CHAPTER

10

BIOBEHAVIORAL ROOTS OF LANGUAGE: WORDS, APES, AND A CHILD

Duane M. Rumbaugh, and E. Sue Savage-Rumbaugh
Georgia State University, Atlanta

"Uniqueness" is the hallmark of taxonomic classification, and each species, including our own *(Homo sapiens)* has its own constellation of defining attributes. Not to be overlooked, though, is the fact that the attributes that define various taxa are rarely unique. Hence, species are differentiated, in the main, as unique configurations of continua that, to varying degrees, characterize other species as well: Each species presents a unique profile of points on continua that, in turn, are the themes and threads of the evolution of life. From a less serious perspective, if there is a dimension unique to our own species, it perhaps is none other than the continuing preoccupation with the search for the defining attribute that sets us apart from others!

Impatient for the results of scientific inquiry, historical and contemporary records are replete with proclamations about our species' distinguishing attributes. One by one, however, these proclamations have been found wanting. For instance, *Homo sapiens* is no longer defined as *the* tool maker, nor is our species the only primate that reasons and transmits culture across generations (see Heltne & Marquardt,

1989). The same is generally conceded for still other attributes once held as bastions of uniqueness for humankind. There is, however, one notable, indeed remarkable, point of distinction that is looked upon by many as the ultimate, irresolute line that demarcates humans from all other animals, and that is *language*.

This human distinction notwithstanding, in this chapter we argue that chimpanzees *(Pan troglodytes)* and bonobos *(Pan paniscus)* can acquire impressive language skills, including the ability to understand the syntax of novel sentences of request spoken to them. Pan's competence for language is optimized if it is reared from birth in a language-saturated environment, one in which members of a social group coordinate their activities through language throughout the course of each day. Being reared thus, *Pan* acquires language without special training and in the same course or pattern that characterizes language development in the human child. Understandably, *Pan* appears not to be capable of all dimensions of human language. A prime limitation is its inability to talk, but its comprehension and use of language, however, is far more advanced than it was thought to be even 5 years ago. Without doubt, future research will continue to define new parameters of Pan's competence for language and the parameters that determine them.

These new data are of paramount significance for solving the classical problem of language origin. Interest in the origins of language has been long standing. On the one hand, it has been asserted that language is the consequence of a mutation unique to our species (see Pinker & P. Bloom, 1990, for a recent discussion). On the other hand, it is argued that language is more probably the product of evolutionary trends that have discernable traces in the capacities of other life forms, notably those most closely related to us—the great apes *(Pan, Gorilla,* and *Pongo;* see E. A. Bates, Thal, & Marchman, 1991; Rumbaugh, Hopkins, Washburn, & Savage-Rumbaugh, 1991, for further discussion on these contrasting views of language origins.)

Because speech is such a salient marker of language in our species, many have come to equate speech with language. We, however, view the equating of speech with language as unfortunate, because it serves to divert attention from the host of cognitive operations that provide the bases for symbolic communication, whether these be operations of speech, gesture, or writing. Without question, speech is the most salient aspect of language, and it is certainly the most highly evolved and efficient means for expressing language. Notwithstanding, it is not

A PERSPECTIVE OF LANGUAGE

We view the emergence of language as resting on a number of interacting nonspeech building blocks, the cornerstone of which is the ability to use an arbitrary symbol to represent something that is not necessarily present in space or time. Such symbols are used socially with other partners and provide references for things and events. It is this provision that, in turn, makes it possible for two or more partners to plan and to coordinate behavior to an advantage. Language enhances one's ability to predict, and hence to prepare for, the behaviors and activities of a social group.

The use of what might have been arbitrary symbols for social communication and the coordination of behavior is, of course, profoundly different from highly predictable, species-specific patterns of behavior (e.g., fixed action patterns; see Alcock, 1984, for a discussion of ethology) brought forth in response to well-defined stimuli and signals (e.g., sign–stimuli and releasers). Although species-characteristic behaviors, such as the new-born gull's readiness to peck at the red dot on its parent's beak to obtain food and a chick's readiness to try to follow its mother, frequently depend upon age-linked experiences and the opportunity to respond–practice; they are predominantly under genetic control. By contrast, the transformation of an initially arbitrary stimulus into a communicative symbol is essentially based on complex learning and cognition.

Genetics and biology *always* play an important role in behavior and learning, but in the case of language their contribution is that of providing the organism with a very complex brain that is, as we clarify later in this chapter, uniquely sensitive to complexities of language during the formative months of infancy.

The Primary Role of Comprehension in Language

In our opinion, the comprehension of symbols, be they spoken or written words, geometric symbols, or American Sign Language (Bellugi, Bihrle, & Corina, 1991) is the essence of language. Even if symbols of a language system are not spoken, as is the case with word–lexigram symbols devised initially for the Lana Project (Rumbaugh, 1977), this does not preclude their acquiring basic semantic value and functioning as spoken words. Lexigrams and other graphic media provide for language, albeit unspoken and silent.

From our perspective it is the competent use of and interpretation of symbols, then, and not speech per se, that are the sine qua non of language. The study of speech has provided us with a great deal of important information about how sounds are produced and heard, but speech produces only sounds, and it is only those sounds, not meanings, that are propagated to the listener. The critical event of a linguistic communication is the assignment of meaning by the listener, regardless of the mode whereby symbolic communications are achieved. Assignment of meaning is contingent on competent comprehension of symbols.

The representational use of symbols (e.g., using them to stand for things and events) is a requisite to all other dimensions of language. Without this competence there can be no syntax or grammar, sentences, paragraphs, or lectures. Unless the participants of conversation are symbol competent, even their verbal exchanges can be no more informative than those one might have with an automatic banking machine that "talks" to us as we address it for the purpose of obtaining a withdrawal or making a deposit of funds. To be sure, such machines are useful, but they are not generally looked to as partners for conversation.

Ape Language Research

The chimpanzee *(Pan)* has been the primate of choice for most research programs addressing the possibility that language might not be unique to our species. The reason for this is that at least the so-called common chimpanzee, *Pan troglodytes*, though not the rare and endangered bonobo, *Pan paniscus*, has been more available than either the orangutan *(Pongo)* or gorilla *(Gorilla)*. *Pan* shares with *Pongo* and *Gorilla* a relatively complex brain and elaborated cortex that provides for the ability to learn via more complex processes than those possible for the lesser apes and monkeys. The evolution of a complex brain has been a very expensive adventure, because it entails relatively long gestation and maturation and high metabolic budgets. That expense has been offset by the provisions that a complex brain can extend to an organism,

10. BIOBEHAVIORAL ROOTS OF LANGUAGE

particularly those for insight, problem solving, rule learning, complex concept formation, and for the positing of cause–effect relationships and language (Rumbaugh & Pate, 1984; Rumbaugh & Sterritt, 1986).

Research at our laboratory (see Rumbaugh, 1977; Savage-Rumbaugh, 1986, for reviews) has documented that particularly the bonobo has a remarkable ability to learn meanings of hundreds of arbitrary visual symbols (e.g., to use lexigrams representationally) and thereby to achieve social communication that otherwise would be impossible. Moreover, research of the recent past indicates that both the bonobo *(Pan paniscus)* and the common chimpanzee *(Pan troglodytes)* have advanced capacities to understand spoken words. In addition, Kanzi (a bonobo) has demonstrated his ability essentially to comprehend an unlimited number of spoken sentences (see Fig. 10.1; Savage-Rumbaugh, 1988; Savage-Rumbaugh et al., 1993). These sentences were novel requests that he had never heard prior to their presentation to him in controlled tests. They were not sentences on which he had specific training; neither were they sentences that others had modeled in his presence. Because of the bonobo and chimpanzee's capacity for comprehension, we have concluded that these chimpanzees can acquire language.

In drawing such a conclusion, however, we intend no claim that chimpanzees have the capacity to master all aspects of human language. For example, it is all but certain that they will never speak as humans do (K. J. Hayes & C. H. Nissen, 1971). Perhaps because of this constraint, they likely will prove to be limited with respect both to linguistic flexibility and syntactic structure (but see Greenfield & Savage-Rumbaugh, 1991).

Fig. 10.1. Kanzi, a bonobo *(Pan paniscus)*, wears his headphones to hear spoken words and sentences. His comprehension approximates that of a 2½- to 3-year-old child.

Thus, even though human language serves many functions not evinced in nonhuman primate communications, chimpanzees have given clear scientific evidence of their representational and referential use and comprehension of symbols. To state it differently, chimpanzees have learned to comprehend the meanings of both lexigrams and spoken words and to comprehend novel sentences of request presented to them via speech.

Roots of Ape Language Skills in Early Experience

Given that *Pan* has evinced competence for acquiring significant dimensions of symbolic language, the question arises as to whether the ape shares a capacity for language with humans that takes other forms in the wild or whether this capacity is uniquely cultivated by ape-human interactions during early life. The following observations address this question.

Observations on Matata, an adult female bonobo with a history of feral living until the age of about 5 years, are instructive. She entered language studies at our laboratory as a young adult. Matata has always impressed us as being a very bright bonobo, particularly when she is traveling about in the 55-acre forest surrounding our laboratory. She, more than the others, can find insect-laden reeds and, given half a chance to do so, catch a rabbit. She is highly sociable and has adapted quite readily to human interaction during cleaning, feeding, playing, and even in giving birth. However, Matata has never excelled at learning the meanings of lexigrams and other tasks readily mastered by other apes in our programs. Even after 2 years of language training, she failed to master reliable use of even seven symbols, even though she used those only to request specific foods.

It is suggested that Matata has failed in these ways because she was introduced to them at an age well beyond that which provides for the structuring of requisite cognitions. Her cognitive structures were laid down for adaptation in the forest, not to the electronics of a modern-day laboratory.

In contrast, even at the early age of 2½ years, Kanzi (Matata's adopted infant) gave evidence that he had acquired mastery of lexigrams quite *spontaneously,* that is, without any specific, food-reinforced, discrete-trial training regimens. His mastery was achieved via observational learning fortuitously made available to him during the daily training sessions given to his mother. In other words, Kanzi was an observer, not an intended student. Notwithstanding, he was the one who learned and learned fairly well!

Evidence of Kanzi's mastery of lexigrams and their meanings became apparent when Matata was separated from him for purposes of breeding. Even from the first day, it was apparent that Kanzi had learned what his mother had not. He was able to use lexigrams to request items, to make comment on activities in which he was engaged, and even to comprehend symbols' meanings when used by others.

Later, it was strongly suggested that he was comprehending the spoken English word. Subsequent controlled tests revealed his comprehension of individual words and novel requests made of him, again without specific training (Savage-Rumbaugh, MacDonald, Sevcik, Hopkins, & Rubert, 1986; Savage-Rumbaugh, 1988).

Confirmation of the bonobo's ability to learn without specific training came from Mulika, born to Matata in 1984 (Sevcik, 1989). Because her eye became infected, Mulika was separated from Matata 4 months after birth and placed in our continuing language project. (We have been reluctant to take infant bonobos from their mothers.) Although at 17 months Mulika reliably made requests with the limited use of only 7 symbols, her receptive skills of both lexigrams and spoken English included 70 other symbols. Of those 70 lexigrams, Mulika had used 30 of them at a keyboard only once, and 2 of them not at all. Observational learning was once again implicated as a powerful, previously unappreciated form of learning in the great apes.

Pan Paniscus and Pan Troglodytes Compared

Because the first instances of apes learning language through observation during infancy were all with bonobos, and because no common chimpanzee had evinced the ability to profit from observation alone, we thought it probable that we had found an important species difference. Consequently, a study was undertaken in which a bonobo, Panbanisha, and a common chimpanzee, Panzee, were coreared from the age of about 6 weeks.

At about the age of 2 years, it was clear that Panbanisha was both learning her symbols spontaneously (i.e., without specific regimens of teaching) and coming to comprehend speech. Notwithstanding, in short order and much to our surprise, Panzee also came to do so, though not nearly so efficiently. Across the years, Panbanisha has remained superior to Panzee in acquiring language skills although Panzee has excelled Panbanisha in other impressive ways—notably in the use of tools and in drawing. Although *Pan paniscus* might be more adroit at language, *Pan troglodytes* has its dominant dimensions of intelligence for mechanical and spatial relations and is not to be viewed as the inferior species (see Fig. 10.2).

Fig. 10.2. Panzee, a common chimpanzee (*Pan troglodytes*) came to learn symbols spontaneously and to understand spoken words, although not as well as did her cohort, Panbanisha (*Pan paniscus*).

Observational Learning of Language Skills

It is clear that for both Kanzi and Mulika, the competent use of word–lexigrams was facilitated by their initial ability to comprehend their use by others. Although their comprehension came about by being reared in a social context that included both humans and apes, it was their observations of others' interactive usages of symbols that cultivated their language learning. Particularly in the case of Mulika (see Fig. 10.3), it is clear that her comprehension of symbol meanings was not contingent upon her actual use of the lexigrams on the keyboards about the laboratory. With comprehension in place, her subsequent productive use of the lexigrams appeared without special training.

10. BIOBEHAVIORAL ROOTS OF LANGUAGE   265

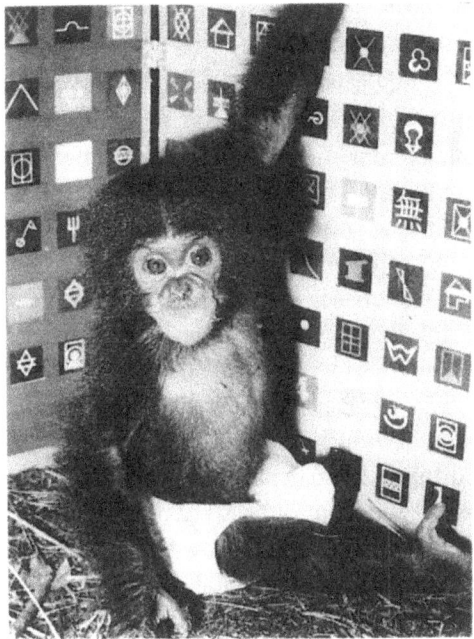

Fig. 10.3. Mulika (*Pan paniscus*) was found capable of understanding the meanings of lexigrams either never used by her or used but once. She was also able to comprehend the meanings or referents for individual words that were spoken to her.

Pattern of Language Learning

The language learning by these chimpanzees (Kanzi, Mulika, and Panbanisha) parallels that of the human child in that comprehension preceded productive use of language (i.e., "production" meaning speech in the child and use of lexigrams in the chimpanzee). Their pattern of acquiring language competence stands in sharp contrast with the language learning by Lana, Sherman, and Austin. Lana, Sherman, and Austin (all common chimpanzees, *Pan troglodytes*) received specially designed training regimens to cultivate specific productive skills with lexigrams (i.e., to request food and activities, to label items, etc.) on the assumption that if they used their symbols, they must also understand their meanings. That assumption was, however, totally incorrect. That chimpanzees can use lexigrams does not mean that the symbols function representationally for them. Neither is it the case that because either a person or a digitized telephone information service talk means that they comprehend the meaning of what they say or what they hear said by others.

Both Sherman and Austin required specific training to come to comprehend word–lexigram symbols (i.e., their referents). That training emphasized the coordination of social behaviors and taught them, for example, to pay attention to one another and to give one another or the experimenter specific tools or foods from an array (see Savage-Rumbaugh, 1986 for a complete description of procedures with an accompanying two-hour-taped documentary). As a consequence of that training, however, they began to make statements about what it was that they were going to do or what it was that they were going to get from an adjoining room or from the refrigerator. They also then started to label activities (e.g., play, tickle, chase, play-bite, etc.) in which they were engaged, the food or drink that they were ingesting, or things that they saw from the window.

Of maximum significance is the fact that Sherman and Austin were then able to label categorically 17 word–lexigrams, each the name of a specific food or tool learned through earlier training, as being either a food or a tool, through use of two lexigrams so glossed, in a tightly controlled test situation. In other words, when shown their lexigram for banana, they called it a "food," when shown their lexigram for screw driver, they called it a "tool," and so on. Their ability to do so was interpreted to mean that these word–lexigrams functioned representationally for them, that is, that the lexigrams were meaningful. In our view, it was because each lexigram, in turn, generated its own representation to Sherman and Austin that they were able to classify them in accordance with the categories to which they belonged. Consequently, their performance evinced at least a basic, though nonetheless elegant, capacity for *semantics*, that is, for understanding and managing the meaning of words.

THE PROBLEM OF SYNTACTIC COMPETENCE

Comprehension of Novel Sentences of Request

A formal controlled test of Kanzi's ability to understand the syntax of human speech was given to him when he was about 8 years old and to a young girl, Alia when she was about 2½ years old. Alia's mother was a member of the research team that worked with Kanzi, and from shortly after Alia's birth and throughout testing her mother worked with her

10. BIOBEHAVIORAL ROOTS OF LANGUAGE

half days in a manner that characterized Kanzi's life. This meant that both Alia and Kanzi had extensive experience in a small social group with the members negotiating and coordinating their behaviors (e.g., determined what they would do, where they would go, what things were, etc.) through use of keyboards embossed with lexigrams. Although they were never required to use the keyboard to obtain an incentive or to engage in an activity, they were always encouraged to observe use of the keyboard and to use it as they wished. Whenever they did use their lexigram-embossed keyboards, their message was always taken at face value; that is, it was responded to by caretakers as though the bonobo intended to "say" whatever they did.

The tests of comprehension included more than 400 sentences and were controlled in that the experimenter was hidden from view (i.e., sitting behind a one-way mirror). In addition, persons who were part of the test procedures and, hence, in the room with Kanzi, wore headphones and listened to loud music so that they could not hear what Kanzi was being asked to do, and thus could provide no supportive cues.

Fig. 10.4. Kanzi is asked to "knife the sweet potato," and does so.

A variety of objects were presented in random collections/arrays both in front of the subject and in other areas to which the subject might be asked to go or to retrieve certain objects. Several different types of requests were posed. Some requested the subject to do something to an object or to do something with one object relative to another. Others requested that something be done with one of two objects designated by their location or that the subject engage in some activity, and so on.

The sentences of request presented to these two subjects were novel and, in many instances, quite unusual (e.g., "Kanzi, can you get the lettuce that's in the microwave?"—where other objects as well as lettuce were placed for the test). This procedure was intended to assure that the subject had never been asked to carry out any of the requests and had never seen another carry out such an action (see Fig. 10.4). Typical questions posed were, "Kanzi/Alia, can you make the doggie bite the snake?" "Go get the phone that's outdoors" "Can you tickle (agent's name) with the bunny?" and so on. The doggie, the snake, the bunny, and similar objects were frequently new toys that had not been used for such purposes in the past.

Analyses revealed that the subjects were much more similar than they were different in their responses. Each subject fulfilled the novel requests with about 70% accuracy; the probability of being correct by chance approximated zero. The subjects also tended to make the same kinds of errors. Alia was better than Kanzi at retrieving two objects upon request (e.g., "Can you give (agent's name) the peas and the sweet potatoes?"). On the other hand, Kanzi was the better in dealing with embedded phrases (e.g., "Can you get the phone *that's outdoors*?).

Never before has a life-form other than a human demonstrated the capacity to comprehend novel sentences of request as has Kanzi. His ability to comprehend must certainly exceed the boundaries of the tests given to him and is, in all likelihood, correctly calibrated at the level of a normal human child of about 2½ to 3 years of age.

With Kanzi's comprehension emerging in advance of his productive (i.e., understanding language before "talking") abilities, we have observed for the first time the pattern of language acquisition in an ape that characterizes that of the human child. There seems to be little doubt that if Kanzi could "speak," he would have much more to say than what is permitted by use of his keyboards.

Grammar and Production

Kanzi has also learned simple grammatical rules modeled by humans, and also has invented his own symbol-ordering rules (Greenfield & Savage-Rumbaugh, 1991). The capacity to learn rules through which symbols may be combined in a potentially infinite number of ways is generally recognized as an essential requisite of competence with human language systems.

In accordance with accepted methodology for studying child language (spoken or sign), all two-element combinations (lexigram–lexigram and lexigram–gesture) for which contextual information was available were classified according to their semantic relations such as agent–action and action–object. Kanzi's behavior subsequent to an utterance was the basis for deciding semantic relations. Thus, it was Kanzi's own behavior, rather than a subjective interpretation of Kanzi's intent, which led to the classification of any given combination. Findings indicated that Kanzi employed a wide variety of semantic relations, and in the majority of these, he tended to use a specific order.

Kanzi's use of the action–object order, for instance, was significantly more frequent than his use of the alternative order. In this regard, he followed the rule or pattern used commonly by his caretakers. Contrary to the claim that chimpanzees cannot make verbal statements but are limited to demands or instrumental requests, Kanzi frequently made statements of what it was that he was about to do. Analyses further indicated that Kanzi made up his own reliable rule for combining agent gesture with action lexigram: His ordering rule, "Place lexigrams first," was in contrast to the ordering strategy expressed by his caregivers' English-based rule. Kanzi's rule, "Place lexigrams first," has considerable generality as well as originality. Kanzi also frequently combined two action lexigrams. From the perspective of human language, these combinations are merely unstructured lists in that they lack the minimum requirements of a proposition (e.g., instead of providing one predicate and one argument, action–action combinations simply chain two predicates). However, these combinations revealed unsuspected regularities that reflected both natural action categories and preferred action orders in social play.

A major limitation of Kanzi's grammar is that it provides no example in which a difference in order signals a difference in meaning. (Claims of this from other laboratories have been single instance reports that lack scientific verification.) A second limitation regards length of utterance: Most combinations were only two elements long, and most utterances were single symbols. (In playing "chase," however, Kanzi would use the lexigram for chase on the keyboard, then lead a person by the hand and place it on the person he apparently wanted them to chase. On other occasions, he would nominate himself as the one to be chased and would scamper off after using the lexigram and pointing to the person nominated to chase after him.)

In summary Kanzi has both learned and invented productive rules for ordering relations between two categories of symbol, and does so with a competence that reflects a productive competence for grammar usually seen in 2½-year-old children.

THE TIES THAT BIND

A new Perspective on Development, Rearing, and Adult Competencies

In our view, the fact that our chimpanzees' language skills appeared normally (e.g., spontaneously as they do in the human child) reflected that they have been reared from birth in a cultural and language-saturated environment. We believe that such an environment allows the chimpanzee's psychological competencies to emerge in novel ways— ways that might be very foreign to their species in the field or in zoos, ways that might approximate those that provide for language in the human child.

Our contention, however, goes well beyond the suggestion that our subjects generally became facile learners (Davenport, Rogers, & Rumbaugh, 1973; Krech, Rosenzweig, & Bennett, 1962) as a result of being reared in "enriched," stimulating environments. It is, more pointedly, because they become adroit at *relational* learning skills, skills that entail more than the specific reward values of a single stimulus in a constrained discrimination–learning situation (Rumbaugh & Pate, 1984). Our chimpanzees' learning entailed the discernment of temporal and causal relationships between responses (e.g., the use of lexigrams by others in a social group) and specific consequences that ensue (e.g., going someplace, getting some specific food or drink, engaging in a game, etc.).

It is very important to note that our chimpanzees gave every reason for us to believe that during infancy, they learn more from observing the consequences of their social partners' use of the keyboard than they did from their own use of it. Such learning extends to the infant chimpanzee opportunities that far exceed its motoric ability to interact effectively with its physical and social environments. Such learning provides the infant chimpanzee a panoply of information from which it abstracts and integrates the basic framework of its language skills, skills that will not manifest until a later age. The chimpanzee's brain does this, not because it is "pellet driven" (e.g., shaped by reinforcers subsequent to motoric responses), but because that is what the advanced primate's brains were selected to do.

That what is learned might be unique to enriched captive settings is made clear when they are compared with learning acquired in feral settings. To the degree that Matata's record is instructive, it tells us that what is learned for survival in the field is not at all applicable to the demands of relational tasks in general or to language learning in particular in a laboratory context.

Specific Contributions of Early Experiences

It is our view that the developmental structures for cognition in apes and humans are quite plastic and have been selected for their sensitivity to the recurring and essential patterns of early experiences. As these structures form, they selectively include records of important observations of others' behaviors and retain them as models for approximate replication at later ages. These structures also organize experiences to serve as bases for the generation of new adaptive response patterns.

It is probably because the ape is so closely related to us that it is sensitive to the identical environments that foster psychological competence, and even language, in the human child, and likely for the same reasons. Being thus influenced, the chimpanzee develops psychological competencies that enable it to thrive as it masters the complex challenges of life in a language-research laboratory. Such adaptation is, however, at the expense of the chimpanzee's ability to adapt later to life in the field, just as we who mature in our technologically laced cities also become unsuited for life in the field. In brief, the specific and recurring pattern of stimulation available to the developing ape and child serves not only to foster relatively specific competencies, but serves to preclude (lock out), and increasingly so across time, the possible development of other, equally impressive dimensions of competence that would serve the interests of adaptation well in some other environment.

To us, it seems likely that as the chimpanzee learns the relational demands of language, it is developing neurological networks that resemble those that were basic to human neuroevolutionary trends and the evolution of language and attendant lateralization (see Riesen, 1982; Greenough, Withers, & Wallace, 1990; and Deacon, chapt. 4, for review of research that supports the plausibility of this view). A definitive answer to this question awaits future research.

Cultural Origins

Our findings and views hold an interesting implication for understanding the emergence of human culture and civilization, implying that the first steps toward culture, presumably by the inventions of adults, had their maximum impact upon the developing cognitive structures of young children who grew up observing each invention–innovation and its merits. Such structures would then serve to channel the creativity and inventiveness of these children as they achieved adulthood. Their creations, in turn, would have provided still better, more focused contexts whereby the intellect of their own infants would be both patterned and directed. Hence, we suggest that cultural gains did not so much evolve as a direct consequence of that inventiveness related to becoming an adult. Rather, cultural gains were made indirectly and quietly as each gain, in turn, served to direct the ever-observant child's cognitive development as it matured, to specific topics for reflection and refinement.

Language may no longer be rationally held as the distinguishing characteristic separating us from animals. Life-forms have evolved to become what they are through the selection for attributes that enhance adaptation and reproductive success. Although as a species we excel over all others both in the mastery and expression of language through speech, language is more than just speech. Moreover, the capacity for language is shared by the apes.

ACKNOWLEDGMENTS

Preparation of this chapter was supported by National Institutes of Health Grant RR-00165 and by Grant HD-06016 from the National Institute of Child Health and Human Development to the Georgia State University. Additional support was provided by the College of Arts & Sciences, Georgia State University.

REFERENCES

Alcock, J. (1984). *Animal behavior, an evolutionary approach.* Sunderland, MA: Sinauer.

Bates, E. A., Thal, D., & Marchman, V. A. (1991). Symbols and syntax: A Darwinian approach to language development. In N. A. Krasnegor, D.M. Rumbaugh, R. L. Schiefelbusch, & M. Studdert-Kennedy (Eds.), *Biological and behavioral determinants of language development* (pp. 29–65). Hillsdale, NJ: Lawrence Erlbaum Associates.

Bellugi, U., Bihrle, A., & Corina, D. (1991). Linguistic and spatial development: Dissociations between cognitive domains. In N. A. Krasnegor, D. M. Rumbaugh, R. L. Schiefelbusch, & M. Studdert-Kennedy (Eds.), *Biological and behavioral determinants of language development* (pp. 363–397). Hillsdale, NJ: Lawrence Erlbaum Associates.

Davenport, R. K., Rogers, C. W., & Rumbaugh, D. M. (1973). Long-term cognitive deficits in chimpanzees associated with early impoverished rearing. *Developmental Psychology, 9,* 343–347.

Greenfield, P. M., & Savage-Rumbaugh, E. S. (1991). Imitation, grammatical development, and the invention of protogrammar by an ape. In N. A. Krasnegor, D. M. Rumbaugh, R. L. Schiefelbusch, & M. Studdert-Kennedy (Eds.), *Biological and behavioral determinants of language development* (pp. 235–258). Hillsdale, NJ: Lawrence Erlbaum Associates.

Greenough, W. T., Withers, G. S., & Wallace, C. S. (1990). Morphological changes in the nervous system arising from behavioral experience: What is the evidence that they are involved in learning and memory? In L. R. Squire & E. Lindenlaub (Eds.), *The biology of memory. Symposia Medica Hoechst, 23* (pp. 159–184). Stuttgart: Schattauder Verlag.

Hayes, K. J., & Nissen, C. H. (1971). Higher mental functions of a home-raised chimpanzee. In A. M. Schrier & F. Stollnitz (Eds.), *Behavior of nonhuman primates* (pp. 59–115). New York: Academic Press.

Heltne, P. G., & Marguardt, L. A. (Eds.), (1989). *Understanding Chimpanzees.* Cambridge, MA: The Chicago Academy of Sciences.

Krech, D., Rosenzweig, M. R., & Bennett, E. L. (1962). Relations between brain chemistry and problem solving among rats raised in enriched and impoverished environments. *Journal of Comparative and Physiological Psychology, 55,* 801–808.

Pinker, S., & Bloom, P. (1990). Natural language and natural selection. *Behavioral and Brain Sciences, 13,* 707–784.

Riesen, A. H. (1982). Effects of environments on development in sensory systems. In W. D. Neff (Ed.), *Contributions to sensory physiology,* (Vol. 6, pp. 45–77). New York: Academic Press.

Rumbaugh, D. M. (1977). *Language learning by a chimpanzee: The LANA project.* New York: Academic Press.

Rumbaugh, D. M., Hopkins, W. D., Washburn, D. A., & Savage-Rumbaugh, E. S. (1991). Comparative perspectives of brain, cognition, and language. In N. A. Krasnegor, D. M. Rumbaugh, R. L. Schiefelbusch, & M. Studdert-Kennedy (Eds.), *Biological and behavioral determinants of language development* (pp. 145–164). Hillsdale, NJ: Lawrence Erlbaum Associates.

Rumbaugh, D. M., & Pate, J. L. (1984). The evolution of primate cognition: A comparative perspective. In H. L. Roitblat, T. G. Bever, & H. S. Terrace (Eds.), *Animal cognition* (pp. 569–587). Hillsdale, NJ: Lawrence Erlbaum Associates.

Rumbaugh, D. M., & Sterritt, G. M. (1986). Intelligence: From genes to genius in the quest for contro. In W. Bechtel (Ed.), *Integrating scientific disciplines* (pp. 309–321). San Diego, CA: Academic Press.

Savage-Rumbaugh, E. S. (1986). *Ape language: From conditioned responses to symbols.* New York: Columbia University Press.

Savage-Rumbaugh, E. S. (1988). A new look at ape language. Comprehension of vocal speech and syntax. In D. Leger (Ed.), *The Nebraska Symposium on Motivation, Vol. 35* (pp. 201–255). Lincoln: The University of Nebraska.

Savage-Rumbaugh, E. S., MacDonald, K., Sevcik, R. A., Hopkins, W. D., & Rubert, E. (1986). Spontaneous symbol acquisition and communicative use by two pygmy chimpanzees. *Journal of Experimental Psychology: General, 115,* 211–235.

Savage-Rumbaugh, E.S., Murphy, J., Sevcik, R. A., Brakke, K. E., Williams, S., & Rumbaugh, D. M. (1933). Language comprehension in ape and child. *Monographs of the Society for Research in Child Development, Serial No. 233, Vol. 58, Nos. 3–4.*

Sevcik, R. A. (1989). *A comprehensive analysis of graphic symbol acquisition and use: Evidence from an infant bonobo* (Pan paniscus). Unpublished doctoral dissertation. Atlanta: Georgia State University.

CHAPTER

11

THE CULTURAL ROOTS OF LANGUAGE

Michael Tomasello
Emory University, Atlanta

Over the past three decades the major obstacle for scientists interested in the psychological aspects of human linguistic competence has been generative grammar. Throughout this period, generative grammarians have claimed, and many psychologists have believed, that the only interesting aspect of language is its syntax, and that syntactic structure consists wholly of mathematical algorithms that are independent of meaning, communicative intention, and other psychological processes (e.g., Chomsky, 1986; Pinker, 1994). Recently, however, a new linguistic paradigm has emerged, and it is much more congenial to the traditional concerns of psychologists. The paradigm of cognitive linguistics, and its companion functional linguistics, is explicitly committed to describing and investigating linguistic competence in psychologically meaningful terms (Lakoff, 1990). Cognitive linguists thus describe linguistic structure in terms of such things as symbols, categories, schemas, perspectives, images, communicative functions, and a variety of other fundamentally cognitive and social processes (E. A. Bates & MacWhinney, 1989; Lakoff, 1987; Langacker, 1987, 1991; Talmy, 1988; van Valin, 1993). With the descriptions of linguistic structure emerging in this new paradigm, we have, for the first time, the possibility of creating a real psychology of language (Tomasello, 1992a, 1992b).

Cognitive linguists have, for the most part, focused their research attention on the conceptualizations that particular types of linguistic expressions encode and how they encode them, for example, the way languages structure space, time, events, agency, and so forth (see, e.g., the papers in Rudzka-Ostyn, 1988). Functional linguists have focused mostly on very general communicative functions such as topic and comment and how these are encoded in various linguistic structures in the many languages of the world (e.g., the papers in Haiman, 1985, and van Valin, 1993). There is another dimension to the psychology of language that these researchers have mostly ignored, however, and that is the cultural context within which languages arise, both phylogenetically and ontogenetically. Over and above a concern with the kinds of things human beings talk about and how they talk about them, it is also important to study the processes of cultural cognition, interaction, and learning that make the acquisition and use of language possible in the first place.

My goal in this chapter is to spell out these cultural processes in some detail, with special reference to the ontogeny of language. Throughout, it should be kept in mind that there are two complementary aspects to each of these processes. On the one hand are the cognitive and social-cognitive processes that constitute the human adaptation for culture: Human children bring to language acquisition a number of social-cognitive and cultural learning skills by means of which they are able to to comprehend and reproduce for themselves adult acts of linguistic communication. Especially important in this regard are children's developing skills in understanding the intentional actions of other persons, including their acts of linguistic reference. On the other hand are the cultural structures and institutions that exist prior to each child's birth: Human adults are adapted to pass on cultural skills to their children. Of special interest in this case are the routine cultural activities and other joint attentional interactions that adults structure for young children, and within which they treat children as intentional agents and use much of their early child-directed speech. Such cultural settings and interactions are an essential ingredient in children's coming to understand the intentional acts and cultural activities of other persons, including language.

In this chapter, I explore these two aspects of language acquisition at each of the two main levels of structure that distinguish language from other forms of animal communication: the level of individual lexical symbols and the level of grammatical symbols. In each case I provide some phylogenetic perspective on the process by making explicit comparisons to the communicative skills of our nearest primate relatives, the chimpanzees—both those that have developed in species-typical environments and those that have developed in human-like cultural environments. I conclude with some speculations on the evolution of culture and language.

LEXICAL SYMBOLS

Deacon (chap. 5, this volume) argued that, despite the great attention paid to grammar as the unique characteristic of human language, linguistic symbols are also uniquely human (at least when we consider nonhuman animals in their natural habitats), and indeed a strong argument can be made that symbols are the key to understanding all of human language. This is certainly the conclusion reached by researchers attempting to teach human-like linguistic skills to apes, as it has quickly become apparent that stringing together communicative behaviors is not grammatical if those behaviors are only conditioned responses and not true symbols (Savage-Rumbaugh, 1986). Even more radically, linguists such as Langacker (1987, 1991) have argued that the grammar of a language not only rests on symbols, but is, in reality, just another form of symbolic functioning: Grammatical symbols are simply symbols that may be used to designate certain kinds of relational or structural meanings. It is thus crucially important to begin any analysis of language by determining something of the nature of symbols and how they might arise both in phylogeny and ontogeny.

In recent thinking about linguistic symbols, two characteristics primarily have been emphasized. From the point of view of cognitive psychology, symbols serve an "information representation" function (Huttenlocher & Higgins, 1978; Premack, 1990). From the point of view of developmental psychology, symbols are communicative behaviors that have become "decontextualized" in that they can be used, not just as a part of an interactive sequence, but to "stand for" it (E. A. Bates, 1979;

Werner & Kaplan, 1963). These two functions of linguistic symbols are clearly an important part of the story. For current purposes, however, I would like to emphasize two related, but different, characteristics of symbols that bring out even more clearly their inherently social–cultural nature. First, of primary importance is the use of linguistic symbols in acts of external reference and, especially, acts of predication (Reed, 1993). In the analysis of Tomasello (1995), an act of linguistic reference is an act in which one individual intends that another individual should attend to some aspect of their shared external environment, in which an act of attention is regarded, according to E. J. Gibson and Rader (1979), as an act of intentional perception. This translates thus: A intends for B to intentionally perceive X. An act of predication simply extends this process as one individual first secures joint attention to some entity with another individual and then expresses an intention that the other should attend to one aspect, of many possible aspects, of that entity.

The second key characteristic of symbols is their reciprocal quality in being communicative behaviors that people both understand and understand that others understand (Mead, 1934). In the analysis of Savage-Rumbaugh (1990), a linguistic symbol is a communicative act that the producer comprehends—in some sense from the perspective of the receiver—as she produces it. This Janus-like quality is what gives linguistic symbols their special role in the evolution and transmission of culture, as both adult and child communicate with each other using the same system of symbols (Herford, 1989).

These two characteristics of linguistic symbols highlight clearly their social–cultural nature, as neither can be described without reference to at least two individuals engaged in certain kinds of social–cultural interactions. For purposes of exposition, these two characteristics of linguistic symbols are brought out even more clearly if we compare language to other forms of communication—more specifically, if we compare the communicative competencies of chimpanzees in their natural habitats, human children in the early phases of language acquisition, and chimpanzees raised in human-like cultural environments. I treat these each in turn, with some concern in each case for both the role of social–cultural cognition (especially the understanding of intentions) and the role of the social–cultural environments involved.

Chimpanzees

Like many other mammals, chimpanzees have a number of more or less involuntary displays that express their mood, for example, piloerection indicating an aggressive mood, penile erection indicating a sexually receptive mood, and "play-face" indicating a playful mood. These evolved displays, and the skills of group members to read them and make correct judgements about their implications for behavior, are an important part of the social regulation of the group. In addition, however, chimpanzees also use a number of gestures intentionally. What marks these gestures as different from involuntary displays is that (a) they are clearly learned, because not all individuals use them (Tomasello, 1990); (b) they are used flexibly, both in the sense that a single gesture may be used in different contexts, and also in the sense that different gestures may be used in the same context, often in rapid succession when an initial gesture does not lead to the desired response (Plooij, 1978); (c) the initiator often waits expectantly for a response from the recipient after the gesture has been produced (Tomasello, George, Kruger, Farrar, & E. Evans, 1985); and (d) particular gestures are chosen or adjusted based on the state of the recipient; for example, gestures requiring visual access are only used when the recipient is looking (Tomasello, Call, Nagell, R. Olguin, & Carpenter, 1994). Even though they are used flexibly in the pursuit of interactive goals, however, these intentional gestures do not seem to possess the two key social–cultural characteristics of linguistic symbols.

With regard to reference and predication, we must note first that chimpanzees in their natural habitats employ basically two types of intentional gesture. First, *attractors* are imperative gestures aimed at activating the actions of others toward the self. For example, a well-known behavior from the wild is the leaf-clipping of adult males, which serves to make a noise that attracts the interest of females to their sexual arousal (Nishida, 1980). Similarly, when captive youngsters want to initiate play, they attract a partner by slapping the ground, poking at a desired partner, or throwing things at a potential playmate (Tomasello, Gust, & Frost, 1989). Chimpanzee attractors are thus invariably used dyadically, to attract others to the self, not triadically, to direct the attention of others to some entity in the environment. Because of this somewhat limited function, attractors most often attain their specific communicative value from their combination with involuntary displays.

For example, the desire to play is most often communicated by means of an attractor that serves to gain attention to a "play-face." The second type of intentional gesture is *metonymic gestures*. These are mostly "intention movements" that serve to initiate interactive sequences. For example, play hitting is an important part of the rough-and-tumble play of chimpanzees, and thus many (but not all) individuals come to use a stylized "arm-raise" to indicate that they are about to hit the other and thus initiate play. Like attractors, most if not all metonymic gestures are imperative in function and used dyadically; that is, they are used to request a behavior of others toward the self, not to draw the attention of others to something in the external environment.[1]

Overall, for neither type of chimpanzee gesture are there any convincing observations of individuals attempting to direct the attention of others to outside objects simply for the goal of sharing attention: so-called "declarative" gestures (Gomez, Sarria, & Tamarit, 1993). Moreover, there are certainly no observations of chimpanzees attempting to direct the attention of others to outside entities in the typically human ways of pointing to them or holding them up to show others. Chimpanzees thus do not seem to be using their gestures in acts of external reference as this concept is traditionally defined.[2]

With regard to the other key characteristic of symbols, their reciprocal nature, the most direct evidence comes from the processes by which young chimpanzees learn their gestures. There are two main possibilities. On the one hand, young chimpanzees might learn their intentional gestures by imitating those of their groupmates. Imitative learning of this type, in which the learner does not just mimic body movements but also learns the functional significance of a gesture, would seem to require that the learner understand the communicative

---

[1] The major exception is food-begging, which is still an imperative gesture used by an individual in order to induce the foodbearer to produce action toward that individual herself.

[2] The well-known observations of Cheney and Seyfarth (1990) on the "referential" quality of vervet monkey alarm call vocalizations do not invalidate these observations. The vervet calls may not be intentionally produced or controlled, and indeed recent observations show that the alarm calls of chickens indicate specific predators in precisely the way that led researchers to call vervet alarm calls referential in the first place (Evans, Evans, & Marler, 1993). Also, Plooij (1978) presented several observations of wild chimpanzees that he believed to be acts of external reference, but each of these may be interpreted in a number of different ways.

intention of the gesturer so that he or she can reproduce the gesture when she has a similar communicative intention. The other possibility is a process called ritualization (or conventionalization). For example, two chimpanzee youngsters might begin to play through play hitting. On some occasion, one individual raises its arm in getting ready to play hit the other individual, who, because of past experience, is able to anticipate the impending hit and so begin the rough-and-tumble play at that early point in the sequence. The initiator then takes note of the recipient's anticipation and connects the raising of his own arm with the beginning of play, thus coming to use his arm-raise in a stylized manner, with no attempt to actually hit, and waiting for a response from the recipient. The arm-raise is now used intentionally, in order to elicit the desired response.[3]

Recent research clearly indicates that chimpanzee gestures of both types are learned through a process of ritualization, not imitation. Most important, in an 8-year longitudinal study involving 2 generations of chimpanzees within the same captive group, Tomasello, Savage-Rumbaugh, and Kruger (1993) found that (a) some youngsters used gestures that no other group member used, (b) some youngsters used gestures that had not been directed to them and that they had had little opportunity to observe, (c) chimpanzees raised only with peers developed many of the same gestures as those raised with adults, (d) individual variability in types of gestures used was equivalent both within and across generations of the group, and (e) there was much individual variability in the way specific gestures were executed. Also, in an ongoing investigation, my collaborators and I have introduced a novel gesture to an individual in this same study (through shaping, outside the observation of other group members), and we have yet to observe the imitative learning of this gesture by others, even though they have had both the opportunity and the incentive to do so.

What is important for current purposes is that ritualization is basically a kind of social shaping process in which each participant learns the effects of its behavior on the other's behavior, sometimes in a complex sequential pattern. If chimpanzees acquire their gestures solely by means of ritualization—as seems empirically to be the case—this might

---

[3]Similarly, attractors may be learned as individuals discover that making noises, creating visual displays, and physically contacting others often succeed in attracting others to the self and its displays of mood.

suggest that they understand their gestures from the perspective of one role only; that is, they understand the effects of the gesture from either the initiator's or the recipient's perspective, depending on which role they played in the conventionalizing interactions. In this scenario, they would not understand their own gestures as reciprocal communicative symbols, but rather as acts that produce certain predictable reactions in others, and they would understand the gestures of others as simple indications of their impending behavior. My only evidence for this admittedly speculative account is that chimpanzees do not imitatively learn their gestures from one another, implying that they do not understand that something they comprehend when another produces it is also something they may produce themselves when they have a similar communicative intention. And the reverse may also be true: They may produce a gesture but not comprehend it. My prediction is that if a chimpanzee had directed to a gesture that she herself had previously ritualized in production, but not in comprehension, she would not comprehend that gesture.

The reason that chimpanzees' intentional gestures are not symbolic in either of these two ways is that chimpanzees do not understand the behavior of others intentionally. First, chimpanzees do not use their gestures to refer to outside entities, much less to predicate things about them, because they do not understand that other chimpanzees may have intentional relations to outside entities. They attract others through various acts, and they even know that others need to be looking at their gestures to produce the desired effects, but they do not know that their conspecifics may attend to—or want or believe or in any way intentionally relate to—something outside their face-to-face relation. Such knowledge is essential (as will become apparent in the analysis of human children's early symbols) for the use of symbols in truly referential and predicative acts. Similarly, chimpanzees do not imitatively learn their gestures, and therefore do not understand them reciprocally, for precisely the same reason. To imitatively learn a new gesture requires that the learner comprehend another's gesture, including the goal toward which it is used, and then reproduce that gesture when she or he has a similar communicative goal. A gesture acquired in this way would presumably be understood reciprocally from the outset (from the perspective of the sender and receiver simultaneously) because understanding of the other's perspective was required for the imitative learning in the first place. If chimpanzees were able to understand directly the communicative intentions of others, they would learn to produce some gestures imitatively—perhaps even on first observation as children seemingly do in the acquisition of many linguistic symbols.

Communicative behaviors that are not used to direct the attention of others to outside entities and are not understood reciprocally are best called something such as "signals," not "symbols" because individuals may produce them intentionally, but not understand them intentionally when others produce them. Thus, signals are understood as spurs to action, and not as an intentional device that could be adopted by the self if needed. It should be noted that this interpretation of chimpanzee gestural communication is fully consistent with recent experimental results on chimpanzee acquisition of tool use, showing that whereas chimpanzees do learn some things by observing others, they do not engage in imitative learning of a type that requires an understanding of the intentions of others (Nagell, R. Olguin, & Tomasello, 1993; Tomasello, Davis-Dasilva, Camak, & Bard 1987). This hypothesis concerning the role of understanding others intentionally in the genesis and use of symbols will be explored and elaborated further as we deal with children and enculturated chimpanzees.

Human Children

Human infants have a number of intentional gestures that are most likely ritualized and understood in the same way that chimpanzees ritualize and understand their gestures, including such things as the "hands-up" gesture as a request to be picked up. Although there is certainly room for disagreement about how children understand these gestures, many of their earliest gestures, before their first birthdays, are not accompanied by the kind of spontaneous gaze alternation and checking with the adult that is typically used as evidence that the child understands the gestures reciprocally and predicatively (Butterworth, 1991). Moreover, in many cases the same may be said of children's earliest attempts at language. Many of children's early "words" are very likely learned through ritualization as well, that is, ritualization in which the child mimics an adult sound (word), with the result that the adult responds in some predictable and interesting way. These so-called presymbolic forms are often characterized as being simply a part of an activity, not a symbol standing for anything else in the activity (E. A. Bates, 1979). We may thus call them vocal signals.

Symbol Use. Children's early words differ from chimpanzee gestures and from their own prelinguistic gestures and vocal signals with respect to both of the key social–cultural characteristics of symbols. First, children's earliest linguistic symbols may be used referentially to designate an outside situation. The predicative use of symbols allows for even more specific forms of reference. For example, upon observing a girl swimming in a pond, a nascent language learner might say to an adult something like "swimming," or "girl", or "water", or "wet", or "raft," or any number of other things. What is crucial in such cases is, first, that the child knows already that she and the adult are jointly attending to the event, and, second, that the child has a choice of which aspect of the event to talk about or comment upon: object, activity, property, location, or whatever. What the child is doing in such cases is choosing a particular psychological orientation or attitude from among other possible orientations and attitudes that he or she wishes the adult to take toward some entity for which they already share attention. The child is predicating something about a shared experience.

Although predication is most often thought of as a linguistically expressed comment on a linguistically expressed topic, a one-word predication is also possible if the child has first secured the adult's attention to a topic nonlinguistically (Tomasello, 1988). When a child holds up a shirt and says, "wet," that is an act of predication if indeed the child has other symbols to use in designating other aspects of the situation if he or she so chooses. Use of a symbol in this way implies that the child understands that the symbol is one among a number of options for directing the attention of the other person to one aspect, as opposed to other possible aspects, of the shared situation. Young children engage in one-word predication defined in this way from before the middle of the second year of life.

Symbol Learning. Excluding cases in which vocal signals are transformed into symbols, children learn their early words by some form of imitative learning from adults. It is thus presumably the case that they understand them reciprocally. This means that when children predicate something of a situation to an adult, they, in effect, understand or anticipate the effect of that predication on the adult's construal of the situation. It also means that they would understand another individual's use of that same symbol. This reciprocity is a natural outcome of the imitative learning process because imitative learning requires that the child understand, not only the adult's communicative intention in using a novel piece of language, but also the fact that he or she may use the same piece of language when she has the same communicative intention.

To understand more precisely how imitative learning leads to the reciprocal understanding of symbols and their use as predicative devices, several recent studies concerning children's comprehension of adults' referential intentions are instructive. First, Baldwin (1991, 1993) had an adult look at one object, while a young child was looking at another object, and then say "It's a toma." In this situation, children did not suppose that the adult was naming the object they were seeing, but rather the object at which the adult was looking. Children were not passively associating a sound and a perceived object. They were actively inferring adult referential intentions. Along similar lines, Tomasello and M. Barton (1995) had an adult announce to 24-month-old children that he or she was going to go find a "toma" in a row of buckets. The adult then approached the buckets, took out two objects and frowned at them, then picked up a third object with obvious glee. Almost all of the children understood immediately that the adult intended for the word "toma" to indicate the third, not the first or second, object chosen. Again, children were not passive participants, but were actively monitoring the adult's intentions (via facial expression and other behavioral cues) to determine the intended referent. Finally, Tomasello and M. Barton (1995) also had an adult announce his or her intention to "plunk" an object, and then proceed to perform one action accidentally followed by another purposefully. Young children understood that the new symbol was intended to depict the action the adult performed intentionally, even though the accidental action was the one performed immediately after the new word was said.

The point is this: To understand novel words in cases such as these, young children use a variety of social-pragmatic cues to determine precisely what the adult is doing and why—what intention was behind the action. Children must understand that the adult using the new word wants them to focus their attention on one specific aspect of the upcoming event out of many aspects that might be possible referents. When the child then uses the word, with the same communicative intention as the adult had in the original learning situation, the reciprocity is apparent. Thus, understanding the exhortations of others that one should attend to a situation in a certain way, and adopting them for oneself in exhorting others to take similar orientations in similar contexts, is called by Tomasello, Kruger, and H. H. Ratner (1993) "imitative learning." It is considered one form—the ontogenetically first form—of a more general process called "cultural learning." The defining feature of cultural learning is its direct dependence on children's ability to understand the intentions of another person who attempts both to direct the children's attention to outside entities and to comprehend their efforts to do the same thing in return. What is unique about language acquisition is that the preexisting set of linguistic symbols provided by the culture offers to adult and child a common medium by means of which they may engage in this form of interaction reciprocally, using a common set of devices to encourage one another to take particular psychological orientations in shared situations. Thus, the fact that young children can imitatively learn novel words in situations in which there are many possible targets for adults' referential intentions indicates that from a very early age their understanding and use of symbols are both reciprocal and predicative.

My explanation for the unique qualities of human children's early linguistic symbols is that children, unlike chimpanzees in their natural habitats, perceive and understand the behavior of others intentionally. Because they understand the behavior of others intentionally, they can also comprehend their communicative intentions in using particular symbols and thus imitatively learn that use for themselves when they have similar communicative intentions. This makes the symbols reciprocal. Similarly, understanding that other persons may intentionally direct attention to various aspects of a shared situation allows children to comprehend and produce linguistic symbols with those persons in a predicative manner. In all, understanding other individuals as intentional agents is the key social–cognitive skill that accounts for the difference between signals and symbols.

It should be mentioned, at least in passing, that further evidence for the view that young children's understanding of intentions is crucial to their acquisition of symbols comes from the emergence of a number of new behaviors at around the same age when young children are learning their first words. Thus, at around their first birthdays human infants for the first time systematically look where others are looking, adopt their emotional attitude toward situations (social referencing), and imitatively learn their instrumental behaviors toward objects. These all require that the young child understand the adult as an intentional agent whose attention or behavior to outside entities may be followed and adopted. Thus the stage is set for language acquisition (Tomasello, 1995). Perhaps even most interesting in the current context, as children begin to learn their first symbols, they also begin to use their gestures in a more interpersonally sophisticated way, often checking with adults to see if they have followed a pointing gesture, for example. Some children even learn a new type of gesture at this age—what has been called the "symbolic gesture" (Acredolo & Goodwin, 1993)—involving such things as flapping the arms to a bird, or blowing toward liquids that are hot. These are presumably learned imitatively and understood reciprocally. It is also important that Petitto (1992) found a distinct difference in the way young deaf children point prelinguistically and the way they point when they begin to do so symbolically in American Sign Language—again at around this same age and also relying, presumably, on imitative learning and reciprocal understanding. The important point is that all of these behaviors evidence the 1-year-old child's emerging ability to understand others as agents with intentional relations to various aspects of the world. The behaviors thus provide further support for the hypothesis that the acquisition of linguistic symbols as reciprocal communicative devices that can be used in acts of predication depends crucially on the understanding of others as intentional agents.

The Cultural Context. Obviously, to learn the use of a new linguistic symbol in its conventional communicative context children must be exposed to others using that symbol. The cultural environment is thus in some sense presupposed by the notion that children acquire their words by means of cultural (imitative) learning. In addition, however, it may be that some more specific aspects of the cultural environment are required. Thus, recent research has demonstrated that children learn almost all of their earliest language in cultural routines or in joint attentional interactions of one sort or another. Joint attentional routines such as feeding, diaper changing, bathing, interactive games, book reading, car trips, and a whole host of other activities constitute the formats within which children acquire their earliest linguistic symbols (see Bruner, 1983, and Nelson, 1985, for summaries). These routines scaffold the initial language acquisition of children in the sense that they create, with no need of a conventional language whatsoever, a shared referential context within which the language of the adult makes sense to prelinguistic children—assuming their ability to understand the behavior of others intentionally.

Even after they have learned their first words, children continue to acquire the vast majority of their language inside nonlinguistically understood joint attentional episodes, and individual differences in the rate at which children acquire their early words are predicted by the extent to which they participate with adults in joint attentional episodes (see Tomasello, 1988, for a review). Again, such episodes, whether or not they are routine, require both a certain type of social understanding on the child's part and certain kinds of participation in the interaction on the adult's part. The nature of routines and joint attentional episodes may vary across cultures to some extent, but there are also certain commonalities in the structuring of routine activities of very different content across different cultures, and it is likely that these commonalities play some role in the early language acquisition of all children (Peters & Boggs, 1986).

Thus, the overall point is that human beings come into the world adapted for intentional communicative interactions with others and that, not surprisingly, cultures are structured in ways that facilitate this process. Although research shows that children learn much of their early language inside routinized cultural interactions, it is still possible to argue from this research that such interactions are not entirely necessary, but serve only to speed up the process somewhat. I would argue for their necessity, however, by insisting not only that routine interactions are necessary for children's early language acquisition—because only in such contexts can their still fragile social–cognitive skills to understand the intentions of others operate—but that children need many months of social interaction with others before language acquisition begins if they are to come to understand others at all as intentional agents (and thus to actively participate at all in cultural routines). Following the arguments of Kaye (1982), I would argue that social interactions of a certain type (i.e., interactions in which infants are themselves treated intentionally) are necessary in children coming to understand other persons as intentional agents. There is, of course, very little direct evidence for this position in research with human children (inferences from wild children and neglected children are notoriously problematic), but research with

11. CULTURAL ROOTS OF LANGUAGE

chimpanzees exposed to human-like forms of symbolic communication provides some highly suggestive findings.

Enculturated Chimpanzees

The first attempts to teach chimpanzees skills of symbolic communication relied on various behavioristic training techniques. Experimenters would do such things as hold up objects, shape chimpanzee hands into signs, and reinforce the connection (production training); or they would themselves give a sign and reinforce chimpanzees for selecting the corresponding object (comprehension training). Subjects trained in such ways did learn to do some very interesting things communicatively, but what they learned may not have been true symbols according to the current definition (Savage-Rumbaugh, 1986). Thus, it turns out that when these pioneer chimpanzees were taught symbols in production, they could not comprehend them, and when they were taught to comprehend them, they could not produce them appropriately (Savage-Rumbaugh, 1990). Their symbols were either production based or comprehension based, depending on how they had been trained. They were not understood reciprocally in the sense that they could mediate communicative interactions in both directions: from chimpanzee to human or from human to chimpanzee.

In contrast, the pygmy chimpanzee (bonobo) Kanzi (and a common chimpanzee since) was raised more naturally in a human-like cultural environment with linguistic symbols appearing as a natural component of his social interactions with humans; he was not conditioned or trained in the use of human symbols in any way. Kanzi was regularly invited into highly structured cultural routines such as changing diapers, preparing food, going outdoors, taking a bath, blowing bubbles, riding in the car, looking at a book, and playing various games. Thus, language (both spoken English and a lexigram board displaying abstract symbols) was used by his human caretakers in these situations in any way that seemed natural to them, presumably in ways comparable to those by which human children are exposed to language. As a consequence of this more culturally saturated and less behavioristic upbringing, Kanzi learned to comprehend and use symbols reciprocally in very human-like ways. Because his productive behaviors were not shaped through reinforcement, Kanzi learned first to comprehend linguistic symbols—as human children do—and only then, with no specific training, did he begin to produce them spontaneously (Savage-Rumbaugh et al., 1993). This initial learning through observation and imitation thus ensured, as it does for human children, that the symbols produced were understood reciprocally.

Savage-Rumbaugh's work would seem to be a very convincing demonstration that routine cultural activities and events help to structure the language learner's experience in a way that is essential to the acquisition of communicative symbols. However, the effect is actually more general than this. Two recent studies compared other social–cognitive and cultural learning skills that chimpanzees develop in cultural environments as contrasted with those that they develop in more typical captive environments. For both imitative learning (Tomasello, Savage-Rumbaugh, & Kruger, 1993) and joint attention (Carpenter, Tomasello, & Savage-Rumbaugh, 1995) enculturated chimpanzees were found to be more similar to 2-year-old human children than they were to their conspecifics who were not raised in cultural environments. Documentation of humanlike behaviors in all three of these domains—language, imitative learning, and joint attention—none of which were the result of explicit training, argues very strongly that through interacting with other persons inside natural cultural routines chimpanzees are not just learning some isolated skill, but rather are coming to learn more generally about the behavior of human beings. They are coming to view humans as intentional agents, and this allows them to comprehend and then to produce appropriately the symbols humans use in their interactions with them, as well as to engage in a number of other humanlike cultural skills.

None of this is meant to imply, of course, that cultural environments create social–cognitive skills de novo. Many animals are raised in humanlike ways and do not develop such skills. The limitations of a cultural environment are even more dramatically demonstrated by the case of autistic children who have been raised in all kinds of cultural environments, with and without specific intervention programs, and who still do not develop any language or imitative learning skills. (This describes about half of all autistic individuals.) It is also important in this context to note that recent research has established that the extent to which autistic children can engage in nonlinguistic joint attentional interactions with adults—implying some understanding of adults as intentional beings—is strongly correlated with extent of their symbolic and linguistic skills (Landry & Loveland, 1986; Mundy, Sigman, & Kasari, 1990).

Lexical Symbols: Summary

Most recent accounts of early linguistic symbols have focused on processes of information representation and decontextualization as their defining features (E. A. Bates, 1979; Huttenlocher & Higgins 1978). Although not disputing that these are an important part of the process of learning to understand and use symbols, I simply do not think they are the whole story, or even the most important part of the story. In my view the kinds of social understandings discussed here—the reciprocal understanding of symbols along with the understanding that linguistic symbols allow choices in the particular orientation or attitude that one might predicate of a situation—are crucial in distinguishing symbols from other kinds of semiotic devices. In the current hypothesis, the understanding of symbols as both reciprocal and as predicating is made possible by the child's developing understanding of other persons as intentional agents. Such understanding allows children to comprehend that when the adult uses a symbol to refer to some aspect of the current situation, the adult intending that the child attend to that aspect. Linguistic symbols also require certain forms of social–cultural interaction with others. Individual organisms do not just come to invent things such as symbols on their own. They must interact with others inside contexts that make apparent the various intentions involved, it is essential that they also have a period of time in which other persons treat them intentionally before they can understand other persons as intentional agents at all.

GRAMMATICAL SYMBOLS

As in the case of symbols, there is a long history of controversy over the proper characterization of grammar. Generative grammarians, for example, have defined grammar and syntax in terms of formal mathematical rules in which semantic and communicative functions play absolutely no role (Chomsky, 1986). The cultural roots of such rules are presumably nil. But the generative view of grammar is not the only possible view. The view of grammar emerging in cognitive linguistics relies not on formal rules but explicitly and exclusively on symbols and categories of symbols (Langacker, 1987). Competence with a language is thus nothing more or less than competence in using symbols, or, more precisely, in using a "structured inventory of symbolic devices," of which there are many types serving many different functions, including grammatical functions (see Wittgenstein's analogy of a tool box, 1953). To construct communicative messages, human beings take symbols and categories of symbols from this inventory and integrate them into larger symbolic wholes that relate in comprehensible ways to the ongoing communicative context.

For current purposes, the cognitive linguistics view of grammar allows us to take our previous analysis of symbols and use it as a foundation for our characterization of grammar. The basic idea is that human beings, including young children, live in a world of events and actions (Nelson, 1985). As they begin acquiring their first symbols, they learn to understand and to predicate symbolic references to different aspects of the same event: the entities, relations, and processes that constitute it. The preexisting language that children encounter in their interactions with adults provides a number of different means for these predications and for coordinating these predications into one coherent description in which the roles of different participants in an event are symbolically marked with grammatical symbols (i.e., into "sentences"). Thus, what we might call lexical symbols designate the elements in a complex cognitive scene, whereas grammatical symbols operate on these elements to designate the structure of the scene—the relation of the elements to one another in the event (Talmy, 1988). The nature of these grammatical symbols is different in varied languages. For example, in some languages speakers mark the agent and recipient of an action by placing them in particular orders. In other languages the order of the elements is not crucial, but there are special case endings. In still other languages there are special symbols (such as some English prepositions) or special intonation patterns (as in tone languages) that serve these same functions (E. A. Bates & MacWhinney, 1989). The point is that grammatical symbols are simply another kind of symbol in the communicative inventory, created and used for purposes of communicating complex messages concerning recurrent and predictable relationships among entities in the shared world of their users.

It is clear from this characterization that the most important cultural roots of grammar are precisely the same as those of individual symbols because grammatical symbols are just another form of linguistic symbols. In addition, however, the combining of individual symbols and the marking of their respective roles with grammatical symbols entails some further cognitive and social–cognitive skills that are cultural in ways that go beyond individual symbols. Again, the best way to explore this issue is by comparing the grammatical skills of chimpanzees, children, and enculturated chimpanzees.

The ability to take an event, parse it into elements, relations, and processes of various types, and then to indicate these elements, relations, and processes with individual lexical and grammatical symbols in one coherent utterance, is an ability that has evolved only in the human species. Chimpanzees in their natural habitats sometimes string multiple vocalizations or gestures together, but they do not use these combinations to create new meanings of any type or to parse (predicate) events into their constituent elements. Most chimpanzee gesture combinations are repetitions of the same gesture or several gestures, all with the same communicative intention (e.g., to request play); they do not contain different gestures playing different roles within a single communicative intention (Tomasello, Savage-Rumbaugh, & Kruger, 1993). Chimpanzee gestural communication thus cannot display a grammar because their gestures are not referential and predicative in the first place.

Human Children

Early Grammatical Skills. Children's grammatical skills begin with their skills of predication. In their very first multiword utterances in their second year of life, human children predicate different aspects of the same event, saying for example, "More juice," and on another occasion of the same event, "Mommy juice." These combinations usually follow closely on the heels of their first one-word predications. In these early word combinations children are not employing grammatical symbols to designate the relation between the lexical symbols, however. They utter the words in a certain order, but they are not actively using that order to designate the roles that individual words are playing: "More juice" does not mean something different from "Juice more," and the children are not explicitly marking the intended relation in any other way. In these early utterances it is up to the listener to infer what grammatical relation among lexical symbols the child is intending. In many cases children follow the adult word order and therefore seem to be using adult-like grammatical marking, but I am aware of no evidence showing that children's early word combinations employ word order or any other grammatical symbols as productive communicative devices.

When children do begin to actively mark lexical symbols for their grammatical functions, they do so in event-specific ways, in which event most often means intentional human action. Thus, children learn first grammatical symbols inside specific cultural activities and events, most typically activities and events about which they have previously predicated different things (Ninio, in press). For example, English-speaking children learn the grammatical symbols for "hitting" in situations such as sibling disputes while eating at the dinner table, swimming at the pool, and deciding who will play with certain toys. What they learn is tied to the specific event and the way adults talk about the intentional actions within that event, for example, that "the hitter" goes before "hit" and "the thing hit" goes after, whereas the "thing hit with" is designated by the word "with." Evidence for this view comes from the diary study of Tomasello (1992a) who found that his subject did not generalize the use of grammatical symbols across different event structures: She had to learn how to parse and grammatically mark the components of each of the different events individually. R. Olguin and Tomasello (1993) provided experimental confirmation for this explanation: the so-called Verb Island Hypothesis.[4] These results mean that the syntagmatic categories of children's early language are event-specific categories tied to the specific participant roles involved, such as "hitter," "thing hit," "kisser," and "thing kissed," not event-general participant roles such as "agent," "patient," and "instrument." It is also interesting and important for current purposes to observe that almost all of these early events serving to organize children's early grammars are the intentional actions of persons, including the child in almost all of

---

[4]It should be noted that children of this age can substitute different objects in a single participant role without having heard that object's name used in that role (e.g., "More juice," "More dax"), providing for some degree of productivity and indicating some early notion of something like a grammatical category of noun (Tomasello & Olguin, 1993).

the early transitive utterances of the subject of Tomasello (1992a), there was an animate actor acting on an inanimate object.[5]

Children's early grammatical skills are thus dependent on their being able to conceptualize and symbolize events, especially intentional actions, and, more importantly, on their ability to predicate different participant roles in those events. Acquiring grammatical symbols to indicate those participant roles—such things as word order and some prepositions in English—depends on the child's understanding of the intentions of others in just the same way as in their acquisition of lexical symbols. Thus, the only way a child can discover that in the language one is learning that the agent of an action is designated by a particular symbol is by entering into a joint attentional interaction with an adult who is using that symbol in an act of intentional communication (Macnamara, 1972). To understand that the two statements,"Mary hit John" and "John hit Mary," are used to designate different situations involving the same action and participants, and thus to infer the communicative function of the different word orders, the child must engage in the same processes of cultural learning that were used to understand adult use of lexical symbols. The child must first understand why (with what intention) the adult uses one ordering of words in one hitting situation and another ordering of those same words in another hitting situation. Then the child must reproduce that ordering with a similar communicative intention regarding another instance of the hitting event. Understanding and learning grammatical symbols is thus effected inside the very same culturally constituted event structures as those that scaffold early word learning, and the child employs, in the process, the very same cultural (imitative) learning skills that depend on understanding others as intentional agents (Tomasello, 1992b).

Later Grammatical Skills. It is possible to agree that children's early grammars are event-based and dependent on the understanding of intentional action, but at the same time to doubt that such an account is useful for children's later grammatical development. More sophisticated grammatical skills begin as children start to use grammatical symbols more generally across events, implying something like a grammatical category of "verb" to designate a generalized event (or at

---

[5] The major exceptions to this generalization were rational words or verbs used to indicate the locations or simple spatial transformations of objects.

least some subset of events, such as transitive actions). Formation of this paradigmatic category makes possible more general such syntagmatic categories as "agent" and "patient" as generalized participant roles across events. With thecategory of verb in hand, children may now understand that the statement, "John is glorping Mary," is intended to indicate that John is doing something to Mary and not the reverse (L. R. Gleitman, 1990). We may now speak of the beginnings of a language system, based on fundamental processes of linguistic categorization, by means of which the child may create and comprehend an infinite variety of linguistic expressions.

The process of linguistic category formation is fundamentally a cognitive process. However, as my central concern in this chapter is with the cultural roots of language acquisition, I would like to point out two ways in which it is also social–cultural. First, in all of the world's languages that have been studied there are certain commonalities in the complex events and participants that young children are first motivated to verbalize. Many of these commonalities are captured in what Slobin (1985) called the "Manipulative Activity Scene": situations in which people do things to objects, often in particular settings and sometimes with particular instruments—such things as giving, bringing, opening, throwing, and a variety of other concrete activities that humans regularly perform on objects and with other people. These actions typically have animate actors (sometimes with instruments) and inanimate recipients of the action (sometimes in a particular setting or with another person). As Bruner (1990) pointed out, this basic schema is very similar to the basic structure of all kinds of cultural narratives in which an actor acts to effect an outcome in some setting with some instrument. What this means is that the most basic participant roles underlying children's earliest grammatical creations—such things as agent, action, patient, instrument, and location—are in reality the very same categories in terms of which they understand the most basic cultural activities. In both language and social–cultural activities in general, children, like their cultures, are concerned with the same basic types of participant roles.

The second way that early grammatical categories are social is somewhat indirect. An important part of early grammar structure is the formation of paradigmatic word classes such as nouns and verbs that license much productivity; a new word identified as a noun (e.g., by the presence of an article) may be used in many appropriate ways in which it has never been heard. In the analysis of Tomasello (1992a) the construction of these categories is based on the subject's reflection on his or her own linguistic productions. This is the same process as that proposed by Karmiloff-Smith (1992), who found that in many cognitive domains children first learn individual procedures (such as lexically specific structures), and then, through reflecting on their activities, construct general principles (redescriptions) on which to base their future behavior. Paradigmatic categories can thus be formed only when the child has reflected on the way he or she has used various concrete linguistic items, just as principles of lexical acquisition can only be formed after the child has learned to use some individual lexical items. But selfreflection, in the hypothesis of Tomasello, Kruger, and H. H. Ratner (1993), is nothing other than cultural learning turned on the self and its behavioral–cognitive products. That is to say, the ability to self-reflect is simply the ability to take the point of view of another individual, real or imagined, as they are observing me. Self-reflection is my acting as if I were another person, looking at my behavior from the outside, using all of my basic powers of human perception and categorization in the process; I am culturally learning from, and thus forming categories of, my own unreflective productions. Grammatical categories are thus formed through a variation on the basic processes that underlie the acquisition of lexical and grammatical symbols.

It should also be noted that later in their language development children begin to use a variety of specialized discourse structures that differ in various ways from the prototypical events of interest to 2-year-olds. Children learn to produce the conventional form of such things as questions, passive sentences, and sentences with embedded clauses. However, it turns out in these cases as well that children learn these structures on an individual basis, relying, for example, on their knowledge that certain kinds of events, by their very nature, structure other events (e.g., think and believe require other events to complete them; see L. Bloom 1991, on the use of specific "wh" words), or on the grammatical marking required when one wants to highlight the patient of an action. The role of the social–cultural environment in children's acquisition of these more complex forms of grammatical competence is an issue that has not received much attention. It seems clear, to me at least, that children must be exposed to these structures in situations in which they have some way of understanding the communicative intentions of the speaker and connecting them with the new form they are hearing (Akhtar, 1995). Evidence that this is indeed the case comes from studies such as those of Nelson (1977) and Farrar (1990), who both found that adults' replying to nonadult-like child utterances by recasting them into adult form facilitates children's acquisition of some types of grammatical structures, presumably because these recastings represent the child's own semantic intentions. Also, E. A. Bates and MacWhinney (1989) have shown how efforts to take the perspective of the listener in discourse (as manifest in topic–comment structure) underlie the basic grammatical category of sentence subject. Also Rispoli (1995) has shown in an even more detailed way how various grammatical structures derive from basic patterns of discourse-communicative interactions. Learning grammatical symbols and structures is essentially the same process as learning individual symbols.

Enculturated Chimpanzees

The story of chimpanzees enculturated in the use of grammar is very similar to the story of their enculturation in the use of individual symbols, once again highlighting the role of the cultural environment. Some early attempts at training chimpanzees in grammar did not work very well. The trained chimpanzees produced "words" and strings of words as they were reinforced for doing so, but for a number of reasons these words did not seem to be grammatical in the sense that they did not parse events and designate symbolically the different participants in the events. Thus, Terrace, Petitto, Sanders, and Bever (1979) showed that many of their subject's word strings were repetitive, almost random, and did not add significantly to the description of the event as more words were added. Even in recognizing such utterances as Washoe's famous "water bird" as creative symbol combinations, it is still very likely that Washoe was not employing word order in this utterance as a productive grammatical symbol; it is most likely analogous to children's first word combinations, which leave it up to the listener to infer the intended relation. Of course, the failure of trained chimpanzees in the domain of grammar is not surprising if indeed their "words" were not symbolic, if they were not reciprocal symbols used predicatively in the first place.

The most convincing evidence for an understanding of grammatical symbols by an ape comes once again from Kanzi. Kanzi clearly understood and used symbols that were reciprocal and predicative; he was thus capable of parsing a single event into its constitutive elements, relations, and processes. In his productive use of lexigrams on a computer keyboard, Kanzi showed some evidence of productive grammatical devices in the form of contrastive word order: different orders of the same lexical symbols mean different things (Greenfield & Savage-Rumbaugh, 1990). Much better evidence that Kanzi was able to understand grammatical symbols came from his comprehension of novel sentences, mostly presented in human speech. In a recent monograph, Savage-Rumbaugh et al. (1993) documented abilities on Kanzi's part that are comparable to those of a 2-year-old human child tested in a similar manner. Thus, Kanzi carried out the appropriate action when asked to "Make the snake bite the doggie" as well as when he was asked to "Make the doggie bite the snake," indicating an understanding of the contrastive use of word order as an event-based grammatical symbol. These grammatical symbols, like children's grammatical symbols, were based on Kanzi's understanding of the intentions of human interactants as they talked to him about biting events and the participants involved across different instances.

It is thus clear that chimpanzees, when raised in human-like cultural environments, can learn to comprehend some types of grammatical symbols. It is possible, indeed likely, that these are tied to individual events and are not grammatical categories implying a knowledge of generalized participant roles (Tomasello, 1994). Why chimpanzees do not go on to construct grammatical categories, if indeed they do not, is an unanswerable question at this point. One possibility, however, is that we simply have not raised them in the right kinds of environments. Another possibility is that chimpanzees do not use their cultural learning abilities to reflect on their own behavior. That is to say, it may be that once chimpanzees have learned to communicate in complex ways about particular events, they may still not reflect on the forms used across individual events use them to create more generalized grammatical symbols. In either case, what we are talking about is not some generative grammar module that chimpanzees do not have, but rather some social–cognitive skill or some aspect of the cultural environment that may differ from that of human children in their natural environments.

Grammatical Symbols: Summary

If we regard grammar as just one of the devices present in human languages for conceptualizing and communicating shared cultural experiences, then we may begin to study the psychological and cultural processes involved in grammatical development. I argue that the development of grammatical competence in both human children and enculturated chimpanzees is cultural in at least three senses. First, the kinds of things they talk about are recurrent cultural activities, parsed into the actors, actions, affected object, instrument, and setting information characteristic of cultural narratives of all types. Moreover, at an early stage for children, and perhaps at all ages for enculturated chimpanzees, these activities serve as the major organizing structures in early grammars. Second, the parsing of events relies on an understanding of lexical symbols as predicative, which, in turn, relies on an understanding of other persons as intentional. Thus, the social–cognitive skills that children use to acquire grammatical symbols are precisely those that have evolved for the acquisition of cultural skills in general: abilities to enter into a joint attentional interaction with intentional agents and to take their perspective on the situation. The ability to reflect on the structures constructed in this way may be essential to grammatical category formation and may derive from cultural learning abilities in general. Finally, the kinds of discourse-communicative functions that arise in linguistic interactions with others are an integral part of the acquisition of the more complex sorts of grammatical competence: question asking, passive sentences, and the like (which may be the exclusive province of human beings). In all, looking at grammar as an extension of human symbolizing skills allows us to view lexical and grammatical symbols within the same cognitive and communicative contexts, and to compare children of different ages and even nonhuman species as they attempt to acquire human adult-like grammatical skills.

THE EVOLUTION OF LANGUAGE

There is a growing consensus among behavioral biologists that what is unique about primate intelligence is the nature of its adaptations to the social environment, and recent research has elucidated many of the ways that primates may understand, predict, and influence the behavior of conspecifics (Byrne & Whiten, 1988; Cheney & Seyfarth, 1990). In this context human beings have developed some of their own unique, species-typical skills of social cognition and social learning that make possible the process by which one generation of human beings assimilates the cultural knowledge and skills of the generation preceding them (Tomasello, Kruger, & H. H. Ratner, 1993). It is the central contention of this paper that human languages have their roots in general cultural skills of this type, and that they are transmitted across generations in the same way as other cultural skills. The kinds of abstract linguistic structures that theorists such as Pinker and P. Bloom (1991) claimed are not transmittable in this way are simply not a part of the structure of language as conceived by a growing group of linguists and psycholinguists, including myself, who reject the mathematical approach to language structure.

Because of their mathematical construal of linguistic structure, generative grammarians such as Chomsky and Pinker cannot really say anything useful about language evolution except that it burst onto the scene rather recently. I think it is important in this regard, though, to remember that individual lexical symbols are uniquely human inventions as well. The generative view of language must then posit two evolutionary saltations if it is to account for the totality of human grammatical competence: one for symbols and another for grammar. Moreover, given their view of grammar, it would seem that generative grammarians have to posit very different kinds of adaptations in the two cases: one psychological and the other formal. Much more plausible, I think, is the view that skills of human communication emerged gradually from skills of primate social cognition and communication, and that as those underlying skills changed, so did the nature of the human communicative system. Thus, intentional gestures of the type used by modern chimpanzees may have evolved at some point in human evolution into something like linguistic symbols as human beings came to understand the intentions and perspective of other human beings more clearly, which then led to the kinds of reciprocal understandings and predications characteristic of 2-year-old children's linguistic symbols. Grammatical symbols may have evolved from this base as humans came to understand that acts of predication made sequentially may be bundled into one coherent utterance in which different aspects of an event are symbolized by different lexical and grammatical symbols.

Obviously, I do not know the specific evolutionary steps and timetable for all of this. An interesting twist in the story, however, is provided by the chimpanzees raised in human-like cultural environments. Our experience with these apes must lead us to ask the question of whether there might be specific types of social interactions—types practiced by all human cultures of the world—that are necessary for the language acquisition of children to proceed normally. Although we do not know for sure, it seems evident by comparing the different procedures used with different degrees of success with human-reared apes that the key element may be the learner's participation in routine cultural activities in which an adult human treats the ape intentionally by directing its attention, encouraging its behavior (including imitation), and the like. Chimpanzees are not capable of creating among themselves these kinds of cultural activities, but they are able participate in and take advantage of such activities. This makes plausible the view that human skills of social cognition and cultural learning have co-evolved with the cultural environment and the way it is structured. It is thus possible that there are kinds of environments—with no people or in which people behave in unpredictable ways—in which human children would not acquire any linguistic skills at all.

To conclude, I will say only that the "scorched earth" policy used by generative grammarians to keep psychologically oriented linguists at bay is working no longer (E. A. Bates, 1984). Cognitive and functionally oriented linguists no longer believe that it is their duty to explain the kinds of mathematical structures that generative grammarians invent with numbing speed and regularity. Before we can discover the psychological bases of human linguistic communication skills, it is necessary first to describe the different structures of the world's various languages in ways that make their connection with human cognition and communication discoverable. Now that that such descriptions are becoming available, it is possible for the first time for psychologists to make these connections in ways that address the kinds of concerns that motivate their discipline. I have proposed here, in a preliminary fashion, some ways that human language acquisition and use depend on, indeed are part and parcel of, the kinds of cultural interactions and understandings that are the reality of human children in their second year of life and beyond.

ACKNOWLEDGMENTS

I thank Nameera Akhtar, Josep Call, Malinda Carpenter, Kathy Nagell, Jennifer Ashley, Andrew Rosner, and Boris Velichkovsky for their helpful comments on an earlier version of the manuscript.

REFERENCES

Acredolo, L., & Goodwin, S. (1993). Symbolic gestures versus words: Is there a modality advantage for the onset of symbol use? *Child Development, 64,* 688–701.

Akhtar, N. (1995). *Early strategies in responding to speech.* Manuscript submitted for publication

Baldwin, D. A. (1991). Infants' contributions to the achievement of joint reference. *Child Development, 62,* 875.

Baldwin, D. A. (1993). Infants' ability to consult the speaker for clues to word reference. *Journal of Child Language, 20,* 395–418.

Bates, E. A. (1979). *The emergence of symbols: Cognition and communication in infancy.* New York: Academic Press.

Bates, E. A. (1984). Bioprograms and the innateness hypothesis. *Behavioral and Brain Sciences, 7,* 188–190.

Bates, E. A., & MacWhinney, B. (1989). Functionalism and the competition model. In B. MacWhinney & E. A. Bates (Eds.), *The cross-linguistic study of sentence processing* (1–78). Cambridge, UK: Cambridge University Press.

Bloom, L. (1991). *Language development from two to three.* Cambridge, UK: Cambridge University Press.

Bruner, J. (1983). *Child's talk.* New York: Norton.

Bruner, J. (1990). *Acts of meaning.* Cambridge, MA: Harvard University Press.

Butterworth, G. (1991). The ontogeny and phylogeny of joint visual attention. In A. Whiten (Ed.), *Natural theories of mind.* London: Basil Blackwell.

Byrne, R. W., & Whiten, A. (Eds.). (1988). *Machiavellian intelligence: Social expertise and the evolution of intellect in monkeys, apes, and humans.* Oxford, UK: Oxford University Press.

Carpenter, M., Tomasello, M., & Savage-Rumbaugh, S. (1995). Joint attention and imitative learning in children, chimpanzees, and enculturated chimpanzees. *Social Development, 4,* 217–237.

Cheney, D. L., & Seyfarth, R. M. (1990). *How monkeys see the world.* Chicago: University of Chicago Press.

Chomsky, N. (1986). *Knowledge of language.* Berlin: Praeger.

Evans, C., Evans. L., & Marler, P. (1993). On the meaning of alarm calls: Functional reference in an avian vocal system. *Animal Behavior, 46,* 23–38.

Farrar, J. (1990). Discourse and the acquisition of grammatical morphemes. *Journal of Child Language, 17,* 607–624.

Gibson, E. J., & Rader, N. (1979). Attention: The perceiver as performer. In G. Hale & M. Lewis (Eds.), *Attention and cognitive development* (pp. 1–37). New York: Plenum.

Gleitman, L. R. (1990). The structural sources of verb meaning. *Language Acquisition, 1,* 3–55.

Gomez, J. C., Sarria, E., & Tamarit, J. (1993). The comparative study of early communication and theories of mind. In S. Baron-Cohen, H. Tager-Flusberg, & D. Cohen (Eds.), *Understanding other minds* (pp. 159–182). Oxford, UK: Oxford University Press.

Greenfield, P., & Savage-Rumbaugh, S. (1990). Grammatical combination in Pan paniscus. In S. Parker & K. Gibson (Eds.), *"Language" and intelligence in monkeys and apes* (pp. 540–578). Cambridge, MA: Cambridge University Press.

Haiman, J. (Ed.). (1985). *Iconicity in syntax.* Amsterdam: John Benjamins.

Herford, J. (1989). Biological evolution of the Saussurean sign as a component of the language acquisition device. *Lingua, 77,* 187–222.

Huttenlocher, J., & Higgins, T. (1978). Issues in the study of symbolic development. In A. Collins (Ed.), *Minnesota Symposium on Child Psychology, Vol. 11* (pp. 92–114). Hillsdale, NJ: Lawrence Erlbaum Associates.

Karmiloff-Smith, A. (1992). *Beyond modularity.* Cambridge, MA: MIT Press.

Kaye, K. (1982). *The mental and social life of babies.* Chicago: University of Chicago Press.

Lakoff, G. (1987). *Women, fire, and dangerous things: What categories reveal about the mind.* Chicago: University of Chicago Press.

Lakoff, G. (1990). The invariance hypothesis: Is abstract reason based on image schemas? *Cognitive Linguistics, 1,* 39–74.

Landry, S., & Loveland, K. (1986). Joint attention in autism and developmental language delay. *Journal of Autism and Developmental Disorders, 16,* 335–349.

Langacker, R. (1987). *Foundations of cognitive grammar* (Vol. I). Stanford, CA: Stanford University Press.

Langacker, R. (1991). *Foundations of cognitive grammar* (Vol. II). Stanford, CA: Stanford University Press.

Macnamara, J. (1972). Cognitive basis of language learning in infants. *Psychological Review, 79,* 1–13.

Mead, G. (1934). *Mind, self, and society.* Chicago: University of Chicago Press.

Mundy, P., Sigman, M., & Kasari, C. (1990). A longitudinal study of joint attention and language development in autistic children. *Journal of Autism and Developmental Disorders, 20,* 115–28.

Nagell, C., Olguin, R., & Tomasello, M. (1993). Processes of social learning in the tool use of chimpanzees and human children. *Journal of Comparative Psychology, 107,* 174–186.

Nelson, K. E. (1985). *Making sense: The acquisition of shared meaning.* New York: Academic Press.

Nelson, K. E. (1977). Facilitating children's syntax acquisition. *Developmental Psychology, 13,* 101–107.

Ninio, A. (in press). *Early syntactic development.* Cambridge, UK: Cambridge University Press.

Nishida, T. (1980). The leaf-clipping display: A newly-discovered expressive gesture in wild chimpanzees. *Journal of Human Evolution, 9,* 117–128.

Olguin, R., & Tomasello, M. (1993). Twenty-five-month-old children do not have a grammatical category of verb. *Cognitive Development, 8,* 245–272.

Peters, A. M., & Boggs, S. (1986). Interactional routines as cultural influences on language acquisition. In B. Schiefflein & E. Ochs (Eds.), *Language socialization across cultures* (pp. 80–96). Cambridge, UK: Cambridge University Press.

Petitto, L. A. (1992). Modularity and constraints in early lexical acquisition: Evidence from children's early language and gesture. In M. Gunnar & M. Maratsos (Eds.), *The Minnesota Symposium on Child Psychology, Vol. 25* (pp. 201–225). Hillsdale, NJ: Lawrence Erlbaum Associates.

Pinker, S. (1994). *The language instinct: How the mind creates language.* New York: William Morrow.

Plooij, F. (1978). Some basic traits of language in wild chimpanzees. In A. Lock (Ed.), *Action, gesture, and symbol: The emergence of language.* New York: Academic Press.

Premack, D. (1990). Words: What are they and do animals have them? *Cognition, 37,* 197–212.

Reed, E. (1995). The ecological approach to language development: A radical solution to Chomsky's and Quine's problem. *Language and Communication, 15,* 1–29.

Rispoli, M. (1995). Missing arguments and the acquisition of predicate meaning. In M. Tomasello & W. Merriman (Eds.), *Beyond names for things: Young children's acquisition of verbs.* Hillsdale, NJ: Lawrence Erlbaum Associates.

Rudzka-Ostyn, B. (Ed.). (1988). *Topics in cognitive linguistics.* Amsterdam: John Benjamins.

Savage-Rumbaugh, S. (1986). *Ape language: From conditioned response to symbol.* New York: Columbia University Press.

Savage-Rumbaugh, S. (1990). Language as a cause–effect communication system. *Philosophical Psychology, 3,* 55–76.

Savage-Rumbaugh, S., Murphy, J., Sevcik, R. A,, Brakke, K. E., Williams, S. L., & Rumbaugh, D. (1993). Language comprehension in ape and child. *Monographs of the Society for Research in Child Development, 58* (3–4).

Slobin, D. (1985). The language making capacity. In D. Slobin (Ed.), *The cross-linguistic study of language acquisition, Vol. 2* (pp. 1157–1256). Hillsdale, NJ: Lawrence Erlbaum Associates.

Talmy, L. (1988). The relation of grammar to cognition. In B. Rudzka-Ostyn (Ed.), *Topics in Cognitive Linguistics* (pp. 165–206). Amsterdam: John Benjamins.

Terrace, H. S., Petitto, L. A., Sanders, R. J., & Bever, T. G. (1979). Can an ape create a sentence? *Science, 206,* 891–900.

Tomasello, M. (1988). The role of joint attention in early language development. *Language Sciences, 11,* 69–88.

Tomasello, M. (1990). Cultural transmission in the tool use and communicatory signaling of chimpanzees? In S. Parker & K. R. Gibson (Eds.), *Language and intelligence in monkeys and apes: Comparative developmental perspectives* (pp. 274–311). Cambridge, UK: Cambridge University Press.

Tomasello, M. (1992a). *First verbs: A case study of early grammatical development.* Cambridge, UK: Cambridge University Press.

Tomasello, M. (1992b). The social bases of language acquisition. *Social Development, 1,* 67–87.

Tomasello, M. (1994). Can an ape create a sentence revisited. *Language and Communication, 14,* 377–390.

Tomasello, M. (1995). Joint attention as social cognition. In C. Moore & P. Dunham (Eds.), Joint attention: Its origins and role in development. Hillsdale, NJ: Lawrence Erlbaum Associates.

Tomasello, M., & Barton, M. (1994). Learning words in nonostensive contexts. *Developmental Psychology, 30,* 639–650.

Tomasello, M., Call, J., Nagell, C., Olguin, R., & Carpenter, M. (1994). The learning and use of gestural signals by young chimpanzees: A trans-generational study. *Primates, 35,* 137–154.

Tomasello, M., Davis-Dasilva, M., Camak, L., & Bard, K. (1987). Observational learning of tool use by young chimpanzees. *Human Evolution, 2,* 175–183.

Tomasello, M., George, B., Kruger, A. C., Farrar, J., & Evans, E. (1985). The development of gestural communication in young chimpanzees. *Journal of Human Evolution, 14,* 175–86.

Tomasello, M., Gust, D., & Frost, T. (1989). A longitudinal investigation of gestural communication in young chimpanzees. *Primates, 30,* 35–50.

Tomasello, M., Kruger, A. C., & Ratner, H. H. (1993). Cultural learning. *Behavioral and Brain Sciences, 16,* 495–552.

Tomasello, M., & Olguin, K. (1993). Twenty-three-month-old children have a grammatical category of noun. *Cognitive Development, 8,* 451–464.

Tomasello, M., Savage-Rumbaugh, S., & Kruger, A. C. (1993). Imitative learning of actions on objects by children, chimpanzees, and enculturated chimpanzees. *Child Development, 64,* 1688–1705.

van Valin, R. (Ed.) (1993). *Advances in role and reference grammar.* Amsterdam: John Benjamins.

Werner, H., & Kaplan, B. (1963). *Symbol formation.* New York: Wiley.

Wittgenstein, L. (1953). *Philosophical investigations.* London: MacMillan.

LIST OF AUTHORS

Bechtel, William, Washington University, Philosophy-Neuroscience-Psychology Program, Department of Philosophy, One Brookings Drive, St. Louis, MO 63130-4899, USA

Bornstein, Marc H., National Institute of Child Health and Human Development, Bethesda, MD 20892, USA

Harnad, Stevan, Cognitive Sciences Center, Department of Psychology, University of Southampton, Southampton SO17 1BJ, United Kingdom

Deacon, Terrence W., Boston University, Department of Anthropology, Boston, MA 02215, and Mailman Research Center, McLean Hospital, Belmont, MA 02178, USA

Friederici, Angela D., Max-Planck-Institute of Cognitive Neuroscience, Inselstraße 22-26, D-04103 Leipzig, Germany

Maryanski, Alexandra, University of California at Riverside, Department of Sociology, Riverside, CA 92521-0413, USA

Piazza, Alberto, University of Torino, Dipartimento di Genetica, Biologia e Chimica Medica, Via Santena 19, I-10126 Torino, Italy

Rumbaugh, Duane M., Georgia State University, Departments of Psychology & Biology; Language Research Center, Atlanta, GA 30303-3083, USA

Savage-Rumbaugh, E. Sue, Georgia State University, Departments of Psychology & Biology; Language Research Center, Atlanta, GA 30303-3083, USA

Scheerer, Eckart, University of Oldenburg, Faculty of Psychology, P.O. Box 25 03, D-26111 Oldenburg, Germany

Tomasello, Michael, Emory University, Department of Psychology, Atlanta, GA 30322, USA

Velichkovsky, Boris M., Dresden University of Technology, Unit of Applied Cognitive Research, Mommsenstraße 13, D-01062 Dresden, Germany

AUTHOR INDEX*

A

Abrahamsen, A. A. 46, 52, 53, 56, 75–77
Acredolo, L. 287, *303*
Agawu, V. K. 27, *42*
Akhtar, N. 298, *303*
Akhutina, T. V. 14, *20*
Akopyanz, N. S. *24*
Alcock, J. 259, 273
Allman, J. 81, *97*
Amaral, D. G. 89, *97*
Ammerman, A. J. 198, *208*
Andersen, R. A. 89, *97*
Andrews, P. 84, *97*
Anglin, J. M. 222, *251*
Antony, D. W. 202, *208*
Aram, D. M. 232, 233, *251*
Arend, R. 159, *169*
Arensburg, B. 5, *20*
Aronoff, M. 235, *251*
Asanuma, C. 89, *97*
Aslin, R. N. 148, *164*
Azumi, H. *166*

B

Bachman, D. 91, 93, *97*
Baldwin, D. A. 158, *164*, 285, *303*
Barbas, H. 81, *100*, 115, *137*
Barbujani, G. 203, 204, *208*
Bard, K. 283, *307*
Barnard, K. E. *164*
Barnes, C. 115, *137*
Baron, G. 82, *101*, *304*
Barss, A. 180, *185*

Barton, D. 221, *253*
Barton, M. 285, *306*
Basso, A. 177, *183*
Bates, E. A. 3, *20*, 77, 142, 156, *164*, *166*, *171*, 258, *273*, 275, 277, 284, 292, 298, 302, *303*
Bates, J. E. 158, 159, *170*
Bayles, K. 158, 159, *170*
Bayley, N. 156, *164*
Beard, C. 82, *97*
Bechtel, W. 2, 4, 11, 12, 45, 46, 49, 53, 56, 76, 77, 78, 211, 212, 223, 237, *251*, *274*
Bee, H. L. 159, *164*
Bellinger, D. 147, *164*
Bellugi, U. 5, *20*, 91, *98*, *101*, 175, *184*, 259, *273*
Beloch, J. 195, *208*
Belsky, J. 156, 158, 159, *164*
Beltrami, M. A. 13, *23*
Benedict, H. 159, *167*
Bennett, E. L. 270, *274*
Benson, D.F. 10, *25*, 120, *138*
Bérard, J. 198, *208*
Berg, T. 230, *251*
Berlin, B. 3, *20*, 34, *42*, *137*, 166, *252–254*, 304
Bernard, J. 192, *210*
Bernhards, D. 13, *20*
Bernstein, N. A. 15, 17, *20*
Bertelson, P. 26, 217, *251*, *252*
Bertranpetit, J. 189, *208*
Bever, T. G. 236, *256*, *274*, 298, *306*
Biben, M. 13, *20*
Biber, D. 214, *251*
Bickerton, D. 5, *20*, 140, *165*
Bihrle, A. 5, *20*, 260, *273*

---
*Numbers in italic refer to reference pages.

Blank, D. S. 65, 78
Blinkov, S. 112, *137*
Bloom, K. 146, 154, *165*
Bloom, L. 297, *303*
Bloom, P. 8, *24*, 258, *274*, 301
Blumstein, S. E. 182, *183*, 232, *251*
Boggs, S. 288, *305*
Bonin von, G. 83, *102*
Bornstein, M. H. 3, 13, *20*, *24*, 34, *42*, 139, 142, 145, 146, 149, 151, 154, 156–159, 161, *165*, *166*, *170*, *171*
Bosch-Gimpera, A. 188, *208*
Boughman, J. A. *170*
Boukydis, C.F.Z. 151, *168*
Bowman, L. L. 155, *169*
Boynton, R. M. 34, *42*
Boysson-Bardies, B. 151, 153, *166*, *167*
Bradley, D. C. 175, *183*
Bradley, L. *254*
Bradley, R. H. 159, *166*
Bradshaw, J. L. 16, *20*
Brakke, K. E. 25, *101*, *274*, *306*
Bretherton, I. 142, 156, *164*, *166*
Bridgeman, B. 6, 10, 11, 17, *20*
Bridges, L. 23, 159, *167*
Brodbeck, A. J. 154, *166*
Brown, C. 180, *184*
Brown, D. R. 202, *208*
Brown, R. 142, *166*, 202
Brownell, H. 16, *22*
Brugge, J. 86, *97*
Bruner, J. 12, 13, *21*, 287, 296, *303*
Bryant, P. 217, *254*
Burling, R. 6, *21*
Burr, D. J. 39, *43*
Burton, D. 90, *97*
Butterworth, G. 283, *303*
Byrne, R. W. 11, *25*, *26*, 301, *303*

C

Caldwell, B. M. 159, *166*
Call, J. 279, 303, *307*
Camak, L. 283, *307*

Cameron, R. F. 231, *251*
Campbell, B. *21*, 88, *97*
Cant, J. 84, *102*
Cappello, N. 187, 189, 195, *209*, *210*
Caramazza, A. 175, *184*
Carew, J. V. 159, *166*
Carey, S. 233, *256*
Carpenter, M. 279, 290, 303, *307*
Carter, A. 235, *253*
Cassidy, K. W. *167*
Castro-Caldas, A. 231, *251*
Catania, A. C. 29, 41, *42*
Cavalli-Sforza, L. L. 7, 8, *21*, 187, 188, 189, 192, 198, 203, 204, *208*, *209*, *210*
Chalmers, D. J. 65, *78*
Chan, A. 158, 161, *172*
Chang, H. 149, *171*
Chapman, R. M. 180, *184*
Chapman, R. S. 141, 159, *166*, *169*
Cheney, D. L. 16, *21*, 87, *97*, 280, 301, *304*
Chernigovskaya, T. N. 16, *21*
Chipman, S. 226, *255*
Cholewa, J. 182, *184*
Chomsky, N. 2, 3, *21*, 27, *42*, 46–48, 56, 69, 75, *78*, 140, 155, *166*, 275, 291, 301, *304*, *305*
Christian, J. C. *170*
Churchland, P. S. 49, *78*
Ciochon, R. 85, *98*, *101*
Clark, B. *164*
Clark, E. 155, *166*
Clifford, P. 201, 202, *209*
Cockerham, C. C. 192, *210*
Coffey, S. A. 178, *184*
Cole, D. 31, *42*
Cole, M. 18, *25*
Conroy, G. 5, *21*, 83, 84, *98*
Contini, M. 205, *209*
Corballis, M. 5, 6, 18, *21*
Corey, L. A. *170*
Corina, D. 91, *98*, 260, *273*
Corruccini, R. 85, *98*
Costa, L. D. 10, *22*
Couvering van, J. 83, *102*

AUTHOR INDEX

Cowey, A. 90, *98*
Cunningham, C. C. 145, *167*
Currier, R. D. 231, *251*
Cutler, A. 174, *185*

D

Damasio, A. R. 231, *251*
Damasio, H. *251*
Damerow, P. 242, *254*
Daniels, P. T. 244, 248, 249, *251*
Darwin, C. R. 139, *166*
Davenport, R. K. 90, *98*, 270, *273*
Davidson, I. 6, *24*, *254*
Davidson, R. 141, *170*
Davies, A. M. 244, *252*
Davis-Dasilva, M. 283, *307*
De Casper, A. J. *171*
De Gelder, B. 217, *252*
De la Coste-Larymondie, M. 16, *23*
De Valois, R. 88, *98*
Deacon, T. W. 5, 6, 10, 11, 17, 18, *21*, 76, 103, 105, 108, 110–113, 115, 133, *137*, 173, 179, 182, *183*, 272, 277
DeFries, J. C. 162, *167*, *170*
Delson, E. 83, *102*
Deutsch, G. 148, *171*
Devoto, G. 195, *209*
Di Rienzo, A. 192, *209*
Diamond, I. 86, *100*
Diamond, J. M. 200, *209*
Dibble, H. L. 240, *252*
Ding, B. Q. 217, *255*
Dingwall, W. 92, *98*
Doherty, S. 5, *20*
Dolan, C. P. 60, *78*
Dolgopolsky, A. B. *21*, 198, *209*
Donald, M. 5, 6, 9, 12, 17, *21*
Driver, G. R. 245, *252*
Druss, B. *167*
Duchin, L. E. 5, *21*
Duhn, F. 195, *209*
Dunaif-Hattis, J. 89, *98*
Dunbar, R. I. M. 11, *21*
Dunn, J. *167*

Durand, C. 153, *166*
Durham, W. H. 7, *22*
Dworetzky, B. 182, *183*

E

Eccles Sir, J. 89, *100*
Edwards, A. W. 192, *209*
Ehlich, K. 244, *252*
Eilers, R. E. 153, *170*
Eimas, P. D. 149, *166*
Ekelman, B. L. 233, *251*
Elardo, R. 159, *166*
Elman, J. L. 67–69, 76, 77, 78
Emde, R. N. 159, *171*
Emmorey, K. 175, *184*
Englund, R. K. 242, *254*
Erting, C. J. 144, *166*
Espir, L. 219, *252*
Essick, G. 89, *97*
Etcheverry, R. 188, *209*
Ettlinger, G. 90, *97*, *98*
Evans, C. *304*
Evans, E. 279, *307*
Evans, L. *304*
Eyres, S. J. *164*

F

Faber, A. 250, *252*
Farah, M. J. 2, *22*, 77, *78*
Farrar, J. 279, 298, *304*, *307*
Fauconnier, G. 14, *22*
Feldman, S. 76, *78*
Feldstein, S. 146, *168*
Fernald, A. 144, 145, 158, *166*, *167*
Ferro, J. M. 231, *251*
Fifer, W. P. 148, 150, *166*
Finnegan, R. 223, *252*
Fleagle, J. G. 82, *100*, *101*
Fodor, J. A. 2, 11, *22*, 29, *42*, 48, 49, 55, 58, 59, 66, *78*, 176, *183*, 225, 226, *252*
Forster, K. 180, *185*
Fowler, A. E. 230, *252*
Frahm, H. 82, *101*

Franceschi, T. 205, *211*
Frauenfelder, K. H. 174, *186*
Frauenfelder, U. 175, *185*
Frazer, B. 219, *252*
Frazier, L. 181, *183*
Freides, D. 88, 90, *98*
Friederici, A. D. 10, 14, *22*, 173, 175, 177, 180, 182–*185*, 219, 232
Frodi, A. 159, *167*
Frost, T. 279, *307*
Fukui, I. *167*
Furrow, D. 159, *167*
Fuster, J. 116, *137*

G

Gabow, S. 93, *98*
Galaburda, A. M. 16, *22*
García, E. C. 218, *252*
Gardner, B. T. 7, *22*
Gardner, H. 16, *22*
Gardner, R. A. 7, *22*
Garnsey, S. M. 180, *184*
Garon, J. 4, *25*
Garrett, M. F. 175, 180, *183*, *185*
Gelb, I. J. 249, 250, *252*
Gelman, R. 155, *172*
George, B. 48, *166*, 279, *307*
Gershberg, F. 182, *183*
Geschwind, N. 16, *22*, 89, 91, *98*, *99*
Gesell, A. 154, *167*
Gibson, E. J. 35, *43*, 278, *304*
Gibson, K. R. 236, *254*, *306*
Gibson, R. H. 87, *102*
Gidley, J. W. 82, *98*
Gilbert, J.H.V. 153, *167*
Gimbutas, M. 200–203, *209*
Gingerich, P. 82, *98*
Givón, T. 218, 219, 239, *252*
Gleitman, H. 159, *169*
Gleitman, L. R. 159, *169*, *304*
Glenn, S. M. 145, *167*
Glezer, I. 112, *137*
Goldberg, E. 10, *22*, *25*

Golden-Meadow, S. 76, *78*
Goldfield, B. A. 142, 143, 159, *167*
Goldman-Rakic, P. R. 115, *137*
Gomez, J. C. 280, *304*
Goode, M. K. 158, 159, *164*
Goodman, N. 27, 30, *43*, *172*
Goodwin, S. 287, *303*
Goody, J. 215, 223, *252*
Gopnik, M. 9, *22*, *185*
Gordon, B. 175, *184*
Gorman, R. P. 226, *252*
Gray, C. A. *164*
Greenberg, J. H. 6, *22*
Greenfield, P. M. 6, 7, 9, 17, *22*, 179, *184*, 238, 239, *253*, 261, 269, *273*, 299, *304*
Greenough, W. T. 272, *273*
Grieser, D. L. 13, *22*
Grolnick, W. 159, *167*
Groothusen, J. 180, *184*
Grosso, J. T. 231, *251*
Gruen, G. E. 159, *172*
Guilford, J. 121, *137*
Gust, D. 279, *307*

H

Haglund, M. 91, *98*
Hagoort, P. 177, 180, *184*
Hahne, A. 180, *184*, *185*
Haiman, J. 276, *304*
Hamilton, M. 221, *253*
Hammond, M. A. *164*, *210*
Hampshire, B. 88, *98*
Hamsher, K. 231, *251*, *253*
Hanson, S. J. 4, *22*, 38, 39, *43*, *44*
Hardy-Brown, K. 162, *167*
Harnad, S. 3, 4, 11, *22*, 27, 29, 30, 33–35, 37–*44*, *165*, *255*
Havinga, J. *184*
Hawkins, J. A. 21, *137*, *183*, 234, *253*
Hayes, C. 79, *98*
Hayes, K. J. 261, *273*
Hearer, A. F. 231, *251*
Heeschen, V. 221, *253*

Heffner, H. 86, *98*
Heffner, R. 86, *98*
Heilbroner, P. 91, *99*
Heltne, P. G 257, *274*
Hémon, D. 201, *209*
Herford, J. 278, *304*
Herrmann, Th. 14, *23*
Higgins, T. 277, 291, *304*
Hill, J. 83, 94, *99, 101, 137, 165*
Hinton, G. E. 4, *23*, 51, 58, 63, 74, *78, 79*, 246, *253*
Hirsh-Pasek, K. 145, *167*
Ho, H. Z. 162, *167, 169*
Holcomb, P. J. 178, 180, *184, 185*
Holloway, R. L. 16, *23*, 85, 87, 91, 92, *99*
Hopkins, W. D. *101, 274*
Horel, J. 89, *99*
Horgan, J. 9, *23*
Hrncir, E. 156, *164*
Hu, Y.-H. 13, *23*, 232, *253*
Huber, W. 9, *23*, 182, *184*
Hunt, K. 84, *99*
Hunter, I.M.L. 222, *253*
Hurford, J. R. 8, *23*
Hutchinson, J. E. 155, *168*
Huttenlocher, J. 291, *304*
Hynes, M. O. 144, *166*

I

Ingvar, D. H. 179, *184*
Irwin, D. L. 154, *166*
Isaacson, R. 81, 83, *99*
Ivanov, V. V. *209*

J

Jackendoff, R. 3, *23*
Jackson, H. J. 9, *23*, 219, *253*
Jacobs, G. 88, *98*
Jacobs, R. A. 74, *78*
Jacobsen, C. *23*, 117, *137*
Jakobson, R. 140, 151, *168*
Jasanoff, J. H. 200, *212*
Jasnow, M. 146, *168*

Jensen, H. 247, 248, *253*
Jerison, H. 25, 82, 96, *99, 137*
Jernigan, T. *20*
Jones, E. 6, 86, *97, 99, 100–102*
Jordan, M. I. 74, *78*
Jürgens, U. 86, 92, *99, 102, 168*
Jusczyk, P. W. 148, *164, 167*

K

Kaas, J. 81, 86, 87, *99*
Kalmár, I. 218, *253*
Kang, K. W. *170*
Kaplan, B. 278, *307*
Karmiloff-Smith, A. 6, 14, 16, *23*, 297, *304*
Karzon, R. G. 145, *168*
Kasari, C. 291, *305*
Kay, P. 3, *20*, 34, *42*
Kaye, K. 145, *168*, 288, *304*
Kellogg, L. A. 79, *99*
Kellogg, W. N. 79, *99*
Kempe, V. 14, 15, *20*
Kendon, A. 6, *23*
Kennedy, L. *20, 167*, 254, 273, *274*
Kent, R. D. 152, *168*
Khanna, S. 86, *99*
Kilborn, K. 175, 177, *184*
Kinsella-Shaw, J. 4, *23*
Klein, R. E. 88, *101*, 149, *168*
Klima, E. 91, *101*
Kolb, B. 120, *137*
Krämer, S. 235, *253*
Krech, D. 270, *274*
Krishtalka, L. 82, *97*
Kruger, A. C 16, *25*, 279, 281, 286, 290, 293, 297, 301, *307*
Kugler, P. N. 4, *23*
Kuhl, P. K. 13, *22*, 145, 150, *167, 168*
Kuhn, T. 42, *44*
Kurosaki, K. 8, *26*
Kutas, M. 180, *184*

L

Lakoff, G. 3, *23*, 275, *304*
Lamb, M. E. 143, *165*
Lancaster, J. B. 41, *44*
Landau, B. 3, *23*
Landry, S. 291, *304*
Langacker, R. *23*, 275, 277, 292, *304*
Lasky, R. E. 149, *168*
Launer, G. A. *24*
Laver, J. 152, *168*
Lawrence, D. H. *20, 21, 23–26*, 35, *43, 44*, 77, 78, *165, 170–172, 251, 253, 255, 256, 273, 274, 304–306*
Lawson, J. 125, *138*
Le Moal, M. 81, *99*
Lecours, A. R. 13, *23, 185*, 231
Lederman, S. J. 87, *102*
Lelikova, G. P. *24*
LeMay, M. 91, *99*
Lenneberg, E. H. 9, *21, 23*, 140, 154, *167, 168*
Lester, B. M. 151, 152, *168*
Lettich, E. 91, *98*
Levelt, W. J. M. 173, *184, 185, 253*
Lewin, R. 8, 9, *23*
Lewis, O. J. 79, 83, *99, 304*
Liberman, A. M. 243, *255*
Lichtman, J. 110, *138*
Lieberman, P. 5, *24*, 151, *168*, 179, *184*
Limborska, S. A. *24*
Linebarger, M. C. 182, *185*
Lisitsyn, N. A. 8, *24*
Livi, R. 195, *210*
Lock, A. 54, *78, 305*
Locke, J. 157, *168*
Locke, J. L. 151, *168, 172*
Lord, A. B. 215, 216, 221, 222, *253*
Loveland, K. 291, *304*
Lovilot, A. 81, *99*
Lubin, J. 4, *22*, 38, 39, *43, 44*
Lucariello, J. 158, *168*
Lucas, M .M. 174, *185*
Lundberg, I. 217, *253*

Luria, A. R. 5, 9, 11, 12, 15, *24, 25*, 222, 232, *253, 254*
Lyon, G. 177, *186*

M

MacDonald, K. 263, *274*
MacLean, P. D. 15, 17, *24*, 81, 83, *100*
Macnamara, J. 295, *305*
MacWhinney, B. 275, 292, *303*
Magoun, F. P. Jr. 220, *254*
Mallory, J. P. 200, *210*
Mann, V. A. *183*, 217, *254*
Manning, F. 118, *137*
Marchman, V. A. 3, 10, *20, 24*, 258, *273*
Marentette, P. F. 152, *170*
Marguardt, L. A. *274*
Markman, E. M. 155, 158, *164, 168*, 221, *254*
Marler, P. 280, *304*
Marshack, A. 18, *24*
Marshall, J. B. 65, *78*
Marslen-Wilson, W. D. 173, *185, 186*
Martin, A. 91, *97*
Martin, R. D. 8, *24*, 82, 85, 88, *100*
Martynov, V. I. *24*
Maryanski, A. R. 11, 14, 15, 79, 94, *100*
Maskowitz, N. 89, *100*
Massaro, D. W. 12, *24*
Masterton, B. 86, *100*
Matas, L. 159, *169*
Mateer, C. 179, *185*
Mazzie, C. 158, *167*
McClelland, J. L. 51, 69–74, 79
McDevitt, T. 147, *169*
McGeer, E. 89, *100*
McGeer, P. 89, *100*
McGowan, R. S. *254*
McHenry, H. 85, *98*
McLaughlin, B. 147, *169*
McLean, M. 217, *254*
McNew, S. 142, *166*

Mead, G. 278, *305*
Meeden, L. 65, *78*
Mehler, J. 13, *23*, 175, *185*
Mellars, P. 240, *252*, *254*, *256*
Meltzoff, A. N. 150, *168*
Menozzi, P. 7, 8, *21*, 187–198, 201, 204, *209*, *210*
Merriman, W. E. 155, *169*, *306*
Messer, D. J. 158, *169*
Mesulam, M.-M. 86, *100*, 115, *137*
Meyer, A. S. 173, *184*, *185*
Michelow, D. 16, *22*
Miikkulainen, R. 74, *78*
Milberg, W. P. 182, *183*
Miller, G. A. 148, *169*
Miller, J. F. 141, *169*
Miller, R. 151, *172*
Minch, E. *210*
Mishkin, M. 118, *137*
Miyake, K. 161, *165*
Molfese, D. L. 148, *169*
Molfese, V. J. 148, *169*
Morais, J. 216, *251*, *254*
Morgan, J. L. 53, 145, *169*
Morton, J. 175, *185*
Most, R. K. 156, 158, 159, *164*
Mountain J. 187, 204, *209*, *210*
Mourant, A. E. 188, *210*
Mundy, P. 291, *305*
Murdock, G. P. 152, *169*
Murphy, J. *25*, *101*, *274*, *306*
Murray, A. D. 152, *168*

N

Nagell, C. 279, 283, 303, *305*, *307*
Nance, W. E. *170*
Napier, J. R. 82, 83, 87, *100*
Napier, P. H. 83, 87, *100*
Nelson, K. E. 157, 159, *167*, *169*, 222, *251*, *254*–*256*, 287, 292, 298, *305*
Neville, H. J. 178, 180, 182, *184*, *185*
Newman, J. 86, 92, *100*
Newport, E. L. 159, *169*

Nicol, J. 180, *185*
Ninio, A. 294, *305*
Nishida, T. 279, *305*
Nissen, C. H. 261, *273*
Nissen, H. J. 242, *254*
Nissen, M. J. 88, *101*
Nittrouer, S. *254*
Noback, Ch. 89, *99–101*
Noble, W. 6, *24*, 241, *254*
Norrick, R. M. 219, *254*
Nowlan, S. J. 74, *78*
Nuzzo, C. 145, *170*

O

O'Leary, D. 111, *137*
Oden, N. L. 203, *211*
Ogle, K. 88, *100*
Ojemann, G. A. 98, 133, *137*, 179, *185*
Olguin, K. *307*
Olguin, R. 279, 283, 294, *305*, *307*
Olivetti, E. 187, 189, 195, *210*
Oller, D. K. 151, 153, *169*, *170*
Olson, D. R. 253, *254*
Olson, S. L. 158, 159, *170*
Ong, W. J. 215, 216, 221, *254*
Osterhout, U. 180, *185*
Otomo, K. 153, *171*

P

Pallottino, M. 195, *210*
Pandya, D. 81, 86, 92, *100*, 115, *137*
Papandropoulou, I. 221, *254*
Papoušek, H. 145, *170*
Papoušek, M. 145, *167*, *168*, *170*
Paquier, P. 177, *185*
Parente, M. A. 13, *23*, 231, *253*
Parker, S. T. 236, *254*, *304*, *306*
Parry, M. 220, *255*
Passingham, R. E. 92, *100*, 118, *138*
Pate, J. L. 261, 270, *274*
Patterson, F. G. 237, *255*

Pêcheux, M. G. *166*
Pechmann, T. *184*
Pennington, B. F. 243, *256*
Perecman, E. 22, *24*, 116, *137*, *138*
Perner, J. 11, 14, 17, *24*
Peters, A. M. 97, 99, *100–102*, 142, 145, *170*, 288, *305*
Petitto, L. A. 152, *170*, *256*, 287, 298, *305*, *306*
Petrides, M. 118, *138*
Pfeifer, E. 180, *184*
Piaget, J. 6, *24*, 117, *138*
Piazza, A. 7–9, *21*, 187–189, 194–198, 201, 203–205, *209*, *210*
Pick, H. Jr. 88, *102*
Picton, T. W. 180, *185*
Pike, K. L. 35, 41, *44*
Pinker, S. 2, 8, 18, *24*, 258, *274*, 275, 301, *305*
Pisoni, D. B. 148, *164*
Plomin, R. 162, *167*, *170*
Plooij, F. 279, 280, *305*
Plotkin, H. 17, *25*
Poeck, K. 9, *23*
Poizner, H. 91, *101*
Pollack, J. 60, 62–65, *78*
Pons, T. P. 87, *99*
Posner, M. 88, *101*
Premack, D. 7, 16, *25*, 277, *305*
Prezioso, C. 144, *166*
Pribram, K. H. 27, *44*
Price, A J. 89, *97*
Prosdocimi, A. L. 195, *210*
Pulgram, E. 195, *210*
Pullum, G. K. 30, 34, *44*
Purves, D. 110, *138*
Pütz, P. 180, *185*
Pye, C. 144, *170*
Pylyshyn, Z. W. 2, *22*, 29, *44*, 48, 55, 58, 59, 66, *78*

Q

Qiou, Y.-G. 13, *23*, 232, *253*

Quine, W.V.O. 11, 28–30, *44*, 155, *170*, *305*

R

Rader, N. 278, *304*
Radinsky, L. B. 82, 83, *101*
Rahn, C. W *166*
Rak, Y. 5, *20*
Ramsey, W. 4, *25*
Raskin, R. 147, *169*
Ratner, H. H. 12, 17, *25*, 286, 301, *307*
Ratner, N. B. 144, *170*
Rayner, K. 181, *183*
Read, C. 217, 230, *255*
Reale, R. 86, *97*
Reed, E. 278, *305*
Rendine, S. 187, 189, 195, 203, 205, *209*, *210*
Renfrew, C. 6, *25*, 198, 202, 203, *210*
Repp, B. H. 243, *255*
Reynell, J. 156, *170*
Reynolds, J. 192, *210*
Richardson, S. 46, 47, *78*, 201, *209*
Riesen, A. H. 272, *274*
Rispoli, M. 298, *306*
Riva, P. 193, *210*
Rock, I. 88, *101*
Rogers, C. W. 90, *98*, 270, *273*
Rosch, E. 3, *25*
Rose, F. 219, *252*
Rose, K. D. *101*
Rose, R. J. 162, *170*
Rosen, A. 182, *183*
Rosenberg, C. R. 226, 243, *255*
Rosenthal, D. 16, 18, *25*
Rosenzweig, M. R. 270, *274*
Rösler, F. 180, *185*
Rubert, E. 263, *274*
Ruddy, M. 156, *165*
Rudzka-Ostyn, B. 276, *306*
Ruffié, J. 192, *210*
Ruhlen, M. 6, *25*

AUTHOR INDEX

Rumbaugh, D. M. 7, 9, 16, 19, *20*, *25*, 49, 80, 90, *101*, 125, *138*, 236, 237, *255*, 257, 258, 260, 261, 263, 269, 270, *273*, *274*, 277, 278, 289, 290, 293, 299, *303*, *304*, *306*, *307*
Rumelhart, D. E. *25*, 51, 63, *79*
Russell, A. 90, *98*, 146, *165*
Russell, I. S. 90, *98*, 146, *165*

S

Saffran, E. M. 182, *185*
Sagart, L. 153, *166*
Sanders, R. J. 236, *256*, 298, *306*
Sapir, E. 80, *101*
Sarria, E. 280, *304*
Savage-Rumbaugh, E. S. 7, 9, 16, *25*, 49, 80, 90, *101*, 125, *138*, 236, 237, *255*, 257, 258, 261, 263, 269, *273*, *274*, 277, 289, 290, 293, 299, *303*, *304*, *306*, *307*
Scarborough, H. 141, *170*
Scarpa, M. T. 177, *183*
Scarr, S. 162, *170*
Scheerer-Neumann, G. 231, *255*
Scheerer, E. 4, 6, 12, 211, 225, 231, 235, *255*
Schepartz, L. A. 5, *20*
Schieffelin, B. B. 159, *170*
Schneider, B. 149, *170*
Schriefers, H. 173, *184*, *185*
Schwarz, M. 182, *185*
Scribner, S. 18, *25*
Searle, J. R. 228, *255*
Segui, J. 175, *185*
Seidenberg, M. S. *185*
Sejnowski, T. J. 226, 243, *252*, *255*
Seldon, H. L. 91, 93, *101*
Seltzer, B. 81, *100*
Seuss, D. 150, *171*
Sevcik, R. A. *25*, 90, *101*, 263, *274*, *306*
Seyfarth, R. M *21*, 87, *97*, 280, 301, *304*

Shallice, T. 4, *23*, 246, *253*
Shaw, R. E. 4, *23*
Shcheglov, Y. 14, *25*
Shepard, R. N. 226, *255*
Sherratt, A. 203, *210*
Siegel, R. M. 89, *97*
Sigman, M. 291, *305*
Simon, H. A. *43*, 50, *79*, 81, *99*
Simonds, P. 88, *101*
Simons, E. 82, *101*
Simpson, G. B. 174, *185*
Sinclair, H. 221, *253*, *254*
Skinner, B. F. 30, *42*, 47, *79*, 123, 124, 140, *171*
Slade, A. 159, *171*
Slobin, D. 296, *306*
Smith, S. T. 6, 14, 16, *21*, *23*, 125, *138*, *172*, *185*, 297, *304*
Smolensky, P. 51, 60, *79*, 225, 246, *255*
Snow, C. E. 142, *167*, *169*
Snowdon, Ch. 87, *101*
Snyder, C. *164*
Snyder, L. 142, 156, *164*, *166*
Sokal, R. R. 201, 203, 204, *208*, *210*, *211*
Sokolowski, R. 234, *256*
Sorce, J. 159, *171*
Soreno, M. I. 10, 14, 17, *25*
Spence, A. J. 148, 150, *171*
Spietz, A. L. *164*
Springer, S. P. *23*, *25*, *43*, *137*, 148, *166*, *169*, *171*, *253*
Sroufe, L. A. 159, *169*
St. John, M. F. 69, 70–74, *79*
Stebbins, L. 86, 93, 96, *98*, *101*
Steklis, H. D. 29, 33, 41, *44*, 87, *99*, *100*, *101*
Stephan, H. 82, 86, 92, *101*
Stern, D. N. 146, *171*
Sterritt, G. M. 261, *274*
Stich, S. P. 4, *25*
Stoel-Gammon, C. 153, *171*, *172*
Stone, G. O. 243, *256*
Streeter, L. A. 149, *171*
Stucky, R. 82, *97*
Studdert-Kennedy, M. *20*, *254*, *273*

Stuss, D. T. 10, 15, *25*, 116, 120, *138*, 180, *185*
Sutton, D. 87, *102*
Sverdlov, E. D. *24*
Swartz, S. 84, *102*
Swinney, D. A. 174, *185*
Symmes, D. 13, *20*, 145, *170*
Syrdal-Lasky, A. 149, *168*

T

Taeschner, T. *167*
Tagifzouti, K. *99*
Talmy, L. 275, 292, *306*
Tamarit, J. 280, *304*
Tamis-LeMonda, C. S. 142, 146, 158, 159, 161, *165, 166, 171*
Tanenhaus, M. K. 174, 180, *184, 185*
Tattersall, I. 83, 84, *102*
Taylor, M. M. 87, *97, 102*
Temerin, A. 84, *102*
Terrace, H. S. 7, *25*, 236, *256*, 298, *306*
Terracini, B. 194, 205–207, *211*
Teuber, H.-L. 233, *256*
Tfouni, L. V. 217, *251*
Thal, D. 3, *20*, 142, *171*, 258, *273*
Thomson, B. A. 203, *211*
Tiller, A. M. *20*
Tilney, F. 10, *25*
Toda, S. 161, *165, 166*
Tomasello, M. 4, 5, 12, 14, 16, 17, *25*, 239, *256*, 275, 276, 278, 279, 281, 283–290, 293–295, 297, 299, *303–307*
Tonndorf, J. 86, *99*
Torgesen, J. K. *256*
Trauner, D. 5, *20*
Trehub, S. E. 149, *170, 171*
Treiman, R. 217, *256*
Trombetti, A. 193, 194, *211*
Tulving, E. 6, *26*
Turner, J. H. 94, *100*
Tuttle, R. 82, *102*
Tyler, L. K. 173, 174, *185, 186*

U

Ueda, S. 8, *26*

V

Van de Sandt-Koenderman, M. 177, *186*
Van Dongen, H. R. 177, *185*
van Gelder, T. 60, *79*
Van Hout, A. 177, *186*
Van Lancker, D. 9, 15, *26*, 219, *256*
Van Orden, G. C. 243, *256*
van Petten, C. 180, *184*
van Valin, R. 275, 276, *307*
Vandermeersch, B. 5, *20*
Vardi, D. *166*
Velichkovsky, B. M. 1, 14–20, *26*, *303*
Vibbert, M. 161, *171*
Vihman, M. M. 151, 152, *166, 172*
Vincente, K. J. 4, *23*
Visch-Brinck, E. G. 177, *186*
Vondra, J. 156, *164*
Vorberg, D. *184*
Vroomen, J. 217, *252*
Vygotsky, L. S. 4, 18, *26*, 77, *79*

W

Wachs, T. D. 158, 159, 161, *172*
Wagner, L. L. *24*
Wagner, R. K. 217, *256*
Walker, A. C. 82, 83, *100, 102*
Wallace, C. S. 272, *273*
Wapner, W. 16, *22*
Warren, D. 88, *102*
Washburn, D. A. 258, *274*
Washio, K. 8, *26*
Wassenberg, K. 146, *165*
Waxman, S. R. 155, *172*
Wechsler, D. 156, *172*
Weinberg, F. A. 162, *170*
Weir, B. S. 192, *210*
Weiskrantz, L. 90, *98, 102*

Weniger, D. 9, *23*
Werker, J. F. 149, *172*
Werner, H. 15, *26*, 278, *307*
Wessels, J. 175, *184*
Whatmough, J. 195, *211*
Whishaw, I. 120, *137*
Whitaker, H. L. 233, *251*
White, D. 147, *169*
White, E. 92, *102*
White, R. 240, *256*
Whiten, A. 11, *25*, *26*, 301, *303*
Whitfield, I. C. 82, *102*
Whitfield, W. 90, *102*
Whorf, B. L. 32–35, *44*
Wilbertz, A. 182, *184*
Williams, R. J. *79*
Williams, S. L. *25*, *101*, *306*
Wilson, A. C. 173, *185*, *186*, 192, *209*
Witelson, S. F. 148, *172*
Withers, G. S. 272, *273*
Wittgenstein, L. 11, 28, *44*, 292, *307*
Woods, B. T. 233, *256*
Wulfeck, B. 182, *186*
Wyckoff, J. *170*
Wynn, T. 240, *256*

Y

Yeterian, E. H. 86, *100*

Z

Zhang, Y.-F. 217, *255*
Zholtkovsky, A. 14, *25*
Zhong, G.-Q. 13, *23*, 232, *253*
Zurif, E. B. 174, 175, *183*, *185*

SUBJECT INDEX

A

Afferent phonemic aphasia 232
Agrammatism 15, 233
Alleles 189
Allometry 108
   cell-proliferation 110
Alphabetic principle 232, 250
American Sign Language 236, 259, 287
Anatomical biases 153
Anthropogenesis 1, 11, 16
Anthropometric traits 189
Aphasiology 184, 185, 219
Artificial intelligence 23, 43, 44, 47, 235, 256
Assertions
   descriptive 37
   ostensive 37
Associationism 48, 56
Associations
   conditioned 124–126
   correlative 132
   cross-modal 90
   habitual 126
   hierarchic 134
   higher order distribution 139
   indexical 125, 129, 133, 136
   learned 123, 132, 133
   lexigram-object 130
   nonlimbic intercortical 90
   nonsymbolic 124
   statistical 134
   symbolic 123–126, 132, 133, 138
Attentional control 13, 19
Auditory system 80, 81, 86, 95, 97, 100, 149, 150
Awareness
   metaphonological 229
   of speech sounds 217
   phonological 217, 229, 230, 233

B

Backpropagation 63, 71
Basal ganglia 17, 100, 108
Behaviorism 28, 30, 42
Biological processes 140
Blood types 189
Boundaries
   linguistic and genetic 203
Brain
   complex 259, 260
   event-related potential 178, 180, 181, 184, 185
   evolution 86, 101, 106, 107, 113, 114, 137, 138
   functional organization 15
   hominid brain expansion 137
   human 107
   language 23, 141, 184
      coevolution 184
   medial frontal damage 120
   neural tube 109
   prefrontal regions 10, 15, 16, 115, 117, 120, 135
   reptilian 17
   size 94, 107, 111, 136, 137
   stem 81, 108
Broca's aphasia 176, 177, 179, 183, 184, 219
Broca's area 10, 16, 91, 92, 96, 179, 180, 182, 233, 239

C

Call system
   emotionally based 95
   species-specific 95
Categorization 3, 5, 11, 12, 14, 28, 29, 32, 35, 36, 38, 39, 41, 170, 171, 240, 296, 297

linguistic 240, 296
Categorization problem 38
Category(ies)
  abstract higher-order 40
  abstract semantic 32
  categorical perception 13, 35
  category membership 36, 39
  concrete 32
  concrete perceptual 32
  grammatical 69, 239, 256, 297, 299
  paradigmatic 296
  psychophysical 39
  syntagmatic 294, 296
Cluster analysis 68
Coevolution 17, 18, 135–137, 183
Cognates 204, 205
Cognition
  cognitive modules 176
  cultural 276, 278
Cognitive style 115
Cognitivism 29
Color perception 34, 88
Combinatorial rules 103, 127
Communication
  emotional 15
Communicative behaviors 283
Connectionism 4, 56, 58, 59, 78, 212, 224, 227, 256
  connectionist
    approach 212
    paradigm 4
Conventionalization 281
Cortex
  association 81, 92
  cerebellar 108
  cerebral 81, 89, 101, 102, 107, 108, 110, 112, 113
  enlarged prefrontal 114
  expansion of the prefrontal cortex 135
  limbic 81, 87, 99, 114
  prefrontal 112–117, 123, 134–136, 139, 179
  temporal 81, 102
Cortical association areas 89

Cues
  acquired distinctiveness 35
  acquired similarity 35
  social-pragmatic 285
Cultural
  cultural-historical psychology 4
  isolation 204
  trait 197, 198
  transmission 14
Culture
  human 1, 4, 19, 33, 272, 302
  oral versus literate 222
  writing 221

D

Decomposition 46, 47, 246
DNA 8, 24, 26, 91, 109, 189, 192, 209
Duals
  perceptual 32
  semantic 31, 32

E

Ecological approach 4, 306
Electrophoretic variants 189
Emergent product(s) 50, 75
Enculturated chimpanzees 283, 290, 293, 300, 304, 307
Environment
  cultural 212
  physical 163, 212, 229, 235, 271
  social 212, 229, 235, 271
Evolution
  biological 1, 188
  hominid 98, 135, 136
  of life 257
  short-term 192
Evolutionary failures 84
External reference 278, 280
External signal systems 228

SUBJECT INDEX

F

Features
  content 144
  lexical 144
  prosodic 23, 144
  redundancy 144
  simplicity 144
Formal symbol manipulation 3, 211, 235, 238
Functional core hypothesis 222
Functionalism 29

G

Gene frequencies 189, 194–197, 200, 201, 205, 210
Genetic
  distance 192, 193, 210
  drift 192, 193
  histories 187, 195, 206
  isolation 205
  structure 198, 205
  system 189
Gesture(s)
  intentional 279, 280, 282, 283, 301
Glossability criterion 29
Glossogenesis 5
Grammar
  formal-combinatorial 228
  localization 10

H

Habituation 158, 162, 167, 173
Heuristics 11, 47
Holophrastic 30, 36, 41
Homeotic genes 109
Hominid adaptive zone 93
Hominoid evolution 97
Hominoid(s) 80, 84, 90, 93, 97

I

Illiteracy
  absolute 215
  functional 215
  partial 215
Indeterminacy 41, 42
Innate universal grammar 105, 140
Intentional communicative
    interactions 288
Interpretation
  multiple 31
Intertranslatability criterion 27
Inverted spectrum conjectures 31
IQ 122, 166
Isonimy 205, 206

J

Joint attentional
  episodes 288
  interactions 276, 287, 291

K

Knowledge
  implicit 130
  innate grammatical 105
Kurgan
  culture 200, 202
  region 203
  waves 201, 202

L

Lana Project 260
Language
  acquisition 3, 8, 13, 14, 23, 132, 140, 141, 149, 155, 157, 159, 163–165, 168, 169, 172, 174, 178, 268, 276–278, 286–288, 296, 302–307
  ancestral 7
  anthropogenesis 1, 11, 16
  ape language research 260

brain organization 233
brain specialization 231
closed class 174, 175, 176
as combinatorial grammar system 8
communities 153, 154
complexity 104
computer language 235
connectionist models of processing 224
development 2, 3, 5, 8, 10, 12, 20, 51, 79, 141–143, 152, 155, 164, 168, 169, 171, 173, 177, 219, 258, 273, 274, 297, 305, 306
evolution 6, 12, 17, 18, 136, 301
functional reorganization 179
genesis 80
grammar and production 270
history 220
Hopi 33
Indo-European 198, 203, 208, 209
language module(s) 46, 49
lexical access 174, 177, 184, 185
living language 219
meta-language 16
monogenesis 7
natural language development 164
need for 96
neurological capacity 85
nonpropositional 221, 230
of thought 42, 48, 49, 78, 228, 234, 253
  theory 225
ontogeny 141, 172, 276
open class 174, 178, 181, 184
oral 79, 80, 212, 216, 219, 220, 222, 228, 229, 235, 237, 241
origin(s) 1, 6, 18, 19, 25, 27–29, 41, 102, 140, 258
phonology 6, 9, 35, 171, 174, 234, 235
poetic 11
presyntactic-pragmatic mode 219, 220, 222, 240
process in comprehension 174
production 270
productive use 265
propositional 219, 221
proto-Indo-European 7, 199, 200, 202, 203
semantics 3, 6, 7, 11–14, 17, 47, 48, 65, 66, 72, 73, 76, 140, 164, 165, 213, 222, 225, 226, 229, 248, 253, 266
sequence in time 173
sign language 22, 55, 103, 144, 154, 236, 237
simple 104, 105, 123
simplified 104
skills 163, 171, 258, 264, 270, 271
spoken 54, 87, 173, 185, 186, 212–216, 22–230, 233, 235–238, 241, 243, 245, 246
substrata 206
symbol-processing paradigm 212, 223
syntax 6
synthetic 30
temporal structure 173
use of language 45, 49, 50, 51, 53–55, 75, 77, 173, 174, 177, 180, 211, 216, 235, 237, 239, 241
written 54, 212–218, 222, 223, 227, 229, 230, 232–235, 237, 238, 240, 244, 247
  linear arrangement 216
  segmentability 213
  spatial arrangement 216
Language areas 233
  functional segregation 233
  left lateralization 233
Language of thought theory 225
Learning
  algorithm 39
  associative 129, 133–137, 139
  combinatorial 137, 138
  correlative 137
  cultural 276, 286, 290, 295, 297, 299, 300, 302
  hierarchic 137, 138
  imitative 280, 307
  relational skills 270
  rote 104, 123, 128, 130, 131

symbol(ic) learning 123, 124, 130, 132–136, 138
Lexigrams 7, 9, 54, 126–133, 236–238, 261–267, 269, 270, 299
Limbic system 81, 83, 90, 94, 99
Linguistic
  atlas 205
  geography 194
  item 76, 197, 207, 297
  motor 6, 87
  motor control abilities 6, 87, 153, 179
  relativity hypotheses 3
Linguistics
  cognitive 305, 306
Literacy 6, 25, 211–215, 218, 221, 224, 229, 231, 234, 251, 252–256
  typographic 215
Localization
  complex 46, 47
  direct 46
Locus of control 47
Logic
  formal 52
  sentential 53
Logograms 245, 246, 248

M

Machiavellian intelligence 11, 25, 26, 304
Memory
  echoic 54, 77
  literate 222
  oral 222, 223
  response inhibition 118
  short-term 118, 121
  working 116, 121
Meta-cognition 18, 230, 235
Meta-cognitive
  coordination 17, 20, 21
  control 17
  operation(s) 16
Meta-linguistic vocabulary 221, 253

Methodological solipsism 11, 226
MLU – Mean and Length of Utterance 141
Modality
  auditory 86, 88
  haptioc 87
  tactile 88
Molecular 204
Molecular techniques 204
Motherese 13, 23, 145, 168

N

Nativism 2, 76
Natural selection 25, 106, 274
Neocortex
  prefrontal lobes 10
  size 11, 22
Neolithic farmers 189, 198, 201, 202
Network(s)
  autoassociative 63
  connectionist 23, 43, 44, 53, 56, 59, 60, 66, 74, 78
  network modeling approach 212
  recurrent 6–69, 74
Neural network paradigm 225
Neuropsychology 5, 9, 23, 25, 78, 117, 139, 171, 231
Normative tradition 141
Notational system 211, 212

O

Operational language unit 246
Oral
  poetry 216, 220, 221
  segmentation 216
Orality 213,–217, 224, 227, 228, 234, 253–255
  primary 215–217, 227, 228
  synchronic 218
Ortholinguistic structure 220

P

Paleolithic period 5, 18, 188, 189, 194
Parsers 47
Pattern recognition 4, 38, 52, 53, 57, 229
Phonemes 13, 35, 80, 150, 173, 216, 230, 239, 256
Phonological awareness 217, 229, 230, 233
Phyletic relationship 91
Pictograms 246
Population
  Basque 188
  Caucasian 193
Poverty of the stimulus 69
Predication 278, 287, 302
Predicative devices 285
Prefrontal
  anatomy 114
  areas 117, 134, 182
  circuits 115
  connectivity 114
  cortex 112–117, 123, 134–136, 139, 179
  damage 117, 119–122
  deficit 117, 118
  enlargement 113, 114, 135
  expansion 17, 114, 122, 135, 137, 138
  functions 10, 11, 18, 114, 117, 122
  human 121
  information processing 114
  lesions 121, 139
  lobes 10, 113, 122
  posterior lateral regions 120
  regions 10, 15, 16, 115, 117, 120, 135
  subdivisions 117
Primate
  evolution 86, 94
  niche 82, 83
  order 82, 84
Problem of induction 38

Problem solving 1, 13, 15, 157, 252, 261, 274
Productivity 48, 59, 236, 297
Prosody 145, 146, 216
Protolanguage
  written 237
Psychophysics 24, 34, 172

R

RAAM – Recursive Auto-Associative Memory 61–66, 78
Radiation
  adaptive 83, 84
  anthropoid 82
  prosimian 82
Realism 28
Recall
  extended verbatim 222
  serial 222
Reference
  indexical 129, 130
  symbolic 103, 123, 126, 129, 130, 132, 292
Referent-object separation 241
Relationship
  combinatorial 126, 129, 133, 135
Representation(s)
  categorical 28, 38, 39, 40
  complex 219, 225
  compressed 62–66
  external 51, 53
  holistic 226
  iconic 28, 38, 39, 40
  internal 38, 48, 55, 59, 60, 66, 67, 73–75, 79, 158, 212, 224, 249, 256
  mental 22, 48, 53, 60
  nonsymbolic 40
  structured 73, 75, 76, 225
  system 55
  uncompressed 63, 65
  visual-symbolic 111, 132
Ritualization 281, 283

SUBJECT INDEX

S

Segmentation deficit 217, 229
Semantics
  external 226, 229
  internal 226, 229
Sensory
  discrimination 32
  modalities 79, 213
Signs
  manual 7, 50, 54
Social referencing 287
Social-pragmatic cues 285
Society
  of intimates 218
  of strangers 218
Speech 5–7, 11, 13, 14, 16, 18,
    20–24, 26, 28, 35, 36, 44, 54,
    67, 74, 75, 77, 79–81, 91, 93–
    96, 101, 141–143, 145–155,
    159–161, 164, 166, 168–174,
    176, 179, 181,
    183–186, 206, 211, 213, 214,
    216, 217, 219, 221, 228, 230,
    231, 233, 235, 239, 241, 243,
    247, 250, 252, 253, 255, 256,
    258, 260, 262, 263, 265, 266,
    272, 274, 276, 299, 303
  analytic approach 233
  metaphorical 11
  perception 24, 35, 92, 96, 101,
    148, 166, 174, 216, 230, 231,
    234, 243
  perception and production
    cerebral control 234
  perception of sound 35
  phonemic
    approach 233
    left-hemisphere dominance 231
  production 230, 231, 234
  propositional 6
  serial 219
  social 219
  social gestures 219
  sound perception 149
    production 152
  synchrony 143

temporal 247
temporal sequence 247
Spinal cord 108, 111
Syllabary 217, 244, 248, 249
Syllabification 228
Syllable(s) 149, 153, 154, 174–175,
    216, 217, 222, 228, 230, 245,
    246, 249, 250, 255, 256
Sylvian
  fissure 91
  point 91
Symbol paradigm 212, 225, 226, 229
Symbol(s) 2, 7, 40, 43, 48, 50–55,
    57, 59, 60, 73, 75–77, 79, 103,
    123, 125, 126, 129, 132, 133,
    136, 211–213, 224, 225, 228,
    234–238, 241–249, 259–266,
    269, 270, 274, 275, 277–280,
    282–286, 288–301, 303
  acquisition 122, 135, 137, 238,
    274, 275
  context-free deep-structure 234
  elementary 228
  external 12, 51–54, 57, 73, 75, 77,
    211, 212
  grammatical 277, 292–300, 302
  graphic 241, 247, 248
  grounding prolem 3, 23, 43
  information processing paradigm
    3, 7, 11
  lexical 277, 292–295, 297, 299–
    301
  linguistic 51, 54, 59, 60, 76,
    277–283, 284, 286–289, 291,
    293, 301
  manipulation 238
  physical 50, 51
  physically segmentable 213, 238,
    249
  primitive 40
  production 236
  reciprocal and predicative 287,
    300
  reciprocal understanding 285, 291
  representational and referential use
    262

system 11, 12, 127, 131, 132, 213, 229, 234
Symbolic
   communication 97, 104, 136–138, 258, 260, 289
   reference system 123
   representational systems 41
Synapses 114
Syntactic processes 138, 174, 179, 180, 182
   N400 180, 181
Syntactic structure
   emergence 218
Syntax 6, 11, 12, 14, 20, 45, 47, 48, 60, 65, 66, 72, 73, 76, 78, 80, 105, 140, 164, 165, 168, 185, 213, 219, 226, 228, 239, 253, 258, 260, 266, 273, 274, 275, 292, 304, 305
   formal-combinatorial 228
Systematicity 48, 59, 64, 236

T

Tectum 108
Thalamus 107, 110, 111
Theory
   of meaning 11, 15, 16, 25
      empiricist 37
   of mind 11, 15, 17, 25
Thinking
   divergent 122
   symbolic 18
   visual thinking 241
Tool use 239
Turing machine 57, 58
Turn taking 143, 146, 147, 155, 167

U

Underdetermination 30, 32

V

Vanishing intersections objection 37
Vocalizations 5, 9, 13, 14, 87, 93, 95, 146, 152, 153, 155, 160, 166, 167, 173, 280, 293

W

Wernicke's area 91, 92, 96, 177, 179, 233
Word
   oral concept 221
Writing 213, 248
   alphabetic 244
   logographic 244
   proto-writing 241, 246
   syllabic 244, 248
Writing systems
   logographic 213, 248
   phonographic 213

Z

Zone of proximal development 12

For Product Safety Concerns and Information please contact our EU
representative GPSR@taylorandfrancis.com
Taylor & Francis Verlag GmbH, Kaufingerstraße 24, 80331 München, Germany

www.ingramcontent.com/pod-product-compliance
Lightning Source LLC
Chambersburg PA
CBHW070736230426
43669CB00031B/2209